ON HIS OWN

Robert F. Kennedy, February 13, 1969, (André Lefebvre, *Paris Match*)

ON HIS OWN
ROBERT F. KENNEDY
1964–1968

WILLIAM VANDEN HEUVEL
AND
MILTON GWIRTZMAN

DOUBLEDAY & COMPANY, INC./GARDEN CITY, NEW YORK/1970

LIBRARY OF CONGRESS CATALOG CARD NUMBER 79–98105
COPYRIGHT © 1970 BY WILLIAM VANDEN HEUVEL
  AND MILTON GWIRTZMAN
PRINTED IN THE UNITED STATES OF AMERICA
FIRST EDITION

To our children, Katrina and Wendy vanden Heuvel
and Matthew Michael Gwirtzman

CONTENTS

ACKNOWLEDGMENTS

In preparing this volume, we have relied primarily on our own notes, observations and recollections made during the four years in which we worked with Senator Robert Kennedy. On issues and events for which our own material was incomplete, we were fortunate to have the assistance and opinions of others who worked with him closely. While this is in no way an authorized biography, and while the judgments are the authors' own, we wish to express our appreciation to the following people whose recollections were most helpful:

Carter Burden

David Burke

Bishop Philip Crowther

Gerard Doherty

Joseph Dolan

Frederick Dutton

Peter Edelman

Richard Goodwin

Thomas Johnston

Frank Mankiewicz

Burke Marshall

Robert McNamara

Lawrence Ralston

Ian Robertson

Jack Rosenthal

Stephen Smith

Phillip Sorensen

Maxwell Taylor

We also wish to thank Paul Michael Green, who compiled the precinct returns from Lake County for the 1968 primary election; Bartle Bull for his valued editorial suggestions; and Burt Drucker who was helpful in countless ways.

Jane Santy and Nancy Levy worked long hours, typing and retyping the manuscript, with great patience and accuracy.

Sandy Richardson, our editor at Doubleday, believed in this book, and his cooperation, confidence, and judgment made it possible. We also thank his able assistant, Emily Miller, for her help, patience, and good humor.

Mrs. Robert F. Kennedy read portions of the manuscript and offered helpful criticisms and suggestions. We gratefully acknowledge that assistance. We hope she knows how much her friendship and encouragement has meant to us.

William vanden Heuvel
Milton Gwirtzman
Rochester, New York
October, 1969

PREFACE

The sky had begun to brighten in the early morning of March 16, 1968, when Senator Edward Kennedy walked up the gray slate path of his brother's home in McLean, Virginia, and entered through the large red door. He was returning from Green Bay, Wisconsin, where he had informed Senator Eugene McCarthy that his brother, Robert Kennedy, was going to announce his candidacy for the Democratic presidential nomination that very day.

The trip had been arranged by Blair Clark, Senator McCarthy's campaign manager, and Richard Goodwin, in the hope that direct discussions, even at this late hour, might find a way to avoid a head-on collision between the Kennedy and McCarthy forces which could only damage their mutual purposes and individual ambitions. Clark and Goodwin accompanied Edward Kennedy on the commercial flight that left Washington at 7 P.M. for Chicago on the evening of March 15. A private plane, arranged and paid for by the McCarthy campaign, then took the trio to Green Bay and waited to return Kennedy to Washington when the conversations were over.

It was an awkward meeting. McCarthy seemed uninformed of its purpose and resentful of the interruption to his sleep. Edward Kennedy sensed the quixotic nature of the visit and tried to make sense out of it for both of them. He intended to review the obvious difficulties in denying renomination to Lyndon Johnson, especially if the forces opposing Johnson were divided. He expected to offer Robert Kennedy's proposal for a coalition effort: Kennedy would help McCarthy win the early primaries, they would both run in later primaries, such as California, Oregon, and South Dakota, but they would not oppose one another where the result would be to help Johnson win. But the atmosphere of the meeting was too negative for any solid discussion of a joint course. Senator McCarthy, buoyed by his New Hampshire triumph, was preparing to continue his campaign alone.

Gone was the diffidence of the man who, in announcing his candidacy on November 30, had publicly stated that he expected Robert Kennedy to be carrying the banner to the Chicago convention. McCarthy was to become an enigma to even his most devoted followers, but at this moment he was the tough, shrewd, confident politician who had never lost an election in twenty-four years in politics. New Hampshire's primary had made him a national figure. Almost alone, he had transformed the electoral possibilities of 1968. He had not always led the millions who despaired of America's involvement in Vietnam, but he walked in front for them at a crucial and dramatic moment. He had nothing to lose when he became a candidate, and he had much to gain by remaining one. If he had any doubts about continuing his campaign, Abigail McCarthy had none, and as his wife, she never hesitated to offer political judgments and ideas.

As Edward Kennedy pushed open the door at Hickory Hill, a friend who had been awaiting a telephone report from him asked: "How did it go?"

"Abigail said no," was the answer.

Robert Kennedy used advisers for advice. He made the decisions. It was not a matter of placing arguments on a delicate scale and then siding with the heavier weight. Generally he kept his own counsel, rarely revealing his own instinct or opinion, so as to encourage the person he was talking with to reflect his own viewpoints, uncolored by what he thought Robert Kennedy wanted to hear. Sometimes he deliberately took a position he knew the other person supported, just to get a reaction. Now, in the most difficult personal decision of his life, he was finally prepared to act. For months he had delayed and reflected; he had been frustrated and encouraged; he had both awaited events and helped make them. He knew all the arguments and sensed all the complexities. Neither luck nor timing had been with him. In many ways, the problem that confronted him had no acceptable solution. Whatever decision he made would spawn its own difficulties. There was only one certainty: No matter what he decided, the months ahead would be as difficult as any he had ever known.

Only hours separated him from the fateful public statement of his candidacy. The disappointing news from Green Bay caused one final review of the alternatives available to him. He breakfasted with four men who knew better than most what the past anguish had been and what the future toll of mind and body would be. He was told that he would have to win all the primaries and spend several million dollars, and then still face an uphill struggle to win the nomination. It was argued that the Democratic Party would never nominate McCarthy as its candidate, that McCarthy's real role was as a protest candidate, that McCarthy would discredit Johnson in the course of the primaries, and that Kennedy could win the convention at this point as the only Democrat with national power, experience, and a chance of winning the election. But he was a Kennedy, transfixed by the legend he had done so much to create, certain that his supporters would accept nothing less than his open willingness to do battle, and sustained by that mystical, irrational confidence that in such a battle he would never lose.

For forty minutes the final debate continued. Kennedy left the room and walked alone with his thoughts. Five minutes later, he reappeared.

"I am going to run. Let's complete the statement." He finished dressing, went over the announcement statement line by line, posed questions and tried answers for the press conference just an hour away. With Ethel and nine of their children with him, with the household staff of Hickory Hill part of the caravan, he drove onto the George Washington Memorial Parkway headed for the United States Senate.

As he walked alone into the Caucus Room of the Old Senate Office Building, the crowd in the corridors respectfully made way for him. Someone whispered to a companion: "Here comes Che."

Eight years before John F. Kennedy had stood in the same room for the same purpose. Now Robert Kennedy began with the identical words of his brother: "I am announcing today my candidacy for the Presidency of the United States."

When Robert Kennedy announced for the presidency at the age of forty-two, he had already made his share of history. In the rest of the world, he was probably the most respected and exciting public figure in America. He was a man of great wealth, who held the loyalty of the poor as no man had since Franklin Roosevelt. He was the heir to the Kennedy legacy, the undisputed chief of a government-in-exile whose talents were said to rival the government in Washington. He was the most charismatic and one of the most controversial figures in the country, a symbol of national opposition on the two most important issues of the day: Vietnam and the crisis of race.

The road to that Caucus Room stretched back five years, to another assassination and to Robert Kennedy's slow attempt to find his own place in American public life. The road ahead was to be a short one, but on it he would stir the public like no one else in the tumultuous year 1968.

This biography tells the story of the Senate years of Robert Kennedy, years of grief and joy and work and growth. It is also the story of what happened in the brief and tragic presidential campaign that began on the Ides of March.

ON HIS OWN

1

"WHAT WILL BOBBY DO?"

No man can predict his future. But he can plan for it, and by the beginning of November 1963, the future of Robert Kennedy seemed to be taking shape. He had been Attorney General of the United States for three years. Now he wished to move to another position in Washington, one which would give scope to his increasing involvement in foreign affairs and still allow him to continue as the closest confidant and principal adviser of his brother, the President of the United States.

Kennedy had accepted the appointment as Attorney General with extreme reluctance. His age was a factor—at thirty-six, he would become the youngest man to serve since Richard Rush in the administration of Thomas Jefferson. His legal experience was in public law, primarily congressional hearings and investigations; he had never tried a lawsuit. His greatest concern was the potential embarrassment the appointment would cause his brother. But President Kennedy wanted him in the Cabinet, and the trust and confidence the President had in him was the ultimate qualification for the sensitive and demanding post of Attorney General.

In the course of his service, his liberal critics became admirers. The New York *Times*, which had criticized the appointment when it was made, praised Kennedy at the time of his resignation as Attorney General in 1964 for having "elevated the standards of the office." Francis Biddle, President Roosevelt's Attorney General for four years, whose brilliant service in the office was the measure for his successors, described Kennedy as "certainly the finest Attorney General in the last twenty years, probably the best in this century." His opposition now came from conservative elements, in the South and in the business community, which opposed the major domestic programs of the Kennedy administration.

Robert Kennedy was proud of the department he had organized and would remain devoted to its work; but after ten years as a prosecutor, investigator and law enforcement officer, he was, as he put it, "tired of being a cop." Increasingly his interests had turned to foreign policy, stimulated by his involvement in the investigation of the failure of the Cuban invasion in 1961, his activities during the Cuban missile crisis of 1962, his frequent contacts with foreign diplomats in Washington and his trips to three continents as a presidential emissary. He could be sure the department would continue its mission as he had defined it, for in Nicholas de B. Katzenbach, he had a successor skilled in administration, and tested in judgment and courage. His plan, as of November 1963, was to resign as Attorney General the following summer, manage his brother's campaign for re-election, which he fully expected to be successful, and then go into the Department of State. The actual post was still unclear,[1] but that was unimportant. No matter what his exact title, he would have a major role in policies and procedures. His task would be to bring new men, methods, and ideas to a department whose inflexibility had confounded President Kennedy.

Then came Dallas and November 22. For weeks after his brother's assassination, Kennedy was numbed by sorrow and depression. He returned to his desk at the end of December, but he could not concentrate. In the middle of a meeting, his expression went blank and he would stare out a window, absorbed in his own thoughts and grief.

[1] On November 2, 1963, President Kennedy—over the opposition of the State Department—ordered the creation of a new post of Under Secretary of State for Latin American Affairs, to give that continent status within the Department commensurate with its importance to the United States and with the President's interest in it. When Rafael Squirru, a young Argentinian at the Organization of American States had suggested to the President he fill the position with "someone of great stature, like your brother," the President joked that he was "running out of brothers." But when Squirru mentioned the possibility to Robert Kennedy, he said, "I'd like to do something like that when I'm through here."

Handed an official paper, he looked at it briefly and tossed it aside. Often he left in the middle of the day to visit the President's children, or go home to his own, or take long walks on the Mall with his Newfoundland dog.

Parallel to his grief was the vacuum caused by the loss of power and motivation. He had been in the center of activities which affected the world. The ancient Greek definition of happiness—"the exercise of vital powers along lines of excellence in a life affording them scope"—a favorite quotation of Robert Kennedy's—was also a description of the life that had been his. Now that life was in disorder. Only the symbols remained. The direct phone to the President's office was still on his desk but was scarcely used. Outside the Department of Justice, he had lost his power to command. In December, concerned with the treatment by the State Department of American students who had visited Cuba, he wrote a memorandum. Before, a phone call would have been enough to bring about quick action.

He talked vaguely, in the months after November, about leaving Washington, taking his family to England for a year, doing some writing, perhaps returning to teach at a university or work with children. "I don't think there's much left for me in this town," he told his Washington friends. So complete was his withdrawal, so scant his interest in his own future in public life, that for a time members of the family felt that the political succession of the Kennedys, by Robert Kennedy's own choice, might settle on his brother, Edward.

But as winter passed Robert Kennedy emerged from his sadness.

His own adjustment was eased by the help he gave Jacqueline Kennedy in her even more difficult situation. He was a frequent visitor at her house in Georgetown. She leaned on him, more than anyone else, for companionship in grief and guidance in rebuilding her life. He had always regarded self-pity as the most corrosive of emotions, destructive to those who indulged in it. "We just can't feel sorry for ourselves" he told her. "We have to carry on." In giving strength to her, he helped discipline himself.

In February, President Johnson, personally upset by "the sorrow on that boy's face," as he put it, was pleased to accept a State Department recommendation that Kennedy be sent to Asia to mediate informally a territorial dispute between Indonesia and Malaysia. For

Kennedy, it was a difficult and absorbing assignment, a welcome change of scene. Ethel Kennedy accompanied her husband on the trip and helped in countless ways to divert him from the sadness that was written so deeply in his features.

By March 1964, he was able to speak again in public. Preparing to keep a long-scheduled commitment to address a St. Patrick's Day Dinner in Scranton, Pennsylvania, he decided to use a poem by John Boyle O'Reilly about the death of the Irish patriot Owen Roe O'Neill, which ended:

> We're sheep without a shepherd,
> When the snow shuts out the sky—
> Oh! why did you leave us, Owen?
> Why did you die?

His assistant, Edwin Guthman, advised against it, saying "You'll never get through it." "I've been practicing," Kennedy said. He had been standing in front of a mirror at home, repeating the lines so he could say them without breaking. "I can't yet, but I will by the time I speak." After Scranton, he was confident he could speak in public once more.

In April, he plunged again into the legislative struggle over passage of the Civil Rights bill. Designed to meet the grievances which had touched off the demonstrations in Birmingham and Selma, Alabama, the bill was the most important piece of legislation in the Justice Department's program. President Johnson, in his address to Congress on November 26, 1963, had asked for its "soonest possible passage" as a memorial to President Kennedy. Defending the bill in congressional hearings and directing the strategy to win the Republican support needed to break the ten-week southern filibuster restored some of Kennedy's zest for work. He decided to stay in office long enough to see the bill passed and he began seriously to consider his future.

He was a major public figure, a recognized talent floating free. And so, in the early months of 1964, his future plans became a steady source of speculation in the press. "What Will Bobby Do?" asked *Newsweek* magazine, sifting every shred of gossip and concluding only that "he would not seek a U. S. Senate seat from New York." His friends and family kept suggesting possibilities. One was to serve as Ambassador to the United Nations. The chance to debate foreign policy with representatives of other nations appealed to him. The heavy social obligations of the office and its subordination to second-level officials in the Department of State did not. Another suggestion was Ambassador to the Soviet Union, a possibility he had actually discussed with President Kennedy.

He was certain of only one thing: He would stay in public life. Except for teaching at a university, nothing in private life interested him. His father had impressed on all his sons that the responsibilities and opportunities of public service were the most rewarding and exciting challenges for men who had wealth. Coaching his brother Edward for a television debate in Massachusetts in 1962, he had come to the question: Why do you want to be in the Senate? "Tell them," he said, "why you want to do that instead of sitting in some office in New York." He said it with a passion that showed how strongly he felt that merely increasing his wealth was a misuse of his abilities.

Other things were happening in the early months of 1964 that were to affect this decision and the rest of Robert Kennedy's life. The night of his brother's funeral, he said to members of his family and his closest associates in government that if there was anything they wanted from the new Administration they better get it quickly, because, "in a few weeks, the Kennedys will be forgotten in this country."

He miscalculated the effect of his brother's career and the impact of his death. In the three months following President Kennedy's funeral, 200,000 people visited his grave and 900,000 sent letters of sympathy to his widow. Schools, streets, public buildings, and airports were renamed in his honor. Out of collective guilt and warm memories, the name of Kennedy, far from being forgotten, was becoming a legend in America. It represented something young and clean, a commitment to excellence, qualities that would be missed in public life.

As he reappeared in public, Kennedy received, for the first time, the reception reserved for national heroes. All the emotions people felt for his brother—the sympathy, the guilt, the hope—were converging on him. He was the first to point out that the adulation was not for anything he had done. Nor did he want it for himself; for more than anyone, he was determined to keep his brother's memory bright. But it was this enduring wave of public feeling, above all else, that would make him a major political figure in his own right, and compel him to pursue a career that could continue what his brother had begun.

Kennedy put it this way, in an interview a year later:

> I began to think about it a lot, continuously in fact, after he died, as a means to continue what he and I had begun together. You see, not the President alone, but we all were involved in certain tasks and certain dreams he wanted to translate into reality. Then, all of a sudden, he was no longer there to do it. I understood that it was up to me to carry them forward, and I decided to do so.

To do this, he would have to run for public office. For fifteen years, Kennedy had avoided elective office. After he left the staff of the Hoover Commission in 1954, his father urged him to move to Massachusetts to build a political base. He took another staff job in Washington instead. Persisting, Ambassador Kennedy suggested he move from Virginia to Maryland where the political climate was more receptive to a liberal Democrat. He refused. After the election of 1960, President Kennedy's Senate seat was vacant, and he suggested his brother might be appointed. Again, Robert Kennedy demurred.

He resisted in part because he was not built to be a candidate. Abrupt, aloof, and shy, he was a poor public speaker, who had not tried to improve his dry and monotonous style. He was the opposite of the "natural" politician. He could mingle with crowds and shake hands with strangers, but he did it almost mechanically, out of a sense of obligation. He never put his arm around someone he did not know well, and stiffened when more gregarious politicians did it to him.

He had been the manager, the administrator, the lightning rod. He had no hesitation about taking on the distasteful assignments men in elective office prefer to leave to others. In his brother's campaigns and in the Administration, he had been the "no-man," the one who told a man he was fired. The superficial camaraderie of politics was dissolved in his insistence on knowing the truth and getting the job done. These very qualities had made him so valuable to his brother.

Beyond his temperament, he had no need to hold elective office. He could serve his country by serving his brother. Whatever desire he might have for power or responsibility was more than fulfilled as the two of them, complementing each other, confiding in each other, weathered the challenges of political advancement and of the Presidency itself.

But now he was on his own. To carry forward what his brother represented he must now choose an office to run for and a time to seek it. For two years, there had been speculation in Massachusetts that Kennedy would come there and run for governor. The major issue of the time was the corruption in the state's government, and the combination of a Kennedy and a prosecutor was irresistible. Kennedy had seriously considered running—not in 1964, when a Democrat, Endicott Peabody, would be up for re-election, but in 1966, when for the first time a governor would be elected for a four-year term.

He had little doubt he could win, but was not sure a governor could make significant progress on the formidable problems of the state. He felt that the governor of Massachusetts had as little voice in the running of his state as any governor in the country. His power was severely circumscribed by the independence of the state legislature, the power of the independent commissions the legislature had created, and the legislature's deep aversion to increasing taxes, which made it difficult to raise money for the programs that were needed. In addition, many of the governor's actions had to be approved by the independently elected Governor's Council, a remnant of colonial times which had come to consist of petty politicians subject to questionable influences.

Reluctantly, Kennedy let it be known that he would not enter the Massachusetts political scene. Not wanting to criticize the state government, he gave as his public reason the fact that it would be awkward for him to come in because his younger brother was already there. Actually, Edward Kennedy had encouraged him, believing that if Robert Kennedy felt he could be an effective governor, his own position should not be a consideration.

From the time he first began to think it through, Robert Kennedy believed that the best position for him would be the vice presidency of the United States. In view of subsequent events, it now seems ironic that he desired to be Vice President under Lyndon Johnson. But the situation as it existed in the first half of 1964 made it a logical objective.

He was influenced by Johnson's repeated commitments to continue John Kennedy's policies. He was impressed by the energy with which Johnson set about to get the Kennedy legislative programs through Congress. Also, the vice presidency was the only position that would keep him near the wide range of problems he had worked on with his brother. It would not require moving from the home in Virginia where his family had lived for fourteen years.

Kennedy did not look upon the vice presidency as an independent office. He realized it involved subordinating one's own views and activities to those of the President. But for him, as for other strong-willed men who had agreed to take the office—including Lyndon Johnson—its strategic position was enough to overcome whatever difficulties the nature of the office involved. Kennedy felt the office would not relegate him to obscurity as it had so many others. In his case, it would help him keep his national constituency, and offer a vantage point from which to gain his party's nomination for the presidency when the Johnson administration ended.[2]

At no time did Kennedy believe that Johnson, deeply desirous of making his own mark, would prefer him as his running mate. But there was the possibility that he would need him. Johnson had relied heavily on the Kennedy lieutenants during the transition of power. Despite his almost thirty years in government, Johnson had only a handful of his own men with enough ability to take over the extensive responsibilities of running the Executive Branch. It was more than the appearance of continuity that led him personally to ask every significant member of the Kennedy White House staff, and every cabinet member, to stay on with him. With the exception of Arthur Schlesinger, Jr., and Theodore C. Sorensen, all of them agreed. Thus there was in Washington a government within a government, held together by a desire to see the thrust of the Kennedy program continue, loyal to the President but also to the Attorney General and privately supporting him for Vice President. "There are hundreds of people around this city in positions of influence," Kennedy told Richard Goodwin in December, 1963, "I'm the most important one because of my name, but I am not

---

[2] Obviously, he also must have thought he would be able to work with Johnson. Later, he was to change his mind, and declare on several occasions that he was glad he had not been selected because such close cooperation between them could never have been possible. A chief reason he offered was the way Johnson, in private conversations, continually belittled the closest and most loyal members of his staff. Kennedy had been trained to believe in personal loyalty as the *sine qua non* of any political operation, something that had to flow reciprocally between worker and chief. He felt these belittling statements demoralized associates and undercut their power, and it would have had the same effect on him.

unique. Sure, I've lost a brother—but other people lose their wives or even their children. The important thing is to do something for the country . . . collective action . . . that's the secret—but how to do it? I haven't figured out how to do it."

The core of his concept of "collective action" was that Johnson was so dependent upon President Kennedy's associates, at least until the next election, that they could trade their willingness to work for him for a measure of influence within his Administration. In this way, they could continue President Kennedy's policies, and perhaps influence the selection of Robert Kennedy as the vice presidential nominee.

But there was no way to bring it about. President Johnson held all the levers of power in the Executive Branch, checked only by his own feeling on the need for continuity of policy. Less than three weeks after President Kennedy's funeral, Johnson appointed his old friend Thomas Mann to direct Latin American policy. Mann was a traditional diplomat, concerned primarily with maintaining the political stability that protected American economic interests. To Kennedy, the appointment was the first signal that Johnson was determined to move independently of the Kennedy group, even if it meant their opposition. As the months passed, it became evident that by continuing on a generally liberal course, Johnson would be able to establish himself firmly enough, in the country and the Democratic party, to be able to choose anyone he wanted for the vice presidency.

There remained the possibility that conditions at the time of the Democratic Convention would be such that Johnson would feel only by choosing Kennedy could he ensure his own election. It was pointed out to Kennedy that Alben Barkley had not been President Truman's first choice as a running mate, nor had Truman been President Roosevelt's. In both cases the decision was forced upon the President by the necessities of the political situation and the pressure of Democratic leaders.

Kennedy was the clear first choice of Democratic voters for the vice presidential nomination. Through the spring of 1964, public opinion polls commissioned by Johnson and others confirmed this. Despite his identification with civil rights, he led in states like North Carolina and Alabama. In the urban states his margin was massive. Northern political leaders, aware of what a national landslide could do for their state candidates, urged Kennedy to make himself available for the ticket. Governors and former governors of three southern states, Terry Sanford of North Carolina, Carl Sanders of Georgia, and Earle Clements of Kentucky, did the same. By the first of June, Kennedy was ready to do what he could to influence Johnson's decision.

One thing he did was add a visit to Poland at the end of a trip to Berlin to dedicate a memorial to his brother. Disregarding protocol, he took himself directly to the people, much to the dismay of the Polish government. His intinerary was not publicized in the state newspapers or on television, but thousands of Poles came out to cheer him, giving him bread and roses in the Warsaw market and choruses everywhere of "May you live to be a hundred years." In the northern cities of the United States, 1964 marked the beginning of the "white backlash." There was considerable dissatisfaction within the Polish-American bloc of the Democratic Party over civil rights developments. The tumultuous reception given Kennedy throughout Poland reminded Democratic leaders that his appeal extended to a broad cross section of Catholic immigrant groups in the United States.

Kennedy's decision to visit Poland was not solely political. A demonstration of affection for an American leader benefited the nation's image in Eastern Europe and elsewhere. But the vice presidency was very much on his mind. To a group of students at Warsaw University he joked, "I am not a candidate for the vice presidency, but if you were in America and could vote for me, I would be."

By mid-July, Kennedy's closest political associates had prepared a list of major Democratic leaders, state by state, who were sympathetic to him as the vice-presidential choice. Another list, reading like a Who's Who of Democratic politics, named those President Johnson would probably consult in seeking advice about his choice. It included labor leaders, publishers, and a few large contributors to the party. The plan was for the men on the first list to urge those on the second, if they were consulted by the President, to recommend Kennedy.

In addition, plans were laid against the remote chance that Johnson would follow Adlai Stevenson's precedent of 1956 in leaving the nomination up to the Convention. Stevenson's decision then had caught the Kennedy forces by surprise. Only the heavy support of southern delegations allowed John F. Kennedy to make it a contest against Estes Kefauver. This time they would be better prepared. The list of delegates to the 1964 Convention would be compared against the lists of pro-Kennedy delegates to the 1960 Convention. A headquarters would be rented in Atlantic City and switchboard facilities installed. The opinion polls, top-heavy for Kennedy, would be delivered to the delegates. Special efforts would be made among congressmen and senators from close districts, whose own prospects would be aided by the Kennedy name on the ticket.

The possibility of success was remote. In all probability, a strong-willed man like Lyndon Johnson would not delegate the decision to the Convention. He would consult widely, but chances were that those he asked would tell him what they believed he wanted to hear. It was purely a contingency plan, compounded of rumors, fed by hopes that the decision might be left open.

But Johnson did not want Kennedy as his Vice President, and, as it turned out, he did not need him. The same poll that showed Kennedy so far ahead as the choice of Democrats also told Johnson that neither Kennedy nor anyone else would add significantly to what appeared to be a comfortable margin of victory over all possible Republican opponents.

On July 20, the Republican National Convention nominated Senator Barry Goldwater of Arizona, thereby assuring that the major battleground in the campaign would be the southern states, where Kennedy was considered to be weakest. On July 29, at the White House, Johnson told Kennedy he was not his choice for Vice President. He said Kennedy was fully qualified to be President, and that he, Johnson, would be happy to help him get elected later on. Johnson asked him to stay on as Attorney General for the time being, and implied there were other positions he could have if he desired them, in the Cabinet and in embassies abroad. Kennedy did not express disappointment. He offered to help Johnson in the campaign, but he said it would be hard for him to do so as Attorney General, a post traditionally removed from overt, active political participation.

Later that day, McGeorge Bundy, special assistant for National Security Affairs under Presidents Kennedy and Johnson, telephoned Robert Kennedy and suggested he announce immediately he was not available for the vice presidency. This would save Johnson the embarrassment of having to eliminate him publicly. Bundy did not normally involve himself in political affairs. Kennedy was irritated with Johnson for using Bundy for this kind of mission, and with Bundy for allowing himself to be used. To withdraw so precipitously would be an insult to all the political leaders who had urged him so strongly to run. He curtly rejected the proposal. He told Bundy he would not fight Johnson's decision, but he would not relieve Johnson of bearing the consequences of it.

The next day, Bundy called again. The President would issue a statement, and he wanted Kennedy's suggestions on what it would say. The President also wanted Kennedy to know that he would select as Vice President whomever Kennedy recommended. Kennedy refused to involve himself further. The repeated attempts to preserve the appearance of harmony mocked Johnson's promise to select "the best man for the country," "the man who could best take over if something happens to me." It made Kennedy regret that he had even wanted to be Vice President.

Johnson went on television that evening to announce he was eliminating every member of the Cabinet, as well as all who sat regularly with the Cabinet, from consideration for the vice presidency. The next day, speaking to a luncheon of Democratic congressional candidates in Washington, Kennedy said he had sent a telegram to his fellow cabinet members, saying that he had heard the President's announcement and he was "sorry I took so many of you nice fellows over the side with me."

Kennedy then went to Hyannis Port for the weekend. He still talked of working in the State Department, but Arthur Schlesinger, Jr., Averell Harriman, and others who were with him, and knew the department's feelings discounted both the possibility of such an appointment and Kennedy's satisfaction with the position. At this point he decided to reopen the possibility of running for the United States Senate from New York.

As early as December of 1963, Edward Kennedy and Stephen Smith, his brother-in-law, had discussed Robert's moving to New York, living there for the three years, and then running for the governorship in 1966. It had been just one of the many possibilities talked about by those who were concerned about his future, including the possibility of purchasing and publishing the New York *Post* which reportedly was for sale. The New York Constitution, however, imposed a minimum residence requirement of five years for the office of Governor. The Senate required only that he be a resident of the state at the time of his election.[3] A memorandum on the subject had been sent to Kennedy while he was on a Christmas skiing holiday in Aspen, Colorado, urging him to run for the Senate, but he had shown little enthusiasm for the prospect.

There had been considerable interest, however, among political leaders in New York. They were looking for a strong candidate to run against Senator Kenneth Keating, a first-term Republican senator from Rochester, who had been elected in 1958 on the coattails of Governor Nelson Rockefeller. One of these leaders was Peter Crotty of Buffalo, the Democratic Chairman of Erie County and one of the most influential Democrats in the State. He had been the first county leader in the state to declare his support for John Kennedy in 1960. On Inauguration Day 1964, Crotty, lunching at Hickory Hill, had told Kennedy that a vacuum existed in the Democratic party, and that he could win the Senate nomination and the election. Kennedy replied by soliciting Crotty's advice on the vice presidency. Returning to Buffalo, Crotty, on his own initiative, arranged for the county committee to pass a resolution endorsing Kennedy for Vice President.

Others took up the discussion[4] during the spring, and by June 1964, there was considerable public speculation about Kennedy making the race. Polls taken by the Democratic State Committee showed him easily the strongest nominee. He was sufficiently interested to authorize Stephen Smith to take informal soundings among the major Democratic County leaders but he felt he must wait until the vice-presidential question was resolved before taking further steps. He did not want to give Johnson any excuse for avoiding the fact of his availability as a running mate. But he could not remain silent without making it appear that he was open to, if not tacitly promoting, a draft in New York.

The occasion for resolution of this difficulty came on June 19, when Senator Edward Kennedy was critically injured in an airplane crash while traveling to the Democratic State Convention in Springfield,

[3] Article I, Section 3 of the United States Constitution provides that "No person shall be a Senator who shall not have attained the age of thirty years and been nine years a citizen of the United States, and who shall not, when elected, be an inhabitant of that state for which he shall be chosen." No state can impose any additional qualification.

[4] Franklin D. Roosevelt, Jr., and John English, leader of Nassau County, publicly suggested Kennedy make the race.

Massachusetts. During the days of agonizing uncertainty following the accident, Kennedy, propelled by instinct and events, issued a brief statement thanking those "Democratic leaders and friends in New York" who had urged him to seek the Senate nomination but saying that "in fairness to them and to end speculation" he would not be a candidate.

Now, six weeks later, on August 2, he told Smith to renew his contacts with Democratic county leaders. That same week, he flew to New York City to seek the support of Mayor Robert F. Wagner, the state's most influential Democrat. Wagner agreed to support him. His course was now certain: he would run for the Senate. It had not been his preference, and had never been his goal, but it was a resolution. After eight months of grief and indecision, Robert Kennedy had a project and a purpose once again.

2

A MAN, AN IMAGE, AND A SYMBOL

Robert Kennedy was thirty-eight when he decided to run for the Senate. He stood 5 feet 10 inches tall, although his slender build and a tendency to stoop made him look shorter. He had a muscular body, hardened by constant athletic competition, and though he liked rich foods and ate chocolate sundaes for dessert, he rarely added to his weight, which was approximately 150 pounds. His dark blond hair showed some gray, and he used glasses for reading, but these, the deep wrinkles in his forehead and the knotted aspect of his hands were the only evidence of his full years.

Unlike his brothers, he had no history of serious illness or chronic pain. He seemed almost to vibrate with nervous energy. He could not sit in one place for long without jiggling a foot or tapping his teeth with the end of a pencil. Generally he slept easily and had learned the political art of sleeping anywhere during a tough schedule when time permitted. He was in better physical condition than most men in their twenties.

Kennedy was good-looking, not with the glamour of his brothers, but with a rugged look, superimposed on the Irish features that marked the members of his family. Cartoonists made the toothy grin and the unruly shock of hair into trademarks long before he let his hair grow to show his rebellious identification with the restlessness of youth. Lampooners sometimes dubbed him "Bugs Bunny," which made him laugh. The most striking feature of his face were his eyes—bright blue, piercing, sometimes steely, often compassionate. Around them, the intensity of his life and the tragedy of his brother's death had sculpted deep, sad lines.

He had the flat New England accent made famous by President Kennedy. Listening to his voice on a broadcast, many people thought it was his brother. In person, his voice was higher, more nasal, more penetrating, and it would rise as he became more animated. At the beginning of his Senate campaign, the exhausting schedule and constant speaking gave him laryngitis. Dr. W. James Gould, a Manhattan throat specialist who had treated President Kennedy for the same problem, explained that Kennedy was not suffering from overuse of his voice but from the incorrect use of it. He was forming his sounds in his throat instead of in the lower respiratory system. The constant pressure, along with the changes in climate, had tightened his throat and caused infection.

Dr. Gould gave him pills to reduce the infection, but more important he instructed Kennedy in the techniques of "thoracic-abdominal" speaking which involves forming words deeper in the respiratory system and learning more effective breathing patterns between phrases. This enabled Kennedy to lower his pitch and develop a more sonorous quality which made him a better public speaker, though when he became absorbed in answering questions his voice tended to rise to the old level.

Kennedy was born to wealth and its advantages, and he used them routinely. He maintained an apartment in New York City, a house in Hyannis Port, another house (until 1967) in Glen Cove, Long Island, and his permanent home at Hickory Hill. He had the perpetual tan of one who could afford to go skiing or vacation in the South during the winter and go to the beach every weekend in the summer. His suits were made in London, or at Lewis and Thomas Saltz, one of the most expensive men's stores in Washington. In the judgment of *Men's Wear* magazine his tailoring was "authoritative, expensive, expansive, very safe, blending unobtrusively into the background." He made large contributions to religious and social charities, often anonymously. He could indulge his interest in American history with expensive purchases, such as one of the twelve copies of Lincoln's

Emancipation Proclamation. Like many wealthy men who rarely travel alone, he often forgot to carry money. He was allowed to sign for the bill at a hotel or restaurant at sight, but his companions were usually left with the taxi bills or other small items, with little prospect of repayment. Once, in church, a friend put a dollar in the collection plate for him, and Kennedy then suggested, with a smile, "Don't you think I should give more?"

A large staff tended to his personal and family arrangements, allowing him to make his way through a hectic schedule which often found him working in two cities on the same day. Edwin Guthman, reflecting on how Kennedy could lead so many lives at once, decided he could, too, if he had someone to buy his clothes, pay his bills, do his taxes, watch his children, mow his lawn, and do all the other tasks of drudgery that consume so much of the lives of ordinary men. Guthman and the rest of Kennedy's staff also understood the hours of drudgery that consumed his time: work days lasting eighteen hours that ran from hearings to dinners, from mountains of correspondence to constant traveling around the country.

Kennedy had a quick and flexible mind but he did not think of himself as an intellectual. Although his qualities of tenacity and concentration were marked, his formal academic record was undistinguished. His primary intellectual development came from the intensive experiences and study that accompanied his growing responsibilities in public life. A compulsion to learn drove him to do things like listen to foreign language tapes while in the bath. He read widely, and when he came across a quote he thought especially appealing, he marked it to be typed up and frequently it appeared later in impromptu remarks. He memorized long passages of poetry, and once bested Richard Burton in recalling lines from a speech in *Henry V*. He quoted his poetry with great accuracy although he sometimes forgot the author and had to begin, "As the poet said . . ."

Watching television, for him, was largely a waste of time. The news shows were part of his work and he admired some special productions, taking time to send a complimentary note to his friend, William Paley of CBS, for example when that network showed its study of hunger in America. He believed—and often told his friends in broadcasting—

that the networks were forfeiting an enormous opportunity to help develop the minds and cultural tastes of the American people.

In public affairs, he could draw from a core of knowledge about most areas developed in his previous work, the field of finance being an exception. Between 1961 and 1963, he had been involved in daily top-level briefings and discussions and had traveled to twenty countries. He could be briefed quickly, orally as well as on paper, and he retained vast amounts of detailed information. His question-and-answer sessions were always impressive performances. He had an instinct for the fact or figure which would most dramatically make his case and a way of stating complicated issues in language mass audiences could understand.

Open-minded and totally accessible to new ideas, Kennedy welcomed the opportunity of learning. His close relationship to his more dispassionate, more intellectual brother, and the experience in governing a nation, had shown him the complexities of public problems and had dissolved whatever sense of absolutes he had about them. Dogmatic and strongly opinionated people disturbed him. The sharpest puncture of his questioning was reserved for them.

He was a man of instinct both about people and problems. If he could see a problem firsthand, he preferred that experience to reading a book about it. He confronted the hunger of Negro children in Mississippi by walking the muddy paths of the delta. He sought to understand the strength of Communism in Chile by going into the coal mines to see the conditions that bred revolution. By seeing and sharing and confronting, he understood, and although he held his political ideas with great self-assurance, none of them was beyond challenge and re-evaluation.

Kennedy had a wry, impish sense of humor that was all his own. For his public appearances he made use of both amateur and professional humorists.[1] With their help he became as effective as anyone in politics in delivering the short one-liners that are professional fare

[1] At various times in his career, Kennedy received suggestions for speech humor from Theodore Sorensen, Jack Rosenthal (assistant director of Public Affairs of the Department of Justice under Kennedy), his Senate press secretary, Frank Mankiewicz, his brother Edward's press secretary, Richard Drayne and comedians Alan King and Joey Bishop.

on television. But his spontaneous humor, in notes or conversation, often topped his writers' efforts. He generally directed this humor at himself, using it to defuse embarrassing situations or make light of political attacks. When a right-wing magazine accused a Democratic candidate for Congress of getting a $25,000 contribution from the Kennedys, he said, "He can't deny it now. He was very appreciative when I met him in the hotel lobby. I gave him the satchel and he gave me a card which said 'Kennedy '68.' "

Once a longtime political associate felt temporarily ignored and blurted some unkind remarks about him to the press. Kennedy sent him a letter saying, "I read you don't like the Kennedys very much because they are such selfish, ungrateful wretches. Oh well, we fooled you for a long time, didn't we?" On another occasion, William Buckley, Jr., the columnist, sent him a copy of a letter from a woman who had canceled her subscription to the *National Review* because she had seen Buckley and Kennedy together in a newspaper picture. He told friends that Buckley lost a customer because he said something nice about him, "but by now he must have gotten her back."

He saved some of his best humor for sensitive political situations. One was the competition that seemed to be developing between himself and Hubert H. Humphrey for the Democratic presidential nomination in 1972. Kennedy and Humphrey liked one another. Each thoroughly understood the other's political course and ambitions, and each knew the other could take a joke. A light-hearted private correspondence developed between them. When a little boy wrote Kennedy asking for "a copy of your Inaugural Address," he sent the letter to Humphrey, as "a typical example of my mail." Humphrey responded with several similar requests he had received.

When Humphrey spoke at a meeting of New York State mayors organized by Kennedy to offer information about programs of federal assistance, Kennedy sent him a formal note of thanks, adding, "Personally, I thought you were a little *too* good." When Humphrey read about Kennedy's exploits on the ski slopes, he challenged him privately to a race with snowmobiles, which are popular in Minnesota winters. And when a letter to Humphrey from the mayor of a city in Alabama was delivered to Kennedy's office and opened by mistake, he sent it along with this note of apology:

Dear Hubert:

It was a mistake, not part of any ruthless scheme to intercept your mail. However, I am somewhat shocked and surprised at the close working and social relationship you are establishing with some people. Needless to say, I shall not breathe a word about any of this to Clarence Mitchell or Whitney Young or anyone like that.

Kennedy was an athlete all his life. He relaxed his mind by exerting his body. In the early mornings he rode a horse named Attorney General, and in mild weather swam in his pool or played tennis. He went about his recreation with the same singleness of purpose that he gave his professional interests. His children, who shared his love of outdoor sports, were forever breaking arms and legs and falling from horses and rooftops. He had suffered only one serious injury since college, a leg broken skiing at Sun Valley, Idaho, in 1950.

Exercise was essential to his life. Late in 1964, he sprained his ankle so badly he had to submit to heat therapy and whirlpool baths. The doctor told him he would have to stay off the leg for a week. Kennedy said this would be impossible; he had to have his exercise on weekends. The doctor told him gently that if he insisted on running around, the injury would never heal. He listened and obeyed. In touch football, the family game, he was a good ball carrier, quick, and deceptive. He liked to call the plays himself. He was only a fair tennis player, having taken it up late in life, but whatever he lacked in skill, he made up in competitiveness. Psychological warfare designed to demoralize his opponents, like running to a net position during a change in service while those on the other side were welcoming a moment to rest, was as much a part of his game as his forehand stroke.

His favorite sports were skiing and sailing. Taking the hard slopes at Aspen, Waterville, or Sun Valley was the kind of test against difficult obstacles that gave him stimulation. He skied without finesse or any discernible style, but he was an instructor's delight because he skied fast even while learning, and had no fear of falling or crashing into the landscape. As a sailor he was equally fearless, heedless of the fog near shore, enjoying the discomfiture of the more timid aboard. Most of his sailing was done on Nantucket Sound off Hyannis, in a Wiano yawl, the *Resolute*. For longer trips along the rocky coast of Maine, he chartered a larger boat, filled it with children, friends, and animals, and set off for whatever adventures the wind and seas would hold.

He played every sport to win. If his team was behind at the end of a game of touch football, he might call for an extra period and drive his teammates until they won. Once, sailing in a race off Hyannis Port, he and Edward Kennedy were involved in a protest at the windward mark. Disqualified from the race, the brothers argued for an hour before the Protest Committee, using little model boats to defend their position with all the force they might have put into an argument before the Supreme Court. They lost the decision.

To some, his competitive nature made him seem combative, eager for a fight, determined to press his views over others. To some, his disregard for danger whether skiing or facing a hostile crowd, was recklessness. But to Robert Kennedy, every challenge—in sports and politics—was an opportunity coolly to measure his abilities against an obstacle. Once he entered a contest, he knew only one way to compete: by running as hard and as fast as he could.

A handwriting analyst once looked at Kennedy's cramped, almost indecipherable scrawl, without knowing whose it was, and concluded his characteristics were "lack of system; careless in small things; more ambitious than practical; cold nature, ruled by head; seldom arrives at conclusions hastily; reticent, even secretive at times; good judge of character; proud, possibly conceited; susceptible to flattery; can be impulsive; fluency of thought, but above all, energy, ambition and ardor." But there were other qualities about Robert Kennedy that marked him apart both in politics, and from most men of his generation. He was at once a private man, a public image, and a symbol, and the three interacted upon one another.

Kennedy the man had been shaped by growing up with two older brothers in a close, hyperactive, strongly competitive family, where the goals of wealth, education, and good manners were easily attained and self-satisfaction was sought through recognition and public service. In personal traits, Kennedy bore a strong inheritance from his father. They had the same strong sense of family unity and personal loyalty, the same disdain for Establishment power, the same zest for combat. At Robert Kennedy's house, the athletic line-up was usually the Kennedys against "the others," even when the others included Shrivers, Lawfords, and Smiths. He passed to his children his father's maxims: "Kennedys don't cry"; or "Kennedys never say can't."

He did not, however, "hate like his father." This phrase was absorbed into the literature about him after a Boston politician had used it in an interview to take out his revenge. It was inaccurate, and unfair to both men. Neither were inclined toward so self-destructive an exercise as personal hatred. Both, however, had more than their share of controversies, fought intensely with those they opposed, and always remembered who had been with them and against them.

Kennedy had a Puritan's sense of right and wrong, good and evil, friends and enemies. He had been attracted to a career of law enforcement because it was the area of public service where these lines were drawn most clearly. Later, the same sense would draw him to the side of the poor. Convinced by his investigations that Teamster Union leader James Hoffa was corrupt, and that his power threatened both honest unionism and the public interest, for six years Kennedy pursued Hoffa with the single-minded zeal of a crusader until Hoffa went to jail. He battled governors who defied federal law regarding integration much as he did racketeers—convinced there was only one right side which had to be upheld.

Yet this intense, electric leader of men was extraordinarily shy, and this is crucial to an understanding of why he seemed so different in private than in public. It was the shyness that made him unable to affect the backslapping, arm-rubbing ritual professional politicians practice on each other, or to have a satisfactory interview with most journalists. He found it especially difficult to talk about himself. He was uncomfortable with public statements that had too many "I's" or "my's." While warm and outgoing with family and friends, he was ill at ease with strangers and in large gatherings. Conversations with him could suddenly founder on long, embarrassing silences, with neither person knowing quite what to say. Those he did not know well were nervous when talking to him because he was a celebrity. Not expecting his shyness, many who met him thought him hostile or indifferent, and this adversely affected his public image.

But this shyness also helped account for his remarkable gift of communication with children. Unlike adults, children met him without embarrassment. He shared their sense of self-consciousness and vulnerability in public and tried to make them as comfortable as possible. Frequently, they walked up to him and put their hand in his. He sometimes put his hands on their heads or shoulders, communicating without words in a way that children understand. In 1963, despite the gloom of Dallas, he insisted that the Christmas party the Justice Department had scheduled for some of Washington's disadvantaged children go forward. At the height of the merrymaking, a little boy rushed up to him and said "Your brother is dead." The room grew quiet. The little boy, sensing something wrong, began to cry. Kennedy picked him up, hugged him and said, "Don't worry, I have another."

Kennedy did not talk about his philosophy of life. He was a pragmatist. His philosophy was in what he did. Theoretical discussions and generalities of any kind bored him. He was impatient with those who understood problems but did not act to solve them. Once a Canadian television interviewer asked him what his values were. "I can't answer questions like that," he said. "Ask me about something specific." If pressed, however, he would have agreed with a philosophy which said "Live life to the fullest, do all you can for others, respect the gifts of life and opportunity, and share them with as many as you can." He was expressing a basic personal conviction when he told the students at Berkeley: "You can use your enormous privilege and opportunity to seek purely private pleasure and gain. But history will judge you, and, as the years pass, you will ultimately judge yourself, on the extent to which you have used your gifts to lighten and enrich the lives of your fellow man."

Kennedy did not talk much about religion either. Whatever inner turbulence he felt about his Roman Catholicism, he kept to himself. Others in his family were more devout in traditional ways, but he never missed Mass on days of obligation, and he always wore a St. Christopher's medal around his neck.

He had been trained as an altar boy and did not hesitate to volunteer if one was needed at Mass. Once while sailing off the coast of Maine, he went to evening Mass at a small church in the remote countryside. As the priest began the Mass, Kennedy went forward to assist him. The reverend father looked with disbelief and later complimented the altar boy on his training.

He had none of the awe or distance with which many Catholics regard their clergy. The Kennedys were the most prominent Catholic family in the United States, substantial benefactors of the Church, with close friends at all levels of the hierarchy. Foremost among them was Richard Cardinal Cushing of Boston, who reflected the ecumenical spirit of Pope John XXIII and, like Pope John, never lost the simple manner of a parish priest.

In Kennedy's opinion, his Church was not sufficiently related to contemporary problems. It was too strongly identified with its own material needs rather than the moral struggles that were tearing the world apart. He once discussed the role of the Church in effecting social justice with Pope Paul VI at the Vatican, and urged the Church to be the foremost champion of improving the living conditions of the poor. Speaking of America, he pointed out that efforts to help the poor, especially the Negro, aroused the fears and hostilities of Catholic groups such as the Irish, the Poles, and the Italians. For this reason, the Church had a special responsibility. Its guidance, in this difficult area, might turn the tide. Kennedy was critical, in that audience, of the hierarchy's leadership, especially in Los Angeles and New York. Few Catholic laymen would have expressed such criticisms to the Holy Father, but Kennedy did not allow his reverence for the Church to overrule his opinions of the men who led it.

The death of John Kennedy had been the first profound tragedy of Robert's life. Joseph Kennedy, Jr., was twelve years older than Robert. The gap of years and the separation caused by the war made him more remote. When he was killed in a bombing mission in 1944, the family, especially the father, was shattered by grief; but for Robert, it was less personal and brutal than what was to come. In Dallas he lost his hero, his daily companion, the focus of his life. He began to read books that dealt with the timeless issues of life. He spent more time struggling with problems of self-identity. Away from his family, he was suddenly a lonely man. He identified with those who had suffered personal tragedy and sought out the company of men like Charles Evers of Mississippi, whose own brother had been assassinated just months before. He sent handwritten notes of condolence to friends and members of his staff who suffered the loss of family members. The zest, humor, and combativeness returned, but melancholy was now his constant shadow. There was a void in his life, a wound that never healed. Anyone who looked into his eyes knew the suffering he had endured.

In these years, Kennedy was more than a personality. He was an image and a symbol. In the torrent of articles written about him, in the comments offered to samplers of public opinion, he was considered to be sincere, energetic, intelligent, and (unlike most politicians) a man of integrity. He was called ambitious, but this trait attaches naturally to men in public life. The one great flaw in his public image was the widespread feeling that he was "ruthless," a label related to his career as an investigator, prosecutor, political manager, and the cutting edge of a national Administration. The label could have been "single-minded" or "hard-driving" or even "tough." The adjective that stuck, however, was "ruthless," which the dictionary defines as "merciless" or "cruel." It was not applied to Kennedy quite so harshly. "It is the conjunction of moral certainty about right and wrong with calculated opportunism" explained political scientist Hans Morgenthau, "which accounts for Kennedy's reputation for ruthlessness. He gives the impression that personal success and the triumph of right are interchangeable."

A public image, by definition, is a picture people have of someone they do not know firsthand. Images break down upon personal acquaintance. Kennedy's friends could never understand how a man so considerate of them and so gentle with children could be considered ruthless. Kennedy himself despaired at ever shaking off the label. Once Arthur Schlesinger, hearing the adjective repeated at countless liberal meetings, suggested Kennedy respond by saying, "I believe deeply in certain things and I work for them. In the course of fighting for these principles, I may have made some enemies, but I am proud of many of those I have made." Schlesinger suggested he mention, among others, Jimmy Hoffa and Governor Ross Barnett of Mississippi. Kennedy was not comfortable with this approach. He thought it too self-laudatory.

As a symbol, however, Kennedy was something far different. He was the embodiment of much of the respect and affection in which the people of the United States, and the world, held the slain President. Crowds mobbed him. When he walked on the street, people gaped. Some approached hesitantly for a picture, a handshake, an autograph, and he would oblige. Those who worked with him each day tended to forget this side of him. They could always be stimulated by going out on the street with him and seeing what he meant to so many people.

There were drawbacks to this. The affection could turn to anger if people felt he were trading on his brother's name. Each of the President's admirers kept their own image of what he had been. All of Robert Kennedy's actions were tested by whether they came up to the legend of his brother. And that legend was different for different people. The crowds which greeted him included those who came to disparage him as well as those who came to adore him. He was proud to have the name Kennedy. But he was a different kind of man from the President, and he knew this better than anyone else. If he were to make a real contribution to American public life, it would have to be as something more than John Kennedy's brother.

3

THE CAMPAIGN FOR THE SENATE

When Steve Smith began talking in earnest to New York's Democratic leaders in August 1964 it was less than a month before the state convention would meet to choose the Senate nominee. Robert Kennedy was still Attorney General, a voting resident of Massachusetts, and unfamiliar with the politicians and the local problems of New York state. But by the middle of August, work had begun on both the substance and politics of his campaign.

On the fifth floor of the Justice Department in Washington, a small group of associates started to assemble a bulky blue briefing book on New York issues: economic problems like housing, employment, and agriculture; foreign policy problems with ethnic repercussions, such as Israel and Cyprus. In each area of domestic interest, the group compiled a list of what the Kennedy and Johnson administrations had done for New York, and what further federal programs were necessary. The book also contained the names of eighteen members of the Senate who had been born in states other than the one they were representing. Because of the unusual circumstances of his candidacy, Kennedy thought he should have commitments from a majority of the delegates to the Convention before officially entering the race. For a few days, all went well. Major leaders, Charles F. Buckley of the Bronx, Stanley Steingut of Brooklyn, William Luddy of Westchester, and of course Peter Crotty and John English, assured Smith of their support. William McKeon, the Democratic State Chairman, switched his support to Kennedy from Samuel Stratton, an upstate congressman who had been the only active candidate. Mayor Wagner assured Kennedy privately he would endorse him at the proper moment. But on August 9, the New York *Times* ran a front-page story which seriously jeopardized the candidacy by identifying Kennedy with what had become the most damaging issue in New York State politics—"bossism."

POWELL SEES GAIN FOR WAGNER FOES
Says He and Others Opposed to Mayor
Will Dictate Senatorial Choice

Representative Adam Clayton Powell predicted yesterday that anti-Wagner forces would dictate the choice of Robert F. Kennedy, or some other favorite of theirs for the Democratic nomination for Senator from New York.

The Harlem congressman said that political leaders opposed to the mayor—including himself—would control the state nominating convention September 1 and pick the candidate.

"Steingut, Buckley, Crotty and I will decide who will be the next U. S. Senator, or at least the Democratic nominee," Mr. Powell said at a news conference at the Abyssinian Baptist Church. He is minister of the Harlem church.

The issue of "bossism" was shorthand for the fundamental ideological conflict that had split the Democratic voting blocs in New York for the past twenty-five years. It has been used by Democrats against each other and by Republicans against their Democratic opponents. It became the major reason why New York, with the largest concentration of Democratic voters of any state in the Union, developed a tradition of electing Republicans to state-wide office.

The Democratic Party of New York is the oldest existing political party in the world. It was formed by Aaron Burr out of the Knights of Saint Tammany and in 1797, after Burr took a trip up the Hudson River with Thomas Jefferson, it became the foundation of the national Democratic Party. In its lifetime, the Democratic Party of New York had given nine of the twenty-six presidential nominees of the national party.[1] But in the years since World War II, New

---

[1] Martin van Buren, Grover Cleveland, Franklin D. Roosevelt; Horatio Seymour (1868) Horace Greeley (1872), Samuel J. Tilden (1876), Alton B. Parker (1904), John W. Davis (1924), Alfred E. Smith (1928).

York Democrats had been so torn by division that they had succeeded in electing only one governor (Averell Harriman), one senator (Herbert Lehman) and one other state-wide officeholder (Comptroller Arthur Levitt). This was no simple factional feud, to be patched up through skilled leadership, or healed with sufficient time out of office. The decline of the party was rooted in the inability of the leadership to hold together its two main voting blocs—the 1,300,000 liberal Jewish voters and the 3,000,000 more conservative Catholic voters—who together comprise almost 80 per cent of the Democratic vote in New York state. United on the domestic economic program of the New Deal and the Fair Deal, these groups had separated over issues such as the Spanish Civil War, post-World War II relations with the Soviet Union, financial assistance to parochial education, and the activities of Senator Joseph McCarthy.*

Statements indicating the sharp divergence of views illustrate this. Catholic views are on the left, Jewish on the right.

* "Recognition of Soviet Russia would be looked upon as treason by the twenty million Catholics in this country . . . the widespread tyranny, cruelty, and persecution practiced in Russia makes reported oppression in Germany read like the hazing indulged in by high school fraternities."

(*Editorial,* The Brooklyn Tablet, *official organ of the diocese of Brooklyn, March 24, 1933*)

"SOVIET RECOGNITION PRAISED IN PULPITS: RABBIS LAUD PRESIDENT . . . Rabbi I. Mortimer Bloom said resumption of diplomatic relations between America and Russia would add great momentum to the movement for universal disarmament. He predicted the rapproachment would be considered in years to come as the crowning achievement of President Roosevelt. Rabbi Jacob Katz said Roosevelt had taken a 'truly American position' . . ."

(*The New York Times November 20, 1933, p. 2*)

"Collaboration with Communism against Nazism is as indefensible as collaboration with Nazism against Communism. Hitler may be the chief menace now. But it is unthinkable that after a war in

"A resolution praising the Soviet Union for 'saving one million and a half of our fellow Jews' and calling on continuous and ever-growing collaboration between the Soviet Union and

THE CAMPAIGN FOR THE SENATE

which the Soviets participate and which they help to win, Communism will not become the primary menace: Alliance with Russia would be a league with death . . . a convenant with hell . . ."

(*Editorial*, The Catholic World, *August 1941, p. 316*)

the United States was adopted unanimously last night by 1,300 persons attending a dinner at the Hotel Commander . . . the resolution was proposed by James N. Rosenberg, honorary chairman of the Jewish Committee for Russian War Relief, seconded by Mrs. David de Sola Pool, president of Hadassah."

(*The national Jewish woman's organization*)

"Francis Cardinal Spellman today rebuked European critics of McCarthyism and said Americans would not be dissuaded from their determination to root out Communism subversion. The Archbishop of New York defended the procedure of a Congressional Committee that investigated Communism . . . 'no American uncontaminated by Communism has lost his good name because of Congressional hearings on un-American activities . . . ' "

(*The New York* Times, *October 23, 1953, p. 25*)

"Jewish groups are disturbed because 42 of the 47 employees suspended or refused clearance at (Fort) Monmouth after the McCarthy hearings are Jewish . . ."

(*The New York* Times, *January 11, 1954, p. 1*)

"One of the most significant facts to emerge from Congressional investigations of Communist infiltration of the schools is the perfect record of American Catholic schools and their teachers, a unique record of loyalty to the democracy."

(The Catholic World, *November 1953, p. 111*)

"The Rabbinical Assembly of America today unanimously called for the granting of 'amnesty in public opinion' to those who clearly dissociated themselves from Communist Fronts before the Berlin Airlift of 1948."

(*The New York* Times, *June 28, 1953, p. 7*)

In the other industrial states of the Northeast and Midwest, the liberal vote is far less significant. There, political leaders of the Catholic ethnic groups had been able to maintain a united front behind the domestic programs of the Democratic Party. In New York, the closer numerical balance and increasing ideological distance between the groups led to the creation of third parties designed to attract liberal voters.

The spiritual leaders of New York's liberals were Franklin D. Roosevelt and Herbert H. Lehman. Roosevelt deliberately created the American Labor Party (ALP) in 1936 so that liberal voters could support him without voting the Democratic line. The ALP was later displaced by the Liberal Party when it came under Communist domination. Lehman, governor of New York for four terms after Roosevelt, was elected to the Senate in 1949 and in the early Eisenhower years became the patriarch of what was then a small band of liberals in that body. Their counterparts in the eyes of conservative Democrats were Alfred E. Smith and James A. Farley. After losing the Democratic presidential nomination to Roosevelt in 1932, Smith broke with him over the liberal trend of the New Deal and opposed his re-election to a second term. Farley had been Roosevelt's campaign manager, chief political lieutenant, and Postmaster General, but Farley broke with FDR over his third term and sought the presidential nomination in 1940 for himself.

The machinery of the Democratic Party in the state was under the tight control of the leaders of the boroughs of New York City, loyal to Farley. These leaders had sufficient votes to control the conventions which nominated the candidates for statewide office. But with their separate constituency of Democrats, the ALP and later the Liberal Party could at least force the "bosses" to bargain with them over candidates, policies, and patronage.

Roosevelt as war President had more important concerns than New York politics. But Farley, though no longer National Chairman, retained his position as Chairman of The New York Democratic State Committee and sought to control the party. The first confrontation came at the 1942 state convention,[2] when the Tammany forces

2 Although the first defection took place in 1936, when Lehman, running for governor, ran 11–15 per cent behind Roosevelt on the Democratic ticket, after Father Charles Coughlin addressed 5000 of his supporters at a rally in St. Mary's Park, Bronx, and heard them each pledge to change ten Democratic votes to the Republican candidate for governor, Congressman William F. Bleakley.

booed Governor Lehman, rejected his personal choice as successor (James Mead of Buffalo), and nominated Farley's man, state Attorney General John J. Bennett. For the first time, the ALP endorsed an independent candidate. Bennett was defeated by Thomas E. Dewey, ending Democratic control of the governor's office that had lasted for twenty years. Four years later, in an effort to regain the support of liberal voters, the Democrats nominated Mead with endorsement of the ALP. This identification with the Mead campaign offended Catholic Democrats who defected to Dewey in large numbers.[3] In addition, Dewey had established an era of progressive Republicanism, which appealed to independent voters, and this, plus the national postwar backlash against the Democrats, helped him to an easy victory.

Out of power, the Democrats fell to factional infighting. Time and again, defections by one group or the other ensured the defeat of the party's candidates. In 1954, Averell Harriman won election as governor by the narrowest margin in the state's history. Most political observers thought his excellent record would win him easy re-election, but in 1958, both Governor Harriman and Frank Hogan, the gentle, independent District Attorney of Manhattan and one of the state's most respected citizens, became classic victims of the split. Carmine DeSapio, the leader of Tammany Hall, was credited with delivering the votes at the Convention that nominated Hogan—and the issue of "bossism" again divided the Democrats bitterly, giving the Republicans the issue they needed to not only defeat Hogan, but displace Governor Harriman with Nelson Rockefeller.

The rule of Democratic self-destruction in New York followed this rough pattern: If the party nominated a man whose background, views and sponsorship tied him to old-line party organization, the Liberal Party would select an independent candidate. Enough liberal voters would defect to ensure the election of the Republican. If the Democrats tried to avoid this by naming a man acceptable to the Liberals, enough conservative Catholic Democrats would switch, to

[3] It was at the opening rally of Mead's campaign that Henry Wallace, then Secretary of Commerce, made the speech that departed from the foreign policy line of the Truman administration and led to his expulsion from the Cabinet. On October 22, 1946, the Moscow radio urged the election of all candidates supported by the Political Action Committee of the CIO. Mead was one of them.

again elect the Republican. The Republicans encouraged this by reject-
ing conservative nominees in favor of progressive leaders such as
Thomas E. Dewey, Nelson Rockefeller, Jacob Javits, and John Lindsay,
who took the conservative Republicans for granted and appealed for
independent Democratic support.

No man could come up through the ranks of Democratic politics
without casting his lot on one side, and thereby becoming unacceptable
to the other. It was no coincidence that the only candidates who
managed to win for the Democrats were Harriman, who had made
his reputation outside of New York politics; Lehman, who had been
governor four times before the conflict had become critical; Robert
Wagner, Jr., who, bearing a revered name from happier times,
picked his way with caution and skill between the opposing groups
when he was mayor of New York City, and Levitt, who established
a reputation independent of the party as state comptroller.

By 1960, many of the liberal Democrats had organized a "reform
movement," with its own clubhouses, strong financial backing, and
the active support of Lehman, then eighty-one, and Mrs. Franklin
D. Roosevelt. Its express purpose was to oust the Democratic leaders
of Manhattan and the Bronx, Carmine DeSapio and Charles Buckley.
To John and Robert Kennedy this was just one more state feud
to be overcome temporarily as part of their campaign for the presidency. Most of the regular Democrats supported John Kennedy at
the Convention. Most of the Reformers backed Adlai Stevenson. To
carry New York, John Kennedy needed support from all factions. As
a liberal, who appealed to conservatives as the possible first Catholic
President, he got it. He was the first Democratic presidential candidate
to carry New York in sixteen years. He was also helped by his
opponent's unpopularity among independent Republicans.

The factions conducted independent campaigns on his behalf.
Robert Kennedy went between the groups, spurring them on and not
concealing his irritation when they let their feuding interfere with
the effort to elect his brother President.

As soon as the 1960 election was over, the Democrats returned to
their fratricide. In 1961, Robert Wagner, seeking a third term as
mayor of New York City, broke with the county leaders and called
for the resignation of DeSapio. By running against "bossism," Wagner
restored his sagging political vitality and won an easy victory.

Thus, the New York *Times* story, by labeling Robert Kennedy as "the bosses' candidate" in 1964, posed a dangerous threat to his candidacy. Kennedy did not want to be the candidate of just one faction. As he saw it, the regular leaders were sufficiently anxious for him to run to give him flexibility in seeking support from the others. He hoped to superimpose himself upon the factions, as a man who could win the election without giving either side an advantage.

First he moved to counter Powell's statement with a strong endorsement from Democratic leaders identified with the liberal wing.[4] More important, he stated flatly on August 10 that "under no circumstances" would he try for the nomination "without the support of Mayor Wagner." To the public, Wagner was then the symbol of the fight against the "bosses." Already assured of Wagner's support, Kennedy confidentially gave Wagner a public veto. In any event, the political options were Kennedy's because he had won enough delegate commitments by this time to win without the mayor.

But Wagner delayed a public announcement for almost three weeks. He had to fend off people who had supported him in the past and were now urging the candidacy of Congressman Stratton or United Nations Ambassador Adlai Stevenson. Wagner talked to Stevenson about running but Stevenson, who had already stated he was not a candidate, was not going to change his mind to fight Kennedy for the nomination. Wagner considered running himself, but decided he could not defeat Keating. But since Kennedy's original sponsors were his strongest enemies, Wagner feared Kennedy's nomination might be interpreted as a defeat for him. Having come to the position of top Democrat in the state after years of anguished effort, however, Wagner was not about to relinquish it voluntarily. From the White House Wagner sought and received assurances that Kennedy's election would not affect his control of federal patronage in the state. From Kennedy and Smith he sought and received assurances that they would do nothing to strengthen the hand of the county leaders against him.

Finally, on August 21, Wagner issued his endorsement, citing

---

[4] Including former Governor Harriman, Mrs. Albert Lasker, philanthropist and close friend of Adlai Stevenson, and Robert Benjamin, Arthur Krim, and Abe Feinberg, leading fund-raisers in New York's Jewish community.

Kennedy's "great public service" and "the dazzling magic of his name." The next day, two months after he had announced he would not run for the Senate, twenty-seven days after Johnson had eliminated him for the vice presidency, Kennedy stood outside Gracie Mansion, the mayor at his side, and began his new career. While pickets marched outside the gate with signs saying BOBBY GO HOME, he read a statement:

"I have decided to make myself available for the nomination of the Democratic State Convention.

"New York is the supreme testing ground for the most acute national problems of our time—the problems of racial harmony, of employment, of youth, of education, and of the quality of urban and suburban life. As Attorney General of the United States, I have been deeply and continually concerned with these problems.

"As a member of the Cabinet and the National Security Council, I also have been concerned with all the questions of peace and security which have confronted our nation. It is my familiarity with these matters and strong convictions regarding them—which are of the utmost concern to every New Yorker—that leads me to believe I can effectively represent the people of New York in the Senate of the United States."

Admitting he was a man who had "left the state and only recently returned"[5] he asserted his candidacy "would wholly fulfill the requirements for membership in the United States Senate which were set forth after solemn consideration by the men who drafted the Constitution of the State of New York as well as by those who drafted the Constitution of the United States." But to those who believed "that where a candidate voted in the past is more important than his capacity to serve the state," he said "I cannot in fairness ask them to vote for me."

Backhanded as it was, Wagner's endorsement had assured Kennedy's nomination. Stratton's support was quickly reduced to a few Reformers and some upstate counties. Kennedy had only to lease a

[5] Kennedy had lived with his family in Riverdale, the Bronx, and Bronxville (Westchester County) from 1926 to 1937. The Kennedys retained the Bronxville home while living in England where his father, Joseph P. Kennedy, was United States Ambassador from 1938 to 1940.

home (in Glen Cove, Long Island), begin to staff his campaign,[6] and wait for the formal nomination to be made. Publicly recorded as a candidate for the Democratic nomination for senator from New York, he now left for Atlantic City and the National Convention. He was uneasy about his decision. On the day of the nominations at the Democratic National Convention, he said suddenly: "Perhaps I should just go over to the Convention on my own—create a spontaneous demonstration. What do you think would happen?" Smith and Crotty talked him out of it. Instead, Kennedy waited until the nominations were over and appeared to introduce a film on his brother. For twenty-three minutes a weeping, cheering demonstration kept him from speaking. But most of those who cheered would have bowed to Johnson's will had Kennedy tried to challenge Johnson's determination to name his own running mate.

The Sunday night before the state convention, Kennedy flew from Hyannis Port, where he had spent the weekend, to John F. Kennedy airport. It was late and the streets were deserted. He had made the long drive into Manhattan many times before, but a man sees familiar sights differently when he becomes a candidate. These were the streets in which he would campaign. These were the people he would be asking to vote—not for someone else, but for himself. As the car entered Manhattan and sped up an almost deserted stretch of Third Avenue, his chauffeur, Ed King said, "This is where the gay crowd hangs out. They'll be strong for you—they

---

[6] As his press secretary, he hired Debs Myers, who had worked in that post for Mayor Wagner. Myers knew most of the politicians in New York City and all the political reporters as personal friends. Advertising was handled by the agency of Papert, Koenig and Lois which had produced effective television commercials for Senator Javits. Its first contribution to the Kennedy campaign was the slogan called "Let's put Robert Kennedy to work for New York." From Washington, he brought Edwin Guthman, his press secretary and closest personal aide at Justice, to travel with him and supervise the campaign from the field. Scheduling was handled by John Nolan, a former assistant at Justice, and Justin Feldman, a New York lawyer who had scheduled several candidates and knew the state. Research and speech writing were handled by the authors, both originally from Rochester, and Benjamin Altman of the Democratic State Committee. Political contacts on the road were assigned to Bernard Ruggieri, whose work in the State Senate had put him on good terms with political leaders around the state. Stephen Smith ran herd on everything and directed the spending of the money. Later the campaign organization was to expand, as they always do in campaigns but these men formed the core.

like your kind of looks." Kennedy shook his head with a laugh and turned back to look out the window.

Two days later, he was in his suite in the Carlyle Hotel watching Kenneth Keating on television accept the Republican nomination in a speech outlining issues and strategy that would appeal to independent Democrats:

"In the past the Democratic party has been able to find its candidates for public office from among the millions, who have lived and worked in New York. We can all take pride in the fact that Franklin Roosevelt, Al Smith, and Herbert Lehman had their roots in this state. Their distinguished careers and accomplishments reflected credit on every New Yorker. But after years of boss rule, the leaders of this party now tell the people of New York that it has no homegrown candidate who is worthy of representing New York in the Senate of the United States. The Democratic party has become the party of opportunism. Its leaders seek not to serve the people of New York but to use the people of New York as pawns in a blatant quest for power. And the man they are promoting comes before our people to ask not what he can do for New York, but what New York can do for him.

"I served with the late President Kennedy in the House and the Senate. I do not hesitate to say in this gathering of Republicans that he was a man of courage, a man of deep conviction. He was, above all, my friend. There was nothing cynical about President Kennedy. He shunned expediency. He was ambitious, but he did not trample upon those who shared his quests. He was determined, but he was not ruthless. He had a strong sense of destiny, but he was prepared to prove himself first by service to his neighbors and fellow citizens in his home state of Massachusetts.

"I am sure that those of you who tune in the Democratic Convention tomorrow will hear an impressive speech. The words will all be just right. There will be the usual clarion call to greatness and the stirring pleas for self-sacrifice."

Kennedy looked down at the ending of his acceptance speech. It read:

"In 1735, Andrew Hamilton said, 'It is not the cause of New York alone that we are trying, it is the best cause, it is the cause of liberty.' It is in that spirit that we will go forward from this room to victory in November."

[37]

"I hope he hasn't cased the rest of my campaign as well as this speech," he said.

The first response to Kennedy's candidacy was heartening. The enormous crowds and wild receptions he had experienced in Poland were repeated across New York. It was a display of emotion never before seen in the state's politics. Appearing in Grand Central Station at rush hour, he caused a near riot. He was mobbed on the Long Island beaches. In upstate New York, his tours created unprecedented political excitement. Thirty thousand people lined the streets for a motorcade into Rochester. In Glens Falls, a town of 18,000 in the foothills of the Adirondacks, 4000 waited until one o'clock in the morning. Packing halls and public squares, lining up behind the fences at the airports, the people of New York struggled to get close to him. Whatever resentment they might have felt about his running for the Senate from their state, whatever strangeness they detected in his Boston inflection, was forgotten in their desire to cheer and touch him and express through him what they felt about his brother.

The emotions cut across the ethnic divisions of New York politics. On one Sunday excursion into Brooklyn, he drew remarkably similar squeals from Irish nuns, residents of the Jewish Home for the Aged, Swedish-Americans, and young Hassidics with their side curls and skullcaps. In the Negro areas, the feelings were so intense it was impossible for him to make a speech. He limited himself to urging the children to stay in school.

Kennedy enjoyed the campaigning, although the long hours, constant traveling, and the crowd pressures were grueling. He developed a bantering manner with the friendly outdoor crowds that was difficult to imitate successfully inside a hall.

He was uncomfortable, though, with the traditional rituals of New York politics, the blintz-and-pizza performance Nelson Rockefeller took to so well. Kennedy went to Nathan's Famous in Coney Island but did not eat the hot dogs. He visited Ratner's, a Jewish delicatessen on the Lower East Side, and wondered why he could not have a glass of milk. One memory of the campaign is Kennedy standing before a crowd in a Jewish neighborhood early in September, grinning awkwardly, looking embarrassed, saying, "First of all I want to wish you all a Happy New Year."

After the first wave of enthusiasm, the campaign ran into difficulty. In the beginning of August, Kennedy had commissioned Oliver Quayle and John Kraft, two of the best political poll takers in the United States, to do continuing, in-depth studies on the progress of his candidacy. Quayle's poll showed that as of the second week in August, Kennedy would defeat Keating 57 per cent to 43 per cent. It also showed that 38 per cent of the voters did not know who Keating was.[7]

During the remaining weeks of August, however, those who opposed Kennedy had the field to themselves. Instead of traveling among the voters as the apparent Democratic nominee, he was forced by his own strategy to stay in Washington waiting for the mayor's blessing. Between August 12 and August 22, the New York *Times,* for example, published three leading editorials attacking Kennedy and his candidacy.[8] In the *Times*'s judgment the best candidate was Adlai Stevenson, whose three and a half years as Ambassador to the United Nations had "given him an authentic claim to local residence." Since Stevenson was legally a resident of Illinois, Kennedy accepted the *Times* editorials as a measure of the animosity he faced.

When his nomination was assured, the *Times* did not relent. "Mr. Kennedy has demonstrated," it said on August 22, "by the ruthless swiftness by which he has put together an irresistible personal political machine in this state that he is a fast learner. The whole procedure reflects the bankruptcy of the Democratic party in this state."

These charges, picked up widely by others, hurt badly. The Kraft

[7] Throughout this book, references will be made to the public opinion polls taken by Kennedy and other political figures. This is done not to indicate that the polls were always accurate, but that Kennedy, like other political figures, was strongly influenced by them. In the 1960 campaign, it was said the Kennedy organization "navigated in a sea of polls." This was true and it continued. Polls are the best techniques yet devised of sampling voter opinion because, for all their defects, they are the closest simulation to an election. They are thus an indispensable technique of modern campaigning and strongly influence the mood, morale, and decisions of political campaigns and political maneuvers.

[8] Said the *Times* on August 15: "Mr. Kennedy appears to have decided his ambition will be best and most immediately served by finding a political launching pad in New York City. Is New York so poverty stricken for Senate material of authentic residence that it has to import a young man so obviously non-resident that he is just about to be a Massachusetts delegate to the Democratic National Convention? Mr. Kennedy needs New York, but does New York really need Mr. Kennedy?"

polls showed that during August Kennedy had dropped 19 points in New York City while Keating had risen by 10. As the campaign began, Kennedy's standing continued to decline. Polling almost daily, Kraft reported Kennedy's initial strong showing upstate and in suburban New York had evaporated. He was losing ground rapidly with a broad spectrum of Democratic voters in New York City. The results of Kraft's interviewing the first week in October were Kennedy 39 per cent, Keating 40 per cent, undecided 21 per cent.

The circumstance of Kennedy's entry into New York politics was only one reason for this decline. The major difficulty was that his abrupt decision to run had not allowed time either to build a campaign organization or to permit him and his staff to familiarize themselves with the complex problems of a state where few of them had ever worked politically. Most men who run for the Senate have either been governors of their states or held some other state-wide office. At the very least, they are long-time residents who have spent months, often years, acquiring intimate knowledge of state issues and personal relationships to local leaders and organizations. In this sense, Kennedy's candidacy was without precedent. Personal tragedy had induced him to find the political haven of New York, but he came without preparation, without the rudiments of a campaign organization, with a research staff that had only begun to find its way through the relevant issues.

His appearances around the state were managed effectively. But the majority of the voters did not see him personally. To them, these appearances came over on television simply as scenes of adulation, with no content or theme save that he was a Kennedy and some people loved him.

His personal organization presented New York Democratic leaders with a new and unfamiliar entity. The channels of communication so important to politicians had not yet been found. They did not know whom to call to have requests and suggestions considered. As a result, the first six weeks of the campaign were even more confused than usual. Averell Harriman, unable to find anyone in Kennedy headquarters who would schedule his speaking engagements, ended up doing it himself. A number of wealthy and reliable contributors waited in vain for several weeks to be asked for money, and decided Kennedy did not want any. Through most of September, the campaign moved in a fog of confusion, missing critical appearances, failing to touch important political bases, buoyed only by the size of the crowds and the energy of the candidate.

But Kennedy was the candidate now, not the campaign manager, and he was convinced that the only way to combat the issue of "carpetbagging" was to be seen personally in as many parts of the state as possible. He demanded an exhausting schedule. In one three-day period he made fifty-one stops in twenty-one cities. This marathon tired him. He had neither the time nor the energy to make effective television commercials or focus on new issues or attend to urgent political problems. From his hospital bed in Boston, Edward Kennedy implored him to take time to make the personal telephone calls which are so important in establishing political relationships. Robert Kennedy rarely had the time to do it.

His unfamiliarity with how campaigns are conducted in New York also led him into a serious mistake of strategy. He felt he could run in New York on the record of the Kennedy administration, which he had done so much to shape. His early instructions to his speech writers were to limit his talks to what he had done in the Justice Department. He was reluctant to campaign in the traditional manner of New York candidates, with a composite of promises and positions tailored to the diverse ethnic and economic groups. Had the crowds in the early days of the campaign come to hear what he had to say instead of to pay homage, they would have learned little. He offered some stock jokes—about his "Long Island" accent, and the fact that he had moved to New York because he had read that the state was being outstripped by California in population. ("In one day, I increased the population of the State of New York by ten and one half.") He offered some general language about the need for moving forward in the tradition of John F. Kennedy. He criticized Senator Barry Goldwater, the Republican presidential nominee. Beyond that, he did little to project himself or any new program.

These tactics inevitably drew the charge that he was running on his brother's name, that his campaign was glamour without substance. Many did not know about his role in his brother's programs, and even those who did were more interested in what he would do for the future. He began to release position papers on a wide variety of subjects, bread and butter issues—solid but not exciting. The press buried them beneath stories of the crowds. The criticism accelerated. Exasperated staffers pointed at the piles of speeches and position papers Kennedy had presented publicly. The press ignored them.

Behind the organizational difficulties and faulty strategy were the stubborn flaws in Kennedy's public image. The most widely heard charge was that he was a "carpetbagger." "People have been standing in line at the World's Fair," said Keating, "longer than my opponent has been a resident of New York." John Kraft pointed out the term "carpetbagger" was a shorthand used by voters "to embrace all their fears regarding the Attorney General." Kraft went on:

> "For a voter to say Kennedy is a carpetbagger is to offer an easy comment. Wrapped up in it are a lot of things: 'He doesn't understand the state,' 'He's using us,' 'We're just a power base,' 'He's ruthless,' and much more . . .
>
> "More meaningful than the comments about carpetbagging or opportunism are those having to do with the possibility that he doesn't appear to ruminate enough, that he doesn't reflect. These gaps feed to 'opportunism' and 'ruthlessness.' If he doesn't have all the answers it would do more good than harm. If he appears to want more time to consider and suggest, this can't hurt."

Kennedy was also subjected to harsh personal attacks from his opponent. Shaken by Kennedy's enormous crowds, especially in his home area of upstate New York, Keating attacked Kennedy personally with issues patently directed to Democratic ethnic groups. Before Negro audiences, he charged that by resigning as Attorney General, Kennedy had run out on the civil rights movement. For Jewish voters he claimed that Kennedy had approved an alien property settlement concerning the General Aniline and Film Company on terms favorable to an international cartel Keating said was owned by former Nazis. Italian voters were told that Kennedy's crusade against the Mafia (especially the arranged appearance of Joseph Valachi, a Mafia functionary, before a nationally televised session of a Senate committee) was intended as a slur on Italian-Americans. A group called Democrats for Keating was organized by author Gore Vidal and ABC News Commentator Lisa Howard, who made no attempt to conceal their deep personal antagonism toward Kennedy. They worked to turn reform-minded Democrats against him, arguing in their literature that Kennedy's election "would be a body blow to the Reform Movement

. . . If he wins," they said, "Kennedy's political victim would be a real liberal—Senator Hubert Humphrey."

Kennedy was reluctant to return the attacks in kind, remembering that Keating was unknown to many voters and that his age and position made him a sympathetic figure. He also felt the ferocity of Keating attacks would eventually rebound in his favor. His reluctance meant that all the negative content of the campaign, in a state where attacks traditionally make up a substantial part of the political dialogue, were being directed at Kennedy.[9]

Piled atop all his other problems, Kennedy was campaigning under considerable emotional strain. He had not fully recovered from the events of Dallas, and as he traveled through the state, reminders of his brother were everywhere. He stared out the window during staff meetings; he shortened his campaign schedule to spend time with Mrs. John Kennedy. He rejected the advice from many quarters that she play a public role in the campaign although he knew she was anxious to help. One day he called on her at her suite in New York City's Carlyle Hotel before beginning the day's campaign schedule. She was late for an appointment and could not leave because the children's governess had not returned and young John would be left alone. Mrs. Kennedy suggested that he take his nephew with him to the Bronx where a visit to the old family home in Riverdale had been arranged. Kennedy never explained young John's presence to the press, even though he knew that the resultant publicity gave his foes a chance to charge his exploitation of the President's family for political purposes.

On September 28, the Warren Commission report was published. Kennedy could not bring himself to read it but he was briefed on its findings and issued a brief statement accepting them. He canceled his schedule that day and stayed in his hotel. Several days later, answering questions from students at Columbia University, he was asked whether

[9] At only one point did Kennedy try to confront his adversary directly. Learning from an Associated Press ticker in his headquarters that Keating was preparing to repeat his remarks about the Mafia and Valachi at an Italian-American banquet in the North Bronx, he decided to go there. "Where are my Italian friends?" he said, and joined by his personal secretary, Angie Novello, his accountant, Carmine Bellino, and Averell Harriman, he set out. By the time he arrived, Keating had already left. He had not made to the audience the charges he had released to the press. The charges were not heard again in the campaign.

he agreed with the commission that Lee Harvey Oswald had acted alone when he assassinated President Kennedy. The question paralyzed him. For almost five minutes he could not bring himself to speak. He turned his back to the audience so they would not see his tears. Finally composed, he spoke hesitantly and softly: "As I said when I was asked this question in Poland, I agree with the conclusions of the report that the man they identified was the man, that he acted on his own, and that he was not motivated by Communist ideology."

By the end of September, it was apparent that Kennedy's hopes depended on reducing the Democratic defection of the liberal Jewish voters, whose opposition or indifference had sealed the fate of so many candidates in recent New York politics. Roughly, they could be divided into two segments, by age and by income: The liberal intellectuals, concentrated in Manhattan and the more affluent suburbs, and the older, less affluent Jewish working people who live in Brooklyn, the Bronx, and Queens. Of all the voting blocs in New York, the liberal intellectuals are the most articulate and demanding, the best-informed but in many ways the most opinionated. They have a long history of suspicion of Irish-Catholic politicians, and Kennedy's relationship to them was to be always uneasy, sometimes strained, frequently perplexing to both sides. They expect firm adherence to liberal policies from their candidates, but they are not attracted to strong political personalities. Accustomed to being on the losing side of power struggles, they put principle over effectiveness. Their ideal candidate had been Adlai Stevenson and would be Eugene McCarthy—men who lost nobly in the name of a virtuous cause. While concerned with issues and programs, they are strongly influenced by the personal and negative side of politics, and thus are easy prey for the catchy pejorative that professes to sum up a man's life and reputation. John Kennedy, prior to the 1960 campaign, had been "all profile and no courage." They had considered John Kennedy insensitive to many liberal issues and dominated by the views of his father. But their opposition faded when the alternative became Richard Nixon, whom they despised for the way he had acted during the McCarthy era.

Keating was no Nixon, and he was holding the support of a large portion of these Democrats. To combat this, Kennedy changed to a more traditional style of campaigning which addressed itself to their concerns. Beginning in early October, he made comprehensive speeches on such subjects as civil liberties, housing, programs for the elderly, and pollution, with detailed programs for each. Next, he emphasized his independence from the county leaders who had been among his original sponsors. He endorsed direct election of county leaders in the Bronx, a proposal Buckley had been fighting for years. Deliberately, Buckley did not appear with him when he campaigned in that borough. He brought West Side Manhattan reform leaders such as Mrs. Ronnie Eldridge, State Senator Manfred Ohrenstein, Assemblymen Albert Blumenthal and Jerome Kretchmer, all of whom had supported him for the nomination, more closely into his campaign organization. In addition, he brought into New York large numbers of former Washington associates, all with impeccable liberal credentials, to testify at clubhouse meetings and coffee hours about the nature and evidence of his liberalism.[10]

Most important, he took the political offensive, making Keating's record the focus of the campaign. Having decided earlier that any criticism of Keating would make it seem that he was bullying an older man, he had spent little time studying his opponent's Senate record. Actually, except in the field of civil rights (where his record had been excellent), Keating had been playing both sides of the street. To keep his ties to his conservative Republican constituents, Keating had split with his liberal Republican colleague, Jacob Javits, on several significant issues. The point was made forcibly to Kennedy in a memorandum dated October 8 from his former Justice Department associate John Douglas, son of Senator Paul Douglas, whose former assistant, Peter Edelman, had joined the Kennedy campaign staff in mid-September and had been researching Keating's voting record in Washington. Douglas said:

> I was appalled to learn you said yesterday that Keating's voting record is good. Every time you make a statement like that you are cutting your own throat.
> Keating's voting record is not good. He is vulnerable in several areas. He voted against President Kennedy's aid to education bill in 1961, against middle-income housing programs, to cut the heart out of

10 Schlesinger's "liberal airlift" included Professor John Kenneth Galbraith, Daniel P. Moynihan, Adam Yarmolinsky, Theodore Sorensen, and Professor Richard Neustadt.

the area redevelopment administration and was a switcher on Medicare.

I don't say his record is bad—only that it reflects lack of leadership or that it is good in some areas but poor in others. After all, Keating is running on his voting record. You can take issue with some parts of this without arousing sympathy towards him; and if you document the differences you will give voters who want to vote for you but feel guilty about turning out an amiable incumbent the right reasons.

The next day, Mayor Wagner addressed himself to these points in an effective television speech which detailed Keating's conservative votes.[11] Pamphlets highlighting his votes were distributed widely in liberal areas. Keating protested his record was being distorted. He had many "liberal" votes to his credit, but the liberal Democratic voters in New York demand consistency, and for the first time they were learning that their junior Senator had not been totally dependable.

The other Jewish voters with whom Kennedy had problems was not as demanding of their candidates, but they had a hard choice in this campaign. Both men appealed to them. They felt a genuine sympathy for the grief, etched deeply in Kennedy's face and bearing, which made him appear so vulnerable. But they admired Keating, who had shown much more interest in their particular concern, the State of Israel, than they felt they could expect from someone of another faith. Senators from New York had traditionally been Israel's

[11] The central documentation of the Wagner speech was contained in this passage: "Senator Keating has voted against housing on 23 separate occasions. In 1959 he voted twice to kill all public housing, urban renewal, FHA home mortgages and special mortgage assistance to veterans. In 1961 he voted to cut 1.6 billion dollars from President Kennedy's housing bill. If his vote had prevailed, it would have taken 800 million dollars away from New York . . . In 1961 Senator Keating voted to cut 60 per cent of the funds from President Kennedy's retraining program for the unemployed. Twice again in 1963 he voted to slash this program. This very year, only a month ago, during the consideration of President Johnson's anti-poverty program, Senator Keating voted to eliminate the Youth Conservation Corps from the bill. Fortunately this move failed. Senator Keating has voted against the distribution of surplus foods to welfare families and against the food stamp plan. In 1947 he even voted against the free school lunch program for school children. In 1960 he voted against the inclusion of retail and service industry employees under the Federal Minimum Wage Law. In 1962, he voted against the late Senator Kefauver's effort to protect the public from dangerous and overpriced drugs . . . His votes on these and other issues explain why in 1961 that extremist organization calling itself Americans for Constitutional Action gave Senator Keating their Distinguished Service Award."

strongest defenders in the Congress, and Keating had been faithful to this tradition. Now, they resented the outside power that threatened Keating with ejection from public life after eighteen years of service.

Robert Kennedy had always been personally committed to the concept of Israel as a national homeland of the Jewish people, and to the security of Israel. He had been there in 1948 during the Israeli War of Independence, and in articles written at that time for a Boston newspaper had predicted Israel would survive and flourish. But Kennedy viewed his commitment as his brother's Administration did: to be honored within the framework of the need to also maintain civil international relations with the Arab states. The Kennedy administration had doubled economic aid to Israel, and for the first time furnished her with anti-aircraft missiles. It did not give Israel everything she asked for, nor did it align itself with every action taken by Israel in securing her position against her Arab foes. It also appreciated the tremendous nationalist pressure on Arab politicians, and tried, through aid programs and personal diplomacy, to turn the resources of these nations to their human needs rather than to wasteful and hopeless war.

But as his political problems grew, Kennedy made concessions to the fact that he was a candidate for senator from a state with the largest Jewish community in the world outside Israel itself. He called for increased economic and military aid to Israel to keep her from becoming the victim of military imbalance. "We must continue to make clear," he said, "to those who threaten Israel that she is not alone. If Israel is attacked we will come to her assistance."[12]

Beginning in October, the Kennedy organization directed a massive effort at the older Jewish voters. A former reporter for the Yiddish-language *Jewish Daily Forward* was placed in charge of public relations for the Jewish press. Harry Golden, a personal friend of the Kennedys and the popular author of memoirs of ghetto life in the Lower East Side of New York City, came from his home in North Carolina to speak and make radio spots. ("This is Harry Golden the writer. I

[12] Even then, he did not go so far as Keating, who urged that Israel be admitted to NATO and proposed that all American shipments of surplus food to Egypt be eliminated unless President Nasser scaled down his military forces to domestic needs. Kennedy retorted that Israel had never asked to join NATO and that the food shipments were a humanitarian responsibility.

know it is a difficult choice between Kennedy and Keating, but as my mother used to say 'it's bad when things are too good.' If we have a Democratic administration, a Democratic senator from New York will again be able to be as effective as the great Herbert Lehman, of blessed memory.") At the urging of Morris B. Abram, then head of the American Jewish Committee, Kennedy even made a campaign statement on deicide, an issue then before the Ecumenical Council in Rome. Kennedy could hardly believe that such a statement could have political relevance, but he bowed to his managers and with some reluctance planned a curbside news conference where he stated:

> It is my feeling, and I am certain that it is a feeling of the great majority of American Catholics, that the Jews should bear no responsibility for the death of Christ—neither those who lived at that time, nor those who lived afterwards. I think a clear statement such as the original version is in keeping with the Ecumenical spirit of Pope John and Pope Paul. It is also in keeping with the effort that all religions in this country have been making to promote brotherhood.

Slowly, all these efforts took effect. By the middle of October, Kraft could report that the Jewish defection to Keating had been slowed. By October 20, it had stopped and a countermovement to Kennedy had begun.

At about the same time, other things were happening to improve Kennedy's standing. Some of the better television spots he had made began to be heavily scheduled. They showed Kennedy on the streets of New York, answering questions from citizens and students. He was spontaneous and frank, far better in this kind of exchange than with any prepared format. "People ask if I am using New York as a steppingstone," he would say. "Let's assume the worst possible answer: Let's say I am. Let's say I want to be senator from New York so I can go somewhere else, which is the presidency of the United States. Well, President Johnson is going to be elected, and I think he's going to be a good President and he's going to be re-elected in 1968. So until 1972 I really couldn't do anything. That's eight years. I will have to be an awfully good senator for the State of New York for the next six years if I want to be re-elected in 1970. And if I have done such an outstanding job in eight years that people all over the country encourage me to run for President, I don't see how New York suffers."

Simply being seen by the voters in their living rooms, talking about the issues and his problems, did much to break down the negative impressions that his early campaign had created. At last, he was getting across, not only as John Kennedy's brother, but as a frank and appealing personality in his own right.

He was also aided by the trend of the national campaign. The Goldwater-Miller ticket was clearly headed for catastrophe in the Northeast. Upstate New York newspapers which had not endorsed a Democrat since before the Civil War urged their readers to vote for President Johnson. To salvage their credentials with the electorate, the Republican leaders of New York State, including Keating, abandoned the national ticket and even refused, up to the day of the election, to say how they would vote. Knowing Johnson would run substantially ahead of the ticket, Kennedy moved to align his campaign with the President's. A cooperative arrangement to encourage straight party-line voting was worked out with Edwin Weisl, President Johnson's personal representative. Down from the buses came the slogan "Let's put Robert Kennedy to work for New York." Up went: "Get with the Johnson-Humphrey-Kennedy Team." Going into the final ten days of the campaign, the trend had reversed. Now it was clearly in Kennedy's favor.

On October 23, however, Keating got his biggest break of the campaign. The New York *Herald Tribune* published the text of a letter to Kennedy from the Executive Director of the Fair Campaign Practices Committee, Bruce Felknor. This committee, a respected guardian of election conduct, drafts and enforces a Code of Fair Practices which is signed by all candidates. According to the *Tribune,* the committee had accused Kennedy of "false and distorted treatment" and "possibly a deliberate and cynical misrepresentation" of Keating's record regarding the Nuclear Test Ban Treaty, approved by the Senate in 1963. It was the first time in ten years of activity that the committee had publically criticized a candidate for public office.

Two weeks before, Kennedy had spoken at Syracuse University and said Keating had "ridiculed" the Test Ban Treaty "throughout the years in which Averell Harriman and Hubert Humphrey and Adlai Stevenson labored to make it a reality." The speech went on to state that while Keating had criticized the treaty before and during its negotia-

[49]

tion, he had supported it when it was submitted to the Senate for a vote.[13] Kennedy himself had embroidered the charge in off-the-cuff statements that day. Several reporters had notes in which he told rallies that "When President Kennedy was fighting for the Test Ban Treaty, Keating never once rose to speak in its favor in the United States Senate." (Keating did not in fact participate in the floor debate over the treaty until the final day, but he had expressed qualified support for it several times in the months before.)

Keating, feeling Kennedy's interpretation of his position would make an effective issue for the closing days of the campaign, filed a complaint with the Fair Campaign Practices Committee. The committee followed its usual practice of requesting the facts from both candidates. Keating sent inserts from the Congressional Record showing his support for the treaty as early as 1961. Kennedy submitted excerpts from the debate in which Keating said that the treaty might actually present obstacles to keeping the peace, and a comment he had made in Rochester in 1961 urging the Kennedy administration to quit trying to get a nuclear test ban treaty and resume testing. The committee staff ignored the evidence. It sent a presumably confidential letter reproving Kennedy in such harsh terms that its objectivity was immediately questionable.

In the past committee letters had never been made public, lest the committee be compromised in its mediation function by the impression it was favoring one candidate over another. The Keating staff, however, felt the letter offered them a major issue. They went to the *Tribune,* prevailing upon a staff member of the Fair Campaign Practices Committee to accompany them with his file. Recognizing a good story, the *Tribune* reporter copied the letter to Kennedy without the knowledge or consent of the FCPC staffer, and it was published in the early evening edition of Otober 27.

Kennedy heard of the story while campaigning in Long Island. He immediately called his campaign headquarters and was assured that

[13] At this point in the campaign, Kennedy's speeches were receiving a final rewrite by a writer for the television show "That Was the Week That Was," a satirical review largely based on political subjects. The writer's job was to simplify speech drafts so Kennedy could speak them more effectively. Interpreting the basic draft to mean that Keating's opposition had been longer and more negative than it actually was, the writer had inserted the word "ridicule" and eliminated the staff's qualifying language.

the necessary documentation to support his charge was at hand. He also learned that Felknor had sent him a telegram of apology, explaining that the letter had been "obtained dishonestly, copied surreptitiously and published without authorization and over our most vehement protests."

The answer rarely catches up with a political charge. Being criticized by a supposedly impartial referee called into question everything Kennedy was saying about Keating's voting record, an issue that had become a vital part of his effort to hold the liberal Democratic vote. More important, this kind of charge reflected the quality of "ruthlessness" he was trying to combat. Keating was already making the letter a major issue, accusing Kennedy of "an utterly unscrupulous campaign, of willfully and deliberately falsifying my record." Unless Kennedy could do something quickly, the incident would hurt him.

Feeling a denial on the merits might not be sufficient at this point, and that the attack must be carried to the committee itself, he personally called several members of the committee's Board of Directors to explain what had happened. He painted a bleak picture of the incident and its consequences, saying that what the committee had done to him was "terribly unfair," and could cost him the election. After talking with Kennedy, two members of the board, Ralph McGill, and Richard Cardinal Cushing, resigned from the committee. Another, famed trial lawyer Louis Nizer, issued a statement attacking the committee's letter as "itself unfair to Robert Kennedy."

Kennedy also instructed two members of his staff to go to the Fair Campaign office with all the necessary documentation, and stay there until they had obtained a retraction. Charles P. Taft, a Cincinnati Republican who was chairman of the committee, resisted the demand of the Kennedy staff for retraction. To do so, Taft maintained, would indicate the committee had no confidence in its staff. He, too, became a recipient of Kennedy's tirade against the committee, which by this time had been polished through a long day of reiteration. After Kennedy and Taft talked, a compromise was struck. Instead of withdrawing the charges, the committee would withdraw the letter. Kennedy's people, with an eye toward the next day's news headlines, suggested the committee's statement say "the letter should not have been written and we hereby withdraw it in full." The next day's papers emphasized the withdrawal. Kennedy claimed "complete vindication." The sting of the issue had been removed.[14]

With less than a week before the election, and with an increasing trend toward Kennedy, Keating's last hope lay in engaging his opponent in a statewide television debate, in which he could show up his superior knowledge of the issues affecting New York and, hopefully, get Kennedy to attack him. A candidate's willingness to debate can be related precisely to how he thinks his campaign is going. Whoever is behind can be counted on to make the challenge, and if the race is close the advisers to the candidates begin seeking delphic signs to guide them in making the appropriate decision. Kennedy had accepted Keating's original challenge to debate on October 10 when he was behind; but Keating, ahead at that time, had tied the matter up in protracted negotiations over format. Now the polls were reversed, and Keating purchased a half-hour on CBS television, challenging Kennedy to show up, saying if he did he would "pin his ears back," and threatening to debate an empty chair if he didn't. Kennedy countered by purchasing the following half-hour.

Although Kennedy's advisers argued that, as the front runner, he should not risk a debate, the thought of showing up on Keating's program intrigued him. He went to the studio on West Fifty-seventh Street and waited in the darkness for a few minutes, intending to keep Keating unaware of his presence until his show was about to begin. As Keating began by pointing to the empty chair and calling it "the symbol of my opponent's ruthless contempt for the voters of New

[14] Early in 1965, the Fair Campaign Practices Committee appointed a special panel to "inquire into every aspect" of the Kennedy-Keating incident. Kennedy filed a long letter in which he stated that he knew, from his own involvement in the attempts to negotiate a test-ban treaty, that "statements made by American leaders who opposed our policies affected the atmosphere of the negotiations and their possibility for success," and how "demoralizing it was to President Kennedy when certain members of Congress publicly criticized the negotiations, urging they be terminated and testing be resumed."

Kennedy's letter did not arrive in time for the panel to consider it before preparing its report. The report concluded his statements were "such as to lead to a substantial distortion in the public's mind as to Keating's position." Nizer, McGill, and Cushing again denounced the conclusion.

As a result of the publicity over the incident, Bruce Felknor resigned as executive director of the committee. His version of the incident, which differs from the authors', can be found in his book, *Dirty Politics*, pp. 189–196.

York," Kennedy arrived at the studio door and requested admission. On the door was a sign that said KEEP OUT—NO VISITORS—KEATING. A CBS official stood blocking the door. Kennedy said to him, "Senator Keating said if I showed up he would pin my ears back. Kindly inform Senator Keating I am here and ready to go on the air." Another CBS man made an appearance, and Kennedy turned to him:

"What is your name?" he demanded.

"Edward Forsling."

"Why are you all out here waiting for me?"

"I am a representative of the legal department of CBS."

"Do you always stand out here?"

"This is Senator Keating's studio."

"Do you know Senator Keating just said I was not here?"

"He can say anything he wishes. It is his program."

"Would you kindly tell him I am here?"

"I cannot interrupt the program."

"Then kindly remove the empty chair from the stage and ask Senator Keating to withdraw his remark about my not showing up."

"I cannot. It is a paid political broadcast."

"Then it is a dishonest paid political broadcast," Kennedy shot back, going to his own studio.

When Keating had finished his show, he was told that reporters wanted to ask him why Kennedy had been excluded. At that point, Keating made the worst mistake of his campaign. He could have said he didn't know Kennedy had been there. He could have challenged him to another debate the next day. He could, if he wished, have gone to Kennedy's studio, where Kennedy had left instructions to let him in. Instead, he and his aides ran out of the building, turning over potted palms and furniture to elude reporters. The next day, every newspaper in New York State carried a picture of Keating pointing to the empty chair and another of Kennedy looking helplessly at the sign telling him to KEEP OUT. The obvious implication was that Kennedy, anxious to debate, had been the victim of an unfair trick by his opponent. A newsman who had chased Keating wrote an article headlined "I Ran The Keating Obstacle Course."

The "Great Non-Debate," as it came to be called, and the withdrawal of the Fair Campaign Practices letter climaxed the campaign and ended Keating's chances. In the last week the candidates merely ran out the clock.[15] On election night, the Kennedys had dinner at the home of Steve Smith and then went to the Statler Hilton Hotel, where preparations had been made to receive early returns from key sample precincts within the state. The first reports came from Buffalo and were optimistic: he was running ahead of his brother's 1960 percentages in Polish and Italian wards. By ten o'clock, it was apparent he was going to win, but he showed no great elation. He called his father and his brother Edward. His sisters were with him at the hotel. He called leaders around the state to thank them. He then retired to a private suite, where he met with the friends and politicians who had come to share the excitement of victory. When Congressman-elect Jonathan Bingham, victor in a primary over Charles Buckley and leader of the reform movement in the Bronx, entered the room, Kennedy ran over and opened up the door to the closet. "OK, Charlie," he said, "you can come out now."

At midnight, he went to the Statler ballroom to thank his campaign workers. He called his victory "an overwhelming mandate to continue the policies" of John F. Kennedy. "This is what I dedicate myself to," he said, "in the next six years for the State of New York." He ended with a quote from Tennyson's *Ulysses,* which he had discovered that day.

> "Come my friends,
> 'Tis not too late to seek a newer world."

It was to become his theme four years later.

The official returns showed Kennedy the winner by 719,693 votes. He had run ahead of the usual Democratic showing among all New York's minorities except the Jews. He had done well in the suburbs, and had carried traditionally Republican upstate New York (north of Westchester County) by 130,000 votes.

Kennedy's majority was the greatest any Democratic candidate for senator or governor had achieved since Herbert Lehman's 818,000 margin in 1938, but Johnson carried New York by a margin of 2½ million votes, and many observers, comparing the totals, concluded

---

[15] A debate was held, the Friday before the election, on the Barry Gray talk show on station WMCA, which commanded one of the large radio audiences in the United States. The candidates were asked questions prepared by the staffs of their opponents, and were allowed to use notes. Considering the emotion generated by the campaign, it was surprisingly tame.

that Kennedy had won because of Johnson's coattails. But the difference between Kennedy's and Johnson's margin was made up of normally Republican voters, who had cut Goldwater, but returned to their party to vote for Keating. Had the Republican presidential candidate been more acceptable to the Republican voters of the state, Keating would have run better, but Kennedy would still have won by 400,000 votes, a very healthy majority in New York.

Kennedy's most impressive source of strength was among the Democratic voters in the upstate areas. Long ignored by their party, they found in him a candidate who could arouse their enthusiasm. Normally, the Democrats lose upstate by 400,000 votes, and drop behind by another 300,000 in New York City's suburbs. The Democratic candidate thus had to carry New York City by 800,000 to win a narrow victory. Kennedy carried upstate and lost the suburban counties by only 61,000. His margin of 720,000 votes in New York City was more than enough for a comfortable win.

The campaign left lasting scars. Its controversies gave fuel to those who portrayed him in terms of partisanship, ruthlessness, and opportunism. The "carpetbagging" issue received enormous publicity outside of New York, raising the question of whether wealthy men could run for the Senate in any state they chose. The antagonism aroused among the newspapers and the intellectuals would hurt him in the future. But he was accustomed to having enemies.

He did not need to win this election to remain a national leader. He would have remained in the public eye had he retired to private life. But by winning a seat in the Senate, he had become an independent political figure, at the center of public affairs. By organizing a victorious campaign from a standing start, he showed he was a powerful political force in his own right. He had proven he could bring his own case to the people, win their support, and with it the ultimate power in a democracy.

Thus, by the first anniversary of his brother's death, Kennedy had been able to conquer his anguish and give new direction to his life and career. How incapacitating his grief must have been, and what an extraordinary psychological effort must have been required to wage a winning campaign and find the strength with which to give hope to others, was something his friends could only begin to understand four years later, when they experienced it themselves.

4

A DIFFERENT KIND OF SENATOR

When Robert and Edward Kennedy were sworn in as United States senators on January 5, 1965, it was the second time in the history of the nation that two brothers had served together.[1] For Edward Kennedy, the ceremony marked his first visit to the Capitol since an airplane crash had come perilously close to crippling him some six months before. He walked with a cane, his posture stiffened by a brace supporting his back which had been broken in the accident. He had made a vow to walk to his seat in the Senate Chamber on opening day. The satisfaction in fulfilling that promise erased the pain and fatigue that were evident as he walked. They entered the Chamber together, greeting colleagues and friends, new and old.

Traditionally, senators beginning new terms take their oaths in groups of four in the alphabetical order of their states. The roll on this day was altered by the presiding officers so the two brothers could be sworn together. At 12:23 P.M., the clerk called "Mr. Kennedy of Massachusetts and Mr. Kennedy of New York." They came forward accompanied by their senior state colleagues, Leverett Saltonstall and Jacob Javits. As the oath was administered, the gallery broke into prolonged applause. A family reception in Edward's office was followed by a large buffet at Hickory Hill. It was one of those

[1] Dwight Foster of Massachusetts and Theodore Foster of Rhode Island served together between 1800 and 1803.

days of celebration that separate the memories of the past from the hopes of the future.

That evening, the Women's National Press Club held its traditional welcoming banquet for new senators. Each was asked to speak briefly and humorously, and Kennedy was ready for a good show:

"First of all I want to say how delighted I am to be here representing the great state of . . ." He stopped, ruffling through his notes, trying to remember the state. He went on to tell how he had found his desk in the Senate placed in the back, almost next to the cloakroom. "I wonder if they're trying to tell me something?" he asked. "And that's not all. Yesterday I found a mouse in my office. I really did! I *know* they're trying to tell me something." He concluded with a word to those who felt he was overly ambitious. "I have absolutely no presidential ambitions," he assured them, "and neither does my wife— Ethel Bird."

Kennedy was assigned an office in a corner suite of the first floor of the New Senate Office Building. It was an undesirable location, next to the building's main entrance with its continual flow of traffic, but suites are assigned by seniority in the Senate, and of the seven-room suites reserved for senators from the largest states it was the only one left. Kennedy's private office was ample, although small compared with his massive offices in the Justice Department. It was furnished comfortably. A portrait of his brother Joseph P. Kennedy, Jr., in pilot's gear and ready to fly a mission, dominated the room. Drawings by his children, stiff-legged people with huge round heads amidst blotches of color, were taped on the wall behind his desk. Family pictures were on the tables. A large stuffed tiger given him by the government of Indonesia stood in front of the fireplace, until it was removed because it scared visiting children.

On a typical day, Kennedy arrived at the office about 9:30 A.M., with a list of things to do and people to call. First, he finished his work on the briefcase full of material he had taken home the previous night—correspondence, memoranda, articles his staff felt he should read. On each of these he wrote a note or an answer to the question in his illegible pinched script. His private secretary, Angela Novello, one of the few who could read his writing, would transcribe the notes and send them out.

The meetings of his Senate committees began at ten, and he would try to attend at least parts of them. The rest of the morning was spent on the telephone, or in individual conferences with members of his staff. He never held staff meetings. When his door was open, anyone with something to discuss could go in.

He usually lunched in his office, preferring to avoid the ornate Capitol dining rooms available to senators so he could continue his telephone calls. He ate little when he ate alone: a bowl of soup or a salad, sometimes a sandwich from the Senate restaurant. Often a friend from out of town or a Washington reporter with whom he was particularly friendly would join him for lunch. Occasionally his cook at Hickory Hill, Ruby Phillips, would send in one of his more preferred luncheon dishes: fish chowder, tuna fish, or cold steak with sliced tomatoes. When the Senate schedule was slow, he would sometimes go home for lunch and work there the rest of the day.

In the afternoons, the phone calls would continue, interrupted by trips to the Senate to vote or to take part in debate. At least twice a week he flew to New York in the afternoon to begin another schedule: meetings, a tour of a school, a speech in the evening. He tried to finish in time to catch the last Eastern Airlines shuttle so he could spend the night at home. If not, he would stay at his Manhattan apartment. As time went on, the trips to New York became more frequent. Often Kennedy made the round trip several days in a row. "I feel like a yo-yo," he would say.

Generally his pace in his first years in the Senate was slower than the schedule he had followed during the New Frontier. In the Justice Department, he rarely ended his day before 9:00 P.M. While in the Senate, he often could go home by 6:30 and have dinner with his family, a change he appreciated.

A great deal of Kennedy's time in these years was spent on business that had nothing to do with the Senate, but related to the requests and obligations that came to him as the acting head of the Kennedy administration. Foreign dignitaries and visitors, American politicians, Cuban-exile veterans of the Bay of Pigs, Soviet poets, and foreign writers came to his office in a steady stream. Most requests for interviews were politely turned down, but enough were accepted to take up an important part of his schedule.

Kennedy had won a reputation in Washington as a superior executive. The New Frontier gave young men large responsibilities, but

Kennedy had had them at a time when old men were in power. In 1957, at the age of thirty-one, he had led a staff of seventy-one through sensitive and highly publicized investigations of corruption. His leadership technique was to pick good people, delegate responsibility freely, demand precision, reject carelessness, give each staff member access to him, and back them up even if they made mistakes. He was tenacious at following up once he had made an assignment. "Will you handle that?" he would say when something came to his attention. From then on, whenever he saw you he would ask how "that" was coming.

His staff appointments were sought-after assignments in Washington. Among the lures were the special attention his activities received and the fact that he was receptive to new ideas, but not the least were the power, dreams, and glory of a potential presidency. As a boss, Kennedy was demanding but understanding. His assistants were overworked and always on call at his convenience. People were stretched to the limits of their abilities and energy, and in the process found themselves producing beyond their own measure of their talents. The office was run informally, with time off given when requested, and with the understanding that staff family matters had the highest priority.

At least one habit made for confusion. Like other members of his family, he would assign small tasks to whoever was around at the time. Often he made the assignment more than once just to make sure it was done. A political leader for whom Kennedy had a message might receive it, the same day, from two or even three of his associates. And they, after working hard on an assignment, could be exasperated to find someone else had already done it. Once an assistant prevailed upon Mayor John Lindsay's office to offer Robert Kennedy, Jr. (who had a special gift for handling animals), a summer job at the Bronx Zoo, only to find that someone else had gotten him a job to work in the National Zoological Park in Washington.

Kennedy drew his top staff primarily from the Justice Department. Edwin O. Guthman, the Pulitizer-prize-winning reporter, who had been Director of Public Relations and Kennedy's chief personal aide in the last two years at Justice and in the Senate campaign, continued those duties for a few months in the Senate, until he returned to journalism as national news editor of the Los Angeles *Times*. He was replaced in his press responsibilities by Wes Barthelmas, a former staffer for Congresswoman Edith Green of Oregon; and later by Frank Mankiewicz, a Los Angeles lawyer and talented writer who had been one of the founders of the Peace Corps. Kennedy's personal secretary, Angela Novello, was almost a member of the family, having served him with total devotion since the days in the Senate Rackets Committee. She handled his phone calls and the traffic that flowed through his office with a protectiveness that he never questioned. His daily schedule and the details of his traveling were also her responsibility. His administrative assistant was Joseph Dolan. Raised in Brooklyn, Dolan had gone West after law school and won election to the Colorado legislature, where he became associated with Byron "Whizzer" White, a long-time Kennedy friend. In 1960, Dolan quit his own promising elective career and joined the presidential campaign. He was appointed Assistant Deputy Attorney General, entrusted with some of the most politically sensitive work of the Justice Department such as the screening of candidates for the federal courts. His laconic manner belied a quick humor and a sharp political insight.

Kennedy's experience had convinced him that young lawyers made the best staff personnel for policy matters. They knew how to absorb large masses of material quickly and deal with new concepts easily as well as carefully; and they had the incentive and energy to work long hours. As his legislative assistants, he chose twenty-nine-year-old Adam Walinsky of the Yale Law School, who had clerked for Judge Carroll Hincks of the Second Circuit Court of Appeals, and thirty-year-old Peter Edelman of Harvard Law School, who had served Justice Arthur Goldberg on the Supreme Court. After working briefly at the Justice Department, they came to New York midway in the Senate campaign, and injected fresh ideas and enthusiasm into the work of the battle-worn research and speech writing operation.

These professionals, together with a large number of typists, clerks, and assistants, went to work to find their way around the Senate, develop legislative projects, deal with the hundreds of phone calls and requests and the 1000 letters that came into Kennedy's office each day. They tried to cope with the unusual attention given him by the press and generally to moderate the chaos that marked Kennedy's office in its first months.

From an abundance of ideas from outside experts in universities and government, his staff winnowed the best and put them in usable form. It could be frustrating work. The overworked, unknown staffers could never tell when some famous New Frontiersman would come bounding in at the last minute with changes in a bill or a speech on which they had labored for weeks. But Kennedy never accepted any one person as the final repository of wisdom. Any project, he felt, could always benefit from a fresh look by someone who was able and informed.

Around the Senate, Kennedy was inevitably a celebrity. When he rose to make a major speech, the press gallery filled up. The standing room for staff in back of the senators' seats was crowded. The atmosphere had the promise of drama and anticipation. Most debate in the Senate plays before an empty house. Kennedy's maiden speech on the nuclear proliferation question drew over fifty senators, and the discussion that followed his remarks was of exceptional quality.

In his years in the Senate, Kennedy made almost three hundred public speeches. They form the permanent record of his evolving views on public issues. In their careful preparation and the caliber of their writing, his major speeches were the best delivered by any member of Congress during that period, rivaled only by the foreign policy speeches of J. William Fulbright. Kennedy's personal writing style was blunt, simple, and direct. It can best be studied in two of the documents he wrote entirely himself: the tribute to Defense Secretary Robert McNamara on his resignation in 1967 and the article on the Cuban missile crisis, published as a book late in 1968. For the rest, he used staff writers extensively, although he kept full command of what was said in his name. He exercised the same control over his statements as a chief architect does in overseeing plans for a building. He would listen to suggestions, and then say "Can I tell you what I want to say?" As he outlined his ideas, his writers would scribble notes furiously. They would then turn his points into a polished statement. The policies and emphasis of the speeches were his. The eloquence and fire came from others—during the Senate years, mostly from Walinsky. Kennedy examined drafts closely, sharpening their focus, having new ones written until they said just what he wished. He thought of speech writing as a misallocation of his time when there were others, with a greater flair, available to do it.

At first, his adjustment to the routine of the Senate was difficult. As with most new senators who had served in the Cabinet, or as governors of their states, Kennedy found the pace extremely slow. It was the classic difference between the Executive and the Legislative branches of the government. The Executive has the feeling of creating, of administering, of seeing something happen. There is little of this dynamic sense of action in a legislature. In the White House there is no respite from crisis and decision-making. The Senate, on the other hand, rarely passes an important bill between January and May, concentrating its work in its committees.

Kennedy's influence as a freshman on the workings of the Senate was minute compared to his influence on the country as Attorney General. He found himself, especially in his first two years there, in the personally unsatisfactory position of speaking rather than doing, introducing legislation to stir interest with slim hope of seeing it passed. The qualities that marked him as an executive—decision under pressure, quick response, and ability to organize the activities of large numbers of men—had little chance to be used. The qualities that mark the behavior of senators toward one another in their elite "club"— the relaxed small talk, glad-handing, and simulated courtesies toward political opponents—were ones for which he had neither talent nor patience. None of this surprised him. Having worked on a Senate staff for five years, he knew what the Senate was like. "I remember and regret the situation that gave rise to my being here," he said, shortly after he had been sworn in. "It will be a totally new life. But I would not be here unless I wanted to come."

So he tried, and gradually he made the necessary adjustment. He went through the routine activities, the time-consuming chores the Senate requires of all its freshmen, such as presiding over sessions. Visitors to the gallery were surprised to see him in the chair, and even more surprised when senators addressed him as "Mr. President." At hearings, he listened attentively, occasionally exercising his old skill at asking witnesses hard questions.

Over time, he learned to get along with and respect senators with whom he often disagreed, like Sam Ervin of North Carolina and James Pearson of Kansas. He made new friends of John Sherman Cooper of Kentucky (who had been a close friend of President Kennedy), Joseph Clark of Pennsylvania, his New York colleague, Jacob Javits, and later Charles Percy of Illinois.

Kennedy developed an especially interesting relationship with Javits.

Javits was something of an anomaly in his own party, an outspoken liberal, less influential in the Senate than his seniority entitled him, a man who persuaded through diligence and tenacity rather than charm. He had survived in a party where his viewpoint was frequently isolated and, perhaps inevitably, he seemed encrusted by a defensive shell that allowed few to know him and sometimes made him appear insensitive. Surrounded in his own state by charismatic figures like Rockefeller and Lindsay, Javits was frequently ignored by them, until election time when they sought his superior strength as a major asset.

Shortly after his election, it was suggested to Kennedy that if he could develop the kind of working cooperation with Javits that John Kennedy had enjoyed with Leverett Saltonstall, in which the two collaborated on programs of concern to their state, it would help both Senators and the interests of New York. Kennedy did not really know Javits at this point and doubted the possibilities of their collaboration because of the differences in their personalities. Their relationship got off to a bumpy start, when their staffs tried various upstaging techniques in matters like announcements of federal grants to New York. When Kennedy opened an upstate office, Javits, who had none, quickly followed suit. But each of them quickly saw it was in their own interest to work together. Javits, in his own words, recognized Kennedy was "the second most prominent political personality in the country." Kennedy discovered that no matter how well he did in the polls in New York, Javits seemed to do better. And Kennedy had some understanding of the effect his highly publicized activities had on Javits. "It's damned tough for him, having had this state all to himself and now having me come in here," he would say.

Kennedy's respect for Javits' ability grew as he saw how he was able to keep the support of all the diverse interests in New York. Through their collaboration, Kennedy learned to know Javits as an engaging and extremely intelligent person. He admired how Javits—born in poverty of immigrant parents on the Lower East Side of New York City—had won political power, earning both wealth and reputation on the way. In Senate committee sessions, he found Javits had done his homework and had some kind of suggestion for almost every paragraph of every bill. Gradually, the two men came to welcome their associations and worked together effectively.

In his adjustment to the Senate, Kennedy received considerable assistance from his brother Edward, who had already served his apprenticeship. In his first months, Edward Kennedy had also chafed at the lethargic pace of the body. For a short time, early in 1963, he talked about leaving the Senate to run for governor of Massachusetts. But he soon found a creative and satisfying role. Through a capacity for hard work and an exceptional gift for getting along with different kinds of people, he won acceptance and then admiration from his Senate colleagues.

Edward Kennedy delighted in his brother's impatience with the Senate's procedures. Once both were attending a committee hearing on a labor matter, which had started at 10 A.M. and promised to go on all day. Robert Kennedy wanted to question the witnesses, but he was anxious to make an appointment in New York that afternoon. Tradition dictated that senators ask questions in order of seniority. By 2 P.M., increasingly impatient, he turned to his brother and whispered: "Is this the way I become a good senator—sitting here and waiting my turn?"

"Yes," said Edward.

"How many hours do I have to sit here to be a good senator?"

"As long as necessary, Robbie," his brother answered.

On another occasion, Kennedy was seeking support for a bill he had introduced in the committee. He approached one colleague who said he would give Kennedy his vote if Kennedy would accept a speaking invitation that had come from his state.

"Is that what you have to do to get votes?" he asked his brother in dismay.

"You're learning, Robbie," the answer came again.

The Senate has a unique institutional life. Personal relationships are close and highly valued. Members take the time to write each other private notes of commendation, concern or apology. The most effective lobbyist on a senator is another senator. To line up support for a significant piece of legislation requires an intricate combination of personal friendships, political commitments, persuasiveness on the merits of the issue, and plain persistence. Kennedy tested these skills in 1965 to secure passage of an amendment to the literacy test section of the Civil Rights Bill, which would allow persons educated in a foreign language in American flag schools to qualify to vote by taking the literacy test in their own language. This amendment enfranchised thousands of residents of New York City who, having been born and educated in Puerto Rico, spoke only Spanish. The bill affected no more than a handful of states, but Kennedy carefully explained it to his Democratic colleagues and helped line up the votes needed for passage.

As the months passed, Kennedy developed a greater sympathy for a legislature's role. He would never be a "Senate man," but he did come to realize that the process of achieving multiple consent for policies, while often slow and cumbersome, helped assure public support for the measures that were enacted, and often served as a beneficial check on the quick decision and action he had come to know in the Executive Branch.

An opportunity to champion the legislative process came during the airlines strike in the summer of 1966. The strike, which went on for over a month, caused a severe policy dilemma. It was not depriving the country of essential transportation service, nor affecting the nation's health or safety—the prerequisites, under existing law, for a court injunction. But it was causing great inconvenience to the small, powerful, opinion-making segment of the public which used air travel, including members of Congress themselves. An emergency bill suspending the strike and providing compulsory arbitration of the issues was introduced. The labor movement, which saw compulsory arbitration as undercutting collective bargaining procedures, felt strongly that the bill set a dangerous precedent. The bill was approved by the Senate Labor and Public Welfare Committee, of which Kennedy was a member, on July 26, 1966, but three days later it was held up when President Johnson dramatically announced that after a negotiating session at the White House, the parties had reached agreement on a new contract. On July 31, members of the union rejected the contract. Tempers in Washington flared. Johnson called the members of both the Senate and House Labor committees to the East Room of the White House. After members of the Cabinet reported on the effects of the strike and the impasse between the parties, Johnson asked the committees to expedite legislation.

The members of the House committee caucused briefly at the end of the room and then rejoined the meeting. "Mr. President," said their chairman, "we support your request for legislation." The Senate members then met at the other end of the room to do the same thing. Kennedy was restive about Congress legislating in the East Room of the White House. He insisted that the committee return to the Capitol and hold hearings in the usual manner, and the other members of the committee agreed. At the hearings the next day, he berated Secretary of Labor Willard Wirtz for the Administration's refusal to recommend any legislation: "Do you know," he asked, "whether the settlement was turned down because of a major factor, or a minor one that can be worked out between the parties? If it is impossible for the parties to come together, I think you should recommend legislation. If it isn't impossible, then you should not recommend legislation."

"If you and the Administration," he said, "which had been working on this for an extended period of time, do not want to express an opinion about whether legislation is warranted, I don't see how this committee can make a decision."

In insisting that Senate procedures be followed, despite the crisis atmosphere that had been created, Kennedy did not speak for either party to the dispute, but for the integrity of the legislative process. In insisting that the Administration make recommendations, he was speaking for the proper relationship between the two branches of government on issues in which the Executive, with its expert knowledge, proposes and Congress disposes. Eventually, the dispute was settled, as Kennedy had hoped, by the parties themselves, without recourse to compulsory arbitration.

Despite his increased participation in Senate affairs, Kennedy remained temperamentally ineligible for membership in the "Club." His wide range of outside activities reduced the time available for Senate life. His national prominence caused envy and resentment among a few of his colleagues. They might have worked on a project for months without attention. When Kennedy spoke about it, the media frequently highlighted his work, not theirs. But most other senators understood why this was inevitable, and welcomed the way their issues were spotlighted by his participation in them.

One of the things that makes the Senate attractive as a political office is its aloofness from the daily clashes of public life. Senators vote and debate on important issues, but the President is held accountable for the frustrations and grievances of the nation, just as mayors are held responsible for the problems of urban life. Even the votes in the Senate are often arranged to avoid clear-cut commitments.[2]

Yet the controversy that attended Robert Kennedy's career did not abate when he entered the privileged sanctuary of the Senate. John Kennedy had not sought out conflict, and this was one of his strengths. Robert Kennedy knew the political benefits of this attitude, but his sense of justice drove him toward disputes where hard, established adversaries were on each side. And once he entered such a fight, he drew the issues more sharply than most. He insisted, for example, that all attacks on him be answered promptly, so that he would "be on record." But frequently such responses drew the issues more sharply and personally.

The issue of cigarette advertising was a typical example of his penchant for a good fight. As a man with a special interest in children and athletics, he was especially disturbed by the way young Americans were encouraged to begin smoking by commercial and social pressures. Under the influence of a constant flood of advertising portraying smoking as an adult trait of strong and admirable people, half a million children were taking up smoking every year.

The cigarette industry had been historically the largest purchaser of commercial advertising. The nation's first successful advertising executive, Albert Lasker, had the American Tobacco Company as his major client. Its president, George Washington Hill, was the model for the client-tyrant in Frederick Wakeman's novel about the advertising industry, *The Hucksters*.

Attempts to regulate cigarette advertising began in 1964. When the Surgeon General of the United States concluded after extensive studies that cigarette smoking was "a health hazard of sufficient importance in the United States to warrant appropriate remedial action," the Federal Trade Commission moved to require all cigarette packs and all advertisements to carry the stern warning that cigarette smoking "could cause death from cancer and related diseases."

Since cigarette companies spent $250,000,000 a year on radio and television advertising, the tobacco industry threw its considerable po-

---

[2] The most difficult issues are often disposed of in committee. On the floor the unrecorded voice vote, the pair and the "absence on official business" are a few of the devices available to protect senators from going on the record.

litical weight[3] behind a law forbidding any government agency to regulate cigarette advertising in any way. To show its good faith, it adopted a much weaker code of self-regulation, administered by the former governor of New Jersey, Robert Meyner, and supported a watered-down version of the FTC's warning (Caution: Cigarette smoking may be hazardous to your health) to go on packages only. In 1965, Senator Maureen Neuberger of Oregon, who had succeeded her husband in the Senate after he died from lung cancer, led a small minority of senators supporting legislation expressly giving the FTC the warning authority it had asserted. Kennedy supported her amendment. When it failed, he was one of five Senators who voted against the bill, and he then urged President Johnson to veto it, on grounds that it would actually weaken federal efforts to warn citizens against the hazards of smoking.

The bill was signed, and both the advertising and consumption of cigarettes increased. Additional studies by the Surgeon General concluded that cigarette smoking was "the principal cause" of lung cancer, the cause of death for 43,000 Americans each year. A survey of 500,000 people by the American Cancer Society showed smoking two packs a day cut the average life span by eight years. The FTC had found the warning approved by Congress had proven ineffective in discouraging smoking.

With Mrs. Neuberger's retirement, Kennedy took up the leadership of the fight for regulation along with Commerce Committee Chairman Warren Magnuson. In so doing, he took on three of America's largest industries: tobacco, broadcasting, and the airlines. He found that industry self-regulation was proving to be, in his words, "a charade." Advertising had been barred from shows produced exclusively for children, such as puppet shows, but it was allowed on all programs in which the share of the viewing audience under eighteen was under 45 per cent. This included professional football games and other sports broadcasts. Commercials showing persons actively participating in sports were barred, but elaborate evasions were permitted, such as showing players smoking after the sports events were over. Persons in

[3] The cigarette industry employs 100,000 workers in twenty-one states. Tobacco is a major crop in half a dozen states and is critical to the economies of Kentucky, North Carolina and Tennessee.

uniform could be shown smoking in the background, though not in front of the commercial.

In May 1967, Kennedy proposed to ban all cigarette advertising on radio and television. He found little support. Three months later he wrote all the major tobacco companies urging them voluntarily to stop advertising on sports programs and all other programs young people were likely to watch.[4]

The tobacco companies showed little interest. The huge audience rating for football programs was too tempting, and besides, they argued, most of the audiences were over twenty-one. Some companies hid behind the legal opinion that were they to agree with each other to limit advertising, they might be violating the anti-trust laws. The American Tobacco Company got to the heart of the issue by charging that none of the "speculation" about the relationship of cigarette smoking to cancer had "stood up to scientific scrutiny"; and that widespread advertising was, in fact, a boon to the public because it could give information about the reduced tar and nicotine cigarettes that had been developed.

Spurred by the negative response, Kennedy went before the World Conference on Smoking and Health in September to charge the cigarette industry had "demonstrated a total inattention to public responsibility" and was "dealing in people's lives for financial gain." He then introduced new federal laws, one giving the Federal Communications Commission the power to determine the kinds of programs and time slots on which cigarette advertising could appear, another taxing cigarettes according to their tar and nicotine content. This would give manufacturers an incentive to develop safer cigarettes, and also allow the public to tell the more lethal cigarettes by their higher prices.

Having failed to move the tobacco industry, Kennedy turned to the broadcasters, requesting each network to accept an experimental one-year ban on cigarette advertising, in effect, to drop their biggest customers. The reaction was predictable. CBS replied that it was fulfilling its responsibility to the public by airing the advertisements sponsored by the Cancer Society and the Public Health Service, which

[4] The ban would have applied to all programs aired before 9 P.M., and would have forbidden depicting of smoking in any way that made it attractive to young people.

gave the other side. NBC was certain citizens were aware of the controversy about smoking and health, and took it into account when deciding whether or not to smoke. ABC urged Kennedy not to put the entire problem on the doorsteps of the tobacco and television industries. "The primary responsibility to the health and welfare of our young people," it said, "begins at home."

Finally, Kennedy wrote each of the major airlines, asking them to discontinue the distribution of free cigarettes on flights. The response was equally evasive. American Airlines pointed out it distributed free cigarettes only to those who asked for them. Other lines said the idea was interesting, but it would require an industry-wide policy so that one line could not get a competitive edge on others, and perhaps Kennedy would like to take up the matter with the Air Transport Association, the industry's trade association. Only Delta Airlines was straightforward: "Our passengers like them," it said.

In stirring new controversies with such powerful opponents, for a cause that had little support in Congress at the time, Kennedy was acting in character. The man who had taken on the labor racketeers and the steel companies found strong satisfaction in such a fight. Unjust advantage was being taken of ordinary citizens by powerful interests. He felt an obligation to protect the public, which was being conditioned to smoke through the subtle techniques of motivational advertising. In the border states, where tobacco is grown and processed, he was accused of undermining the economic well-being of the people. He felt sympathy for those who, tied to the tobacco economy, had been led to believe they were doing good for the country. He knew he was making powerful enemies—and he was to pay the price. Running for President in 1968, he was unable to get a single major political figure to support him in either Kentucky or North Carolina.

In one article about Kennedy, a senate colleague was quoted as commenting that "he's just boarding here." If the comment meant Kennedy did not intend to make the Senate his career, it was accurate. If it meant he was merely occupying space, biding his time in the Legislative Branch, it was off the mark. In his first two years in the Senate, Kennedy carved a respected place for himself; and in the remaining time he used his position to help turn the Senate itself to the national issues that were increasingly to occupy his attention.

5

THE POOR, THE BLACK, AND
THE YOUNG: PART I

The years in which Robert Kennedy served in the Senate were a time of fundamental political change in the United States. The shift in the economic condition of the majority of Americans from poverty to affluence, which had been taking place gradually since the end of World War II, began in this period to alter their attitudes toward government. For the twenty years after Franklin Roosevelt's first election, the domestic issues of American politics had centered on the redistribution of resources from the elite, wealthy minority of America to the poor, disadvantaged majority. Social Security, union security, minimum wages, unemployment compensation, and guaranteed farm prices, all instituted after fierce political struggle, were part of this trend. The redistribution of wealth had overtones of the class divisions that had been present throughout American history. As late as 1951, President Truman could align his government and the Democratic party with the "common people" of the country against "the special interests."[1]

The consequences of the increasing affluence of the majority could be discerned even before the New Frontier began. The labor move-

---

[1] The demise of this historic Democratic battle cry began with the election of 1960. President Kennedy was uncomfortable with the outdated class appeal. He did not even use it when rallying public support in his fight to reverse the Big Steel price increases. When President Johnson tried to include all interests within his consensus, the issue dropped from the arsenal of all Democratic politicians except some who represent rural and populist sections of the South.

ment stopped growing, its militancy dimmed. No longer did most American workers see a conflict between their well-being and that of the corporation for which they worked. Redistribution programs, such as welfare and farm supports, came under increased attack, as voters saw themselves more and more as taxpayers rather than as recipients of tax-supported programs.[2] As the ranks of the impoverished thinned, programs to help them were opposed by groups lately risen from poverty and still insecure in their new status.

The last two Democrats to represent New York in the Senate were Herbert H. Lehman and Robert F. Kennedy. The social revolution that had taken place in the fifteen years that separated the beginning of their service can be measured by the difference in the issues for which they fought. Herbert Lehman, the epitome of New Deal liberalism, was a champion of non-discriminatory immigration legislation, defender of the intellectual community against the assault on civil liberties led by Senator Joseph McCarthy, the protector of minority rights (by which was meant the constitutional and economic interests of the Jews, Catholics, and Italians, as well as Negroes). By a combination of growing prosperity, presidential concern, Supreme Court decisions, and Congressional action, these issues lost their urgency. The issues of criminal justice, race relations, and poverty played a minor part in his Senate career, and the problems of Negroes in his own northern section of the nation were of minor importance. To say this is no reflection on Lehman or the liberals of his time. It is a reflection only of the dramatic swiftness of the tides of change.

The most critical domestic problems during Kennedy's years in the Senate were the results of the gap that had appeared between the affluent majority of Americans and the poor and dissatisfied minority. The poor could not make the levers of the electoral process work for them. Their view of free government became increasingly cynical and among the Negro poor often resulted in riots and civil disorder.

[2] One significant exception was defense spending, which in the twenty-three years after World War II accounted for $908 billion of government expenditure, or 57 per cent of the federal budget. Because defense spending was related to the security of the country and went to domestic corporations which employed millions of workers, it was exempted during Kennedy's lifetime, from the decline in support other programs suffered. Shortly afterward, the assault on the military budget was to begin, with the efforts to stop deployment of the antiballistic missile and cut the fiscal 1970 defense budget authorization, both unsuccessful.

By adding the element of physical fear to the racial and cultural differences already present, the disorders made the conflict even more intense.

Some observers wrote that Kennedy's interest in the poor was designed to create a new constituency on which he could draw when he ran for President. This both amused and irritated him. If politics were his purpose, there was no more disastrous tactic than to alienate the middle-class majority in order to court a minority that would support him anyway. What made Kennedy seek out the problems of the poor was their need for a champion and his personal need for their kind of cause. Their plight became the major new outlet for his sense of right and wrong and his strong feelings about injustice. Just as it had been wrong for union members to be betrayed by their leaders and for the public to be robbed by organized crime, it was wrong, to him, for the poor to be exploited by society at large. This problem would command more of his time and personal effort than any other.

From the beginning of the twentieth century, the effort to help Negroes through government action had concentrated on legal and legislative activity to protect the physical safety and civil rights of black people in southern states. The work was undertaken by the more privileged members of Negro society, with financial help and guidance from white liberals, but the Negro masses were largely uninvolved. A principal objective beginning in the late 1930s was to break up, again through legal action, the network of separate, segregated facilities that had been established after the Civil War in the southern and border states.

Today these goals seem limited. But they were responsive to the needs felt and expressed by Negroes of the time. Until the 1960s, two thirds of the Negroes in the United States lived in the South, in an atmosphere of almost total segregation, with local law enforcement under hostile white control. Legislation to make lynching a federal crime, for example, meant something in the daily lives of blacks who lived in fear of white mob violence.

If a single date can mark the beginning of the modern black revolution, it is May 17, 1954, when the Supreme Court handed down its unanimous decision in *Brown* v. *Board of Education,* finally destroying the constitutional basis of the "separate but equal" doctrine which had compelled Negroes to live in a status of inferior citizenship. In 1955, Dr. Martin Luther King led a bus boycott in Montgomery, Alabama. Later came a wave of sit-ins, begun by college students in North Carolina. Street demonstrations swept Birmingham, St. Augustine, and many other cities. New organizations, with new methods and leadership, offered competition to the NAACP, which had been the unchallenged spokesman for Negro rights for half a century.

All of this signaled a basic change in civil rights strategy. A program of legal action pointed exclusively toward the southern states and directed by an integrated leadership gave way gradually to a social and economic effort, using political techniques, in the North as well as the South, under increasingly black leadership. Probably most significant was the fact that for the first time great masses of the Negro poor became involved in civil rights activities. The message of the "revolution of rising expectations" which government officials were preaching in all corners of the world had a special echo for black Americans. The emergence of the independent African states had given them a sense of identification. The slow economic improvement of black Americans since the Depression, in all areas but the rural South, had raised them from a numb and hopeless proletariat to a people with the same aspirations as whites, increasingly unwilling to accept a subordinate position in the white man's world. During World War II, Joe Louis, the most prominent Negro in the country, could say he would "rather be a Negro in America than a white man anywhere else in the world," and the Negro of the time would accept this as patriotic gospel. Now it was not enough.

Kennedy believed that television played as profound a role in broadening the black revolution as any other force. It brought into the home of every family the picture of immense wealth and opportunity that portrayed the country. Seeing this, Negroes resented the denial of equal opportunity to them and their children. They were no longer willing to listen to the poetic cadence of the American dream while being forced to live in a nightmare of bleak poverty. The demand for equal rights now—not tomorrow—became the battle cry of the young blacks who resented the passivity with which their parents had accepted exploitation.

The involvement of the black poor changed both the goals and pace of the movement. Especially in the North, they were far less interested in integrating with white society than with improving their lives where they were. They had little patience for the rituals of the courts and the delays of a remote Congress. They wanted action from the white power structure of their own communities; and if their white allies would not help them, they would go it alone. In his letter from jail to white Birmingham clergymen, Dr. Martin Luther King observed that the "white liberal prefers a negative peace, which is the absence of tension, to a positive peace which is the presence of justice . . . Shallow understanding," he said, "from people of good will is more frustrating than absolute misunderstanding from people of ill will." The religious tradition of blacks, and the sense of solidarity which most other American ethnic groups had lost, allowed responsible leaders like Dr. King to teach the methods of non-violent direct action, especially in the South. But the ghetto isolation of the urban areas of the country fed the smoldering hostility against white people and permitted demagogic leaders to preach violence as the only means to social justice.

All these changes were just beginning when Robert Kennedy was Attorney General. He came to the office with no special commitment to this cause. He saw problems of civil rights as just some of the many injustices which he had the power and responsibility to help alleviate. The most important civil rights activities of the Kennedy administration were in the traditional pattern: legal, integrationist, and directed at the South. Robert Kennedy enforced court orders to integrate the universities of Alabama and Mississippi, reluctantly using federal marshals and troops. When the young "freedom riders" deliberately rode segregated buses to dramatize the need for integrating transit facilities, he protected them. He brought dozens of cases on behalf of Negroes denied the right to vote, and pushed for authority to enforce voting rights by allowing federal registrars to enroll Negroes on the day of the election. He and President Kennedy dealt primarily with the traditional Negro leaders, who had less rapport with the emerging groups. The President and the Attorney General felt some of the demonstrations in southern cities were ill-timed for the results they wished to achieve. Their initial reaction to the proposal for a March in Washington in August 1963 was a fear that it would lose votes for passage of the civil rights bill, but they worked with the leaders of the March to make it non-violent and successful. Despite what looked like timidity to some civil rights advocates, the name Kennedy became anathema to Southern diehards, and Robert Kennedy as the chief enforcement officer of Negro constitutional rights became a special target of their abuse.

As Kennedy sensed the new direction of the civil rights movement, he directed the Justice Department to relate itself to it. He was the motive force behind the President's Committee on Juvenile Delinquency, which became the first federal agency to work directly with indigenous leadership in poverty neighborhoods. He ordered his U. S. Attorneys not to require bail for indigent defendants, criticizing the system which discriminated against the poor by forcing them to go to jail pending trial while more affluent defendants went free. He saw the emerging problems of the ghetto in the city of Washington. Sensing the dangers in chronic, enforced idleness, he established playground and recreation programs in black areas of the District of Columbia. Realizing the permanent damage of dropping out of school, he spoke at high school assemblies to urge students to stay in school. He focused attention on the inadequate facilities in the public compound for orphaned and abandoned children, Junior Village. In the last months of his tenure as Attorney General all this experience was gathered together as the Justice Department led in the formulation of the first attempts at a federal poverty program.

With few exceptions, the New Frontier programs did not go directly to the hard-core problems of jobs, education and housing in the ghetto.[3] They predated the growing demand for "black power"—separate institutions under Negro control for the exclusive benefit of Negro constituencies. Most important, they did not require any change in the attitudes of the great majority of white citizens outside the South, who had no real sense of the appalling living conditions to which Negroes in their own community had been relegated. They could sympathize with young southern demonstrators pitted against the dogs of Sheriff Bull Connor of Birmingham and the brutality and indifference

[3] Title I of President Kennedy's education bill of 1961 did propose that 10 per cent of the funds be reserved for "hard core" areas, including ghettos and areas of rural poverty.

of Sheriff Rainey of Neshoba County, meanwhile speeding to work on superhighways built over the ghettos and living within a social framework structured to insulate them from any significant contact with Negro citizens. They could applaud the old civil rights struggles without having to face their own deep-rooted prejudices, or consider what they would do if black demands directly affected their own lives.

Robert Kennedy's first real awareness of the change in Negro attitudes came in the spring of 1963, when Burke Marshall, his assistant Attorney General for Civil Rights, went to Birmingham to try to find common ground between the Negro protestors and the white leadership. Marshall asked the Negroes a basic question: "What do you want?" At first, the response was confusion. Much of the protesting had been against oppressive and humiliating discrimination, and no one had really considered the possibility of affirmative demands. When the discussions were over, the demands essentially were for power—political and economic—that would entitle Negroes to share in their government and in the material wealth that could assure them independence.

Shortly afterward Kennedy and Marshall held a meeting in New York with Negro intellectuals and entertainers, to solicit their ideas for new programs for the urban areas. The Attorney General was not prepared for what met him. A sharp exchange between him and a young freedom rider, who had been beaten in the South, brought forth a torrent of insults directed at him personally and as a representative of the white power structure. His efforts to explain the difficulties of getting civil rights laws through a Congress dominated by Southerners were met with derision. He thought of himself as one who had defended Negro interests at great personal and political risk to himself. The leaders who met with him would not dispute his commitment to civil rights, but for the most part it was irrelevant. They were not interested in what they regarded as crumbs of progress, nor sympathetic with the political difficulties of their white liberal allies. They were speaking for a people who were no longer content to wait. The late Lorraine Hansberry, the gifted playwright, told him many Negroes were disinterested in integration, preferring their own institutions to participation in a society they felt was hopelessly rotten. Kennedy was angry. He resented the way he had been treated, but he learned from the meeting that the temper among Negro intellectuals was separatist, impatient, and bitter.[4]

Events during his last months as Attorney General emphasized the potential for racial violence in the North. In the spring and summer of 1964, the Justice Department monitored hundreds of minor disorders properly labeled as civil rights demonstrations which might have developed into riots. Serious violence did break out in Cleveland, Rochester, Jersey City, Chicago, Philadelphia, and New York City. Kennedy had always been careful, in his speeches as Attorney General to ask northern audiences to examine conditions of possible violence in their own communities before judging too harshly the actions of their southern brethren. During the Birmingham crisis in 1963, he met with northern businessmen, newspaper publishers, and civic officials and warned them that they faced even more difficult problems in their own cities. Not one would accept the possibility.

By 1964, the dormant racism of the North began to be aroused. The open-housing provisions of the Civil Rights bill of 1964 had to be abandoned, after Democratic congressmen from urban centers found their constituents vehemently opposed. In the white neighborhoods, the riots stirred fear and demands for stronger police action. Urban politicians who had happily championed "civil rights" were now under increasing pressure to choose between Negro demands and the anti-Negro resentment of a large part of their white constituencies. Many chose the latter.

As a candidate for the Senate in 1964, Kennedy faced the same pressures. He handled his first test cautiously, if not ambiguously. It concerned a proposal of the New York City Board of Education to bus Negro students into schools in white neighborhoods, an issue tinged with deep emotion. Hundreds of militant white women demonstrated against it. White liberals endorsed it. Asked for a position, Kennedy deliberated, then came out in opposition to busing children over long distances to schools outside their neighborhoods. It was essentially the same position he had taken on the general issue as

---

[4] When one participant told him afterward he had done more for civil rights than any other Attorney General, Kennedy said, "Why do you say this to me? Why didn't you say this to the others?" "I couldn't say this to the others," came the reply. "It would affect my relationship with them. If I were to defend you, they would conclude I had gone over to the other side."

Attorney General. His opponent, Kenneth Keating, offered practically the same statement, so busing did not become an issue between them in the campaign.

Later in the campaign, however, in a speech to the NAACP convention in Buffalo, Kennedy sounded the themes of the new Negro movement. The advance in civil rights in the South, he said, must now be matched by improvements in education, housing, and job opportunities in the North:

> I am for programs which meet these problems head-on. I am for federal participation to the full extent it is needed. The cost of these programs, high as it may be, can never be as high as the costs in welfare payments, in crime prevention, in the loss of manpower, in the loss of people to our society that we accept when we tolerate slums, joblessness, school dropouts, and racial discrimination. We cannot accept the status quo, I know we can do better . . . You and I did not labor to destroy segregation of one kind without attacking the more tenacious and difficult discrimination that lies beyond it.

At the beginning of his Senate career, Kennedy believed the most important single program to end racial inequality was education. After his election, he made frequent visits to ghetto schools in New York and other states, talking to children, teachers, and administrators. By acquiring basic learning skills, he felt Negro children would have a chance, at least, to lift themselves out of the life that had imprisoned their parents. As it was, this opportunity was denied them. Schools in Negro sections had steadily declined in quality; Negro children in the sixth grade actually scored lower on I.Q. tests than they had in the third grade. New techniques of learning had been developed, but old-line administrators were reluctant to adopt them. The public school, which, more than any institution, had assimilated the children of European immigrants and given them the tools of self-advancement, had failed in the same task for black children.

As Attorney General, Kennedy had been instrumental in setting up the Model School Program in the all-black Cardozo area of the District of Columbia. Textbooks irrelevant to the life of black children had been scrapped in favor of materials and activities adapted to their needs. Peace Corps returnees and others committed to the education of disadvantaged children were added to the teaching staff. Women from the Cardozo community had been used as teacher's aides. Partially to advance these methods on the national level, Kennedy joined the Education Subcommittee of the Senate Committee on Labor and Public Welfare, which would write the Elementary and Secondary Education Act of 1965. In subcommittee, he sought extra funds for compensatory programs for children in poverty neighborhoods. He also inspired amendments to the bill requiring testing and evaluation so that federal educational authorities could have a measure of the effectiveness of the new programs, and some certainty that funds were being channeled intelligently.[5]

Experience soon showed, however, that improved schools could not alone solve the multiple problems of the ghetto. A black child's ability to learn was already extensively damaged by the age of three. There were no significant pre-school programs for such children. With little opportunity for employment upon the completion of schooling, they had little incentive to learn. Better schools and educational methods helped, but were hardly enough. Kennedy decided he must find other solutions to the problems of the ghetto.

In the middle of August 1965, came the riot in Watts, a Negro community in Los Angeles. The violence, touched off by an apparently routine arrest of an intoxicated Negro, continued for seven days, with widespread looting and arson, and massive counteraction by police and federal soldiers. The riot scenes raged on television. In surrounding neighborhoods as far away as Beverly Hills, fearful whites purchased firearms for protection. The trauma of Watts jarred the nation and set the pattern of racial unrest to come.

Kennedy was deeply disturbed by what happened in Watts. The outpouring of Negro rage was comprehensible, but the harsh and bitter white reaction alarmed him. The enormous publicity given the riot had, he felt, emphasized Negro violence without explaining its reasons, contributing to the impression among the whites that Negroes rioted aimlessly and irresponsibly. "Somebody has to tell the other side," he said. "A lot of those looters are just kids in trouble. I got in trouble when I was that age."

---

[5] The amendment was worked out in Kennedy's office but officially added to the bill in subcommittee by Congressman Hugh Carey of Brooklyn, a subcommittee member in the House.

A week after the riot had begun, with Watts still smoldering and troops still in the streets, Kennedy spoke on the subject to a convention of the International Association of Oddfellows at Spring Valley, New York. It was not the first analysis of Negro rioting by a prominent public figure,[6] but it marked the first time any white political leader had tried to explain to whites why violence threatened their urban security.

Watts was not the first riot, he said. It would not be the last. All over the county "riots were waiting to happen." Southern Negroes, who migrated to northern cities to escape the hopelessness of their poverty, found themselves unprepared and desperately frustrated by the cultural shock of urban life.

Departing from his earlier view of education as the single most important element, Kennedy saw it now as jobs:

> We say to the young, stay in school—learn and study and sacrifice —and you will be rewarded the rest of your life. But a Negro youth who finished high school is more likely to be unemployed than a white youth who drops out of school and is more likely to find only menial work at lower pay. One leader of the Watts riot was a biochemistry graduate. We should not be surprised.

Then he tried to explain why it was that Negro demonstrations in the North were not going to be the dignified confrontations whites were used to seeing in the South.

> In the South the movement had been strongly led and relatively disciplined. Many of the leaders have been ministers, all have preached and practiced non-violence. But northern problems are the problems of everyday living. They affect too many people too directly for involvement to be restricted to those with the patience, the discipline and the inclination to practice non-violence. The army of the resentful and the desperate is larger in the North than in the South—but it is an army without generals, without captains, almost without sergeants. Civil rights leaders cannot, with sit-ins, change the fact that adults are illiterate. Marches do not create jobs for their children. So demagogues have often usurped the positions of leadership—each striving to

[6] President Johnson had offered a brilliant exposition of the problems of Negro society, a month before, at Howard University. The President referred to Negro despair, caused by blighted hope, as "the source of destructive rebellion against the fabric of society." But he tried neither to explain nor justify Negro behavior to white people.

outdo the other in promise or threat, offering unreal hopes and dangerous hates. During and after every riot, city and police officials have pleaded for representatives of the Negroes who could negotiate an end to the violence, and establish a channel of communication to the rioters. Each time Negro civil rights leaders have frankly acknowledged their inability to lead the mobs or the neighborhoods from which the mobs have come.

To understand the deprivation and suffering of the ghettos, Kennedy urged his white audience to see them not as Negro problems, but as the problems of human beings. He pleaded that blacks be given some indication that their problems would become part of the public agenda.

It is only when they are being dealt with in the political process that we can expect to channel people's frustration and resentment and insecurity into constructive action programs. The drive for Negro voting in the South has been peaceful in large part because peaceful protest found in the federal government an audience and an authority capable of taking action and willing to do so. Unemployment among Negroes in the North has resulted in more riots than peaceful protests, in large part because government has not had the tools to affect directly the wide margins between Negro and white unemployment rates.

Finally, he struck a note which, at the time, was only rhetorical, but which would become central to his efforts in this area:

There will be much to be done at the state and local level—especially in giving to the poor a voice in the decisions which affect their daily lives. Only by affording them such a voice can we offer them an alternative to the streets. Only by inviting their active participation can we help them develop the leaders who make the difference between a political force—with which we can deal—and a headless mob with which no one wants to deal.

There was another concept in the speech that was the most difficult of all for white Americans to understand. To people who had been brought up to obey the law and respect its enforcers, the sight of rioting and looting on television suggested the need for stronger police action to preserve public order. Out of Watts and the riots that followed came the "law and order" theme which was to influence domestic politics for the rest of Kennedy's life. His speech took a different view:

> Just saying obey the law is not going to work. The law to us is a friend, which preserves our property and our personal safety. But for the Negro, law means something different. In the South it has meant beatings and degradation and official discrimination. Law has been his oppressor and his enemy. The Negro who has moved North with this heritage has not found in the law the same oppression as in the South. But neither has he found a friend and protector. The laws do not protect them from paying too much money for inferior goods, from having their furniture illegally repossessed, from having to keep lights turned on the feet of children at night to keep them from being gnawed by rats. The law does not fully protect their lives, their dignity or encourage their hope and trust for the future. We have a long way to go before law means the same thing to Negroes as it does to us.

What little press attention the speech received emphasized this last point. "Kennedy Says Law Is Negroes' Enemy" read some headlines. For a former Attorney General of the United States, whose entire career had been devoted to law enforcement, to make such a statement seemed astounding. But Kennedy felt that unless whites realized this fact, they could never comprehend what was going on in the ghetto. Kennedy was not condoning violence. He often stated that "those who lead others to burn and loot must feel the full force of the law."

By "the law" Kennedy did not mean the police. He was sympathetic to the problems policemen faced in ghetto situations—problems created by the color of their skins, their lack of prior training in dealing with this kind of disturbance, the ignorance they shared with other whites of conditions of Negro life. Later, he would strongly support the recommendations of the President's Crime Commission to improve the work of the police and would suggest a plan by which young men who committed themselves to three years of police work would get draft deferments—a proposal endorsed by police officials all over the country. And while he opposed the harsh and regressive District of Columbia Crime Bill, he did introduce legislation of his own to make sure that those acquitted of crime on grounds of insanity would not be released to commit additional crimes if still insane at the time of acquittal.

What he felt was oppressing the Negro was not the criminal statutes or those who enforce them, but procedures such as wage garnishment which harassed the poor, and the network of legal advantages enjoyed by the wealthy and the merchants.

The Spring Valley speech, given only eight months into his Senate term, was the philosophical fountainhead of most of Kennedy's later utterances on racial problems, and a significant landmark in Kennedy's career. Within his first year in elective office, he had taken on the nation's most critical domestic problem, and aligned himself with the most abused group in the United States. He would continue on this path until his public statements and actions made him the chief advocate of the Negro among white political leaders—a course he recognized, as he remarked time and again, to be contrary to his political interests.

Had he deplored the rioting, called for more police, spoken generally of the need for better opportunities, he would have been in tune with public opinion in his state and the nation. Nor did he have to take this approach to improve his standing with Negroes, who were already his ardent supporters. He took it because he realized that the growing fears and the growing conflict between the races were tearing the country apart. Few white voices would be raised on the side he advocated. The rigid attitudes of the white majority made it difficult for politicians to take what looked like an excessively "soft" or generous position on issues related to the riots. But he was in a unique position from which to speak out. Of all the public figures in the nation, he spoke to lower-income whites from the sturdiest base of personal popularity. His programs might have been unpopular with them, but his personal attraction was strong. The respect for his name and his identification with law enforcement, gave him special standing among northern whites most vehement against the Negro.

The Spring Valley speech, drawn up to meet the moment, did not offer any program to match its analysis. That was Kennedy's next step. He increased his tours of black slums in New York and elsewhere. He kept in close touch with John McCone, an old friend and a Republican, whom President Kennedy had chosen as Director of the CIA. McCone had returned to private life and was Chairman of the blue-ribbon commission appointed by the governor of California to investigate the causes of the Watts riot and make recommendations.

In December 1965, Kennedy asked his legislative staff to draw up a civil rights program for the next session of Congress. Still thinking in terms of the old struggles at the Justice Department, Peter Edelman, with the help of Burke Marshall, compiled a series of recommendations aimed at protecting Negroes and civil right workers in the South from official brutality and coercion. This was not what Kennedy wanted. "I want to make proposals about northern problems. This is where the real difficulties are going to be," he said.

For the next two months, Kennedy, working with Edelman and Walinsky, tried to think through a comprehensive program for the urban Negro crisis.[7] Dozens of proposals were already available, from a guaranteed income program, to organized resettlement of ghetto residents in white neighborhoods. The senator was quick to realize that a laundry list of recommendations would have no impact. A new framework was needed to mold the recommendations into a coherent strategy for the ghetto.

First, Kennedy and his aides had to face a central issue being debated within the black community: Should the Negro seek improvement through separation or integration? It was an issue as old as emancipation; it was a vital part of Marcus Garvey's "return to black Africa" movement and the "separate but equal" doctrine enunciated by the Supreme Court in 1896. Given the distinctive culture of the ghetto and the existing levels of education and job skills, was it possible for black people to be integrated at any significant level into a white-dominated society? Even if so, could it be done in view of the stiff resistance to open housing in the North and to desegregation in the South? The alternative of improving the neighborhood (or "gilding the ghetto" as it was called by its critics) would command much

---

[7] While Edelman and Walinsky worked closely together on Kennedy's racial proposals, they had quite a different personal commitment on the issues involved. Edelman lived in an integrated section of Washington and, while working for Kennedy, met (and later married) a black woman, Mississippi civil rights attorney Marion Wright. Walinsky lived in an all-white neighborhood in the suburbs and once surprised Kennedy by asking him to intervene with officials of the Potomac School to get his son admitted. Potomac is one of the most exclusive and, during Kennedy's lifetime, was one of the most segregated private schools in the Washington area.

wider support among whites. What were the moral values involved? Many sociologists maintained that a segregated way of life, no matter what its quality, could never offer blacks the opportunities of an open society. Were Americans willing to deal with the underlying issue of white racism in their national life? In any event, whether the preferred solution was integration or separatism, this was a time of awesome public resistance to new domestic spending. This presented a further political problem: How could the solutions be related to a more general effort to uplift the entire country, carrying the Negro minority with it?

In a series of three speeches at the end of January 1966, later refined in his testimony before Senator Ribicoff's urban hearings in August, Kennedy offered his answers. His program was to become the core of his appeal to the American people in the campaign of 1968.

It began with the recognition that the earlier efforts of the New Deal, the Fair Deal, and the New Frontier were no longer working. Federal slum clearance had been going on for almost thirty years, yet almost half the housing in the ghettos was still substandard. Public housing had been the main hope for progress when enacted in 1946, on the theory that getting a family out of its hovel would *ipso facto* change its life. The program had failed to meet its expectations. Between 1947 and 1966, 800,000 housing units had been built but 900,000 had been torn down. As Kennedy argued in the speeches, housing projects had been built "without relevance to the underlying problems of poverty, unemployment, social disorganization, and alienation which caused people to need assistance in the first place. Too many of the projects have become jungles—places of despair and danger for their residents and for the cities they were designed to save." The welfare program, also conceived with compassionate intentions, had become mere subsistence, degrading and demoralizing to those who had come to depend on it, contributing to, and often forcing, the breakup of families. Programs of job training had been focused on job opportunities in modern factories which required skills black migrants from the South did not have the background even to learn. Negro unemployment had risen sharply since these programs were instituted. Worst of all, government efforts had fallen far short of the needs of a growing population. Their mere existence had given the white population a false sense that conditions were improving. If they were not, it was felt, the Negro was to blame.

Next, Kennedy came to grips with the central question of whether to emphasize integration or ghetto improvement. He decided the two goals were interdependent. In his January speeches, he had stressed "breaking down the massive housing segregation of the ghetto." He proposed several ways to give Negroes a free choice of where they would live, including compulsory desegregation of urban renewal projects; outlawing of discrimination in the sale and rental of housing in suburbs as well as cities; home ownership for low-income families in "new towns" financed with government funds; and federal assistance to the hundreds of private groups helping to achieve desegregation in their communities. But before many blacks would even wish to move into predominantly white neighborhoods, they would have to experience better opportunities in the ghetto and free themselves from what he called their "pattern of fear" of a more integrated life. As he put it in his testimony at the Ribicoff hearings:

> Questions of technical or surface integration are far less important now than is the building of self-sufficiency and self-determination within the Negro community. It is important that Negroes who have achieved financial and social security should have complete freedom to choose where to live. But it is far more important that the vast majority of Negroes be enabled to achieve basic financial and social security where they live now.

To Kennedy, the various problems of the ghetto made up "a seamless web." No one problem could be called the key to solution of the others, but if there was one place to start, it was with employment. Studies in Watts, Harlem, Oakland, and other ghettos had shown the number one Negro demand to be jobs. Massive unemployment, especially among young people, as much as 40 per cent in some slum areas, was the one condition no government program had attempted to deal with. The debilitating effect of being out of work, and thus without purpose in the community, was a major reason so many Negro men seemed shiftless in white eyes, and why some turned into rioters. As Kennedy put it:

> More than segregation in housing and schools, more than differences in attitude of life styles, it is unemployment which marks the

Negro of the urban ghetto off and apart from the rest of us—from Negroes who have jobs almost as much as from whites. Unemployment is having nothing to do, which means having nothing to do with the rest of us.

When he had toured Watts two months after the riot, he talked to an old man sitting on a corner. "What's the problem?" he asked. "Frustration," the man said. "What do you mean?" "Man, when you get to be over fifty, you can't find a job noways."

A call for jobs had popular appeal as well as value as a strategy. Work is a fundamental part of the American ethic. No one could oppose giving a man a chance to work.

But where to find the jobs? Shortly after joining Kennedy's staff, Walinsky had sent him a memo containing ideas he had developed as a member of the Justice Department's task force on the poverty program.

> Suppose, for a moment, that we could stop thinking of the unemployed, the school dropouts . . . as idle hands for whom work, any work, must be found. Consider this, instead, as simply an inventory of raw material . . .
>
> Now ask if there are things that should be done in our cities—forgetting for the moment the question of cost. First we might want to fulfill the declaration of policy of the Housing Act of 1959: "The goal of a decent home and suitable living environment for every American family." We might also, of course, want to build new schools . . . and hospitals and clinics. Take all the unemployed and underemployed . . . start with housing . . . recruit from the schools of architecture every third and fourth-year student; have them design the new buildings and plan renovation of the old, stretching their talents and their imaginations . . . Then bring in thousands of trained construction workers, mostly those too old to work. Put them to training the men and youths in the tasks of building and renovation . . . Take others of these men and boys, and put them to furniture making; the new houses will need new insides as well . . .
>
> As housing is built and upgraded, an ever-expanding force of trained labor will be made available for other tasks—the building of schools, hospitals, playgrounds, community centers.
>
> The difference between this and earlier "public works" programs is that unlike dams or forests, the rebuilding of cities has immediate reality for urban workers . . . Moreover, it has immediate reality for

their neighboring fellow-citizens, whose perception of the worth of any individual is in large part derived from the importance of that individual's work to them. Taking youth to forest camps is likely to be perceived, by the middle class, as a way of getting them off the streets and out of the poolrooms; thus it preserves their status as people with whom something must be done. On their return, they are the same as before. But putting them to work on building schools and playgrounds for all the city's children is in fact making them important to all the city's parents . . .

Walinsky's theory became the core of Kennedy's job proposals. The unemployed would be put to work on the massive task of rebuilding the ghettos. Priority for employment would go to those who lived in the areas where the work was undertaken. An attempt would be made to break out of the confining traditions of the educational system by joining it to the rebuilding effort. If, for example, a high school student wished to drop out of school to join such a program, he would be allowed to do so. Hopefully, the experience would give him the incentive needed to finish school later, as he learned that useful opportunity did exist at the end of the classroom road.

As with most good theories, this one encountered difficulties in practice. A few types of skilled construction work were too complicated for the ghetto jobless. There were many more skills the white construction unions wanted to keep for themselves. Attempts to use neighborhood labor to rehabilitate housing in Manhattan were picketed by both blacks, who wanted no white labor on the job, and by unions, which wanted certain jobs reserved for their members. Nevertheless, it was a new approach that offered a common basis for support among the blacks, who would have to participate in it, and the whites, who would have to pay for it.

To this scheme, Kennedy added an element to meet the growing need for black-controlled institutions. One of the major drawbacks, to previous plans for ghetto improvement was that blacks, in the phrase of Professor James Wilson of Harvard, were "the objects rather than the subjects of civic action. Things are done for or about or to or because of Negroes but they are less frequently done *by* Negroes." Malcolm X had put it more sternly: "We must control the politics and politicians of our community; we must no longer take orders from outside forces."

Kennedy had come to the same conclusion in the Justice Department. The most successful projects funded by the President's Committee on Juvenile Delinquency had been the HARYOU-ACT community program in Harlem and Mobilization for Youth on New York's Lower East Side. HARYOU-ACT involved thousands of young people in summer programs of employment and neighborhood improvement. (Later, it foundered on financial mismanagement, lack of adequate support from Washington, and interference by some Harlem politicians, but the initial concept was sound.) Testifying before Congress in 1964, on the Community Action portion of the poverty bill, Kennedy had used these demonstration projects to illustrate the fact that "the institutions which affect the poor are huge, complex structures operating far outside their control. They plan programs for the poor, not with them. Part of the sense of helplessness and futility comes from the feeling of powerlessness to affect the operation of these organizations. The community action program . . . must give the poor a real voice in their institutions."

Where these principles had been applied, as in the East Columbus, Ohio Community Organization (ECCO), they had shown great promise. Community action had caused controversy, but as Kennedy said:

> It has been a long time since most leadership in this country has spoken to the poor and tried to understand the problems of their existence. We should not fear the conflicts that have arisen as new power groups contend with old, as political leaders are forced to meet the slum dwellers instead of the wardleaders. Every department of city government dealing with social welfare programs should feel challenged to justify their traditional response to the problems of the poor. They may not like it, but the price of their discontent will be stronger and safer communities for our children and ourselves.

In his urban program, Kennedy went beyond the "maximum feasible participation of the poor," the ambiguous phrase in the Poverty Act which had allowed city halls to assert control over poverty programs, frequently making them little more than handouts from the white community. He asked for "full and dominant participation by the residents of the community concerned." The community was to be that geographic neighborhood within the city that residents considered their own:

In the supposed interests of efficiency we have thus far provided municipal services only on a citywide basis; using the same kind of organizational structure, whether the city had 2,000 people or 2 million. This technique has proven unable to meet the special needs of the ghetto and should be replaced by a system which allows a recognizable community to organize and secure those services which meet its own unique needs.

The device to achieve this was the community development corporation. More than any other institution or government program, these corporations, Kennedy hoped, would transform ghettos from vast, undifferentiated masses into real communities, in which residents would have a sense of control over their lives, and feel, for the first time, part of the American experience of self-determination.

Kennedy knew the work of these corporations would be far too costly for government. Mayor Lindsay estimated in the 1966 Ribicoff hearings that $50 billion in federal funds would be needed over a ten-year period for the physical rebuilding of New York City alone, a federal share Kennedy called "totally unrealistic." He sought, therefore, to bring private resources into the process. Even they could not furnish all the money that was needed, but given the fiscal limitations caused by the war in Vietnam and public reluctance to pay for major new ghetto programs, they could do much more than government alone to meet the urgent needs and they could do it in ways that made money. This, rather than the production of goods and services for the affluent, could be the new frontier of the free enterprise system in the building of America.

The year before, Tom Johnston and David Hackett had proposed that he help organize a comprehensive program for Harlem and Bedford-Stuyvesant. This suggestion became the basis of the community development corporation Kennedy wanted to establish in his own state, as an example of how his proposals could work. He was hesitant to move in Harlem. The highly structured political leadership and the strong influence of the militant anti-white groups would create barriers, as would his own arms-length relationship with Adam Powell, who at the time was chairman of the House Education and Labor Committee. But Bedford-Stuyvesant was different. Although its 300,000 people made it the most populous ghetto in the country (except for the South Side of Chicago), it was predominantly a residential, non-tenement area, physically much more like Watts than Harlem. It had a far higher proportion of home ownership than other black ghettos. It had no congressman of its own, its borders having been cut up and distributed among three congressional districts represented by whites. With no dominant Negro leaders, it seemed much more receptive to a program led partially by outside figures.

Beginning in early 1966, Kennedy began to visit the area and talk to its spokesmen. In June, he went there to help dedicate a city swimming pool, the only one in the area. While his reception was friendly, one woman had berated him about the politicians "who come in here and make promises and then nothing happens." He told his staff he did not want to return until he had something tangible to offer.

He saw the need for two parallel corporations, one reflecting the community, the other composed of white business leaders whose experience and influence could assure the private resources needed for economic development. First, the community corporation was organized to act as the applicant for federal funds and as the central management body for the activities and programs planned in the Bedford-Stuyvesant area. The structure was intended to be representative of the community and have its confidence. As its chairman, Kennedy settled on Civil Court Judge Thomas Jones, a former state senator, an eloquent speaker, and a respected figure in the area. For the corporation directed by the white business leaders, Kennedy turned first to André Meyer, the dominant figure in the international banking and investment firm of Lazard Frères. Meyer was one of the authentic captains of finance in the world. Kennedy had met him through his sister-in-law, Jacqueline Kennedy, who trusted him as a financial adviser and good friend. Meyer was a shrewd and talented businessman of the old school. Kennedy sometimes compared him to his own father. If Meyer believed the project was practical, that would be the best recommendation to other business leaders.

In September 1966, he laid his proposal before Meyer and asked for his help. "I'll look into this seriously if you look into Vietnam seriously," said Meyer. After some study, Meyer told Kennedy that his underlying concept was sound, that the white business and investment community had reason to be interested, as a business proposition, in involving themselves in the improvement of the ghetto.

As additional sponsors, Kennedy suggested Douglas Dillon, former Secretary of the Treasury; Thomas J. Watson, chairman of the Board of IBM; William S. Paley, chairman of CBS; and Roswell Gilpatric, former Undersecretary of Defense. Meyer suggested others, such as David Lilienthal, former chairman of the Tennessee Valley Authority, still heavily involved in economic development; banker George Moore; investment banker Benno Schmidt; and insurance executive James Oates. In the course of one day, Kennedy visited each of these men in their offices, explaining the proposal and its significance. They were accustomed to being asked for money for worthy projects. Kennedy asked for much more—their time, their judgment, their influence. They were to be working members of a group responsible for mobilizing white investment in the projects the black leadership decided were needed. Impressed with the detailed planning and by Kennedy's own fervor, all of them agreed.

With these key pieces in place, Kennedy quickly rounded out the project by getting support from the city of New York, planning grants from foundations, and pledges of technical help from universities in the Brooklyn area. With Senator Javits, he sponsored an amendment to the poverty bill providing $45 million in "special impact" funds for a comprehensive approach to job training and economic development. Bedford-Stuyvesant became one of the first applicants.

The first months of the project's life were difficult. Organizational snags and personal differences added to the underlying tension between white and black. Leaders of established organizations in the ghetto saw it as a threat to their influence. The white participation was resented by some. While the neighborhood corporation stood in awe of the captains of industry and tended to follow their suggestions without question, the more militant separatists saw the project as another effort by "the Man" and "his Toms" to do just enough to stave off the revolution they felt was necessary. One college educator, who had worked hard to develop a plan for a "university of the streets," was told by his neighborhood advisers that his first step should be to resign in favor of a black man. At one point, some of the neighborhood groups threatened to discredit the project, but Kennedy and Jones turned them back by broadening the membership of the community corporation to include younger and more militant elements.

The Bedford-Stuyvesant project survived its problems, and, by 1968, had begun to show results. The Sheffield Farms building, a large, abandoned structure in the center of the community, for years the symbol of decay, was being rehabilitated by the residents as a headquarters for community services. Eighty banks and insurance companies, which had previously provided mortgage money in Negro neighborhoods on only the stiffest conditions (short terms, large down payments) agreed to offer conventional mortgages for rehabilitation on the basis of an FHA guarantee alone. IBM was building a plant to employ 300 people. Several local businesses were expanding. Over 300 brownstone homes had been renovated, and unused residential blocks were being turned into recreational areas. By 1968, Bedford-Stuyvesant was beginning to deserve the premature accolade it had received from *Newsweek* as "the most sweeping and comprehensive rehabilitation effort ever brought to bear on a single American community."

The most important element in Bedford-Stuyvesant's survival was Kennedy's own involvement. He considered it a personal responsibility, attending almost every meeting of the Development and Services Corporation Board. Several members of his New York staff were assigned to the project. Kennedy's personal interest enabled the project to get leadership of the caliber of former deputy police commissioner Frank Thomas, as director of the community corporation; and of the former head of the Justice Department's Civil Rights Division, John Doar, in charge of the Development corporation. It was Kennedy who signed them up. For him, the project was more challenging then any of his activities in the Senate. It gave him the chance to test the validity of his solutions to the nation's most urgent domestic problem, and the personal satisfaction of using his executive skills. Later he would say, "If I could do what I really wanted to do, I would resign from the Senate and run Bedford-Stuyvesant."

As the Bedford-Stuyvesant project took form, Kennedy decided to extend its lessons in an upstate community. The election of a political ally, Dominic Assaro, as mayor of Utica made that possible. Kennedy assigned Carter Burden, his legislative assistant in the New York office, to devise a plan for a community development corporation with Mayor Assaro's staff. By June 1968, Burden had worked out a prototype that could be used in communities throughout the state.

With Bedford-Stuyvesant showing the possibilities for private investment in the ghetto, Kennedy tried to develop legislative incentives for companies to do it nationwide. As he expressed it, "private enterprise has created jobs for over 60 million Americans, but it has not rebuilt the centers of poverty, nor put their people back to work, and in my judgment, this is the principal cause of our failure to solve the problem of unemployment in urban poverty areas." Business had considerable influence over public opinion, and was held in great respect by the newly affluent majority. It could be a mighty ally in the war against poverty.

Kennedy suggested an FHA program of guaranteeing private bank loans for the ghettos so that builders and developers could get long-term, low-interest (2 per cent) loans in return for building low-rent housing. He developed an even more unique scheme to encourage jobs. Any company that agreed to create at least fifty new jobs in a poverty area, and fill at least two thirds of them with residents of the area would get a 10 per cent tax credit. It was an attempt to focus the Kennedy administration's tax-credit approach, originally directed to industrial recovery in general, on ghettos exclusively. In addition, firms would receive accelerated depreciation and a 25 per cent tax deduction for the salaries paid these new workers while they were training.

Undoubtedly, the use of the tax laws was a bonanza, designed to make it financially attractive for businessmen to involve themselves in parts of the city they had previously ignored. It contradicted the philosophy that the tax law should be for raising revenue only, not for social purposes. But Kennedy cited many instances where tax laws promoted certain kinds of investment—the oil depletion allowance, credits for construction of grain storage facilities, and the capital gains tax itself, which encouraged investment by taxing its profits at only 25 per cent if held for six months. If accelerated depreciation could be used to build bins for farmers' grain to avert a crisis of abundance, he said, it could help create jobs to solve a much greater crisis of need.

The other ghetto problem Kennedy emphasized in the Senate was the welfare issue. But, instead of a new approach, this was a holding action against an assault on existing programs. For years, white liberals and conservatives had disputed whether welfare was a humanitarian necessity or a wasteful series of handouts. Neither side was aware of the strong reaction that was developing against the welfare program among the poor.

The system by which the federal government put up most of the money for state relief had been established during the Depression, as a device to generate income and redistribute wealth. At a time when few could get work, welfare was a vital means of financial support for poor people, black and white. But in a society which had always put a premium on work, welfare tended to encourage dependency, creating a self-perpetuating class of dole recipients. With job opportunities so scarce among Negroes, the difference between what a black man could earn by working and what he received on relief was so small as to make work seem unappealing, especially since every dollar earned was deducted from the welfare payment received. Those who continued to work at the low wages available did not make enough to support their families; yet most states denied welfare to families if a working person lived in their house, and this fact encouraged broken homes in ghetto areas.

Another source of grievance among ghetto dwellers was the tendency to treat welfare recipients as social problems. An army of white social workers invaded the ghetto, prying into people's private lives and trying to get them to "adjust" to white society. To more perceptive Negroes, as well as to the militants, the welfare system seemed little more than a system of bribes, designed to keep the black population in its place.

After a series of scandals in the local administration of welfare payments in the 1950s (such as the newspaper exposé of the "Lady in Mink" who lived in luxury in a midtown Manhattan hotel on her welfare payments), stiff regulations and inspections were instituted to try to prevent fraud. Families had to submit to means tests. If a welfare recipient wanted a new coat, for example, the social worker would decide whether the old coat would do. In twenty-nine states, to stay on welfare women had to swear they had no husband living at home, and inspectors would often break in at night to see if they were telling the truth.[8]

[8] In some states, a woman was denied welfare if a man not her husband was living with her and if the welfare worker decided he was financially responsible to the children.

By the 1960s, welfare had become the whipping boy of both black and white. Taxpayers resented its mounting costs and the way it seemed to encourage "idleness" and "shiftlessness." As Negroes moved north from southern states, the tax burden mounted. Blacks resented the well-meaning social worker, the prying investigator, and the system which required women to lie, cheat, or break up their homes to get food and clothing for their children.

Beginning in 1967, Kennedy gave special attention to reform of the program. His basic principle was that welfare should be granted on the basis of need alone. He urged that uniform federal standards be established for eligibility, similar to those President Kennedy had recommended for unemployment compensation. He advocated mandatory aid to families with unemployed fathers living at home, simpler processing requirements for applications, and permission for people on welfare to earn more money before losing benefits.

Another battle developed in Congress in 1967, unrelated to his own proposals. The House of Representatives passed a bill freezing the total number of children under the Aid to Dependent Children (ADC) program to that precentage of its children that a state was assisting as of January 1, 1967. If 18 per cent of New York's children were ADC beneficiaries as of that date, that percentage would be the upper limit of future assistance, no matter what the actual need. All welfare recipients, including unmarried mothers with small children, were required to enroll in work training programs for future employment.

The Senate, at the urging of Kennedy and Senator Fred Harris of Oklahoma, had passed a far less restrictive bill. In November 1967, when a Senate-House conference committee was called to reconcile the two bills, the Senate conferees, senior members of the Senate Finance Committee unsympathetic to welfare reform, agreed to almost every provision of the House bill. When the conference report came back to the Senate, Kennedy and his liberal colleagues threatened to filibuster. Since the session was about to adjourn, and the bill also included a 13 per cent increase in Social Security benefits, there was little support for a filibuster and the bill became law.

6

THE POOR, THE BLACK, AND
THE YOUNG: PART II

Kennedy's growing concern with racial tensions and the problems of the poor was gradually transforming him, as a person and as a politician. He had always preferred understanding an issue by personal contact with it. As Attorney General, directing a vast operation from a central office, problems came to him through briefings and memoranda. As a senator, he took to the field. He rode through the tense streets of Spanish Harlem on a night that riots had erupted. He went into slum tenements to see children whose faces had been scarred by rat bites. He saw the remnants of the Depression among whites in eastern Kentucky.

The experiences had a major affect on his public message. After Watts, his appearances before community groups were invariably highlighted by vivid recitals of the problems of poverty, usually touched off by a question that indicated lack of understanding. Before, he had tried to adopt President Kennedy's technique of cool, unemotional argument laced with impressive statistics. But in the face of such massive indifference about conditions among the poor, cold numbers were inadequate to express his outrage. An urgent new rhetoric appeared in his speeches. He talked about "children old and withered before their time," of others "crowded with adults into one or two rooms without adequate plumbing or heat, each night trying to defend against marauding rats." Answering the common white opinion that Negroes were "pushing too fast" for progress, he said: "If any man claims the Negro should be content or satisfied, let him say he would willingly change the color of his skin and go to live in the Negro section of a large city. Then, and only then, has he the right to such a claim."

Government programs for the poor were underfunded because the affluent majority balked at paying higher taxes for this purpose, preferring to use the money to increase their own living standards. For thirty years, the nation's leaders had taken pride in every increase in the gross national product. It had been the proudest measure of the country's progress. Kennedy sharply questioned this national pre-occupation with material goods:

> "Do we stand for our wealth—is that what is important about America? Truly, we have a great gross national product, now soaring beyond $800 billion a year. But that counts air pollution, and cigarette advertising, and ambulances to clear our highways of carnage. It counts special locks for our doors, and jails for the people who break them. It counts the destruction of the redwoods, and equipment for police to put down riots in our cities. It counts Whitman's rifle and Speck's knife, and television programs which glorify violence in order to sell toys to our children.
>
> "The gross national product does not allow for the health of our children, the quality of their education, or the joy of their play. It is indifferent to the decency of our factories and the safety of our streets alike. It does not include the beauty of our poetry or the strength of our marriages, the intelligence of our public debate or the integrity of our public officials. It measures neither our wit nor our courage, neither our wisdom nor our learning, neither our compassion nor our duty to country. It measures everything, in short, except that which makes life worthwhile; and it can tell us everything about America—except whether we are proud to be Americans."

Both as Attorney General and senator, Kennedy came into contact with Dr. Martin Luther King, Jr., foremost among a new generation of black leaders. Kennedy and King were never close collaborators, though their careers and objectives often touched one another. In the days of the New Frontier, they had separate purposes: King was leading a cause and Kennedy was leading a government. They had to move toward similar goals in differing ways. Achieving gains in civil rights through the established legal processes, which necessarily was Kennedy's mission, was too slow a process for King. Non-violent, direct action to achieve concessions, King's unique contribution, was something Kennedy could not embrace while Attorney General.

But as Kennedy became increasingly preoccupied with the causes of growing racial conflict, he gave greater support to King's solutions. As violence flared in the ghettos, he expressed the feeling that the only hope for peaceful resolution of racial conflict in America lay in the goals and methods King advocated, and in the success King and others had in keeping the majority of the black community behind them.

One of Dr. King's closest associates was the Reverend Andrew Young, a brilliant, devout and dedicated disciple of the non-violent movement. Kennedy's aides and Young were in frequent communication during the Senate years. Reverend Young wrote a letter after the death of both men describing Dr. King's evaluation of Kennedy:

> There was a strange attitude of both admiration and caution in Martin's conversation about Robert Kennedy. He was extremely impressed with Kennedy's capacity to learn, to grow, and to deal creatively in any given situation. He appreciated and envied Kennedy's use of staff and advisors. Martin tended to feel overly humble about his own accomplishments and somewhat afraid of "power." He felt inadequate in his "political" actions and saw Kennedy as a man of both moral courage and a keen sense of political timing . . . Martin was clear on the moral issues, but anguished over their implementation. He admired Kennedy's blend of "crusader" and realistic politician.
>
> Closely related to this was the Kennedy "efficiency mystique." "Bobby knows how to get a job done as well as talk about it . . ."
>
> In spite of the deep admiration of Kennedy personally, Martin tended to reserve any commitment or alignment because he thought it dangerous for any leader to feel that he can take the black vote for granted. He worked with John Conyers, Harry Belafonte and others in an attempt to secure himself and his influence from an easy endorsement of the Senator, but in truth he knew there was no choice.
>
> After the White House years, they met very seldom, if at all. The only occasion I can remember was a casual meeting at the hearings of the Ribicoff Committee.
>
> Partially this distance was dictated by the attempts to link the statements and actions of these two men through some direct financial or political alliance. Neither man could profit by such an overt rela-

tionship and both avoided any direct association. Yet they continued down parallel paths of opposition to racism, poverty and war.

Theirs was a distant camaraderie which needed no formal tie or physical link—a bridge across lines of race, class and geography which nevertheless led them to common faith, hopes, and at last a common tragic destiny . . .

As Kennedy set out, almost deliberately, to champion the disadvantaged, he found groups of Americans who had long been hidden from public attention. Among them were the agricultural migrant workers. When fruit and vegetable farming changed from a family farm enterprise to a large scale commercial venture, migrants were imported to harvest the crops. To the farms in upstate New York, they came from the South and the islands of the Caribbean. In the fruit and vegetable belt of the Southwest, they were imported from Mexico. Picking tomatoes and grapes at harvest time, going on relief the rest of the year, agricultural migrants were among the lowest paid, worst-housed, least-educated, and least visible of all Americans.[1] The power of the farm operators and the indifference of organized labor had excluded them from all protective labor legislation. Even the minimum wage bill submitted by President Kennedy in 1961 ignored them.

In 1960, the veteran poverty organizer, Saul Alinsky, set up a community organization for migrant workers in and around the city of Delano in California's Central Valley. On his staff was a Mexican-American named César Chávez, whose family had come to the valley during the Depression and who had worked on voter registration for John F. Kennedy in Spanish-speaking sections of Los Angeles. Using Alinsky's techniques, Chávez formed the Farm Workers Association, which taught newly arrived Mexican-American migrants to read English, buy goods, and manage their money. In 1964, Chávez organized several strikes on some of the large grape farms, demanding recognition of his association and higher wages. Within a few months he received financial support from the United Auto Workers (the first major union to show interest in migrants) and backing from local clergymen, civil rights organizations, and students at California colleges, who helped organize grape boycotts in cities.

[1] The average family earned $1200 a year from farm work and another $600 from whatever work they could find out of season.

Chávez's organization was not a union in the craft or industrial sense. In its emphasis on self-improvement, it was like a community-action organization, even more like one of the old "beneficent organizations" from which unions developed in the nineteenth century. Nor did the strikes resemble those in factories. There were no plant gates where workers gathered—only the fields. The local police restricted the strikers' picket lines to the highways. They marched up and down the road shouting *"Huelga"* ("strike") to those working in the fields, hoping they would lay down their baskets and join them. But strange and diffuse as the strike appeared, Chávez was fighting the most fundamental of labor-management battles—for the right of workers to organize a union which would speak for them in negotiations with employers.

The growers reacted with a ferocity equal to the most militant anti-union companies of the thirties. Local sheriffs were used to discourage strikers from communicating with one another. Speeding cars threw dust in the faces of the strikers as they marched along the road. Strikebreakers were bused in from other regions. To the *California Farmer,* official magazine of the growers, the strike was "a vicious and amoral organizational compaign, spearheaded by extremist elements of the way-out left, cloaked in the robe of respectability by clergymen who are misguided, misinformed or unbelievably gullible."

This battle in a small industry in an obscure section of California drew almost no national attention until early 1966, when the United Auto Workers persuaded the Senate Migratory Labor Subcommittee to hold hearings in Delano on the tactics being used to frustrate the attempt to organize. While Kennedy was a member of the subcommittee, he was reluctant to fly across the country for hearings. He was busy defending a controversial speech he had made on Vietnam and preparing new recommendations on urban problems. It took an urgent call from a top UAW official to persuade him to take a personal interest.

On the flight to California, he kept asking his assistant why he was going there. When he arrived, he understood. In this hot and fertile California valley, Kennedy found what he had seen in American slums: the hostility of the entrenched system and the desire for recognition and participation by people who had been exploited. The descriptions of their poverty and working conditions appalled him. For the first time, migrant workers were organizing to help themselves. To have the official interest of a Senate committee and the personal interest of the brother of President Kennedy, gave them new encouragement.

At one point in the hearings, Kennedy asked a local sheriff why he had arrested men who were picketing:

"Why, they could get into a riot and start cutting up people," the sheriff answered.

"I'm not talking about that," Kennedy said. "Once they get into a riot, I understand that, but before, when they're just walking along, what did you arrest them for?"

"Well, if I have reason to believe that there's going to be a riot started and somebody tells me that there's going to be trouble if you don't stop them, it's my duty to stop them."

"Then do you go out and arrest them? What do you charge them with?"

"Violation of unlawful assembly."

"I think that's most interesting. Who told you that they're going to riot?"

"The men right out in the field that they were talking to said, 'If you don't get them out of here, we're going to cut their hearts out.' So rather than let them get cut, we remove the cause."

"This is the most interesting concept, I think. Somebody makes a statement about somebody going to get out of order, perhaps violate the law, and you go and arrest them. They haven't done anything. How can you go arrest somebody if they haven't violated the law?"

"They're ready to violate the law."

At that point, Senator Williams of New Jersey, Chairman of the Subcommittee, suggested the hearing recess for lunch.

"Can I suggest," Kennedy said, "during the luncheon period that the sheriff and the district attorney read the Constitution of the United States."

Kennedy returned to Washington determined to help the migrants. He looked into conditions in other areas, such as the Rio Grande Valley in Texas, where strikers had been beaten and arrested by state rangers. He dared the Texas growers to hold a union election, ridiculing their claim that no dispute existed between themselves and their workers. He took field trips to migrant labor camps on Lake Ontario and the Finger Lakes country of his own State of New York, where he found migrants living in fly-infested shacks, abandoned buses and, in one case, a chicken coop. He called upon Governor Rockefeller to enforce decent health conditions in the camps. Later that year, Kennedy joined Senator Williams in introducing legislation to bring farm workers under the protection of the laws permitting collective bargaining and outlawing child labor. He sought to raise the minimum wage for migrants and increase the number of workers the law protected.

Always, however, he kept returning to Chávez, the symbolic personality who had affirmed Kennedy's belief that one man can galvanize a movement. After slow, painful effort Chávez had organized some of the farms that raised grapes for wine, and was turning to the producers of table grapes. Kennedy became Chávez's conduit and protector in Washington. When he discovered the Labor Department and the Immigration Service were allowing large farms to recruit strikebreakers in Mexico through lax enforcement of the law which forbids issuance of entry permits (called "green cards") to workers bound for areas where a labor dispute exists, Kennedy made a strong protest to the government. He watched Chávez struggle with some of his own followers who, frustrated with the slow progress, wished to use violent direct action as a weapon. He was in Delano in March 1968, when Chávez broke his fast, undertaken for twenty-five days to inspire his followers and emphasize his own commitment to non-violence. ("What do you say to a man who's on a fast?" Kennedy asked Paul Schrade, the west coast UAW chief. "Just say, 'Hello César,'" Schrade advised.)[2]

On the second anniversary of the strike, shortly after Chávez had won elections on almost every ranch, despite the lack of protection of federal law, Kennedy returned to Delano for the celebration. *"Buenos tardes, es para me une garnde plaisair esta aqui con ustedes en este dis ton especial,"* he made an effort to say. They laughed but

---

[2] Months later, when the California primary was in full heat, McCarthy supporters taunted Kennedy campaigners by asking "Where was he in New Hampshire?"—Chávez answered by shouting, "He was walking with me in Delano!"

applauded his attempt at their language. He urged them, as he had disadvantaged groups all over the country, to reject the alternatives of violence in favor of "a patient, careful building of a democratic organization."

"Along that road," he shouted, "lies success. Along that road lies the building of community, solidarity and brotherhood, the building of institutions and cooperative businesses, of clinics and schools and homes."

And he concluded:

"You are winning a special kind of American citizenship. No one is doing it for you—you are winning it yourselves. And, therefore, no one can ever take it away.

"So when your children and grandchildren take their places in America—going to high school, and college, and taking good jobs at good pay—when you look at them, you will say, 'I did this. I was there, at the point of difficulty and danger.'

"And though you may be old and bent from many years of labor, no man will stand taller than you when you say, 'I marched with César.'

"Viva la Causa."

Out of sight of the American public, the Negro sharecroppers of the Mississippi Delta had been suffering a catastrophic depression. The shift from production of cotton to crops that could be harvested almost entirely by machine had thrown 40,000 people out of work. Thousands more had been discharged by planters who did not wish to pay the rate of $1.25 an hour set by the new agricultural minimum wage, effective in 1966. In the eighteen Delta counties in Mississippi, unemployment averaged between 50 and 60 per cent of the labor force. Destitute families turned to relief, but the state's average welfare payment was $38 per month, too small to give much help. So low a priority did welfare have in Mississippi that the state had passed up $75 million a year in federal aid rather than put up the required $15 million in matching state funds. Old-line federal agencies, staffed by southern whites hired during the New Deal, showed little flexibility or sympathy as they dealt disdainfully with poor families. A free food-surplus-distribution program had been replaced by a food-stamp plan, which required poor families to pay cash for stamps.[3] Delta Negroes, many of whom had no cash income, were being reduced to starvation.

The Delta had been a center of intensive civil rights activities aimed at stimulating voting and community development, but the tide of economic decline was so severe that little was accomplished. The chief result was to embitter the white population, ending whatever paternal concern they had previously shown toward their Negro workhands. With Negroes no longer needed in the fields, many whites encouraged them to go to the northern cities. Migration became a wave, especially among the younger, more ambitious Negroes.

In April 1967, Robert Kennedy visited the Mississippi Delta for Senate hearings. The poverty bill was to expire that year, and the hearings were designed to build public and Congressional support to salvage it in the face of growing opposition. He went on a field trip up the Mississippi Delta into possibly the worst poverty area of the United States. Kennedy had known that income in the Delta was extremely low, but, like most city people, he assumed rural residents could get along on less cash because they could grow their own food. He was not prepared to see the abject poverty and chronic hunger, adults permanently unable to perform prolonged work because of physical decay, children with swollen bellies, too weak from hunger to learn in school. He remarked that the conditions were the worst he had seen in America.

When, in addition, he saw government officials seemingly indifferent to the conditions, the shock of his experience turned to outrage. He could not understand how any public authority could allow near-starvation to go on in its area, or how the Department of Agriculture, which had food to distribute, could hold it back. In a hearing in Washington in July 1967, Mississippi's senators defended the state's system and denied there was any policy, official or implicit, to drive Negroes out of the state. "If the Negroes move out," Senator James Eastland said, "I will move out with them." Senatorial courtesy kept

[3] A family of six making $55 a month had to pay $22 or 40 per cent of its income for food stamps, and in some cases in Mississippi, the total payment was $33 a month or 60 per cent, because families had to borrow the cash from plantation owners until welfare checks came in, and paid 50 per cent interest on the loans.

Kennedy from pursuing the point, but when an official of the Mississippi State Board of Health said he could not authorize emergency medical volunteers unless they were licensed by the state, Kennedy replied sharply: "Children are dying, and you're talking about licenses."

The American people had been oblivious to this situation. They believed the problem of hunger had disappeared with the breadlines of the thirties. But out of Kennedy's trip and the later hearings came the investigation organized by the Citizens Crusade against Poverty. The Crusade reported that three hundred of the poorest counties in the country received no food assistance, while at the same time funds available to the Department of Agriculture for food distribution were being returned to the Treasury unused. From this report came the CBS television documentary on Hunger in America, which roused the nation's conscience. Startled by the exposure of bureaucratic indifference in his own Department, the Secretary of Agriculture announced he was reducing the cost of food stamps for families with monthly incomes of under thirty dollars from two dollars per person in the family to fifty cents. Eggs, fruit juice, and other nutrients were added to the surplus-food program. On June 3, 1968, the Department of Agriculture announced it had finally created machinery to get surplus food into each of the one thousand poorest counties in the United States.

There was one other group of Americans to whom Kennedy directed special attention—the American Indians. They were the nation's oldest "problem." Once considered enemies to be pacified, for the last eighty years they had been wards to be ignored. Shut away on their reservations, they shared none of the progress of their native country. Many left for the cities but found the strain of cultural adjustment too great and returned to their reservations. Accordingly, Indians were the poorest of America's poor, with incomes 75 per cent below the national average, unemployment ten times the national rate, dying in astonishing numbers from tuberculosis and other diseases, long since conquered in the rest of the country.

Officially, Indians were wards of the United States Government, but they received only routine attention. President Kennedy's appointees to the Bureau of Indian Affairs did not change the welfare-caseworker mentality of the agency. Congress showered empty honors on the Indians (thirty-three senators, including Robert Kennedy, co-sponsored a resolution in 1965 to establish National Indian Day to "honor the contribution and remind the Americans of the respect and dignity to which the Indian is entitled") but did nothing about their grave problems of daily existence.

In 1965, Robert Kennedy had assigned a member of his staff to work with the tribes of New York, which ranked eighth among the states in Indian population. He kept saying he wanted to do something about the Indians, but did not get started until late in 1967, when he and Senator Paul Fannin of Arizona persuaded the Senate to establish a subcommittee to conduct a three-year study of Indian education. Almost 20 per cent of the 600,000 Indians in the country were children, being "educated" in federally-funded or federally-operated schools. The schools had low achievement rates and high drop-out rates and surveys found that a fourth of the teachers, by their own admission, would prefer to be teaching elsewhere. Many of the teachers did not speak the Indian languages.

Kennedy's field trips found conditions were even worse. Uprooted from their homes to go to the federal boarding schools far away, Indian children committed suicide at a higher rate than any comparable group. In his first trip to the Fort Hall reservation in Idaho, he asked where the library was. He was shown a large closet with about 500 books. "Are there any books about Indians here?" he asked. Rustling through, one was found—"Captive of the Delawares." The cover picture showed a blond child being scalped.

Kennedy became chairman of this subcommittee four months before beginning the 1968 Presidential campaign. Most of the field investigations were conducted during the campaign. Of all the primary states, only South Dakota had an Indian voting bloc, and most of the reservations he visited were in remote places only a few reporters and no television could reach. His schedulers kept taking these visits off the itinerary. He kept putting them back on. There were no votes among Indians, but Kennedy had made a commitment and was determined to carry it out.

Robert Kennedy deliberately sought out the kind of shattering personal experiences among the poor and despairing that wealthy men for centuries have tried to avoid. He offered them what comfort he could and drew upon the experiences in making his case for reforms. It was not politics that caused Kennedy to go to the poor. It was their lack of a champion, and his personal need for their kind of cause. They gave him a new outlet for his old passion against injustice. Other economic problems he saw as narrow battles of self interest between affluent and affluent. Only these raised basic questions of social justice and equality, and of the vision of what America should be. In this sense, whatever his political caution, Robert Kennedy was a revolutionary figure in American public life.

Kennedy enjoyed his greatest popularity among people under thirty. He was the only political figure who talked their language, appreciated their styles and shared some of them, understood their doubts and concerns about America, and spoke of a world they hoped to create. It did not matter that he was over forty, had gray in his hair, and had children almost as old as they were. He was fearless in a society that valued security, and existential compared to the patterned conformists who dominated the politics of his time. Young people who wanted to "do their thing" saw in him a leader who admired their quest and shared their anger.

Kennedy's involvement with these young people was differently motivated from his interest in blacks and Mexican-Americans. The condition of the poor and minorities touched his sense of justice and rage. The young challenged his own attitudes and opinions. He was drawn toward the poor because they were forlorn. He was proud of the young because they were idealistic and brave. The alienation of the two groups from society came from almost opposite sources. The poor desperately wanted a larger part of American materialism; the young rejected what materialism had produced. Their alienation was partially a product of their privileged status.

Politically, his strong identification with young people was probably a drawback. It became a handy peg for his critics. Cartoonists pictured him in short pants. He was called the "pied piper of the young"; President Johnson called the Kennedy brothers "a couple of kids" when they criticized his policies on Vietnam. Even objective analysts wondered whether he was not deliberately building a constituency for the day he would be running for President and these young people could vote. Voter profile surveys showed one of the strongest negative features in his image was his long hair which made him "look like a hippie." More important, it deepened the impression that he was too young and immature to be entrusted with the responsibilities of the presidency.

Thousands of people wrote in asking him to get a haircut. When one New Jersey boy was suspended from school for wearing a Beatle hair style, his lawyer's defense was that the hair was no longer than Kennedy's. Newspapers nationwide ran a picture of his head of hair alongside that of the embattled boy, with headlines like: "OK in Senate—but not in school." The more protests he received and the more pressure from his political friends to cut his hair, the more stubborn he became about letting it grow longer.

Kennedy had been an indifferent student, more interested in sports and friends than social change or curriculum content. In retrospect, he regarded his college years as largely a waste. Over and over again he would emphasize to students the opportunity and responsibility their college education had given them. At Berkeley in 1966, he expressed it by saying:

> ". . . by coming to this school you have been lifted to a tiny, sunlit island while all around you lies a dark ocean of human misery, injustice, violence and fear. You can use your enormous privilege and opportunity to seek purely private pleasure and gain. But history will judge you, and, as years pass, you will ultimately judge yourself, on the extent to which you have used your gifts to lighten and enrich the lives of your fellowman."

He sought out young audiences and welcomed student groups to his office because he was comfortable with their idealism and their undogmatic search for truth. There was always time for question-and-answer sessions, where he took the teacher's role. Six years before Senator Edmund Muskie won admiration by asking student hecklers to join him on the platform, Kennedy did the same thing at Wasada University in Tokyo, Japan, when a small group of radical students called Zengakuren, tried to prevent his speaking. He stepped into the audience, led the loudest heckler to the stage, and offered to share the microphone with him.

John and Robert Kennedy were the youngest men to assume

leadership of the United States since the founding days of the Republic. They accepted change as part of growth both for themselves and for their country. A man's age was not nearly as important as his attitude in judging his capacity to lead. Robert Kennedy described his admiration for "youth" in 1966 at Cape Town, South Africa:

". . . Our answer is the world's hope; it is to rely on youth— not a time of life but a state of mind, a temper of the will, a quality of the imagination, a predominance of courage over timidity, of the appetite for adventure over the love of ease. The cruelties and obstacles of this swiftly changing planet will not yield to obsolete dogmas and outworn slogans. It cannot be moved by those who cling to a present that is already dying, who prefer the illusion of security to the excitement and danger that come with even the most peaceful progress. It is a revolutionary world we live in; and this generation, at home and around the world, has had thrust upon it a greater burden of responsibility than any generation that has ever lived."

Kennedy far preferred student activists to the "hippies" who had turned themselves off rather than fight the social values and institutions they resented. It took personal courage to stage the southern sit-ins and freedom rides, to march with Martin Luther King in the streets of Chicago, to stand alone as a conscientious objector to the war in Vietnam. The young people who did these things deserved to be heard and admired.

The great majority of students, though, were non-involved—and this disturbed him. The crowds which stoned civil rights marchers in Chicago were made up largely of young people, as were the couples who moved out to suburbs to widen the distance between themselves and the Negro. The great majority of young people were apathetic, willing to take their place in the white affluent society as it was developing. In the fall of 1966 he returned from a speaking tour through Oregon and California. His audiences had been large and primarily youthful. "Most of the kids there just don't care about poor people," he said. "They come to the political rallies in their own cars. What a difference from when I was in college. Only kids like me had cars."

But Kennedy chose to identify publicly with those who did care, to explain their actions and protect their rights, just as he did with the poor. In the fall of 1966, he went to the seed-bed of the student rebellion, the University of California at Berkeley, which he called "the first college to become a major political issue since George the III attacked Harvard for being a center of rebellion for subversion —and he was right." He told an overflowing amphitheater audience:

> . . . It is not enough to allow dissent. We must demand it. For there is much to dissent from. We dissent from the fact that millions are trapped in poverty while the nation grows rich . . . from the conditions and hatreds which deny a full life to our fellow citizens because of the color of their skin . . . from the monstrous absurdity of a world where nations stand poised to destroy one another, and men must kill their fellow men . . . from the sight of most of mankind living in poverty, stricken by disease, threatened by hunger and doomed to an early death after a life of unremitting labor.
>
> We dissent from all those structures of technology and of society itself—which strip from the individual the dignity and warmth of sharing in the common tasks of his community and his country.

In February 1967 he chose an audience of older activists, at an Americans for Democratic Action dinner in Philadelphia, to defend the new political movement. The speech was the frankest attack on the American establishment he ever made. Calling the contemporary generation of young people "the brightest, best educated, most highly motivated generation we have had since the founding of the Republic," he noted that adults "were now profoundly troubled by them."

> For the gap between generations, always present in the past, is suddenly widening; the old bridges which span it are falling; we see all around us a terrible alienation of the best and bravest of our young; and the very shape of a generation seems turned on its head overnight.

He urged adults to listen to these criticisms and find the reasons for the alienation, for "among adults as among the young the sharpest criticism goes hand in hand with the deepest idealism and love of country."

He expressed their disillusion with some of the most entrenched institutions of American society—"the great corporations which . . . play so small a role in the solution of our vital problems . . . labor unions, which young people see have grown sleek and bureaucratic with power, sometimes frankly discriminatory, occasionally even corrupt and exploitative; a force not for change but for the status quo, unwilling or unable to organize new groups of members . . . universities which have become "corporate bureaucracies."

> . . . If we add to the insincerity, and the absence of dialogue, the absurdity of a politics in which a Byron de la Beckwith[4] can declare as a candidate for Lieutenant Governor of Mississippi, we can understand why so many of our young people have turned from engagement to disengagement, from politics to passivity, from hope to nihilism, from SDS to LSD.

The ADA speech, reprinted widely, became an underground document among young people. Letters requesting it came from all over the country.

Kennedy was not as optimistic as the young about the tensions in the world. One sharp difference of opinion with the college generation arose out of the revelations, in early 1967, that activities of the National Student Association and other youth groups had been subsidized by the Central Intelligence Agency as part of its program to counter the activities of Communist "youth" organizations. He had approved these programs during his brother's administration, although he did not know that some young people had joined them without knowledge of their true sponsorship. At the time, the activities seemed necessary and right, and he refused to condemn them now because the climate of opinion had changed. "We must not forget," he said, "that we are not dealing with a dream world, but with a very rough adversary." He pointed out that the decisions were not made by the CIA alone, but by three administrations, beginning with President Eisenhower's; and he told Richard Helms, head of the CIA, that he felt the agency was being treated unfairly by the publicity over the incident.

At other times, his sympathy with youthful protest gave way to political necessity. Campaigning for Democratic congressmen in 1966, he often found himself being opposed by independent anti-war candidates strongly backed by local students. The daughter of a Senate colleague wrote him that she was one of his admirers but found it hard to understand his speaking for candidates who supported

---

[4] de la Beckwith had been indicted for the slaying of Medgar Evers, but acquitted by an all-white jury.

Johnson's war policies. It bothered him too, and he replied by saying that he admired what she was doing and regretted that they were temporarily on different sides. He added a quote from Shakespeare:

"When we shall meet again, we shall unite."

His championing of the young did not impress the radical left minority, which saw him as an orthodox Cold War politician trying to lure young people into supporting him. Robert Scheer, one of the leading figures of the new radical left, expressed this view in an article in *Ramparts:*

> The Kennedy people have raised cooptation to an art form. The Kennedy rhetoric is dangerous precisely because it provides the illusion of dissent without its substance. Hubert Humphrey is a bad joke to most young people, but Bobby is believable, and for that reason, much more serious. He could easily coopt prevailing dissent without delivering to it.
>
> Bobby Kennedy, for all his youth, charm and spontaneity, remains a very orthodox political figure. He shares the prevailing view of the Cold War and the benevolent workings of modern capitalism and very carefully avoids any fundamental criticism of either. In his reliance on private investment as a panacea for the ills of American ghettos and underdeveloped countries alike, he is clearly to the right of the New Deal. He has also been unwilling to deal with the problem of our massive military industrial complex and to talk about conversion from a war economy to a peacetime one. For all the zest of the Kennedy men, they have carefully cultivated an aura of youth as an alternative to political integrity and commitment. It is a stance which provides the illusion of change without its troublesome substance.

For his part, Kennedy preferred to avoid "the beards," as he called them and saw in the more radical members of the New Left the same lack of tolerance and open-mindedness they had come to distrust in others. He wanted students to prove their own commitment by working actively to improve conditions, rather than just protesting them. He told the students at Berkeley in 1966:

> . . . Dissent which consists simply of sporadic and dramatic acts sustained by neither continuing labor nor research—that dissent which seeks to demolish while lacking both the desire and direction for

rebuilding, that dissent which contemptuously or out of laziness casts aside the practical weapons and instruments of change and progress —that kind of dissent is merely self-indulgence. It is satisfying, perhaps, to those who make it.

But it will not assist those seriously engaged in the difficult and frustrating work of the nation. And when it is all over, it will not have brightened or enriched the life of a single portion of humanity in a single part of the globe.

Kennedy did not live to see the spread of disruptive tactics to the campus, or the adoption of terror tactics by both student militants and the police sent to control them. He foresaw dimly what was to happen, when he told the ADA:

Whatever their differences with us, whatever the depth of their dissent, it is vital—for us as much as for them—that our young feel that change is possible; that they will be heard. If we cannot help open to them this sense of possibility, we will have only ourselves to blame for the disillusionment that will surely come.

As one whose career was devoted to achieving change through the peaceful processes of free government, Kennedy would have condemned the use of violence on campus, whether in pursuit of reform, or as a means of repression. Rather than despair, or turn to violence or cynicism, he would have urged young people to work hard and imaginatively, but peacefully, to build a better world.

7

SENATOR FROM NEW YORK

By the time Robert Kennedy came to represent it in the Senate, the State of New York no longer occupied the dominant position it had enjoyed for the previous 175 years of American history. The westward migration and the development of the other regions had created new centers of economic power, independent of Wall Street and the corporate giants which made their home in New York City. New York's decline, however, was only relative. Most of the population movement out of New York City after the Second World War had stayed within the state, going to the metropolitan suburban areas of Long Island and Westchester County. The state had held its own in the development of modern, technological industries and the university resources to which these industries gravitate.

New York City had maintained its dominant position in entertainment, culture, publishing, art, and fashion. In the mid-1960s, it was still the primary place where the styles were set and the fads begun. Because it was also the home base of the television networks, news events occurring there were publicized throughout the nation. Not all Americans liked what went on in New York, but they all knew about it, and to them "New York" meant the city, not the state.

Most New Yorkers north of the metropolitan area lived in a series of urban centers stretching from Albany to Buffalo along the old Erie Canal, which had become the main route of the New York Central

Railroad in the 1830s. The railroad had brought the immigrants to the cities. Each of these communities jealously kept its own identity, and most citizens had little interest in any but their own area. Nevertheless, each absorbed the same waves of migration that came to New York City and each contained, in microcosm, most of the problems of New York City itself. Robert Kennedy quickly developed a special feeling for the people of the upstate area. They lived simpler lives, their pace was slower, and they had a chance to enjoy the out-of-doors. Their problems were more manageable than the city's, if only because the size of the problems was smaller. They were the kind of urban northeastern voters who had given strong support to his brother in his campaign and throughout his presidency. They were less demanding of him, ideologically, than the New York City Democrats. He had run especially well upstate in his Senate campaign, and because the people were not accustomed to celebrities on their streets, his visits, long after the election, were treated as major events by the citizens and the media.

The first trip Kennedy took after his election in 1964 was upstate, to meet with civic leaders to discuss what federal assistance their communities needed. In Rochester, he discussed programs to cope with causes of the recent riots. In Poughkeepsie, where there was an urgent need for recreation facilities for young people, he pointed out new sources of federal money. Wherever he went, he drew on his experience in the Justice Department to urge that more be done to give poorer citizens, white and black, a sense that government cared about their well being.

To emphasize his interest in upstate problems, he opened an office in Syracuse, directed by Gerald Bruno. Bruno had worked for John Kennedy and Lyndon Johnson as an "advance man," planning the routes, making the arrangements and attracting the crowds in campaign and presidential travel. He was the best in the business.[1] Although he had lived in Wisconsin for over thirty years, by background and accent Bruno fit in well with upstate New Yorkers. He was the principal contact for the political leaders of the upstate counties.

[1] Kennedy could always tell a campaign trip Bruno had advanced personally. At every schoolhouse along the road, the children would be waiting to cheer him, waving Kennedy posters and American flags. It was the Bruno "signature" on an "advance" assignment.

Kennedy gave close attention to the substantive problems of New York State. No matter what his prominence in the nation and the world, he held office by sufferance of the people of his state, and because of the special circumstances of his political entry, he knew he had to demonstrate that he cared about the concerns of his constituents and that he could offer them effective help.

The first amendment Kennedy introduced in the Senate in 1965 brought thirteen low-income counties in the southern tier of upstate New York within the scope of the federal development program being created for the Appalachia region. While they were geographically part of the Appalachia region, and shared many of its problems of underdevelopment, no state official had been sympathetic enough with the Appalachia program to seek to include them. With the other members of New York City's congressional delegation, he protested the Defense Department's decision to close the Brooklyn Navy Yard. The closing of the Yard, which employed 10,600 workers, was announced shortly after his election, and many employees looked to him, as a former colleague and close friend of Secretary McNamara, to turn it around. But the Department's decision was firm. Kennedy had no hope the Yard would be kept open, and was not even sure it should be. But as long as a case could be made, he had promised during the campaign that it would be considered at the highest level and he went to see McNamara about it the day after the election.

In his first years in the Senate, he pleaded for federal funds for such purposes as deepening a channel near Staten Island and preserving the wetlands of Long Island. He made a major speech on the prevention of future drought conditions in the Northeast. He fought to remove restrictions on imports of home heating oil, sponsored conferences of those concerned with pollution of New York's lakes and rivers, lobbied the Department of Agriculture for increases in the price of wholesale milk, and held conferences at which counties in the Adirondack Mountain area learned how to apply for development grants from the federal Economic Development Administration. He even urged controls on the export of walnut logs, which were needed by New York manufacturers. But he did not spend time on "pork barrel" projects for his state, and he gave very low priority to New York firms competing for government contracts, knowing that this kind of congressional pressure, except when exercised by an exceptionally powerful legislator, usually did little good.[2]

In these activities, Kennedy relied to a large extent on his staff. His personal interest tended more to local problems with humanitarian overtones. Continuing his interest in juvenile delinquency, he sponsored several programs for criminal justice reform and narcotics rehabilitation in New York. He pursued his concern for the care of the mentally retarded with a special energy, using the availability of federal benefit programs as justification for his involvement. When the Department of Defense closed three upstate veterans hospitals in 1965, he flew up to visit them. "I can't promise you I'll keep this installation open," he told the patients at the hospital at Bath, New York, "but I promise you I will fight and struggle to keep it open and you are entitled to no less." At a special hearing of the Senate Committee on Veterans Affairs, he made a strong case that the closings violated the VA's own standards as to whether hospitals were necessary or whether they were obsolete. He succeeded in keeping two of the hospitals—at Bath and Castle Point—open. When the VA affirmed its decision to close the hospital at Tupper Lake, Kennedy helped have it converted into a mental hospital.

Kennedy's activist approach toward New York's problems found its fullest expression in the work of his resident office in New York City. It was an operation unlike any that a senator had ever mounted in his home state. All senators keep a trusted assistant and a small staff in a field office in the largest city of their state, to process requests from constituents who wish to contact their representative in person but find it hard to travel to Washington. In a city the size of New York, there were thousands of citizens who felt a man as important as Senator Kennedy could help them, not only with their social security or veterans' claims, but with such matters as evictions, lack of heat in apartments, and even their domestic problems. It was

2 After years of being lobbied by individual congressmen on behalf of constituent firms seeking government orders, the Defense Department is said to have devised this rule of thumb: If the congressman merely sends a letter on the matter, it means he is just going through the motions to pacify his constituent, and it is ignored: if he makes a personal telephone call, the officer or civilian official in charge hears him out patiently, assures him it will be given priority, and still does nothing. Only if the congressman comes to the Pentagon personally and pounds on the officer's desk will he *really* get attention.

not uncommon for Angie Cabrera, who handled the requests from Spanish-speaking constituents, to receive a frantic call from a Puerto Rican lady who had just had a spat with her husband and wanted Senator Kennedy's intercession.

It soon became obvious that in a state as populous as New York, a single government official, no matter how hard-working, could not materially affect the lives of a substantial number of citizens through individual casework alone. While not neglecting casework obligations, Kennedy searched for a broader approach. He told the director of the office, Tom Johnston, that he did not want him to spend his time answering mail and talking to constituents and politicians, but to identify the kind of projects that would be of wider-ranging service to broad groups of citizens, especially the underprivileged. Largely through personal funds, he provided enough staff help so that the New York office could apply itself to several such projects at once.

Johnston was an ideal director for such an office. He came from a prominent Kentucky family, was a graduate of Yale where he did special work in drama and play writing, and made his first political effort by joining the 1964 Senate campaign. He left a career in broadcasting to join the senator's staff. Johnston, combining humor, common sense, and diligence, won Kennedy's personal and professional regard. The office he administered, filled with both paid staff and volunteers, was on the fourth floor of the Post Office building at 110 East Forty-fifth Street in Manhattan. It was like a beehive. Senator Javits' New York office was on the fifth floor of the same building. One person who visited both said the comparison was between a wedding and a wake.[3] Over the years, the office became a quasi-governmental social service organization. It helped establish new playgrounds, assisted the city's schools for disadvantaged children to get funding for more text-

[3] Assisting the senator in New York were Carter Burden, a Columbia Law School graduate who brought imaginative insight and a talent for hard work to his general responsibility for New York City's legislative problems; Earl Graves, who served effectively as Kennedy's liaison to much of the black community and was an important factor in organizing the Bedford-Stuyvesant project; and Dall Forsythe, whom Kennedy convinced to stay with him as a staff assistant rather than continue his graduate studies at Stanford. Polly Feingold handled casework in the early years. Swanni von Heinnig became the "girl Friday," working endless hours, always efficient, unfailingly thoughtful, and deeply devoted to the Senator and Mrs. Kennedy. Angie Cabrera combined secretarial duties with a special liaison role to the Puerto Rican community.

books and hot lunches, sponsored skating parties and Christmas parties for ghetto children, served as a contact point for complaints and community organizing efforts, and tried to bring neglected institutions together with experts who could help them.

Kennedy's identification with New York also grew through the wide attention given his non-political activities. In a city which took the famous for granted and generally ignored them, his comings and goings continued to get attention. On occasion, he could be seen playing with his nephew, John Kennedy, Jr., in Central Park, or dining with Ethel Kennedy at superb restaurants like La Grenouille, Cote Basque, the "21" Club, and The Four Seasons, sometimes with his father at the family favorite, La Caravelle. Late at night, with whatever friends he had accumulated during the evening, he went to Sardi's for a steak and a chocolate ice cream sundae or for a hamburger at P. J. Clarke's on Third Avenue.

He and Mrs. Kennedy enjoyed the theatre, especially when friends were performing, like Lauren Bacall in *Cactus Flower,* or Carol Channing and Pearl Bailey in *Hello, Dolly.* He found great pleasure in classical theatre, especially if it had contemporary significance. The Greek tragedy, *Iphigenia in Aulis,* which Irene Papas and Michael Cacoyannis revived with Ted Mann as a protest against the military junta in Athens was a special favorite. He was intrigued by *Marat/ Sade,* and the originality of its director, Peter Brooke, and its star, Glenda Jackson. Among the friends he saw as often as possible were Dame Margot Fonteyn and Rudolf Nureyev, and through them he became fascinated with ballet. When the Bolshoi company was in New York, he was introduced to its prima ballerina, Maya Plisetskaya, and talked with her for hours (through an interpreter) about life and culture in the Soviet Union.

Kennedy had no social circle in New York. Given his intense and crowded existence, there was little time for social life. What private hours he had he preferred to spend with his family and close friends. At parties, he was not a relaxed host. His shyness made him uncomfortable when meeting new people. He resented being put on display as a "catch" at someone's soiree, and he had no use for the gatherings of the "beautiful people" who met to see and be seen in their fashions and jewels. He would rather have a drink at Toots Shor's with columnist Jimmy Breslin or sportscaster Frank Gifford than go to any benefit or cocktail party. He would drop by parties given by his sisters Jean Smith and Patricia Lawford, who maintained apartments in New York, and he would often dine at Jacqueline Kennedy's. But most of his free time in the evenings in New York City was spent with old friends.

Kennedy loved the poetry and power of New York City but it was not the place he would have chosen to live his life. There was something too degrading about its poverty, too intense about its conflicts, too cold about its personal relationships, too materialistic about its values to fulfill the life and meaning he sought.

Robert Kennedy's solid victory in the senatorial election projected him into a central but awkward position within New York's political framework. He was the only Democratic state-wide officeholder, except for Arthur Levitt who, as state comptroller, was an unbeatable, non-partisan symbol of fiscal integrity. As a future presidential contender, Kennedy had to be confident of his own political base and this required a strong assertion of leadership. He felt a further obligation—and pressure—to do so since his campaign had raised the hope that the fractured, bankrupt party structure would be reorganized and given new direction.

But in realistic political terms, Kennedy lacked the power to impose his will upon the leaders of the party. Senators are rarely the dominant political forces within their states, and with good reason. They have little patronage to dispense; and their work requires their presence in Washington, away from the home communities where the foundations of political power are laid.[4] A further handicap in Kennedy's case was the attitude of the White House, which operated as independently of him as possible in the appointment of New Yorkers to the federal government. His power to recommend appointments was more severely limited than any Democrat in the Senate. Administration patronage continued to go through Mayor Wagner (until his retirement), Dem-

[4] Notable recent exceptions have been the late Senator Harry Byrd of Virginia, Richard Russell of Georgia, Hubert Humphrey of Minnesota, and Edmund Muskie of Maine. Most of these men, however, had previously served as governors of their state and the political power and organizations they built during their tenure remained intact afterwards.

ocratic National Committeeman Edwin Weisl, and a few upstate county leaders close to the White House. Kennedy was allowed to recommend candidates for federal judgeships, and through the tradition of senatorial courtesy he held a veto power over presidential appointments "personally offensive" to him. The appointment of a Regional Director of the New York Post Office, for example, was delayed for eighteen months because Kennedy's candidate (an able Nassau County businessman named Gerald McDougal) was not cleared by the White House and Kennedy refused to accept the White House choices. Kennedy's real power lay in his popularity among Democratic voters, but even here, the state's electoral machinery was dominated by the county organizations whose criteria for nomination generally emphasized parochial loyalty and prior party service rather than a capacity to attract the independent vote which was essential to victory.

In terms of his own political interests, non-involvement in intra-party disputes was the logical strategy. Kennedy's national strength was dependent not on the management of the Democratic party in New York State, but on his performance as a senator and his leadership in the issues that affected the country. But the logic did not work. Once the Republicans won the mayoralty of New York City in 1965, he was the only Democrat in the state who could force the local politicians to even listen to the urgent cries for reform. He did not have the power to compel support for his proposals but he did have a position that obliged him to speak and to act.[5]

He was reconciled to living with this dilemma. He believed it would take at least a full term as senator to see the basic changes that would permit real reform. The two paramount considerations, as far as his personal position was concerned, were his re-election as senator in 1970 and his control of the delegations to the National Convention

[5] The one instrument of the party susceptible to his leadership as the most prominent Democrat was the state committee. Its powers were extremely limited, but it could serve as another party spokesman and help mediate intraparty disputes. When Kennedy was elected, the state committee was bankrupt, both financially and in leadership. His choice for chairman was John Burns, mayor of Binghamton who had been the party's candidate for lieutenant governor in 1962. A generous man, with a fine sense of political mechanics, Burns proved a wise choice. His greatest strength was his ability to deal with all party factions. The committee became Kennedy's chief vehicle in state politics, and Burns one of his chief lieutenants. Burns would try to compromise attitudes rather than confront them, providing a perfect complement to Kennedy's approach.

in 1968 and 1972. As he looked at the larger problems of the party, he thought the crucial turn-around would come in 1970, when he would be a candidate for re-election and could help elect a Democratic governor whose nomination he would have helped assure. The new governor, working in alliance with Kennedy, could unify and reorganize the party; and Kennedy would then be free to concentrate on the leadership of the national party and the nomination in 1972.

No sooner was he elected in 1964 than the party split apart over the choice of legislative leaders in Albany. The Supreme Court's "one man-one vote" reapportionment decisions had broken the Republican domination of the state legislature. Combined with the results of the Johnson landslide and Kennedy's own intensive campaigning up-state, they had given the Democrats control of both houses of the legislature for the first time in twenty-five years.

The struggle that ensued revolved around Robert Wagner, the mayor of New York City. His candidate for Speaker of the Assembly was Anthony Travia of Brooklyn; for majority leader of the Senate he favored Joseph Zaretski of Manhattan. The anti-Wagner forces nominated Stanley Steingut of Brooklyn for the Speaker's post and Julian B. Erway of Albany for the Senate position. Kennedy saw no purpose in identifying with any of the candidates. The fight was much more complicated than the newspaper description of Steingut and Erway as "the bosses' candidates" indicated. It involved the traditional up-state-downstate mistrust, with many newly elected legislators from traditionally Republican areas anxious to avoid control by Wagner and the New York City interests he represented. Many of the city reformers sided with Steingut, no longer fearful of the mayor's waning power and anxious to negotiate their own position of power and influence in Albany. Wagner had not yet decided whether to seek re-election, and with the emergence of Kennedy, he felt it necessary to reassert his position. The senator, approached by all sides, tried to play a limited role as arbiter.

The leadership battle lasted six weeks. On January 16, 1965, Kennedy joined Wagner, Levitt, Weisl, and other prominent Democrats in urging that the issue be resolved by a secret ballot among the Democratic legislators. Since the preliminary votes among this group had given a clear majority to Steingut, the suggested solution seemed a victory for the anti-Wagner forces, but within twenty-four hours, it was clear that the Mayor had no intention of quitting the fight, and that his public statement urging a secret ballot had no meaning. Hurling charges of lies, political blackmail and bribery against his Democratic opposition, Wagner reached out for the Republican votes required to elect his legislative candidates. Rockefeller needed the votes controlled by the Mayor to pass his controversial tax program. So an alliance was made. After twenty-eight ballots and with the help of forty-six Republican votes, Travia was chosen Speaker of the Assembly. After twenty-six ballots and with the help of twenty-five Republicans, Zaretski was elected president of the Senate. Kennedy commented ruefully that it was "unfortunate that things have developed to the point that the leadership of the Democratic party is decided by Republicans." But he had made his first journey as senator in New York politics. This was no golf course with regulations for players and an occasional sand trap to test their skill. This was a jungle where quicksand swallowed the naïve and where the animals changed their spots before your eyes.

As the staff appointments were being made by the new legislative leaders, Kennedy was disturbed that the old patterns of patronage were being followed. His friends in the reform movement asked him to intervene, as did some of the upstate county leaders who were being punished for being on the wrong side. Kennedy sent a rather pompous, presumptuous letter to Zaretski and Travia, reminding them of the manpower search he had helped organize for the New Frontier which "brought such distinguished men as David Bell, Douglas Dillon and Robert McNamara to the government." The curt letter, which offered advice, but no congratulations, brought a reminder from Zaretski of the "difference between legislative staff positions and positions of administrative duties in the executive branch of the government." Travia was even more to the point: "Senator," he wrote, "out of respect for your office and in expectation of the closest cooperation in the future in legislative matters of common concern, I have refrained in this letter from the spirited reply that might have been justified. There is, however, a tradition of comity between legislative bodies. I would not undertake to tell you how to run your office." The point was well taken and Kennedy knew it. He decided to make a special effort to develop a working relationship with the new leaders.

Both Travia and Zaretski cooperated. Within months, they were among the most effective political allies Kennedy had available to him in the state, working together to win legislative victories for Medicaid and public power.[6]

The leadership battle had hardly been digested when Wagner announced his retirement as Mayor. After twelve wearing, abrasive, achieving years he was ready for private life. The Democrats had taken New York City for granted, relying on their lopsided registration to heal the wounds of their perennial factional wars.

The war of succession of 1965 was a classic study of the problems of the Democratic party. The liberal, independent and non-organization Democrats divided their votes among three candidates.[7] The regular organization chose Abraham Beame as its candidate. Beame had been an able budget director of the city and had been elected comptroller on Wagner's "beat the bosses" slate in 1961. Now he was tagged as "the bosses'" candidate. Beame won the nomination with less than 45 per cent of the vote, but in the process the coalition necessary for victory was shattered. The reformers preferred a defeat to anything that might strengthen the regular party organization. Wagner did not want to lend his prestige and support to the forces that had tried to oust him from office four years before. The Liberal party bolted its traditional support of the Democratic candidate to join a fusion effort for the Republican candidate, Congressman John Lindsay.

Beame's managers had won the nomination but were hardly prepared to run a campaign that appealed beyond traditional Democratic party loyalties. In this situation, they reached out for as much of the

[6] Travia remained unchallenged as Speaker of the Assembly until early in 1968, when Kennedy acceded to his frequent requests and recommended him for appointment to the Federal District Court. It was a commitment Kennedy had made in 1966, but which he discharged slowly because he did not want another battle to open up for legislative leadership, nor did he want to lose the active cooperation of the most prominent Italian-American politician in the State. Most of all, however, he was reluctant to lose a tough and loyal friend. He finally sent the recommendation forward because Travia, having won Bar Association approval, was anxious to put the mayhem of Albany behind him.

[7] Paul Screvane, president of the City Council and Wagner's choice; Congressman William Fitts Ryan; and City Councilman Paul O'Dwyer, brother of former Mayor William O'Dwyer.

Kennedy apparatus as possible, making an urgent request to Stephen Smith to run the general election campaign. Kennedy endorsed Beame as a matter of party loyalty. However, not having been responsible for the choice of the candidate and knowing that forces hostile to him would be credited with the victory, he did not want to be left with the responsibility for the defeat. He knew too little about Beame and was dismayed at the tone and quality of the campaign. Kennedy also knew that the workers loyal to him could not be persuaded to become a façade for a campaign whose candidate was sincere and able, but which was controlled by forces that basically resented his independent approach to political and governmental problems.

Smith and a number of Kennedy associates did join the campaign at the senator's behest, but their role was never more than technical and advisory. At a meeting with Beame's campaign directorate in the middle of the campaign Kennedy was frankly critical of the campaign's lack of a theme and its failure to appeal to the independent Democrats whose votes would decide the election. He urged Beame to campaign in the ghetto areas, to convince the solid Democratic elector-ate there to get out and vote for him because his administration would serve its aspirations. He stressed the need for Beame to show his independence from the party organization. Kennedy left the meeting only to learn that it had reconvened shortly thereafter to discuss campaign strategy with Roy Cohn, who presumably was organizing an important part of its financial support. Kennedy and Cohn had been bitter antagonists since 1954 when Cohn worked for the late Senator Joseph McCarthy and Kennedy for the Democratic minority on McCarthy's committee, and the two had almost come to blows after one session of the Army-McCarthy hearings. Since Beame and his advisers knew Cohn opposed everything Kennedy represented, the senator was left with no illusions about his own role and interests in the contest.

The Democratic campaign was besieged on every side. William Buckley, the candidate of the Conservative party, was receiving strong support in the boroughs of Queens and Richmond. Lindsay was show-ing himself to be a charismatic candidate, campaigning in the streets in the Kennedy manner, enthusiastically supported by young volunteers, appealing to independent and reform-minded voters who disdained party labels. Although Democrats outnumbered Republicans three to one in the city's registration, Lindsay was obviously making inroads. He was drawing heavy support among Jewish voters, despite that fact that Beame, if elected, would be New York's first Jewish mayor.

The symbolic blow came when Beame sought an endorsement from President Johnson. Beame had based much of his campaign, at Kennedy's suggestion, on the argument that as a Democrat, he could better negotiate the federal funds the city desperately needed. Kennedy had called a meeting in Washington between Beame and the New York Democratic congressional delegation, announcing that "Abe Beame will have a direct line to Washington on New York City's problems." Despite repeated requests, however, there was still no endorsement from the White House. When Vice President Humphrey came to New York for a fund-raising dinner on October 26, bringing with him what everyone anticipated was to be the presidential blessing, he conveyed only the President's "warm regards," and he did that on his own initiative. Beame flew to Washington the next day and met with White House political aides, but he could not get a personal appointment or an endorsement from the President. Obviously, Johnson was unwilling to be identified with what he had been told might be a losing cause, and because of his reluctance, the cause was in greater danger of being lost. In desperation, prominent New York Democrats besieged the White House with telephone calls. The final result was a statement three days before the election from presidential press secretary Bill Moyers, saying the President endorsed Beame, as he did "all Democrats." The incident was a staggering blow to the campaign.

Kennedy did his duty, but little more. He stumped each borough with Beame, urging his election. The crowd reactions confirmed his fears about the outcome. "I know the people of New York City. I can tell when they're with me. I've never seen them so cold," he said. He also knew that his dutiful performance was costing him something among his own supporters. "It will take me six months to get anyone to speak to me again," he commented wryly.

The election proved closer than expected. Lindsay won by 136,000 votes. Although Buckley received fewer votes than expected (his vote was approximately the same as that given the third party conservative candidate, Lawrence Gerosa, in 1961) most came from people who would have supported Beame had Buckley not been in the contest.

Kennedy felt that greater effort among the black and Puerto Rican minorities might have held enough Democratic votes to offset the Buckley drain.

The election left Kennedy the major Democratic officeholder in the state, increasing the pressure on him to direct the party. It also projected Lindsay nationally as his rival in New York. The two men had the same ultimate political goal, and approximately the same timetable. There were some who thought that the most dramatic way for Lindsay to begin his pursuit of the Republican presidential nomination in 1972 would be by challenging Kennedy in the Senate race of 1970. Kennedy recognized Lindsay's political appeal. "There's something about his looks," he said, "that make people want to see him succeed." But he dismissed the talk of a possible Lindsay challenge as just one of countless hurdles in his own political course. His attitude was that if he could not be re-elected running against Lindsay, he had no right to seek his party's presidential nomination. He was not worried about the result of that contest.

To the extent that there was a rivalry between Kennedy and Lindsay, it was a muted one. Whatever political collison might come was years away. Both men saw the necessity to create better opportunity for minority citizens. They were the only major politicians in either party to take this concern personally into the ghettos, and the ability to keep the ghettos "cool" was to be Lindsay's greatest strength.

Because they shared the same hopes for the city, Kennedy avoided criticizing Lindsay in public. But in city problems where Kennedy was involved—welfare, the poverty program, labor relations, the public schools—he felt Lindsay showed an administrative weakness that Kennedy did not regard as excusable because of the immensity of the tasks confronting City Hall. Lindsay did not have the gift that Kennedy described as essential to a good administrator—the capacity to choose able assistants and inspire the maximum commitment of their talents. That was one of the reasons for the unusual number of resignations of city department chiefs that marked the first three years of Lindsay's administration. One of the men who resigned was Sam Kearing, a former marine and a Republican whom Lindsay had put in charge of the Sanitation Department. Kennedy had had a lengthy discussion with Kearing about creating private sanitation districts to assure better garbage disposal in ghetto areas, and he was impressed by Kearing's intelligence and energy. But Kearing found himself in competition with James Marcus, the Water Commissioner, for the leadership of the new superagency which was to combine their two departments. Lindsay sided with Marcus. A story was leaked to the newspapers about laxities in garbage pickup, a move designed to cut Kearing's support. When Kearing complained, Lindsay fired him summarily, accusing him of "insubordination." Kennedy was astonished Lindsay would publicly demean associates in this way. "It's not as though he is the President firing MacArthur," Kennedy said.[8]

More damaging, in Kennedy's judgment, was the way Lindsay handled the collision of opposing forces within the city on problems involving labor relations and racial issues. Kennedy's approach in these situations, as illustrated in Birmingham in 1963, was to bring the opposing forces together, to find what common ground existed between them. Lindsay, he felt, took unnecessary public postures that tended to polarize the opposing sides. Kennedy believed, for example, that the debilitating fight in 1967, over substitution of civilians for police officers on the Review Board that heard citizen complaints against police officers, need never have occurred. The issue aggravated tensions without resolving any major problem; it reinforced the ghetto's dislike of the police, harmed the morale of the force, and gave a public forum to the fear of "crime in the streets." After all, the power of the proposed Civilian Review Board was very limited. The Police Department retained final authority over discipline. The board gave only the appearance of change. Making a public issue out of it, in the prevailing atmosphere of fear and frustration, Kennedy felt, was certain to give the right-wing forces in the city a major electoral victory. Although he campaigned with Lindsay during the Review Board referendum, he believed the confrontation could have been avoided by trying to work out with the police a more responsive board which would include citizen participation.

Lindsay, for his part, kept an equally arm's-length relationship with Kennedy. The two cooperated on many projects for the city, such as the conversion of the Brooklyn Navy Yard. The mayor's assistance

[8] Lindsay had backed the wrong man. Shortly after being promoted over Kearing, Marcus was arrested in the first of a series of scandals involving trading influence for money.

was essential to the success of the Bedford-Stuyvesant project, which Lindsay understood and supported immediately. They worked together to find federal funds to establish a program (under the sponsorship of the Vera Institute of Justice) where certain persons charged with crimes could be offered rehabilitation as an alternative to imprisonment.

In one incident Kennedy felt Lindsay was justifiably annoyed with him. During the 1966 transit strike, the senator was under strong pressure to take a position. He kept in close touch with the situation, discussing it with Lindsay at City Hall as the negotiations were nearing a successful conclusion. At the end of their conference, Kennedy and Lindsay appeared together before newsmen, and the mayor acknowledged the visit as "a sign that all good men pull together in times of difficulty." The strike ended the next day and some stories indicated Kennedy's visit helped break the stalemate. The credit was not deserved. It was Lindsay's strike and Lindsay's settlement. Art Buchwald caught the mood of City Hall in a satirically humorous column entitled "Bobby Saves The Day." He wrote: "Sources close to Mayor Lindsay say the Mayor's warmth and gratitude to Senator Kennedy for coming in at the end of the strike has never been higher. The Mayor just has no words to express it."

During Kennedy's Senate years, Lindsay's popularity survived the disastrous strikes and racial tensions that were threatening every major city. Kennedy felt that part of the reason for Lindsay's undiminished popularity was that the Democrats were not organized to offer responsible opposition and appropriate critical analysis. He thought the Democrats could defeat Lindsay in 1969 if they did their issue homework and chose a candidate who could offer accomplishment, if not charisma. To that end, he privately encouraged a small group to organize in May 1967, to develop the issues and begin a public debate on the merits of the Lindsay administration. The group was organized around the experience of its individual members—men like labor mediator Theodore Kheel, former Police Commissioner Vincent Broderick, and civil rights lawyer Morris Abram, later president of Brandeis University. Kennedy felt this kind of "watchdog" operation could issue statements that would command public attention because of the credentials of its spokesmen—and that hopefully, some of them would consider running in the Democratic primary for mayor. The *ad hoc* group hired a full-time staff member and began a careful program of research, but the effort lapsed without a public statement having been made as Kennedy turned to the presidential campaign.

To Kennedy, the Democratic defeats in New York State reflected in large measure the failure of the party organization to understand the political revolution that was taking place. A growing segment of the Democratic electorate which was affluent, educated, and suburban, regarded social and political reform as more important than party loyalty. Television was the basic weapon of the revolution. The voters could see their candidates directly and form their own judgments about their sincerity, capability, and personality. The politics of patronage and reward were not only irrelevant to the needs of these voters, but actively antagonized them. When they voted for Democrats, it was for men who had made their reputations outside of the political organization.[9]

Reform leaders advocated a state-wide primary instead of the convention system, so that the party members rather than the leaders would select the nominees. Although Kennedy supported the direct primary, he did not see it as a panacea. It would involve large numbers of talented people in the elective process, the kind of people who were repelled by the squalor of party politics, but who had a basic interest in government and a desire to participate in public life. It would also help the Democratic Party free itself from the issue of "bossism." But he had reservations about primaries, because they made it practically impossible to choose candidates other than those who had a consuming ambition to run for office. Franklin Roosevelt, for example, would never have entered a primary in 1928; but he reluctantly accepted the Democratic Convention's nomination for governor because Alfred E. Smith wanted him and Smith could lead the party to support his choice. Primaries also added greatly to the immense cost of running for high office and made it even more difficult for men of modest financial resources to seek nominations.

Kennedy sought to enlarge the party's base by changing it from an

[9] Examples were Democratic congressmen like John Dow, Jonathan Bingham, Richard Ottinger, Otis Pike, William Ryan, and Samuel Stratton. All depended on their personal organizations and popularity rather than the regular party structure.

organization preoccupied with privileged political power and the dispensation of patronage to one involved in the social betterment of the community. In February 1965, he told the Lexington Democratic Club in Manhattan, a pioneer reform organization:

> I think the Democratic party can be a non-governmental community action program; working not just at election time, but all year round; working not just for success within the present political system —but for the creation of a politics more true to the ideals of its founders and our dreams of its future. We must not be satisfied with setting out programs once every four years. We must take an active part in the way those programs are implemented—in the schools, in the welfare department, in law enforcement and housing repair.

In January 1967, Kennedy urged party leaders at a meeting in Albany to organize a Community Service Corps, to provide an outlet for the energy and enthusiasm of citizens who wanted to be active politically, without being clubhouse members. He saw the possibility, for example, of organizing volunteers to teach in the ghettos, to be companions for retarded children in institutions, to sponsor Little League athletic activities, and to collect books for public school libraries. He was advocating participatory democracy, organizing political energy through concern for social problems.

At the same time that he was urging the regular party to broaden its base, Kennedy tried to strengthen his alliances with the leaders who spoke for New York's liberal and independent voters. First there was the reform movement. Kennedy was most comfortable with its Westside Manhattan leaders, who had supported him for the Senate nomination and worked hard in his campaign. Of all the reformers, they were most attuned to his conception of what the party should be and should do. They represented both open politics and ideological commitment, and they knew how to win elections. In the years after his election, he and Stephen Smith frequently consulted with these reform leaders, and many of them worked closely with Kennedy's office on political and substantive projects. In 1966, the senator intervened with the Democratic legislative leadership in Albany to block a proposed redistricting bill which would have put the reformers at a political disadvantage in their fight with the organization. He tried to promote Assemblymen Blumenthal and Kretchmer to leadership positions within the legislature, and later supported a futile attempt to elect Mrs. Ronnie Eldridge as leader of Tammany Hall.

Generally, Kennedy felt the reform groups were outdone in intra-party maneuverings because they had little taste for the mechanics of party leadership and too often allowed conflicting personal ambitions among them to split the strength of a united front.[10] The reformers respected Kennedy and constantly sought to involve him as an ally in their political wars. Some were disappointed that he refused to give public support to their efforts to unseat Charles Buckley as Bronx county leader. There were others whose personal friendship he could never win and who preferred a working alliance with the Johnson forces to any relationship that might further Kennedy's interests.

In 1960, the vote on the Liberal party line gave New York's electoral votes to John Kennedy, and Liberal support in 1964 was a significant element in the coalition that elected Robert Kennedy to the Senate. The Liberal party capitalized its basic union strength, primarily the International Ladies' Garment Workers' Union, by proposing to serve as "the conscience of the Democratic party," thereby attracting the dissident voters who resented the clubhouse control of candidates. In fact, the Liberal party was a much tighter and more effective machine than its Democratic counterpart. A handful of leaders dominated the decisions of its Executive Committee, and they were shrewd and experienced tacticians.

Foremost among them were David Dubinsky and Alex Rose. For forty years, Dubinsky had been the most prominent Jewish trade union leader in the United States. He was a diminutive, fiery man of great warmth and charm, and one of Kennedy's favorite public personalities. He admired the courage that marked Dubinsky's career, the candor that typified his speech, and the toughness of his leadership. Dubinsky talked with a Yiddish accent so compelling that those talking to him, including Kennedy, would almost automatically begin to imitate the inflections of his voice. There was an easy humor between them that was illustrated by a cable Kennedy once sent Dubinsky who was aboard

[10] New York *Post* columnist James Wechsler described the problem by writing: "The reform movement's will to lose is insistent and possibly incurable, perhaps because it is too divided in aims to recognize the nature of victory."

ship en route to Europe: "With you in midocean, have seized control of the Liberal party. What do I do now?" Dubinsky cabled back: "Support the best candidate of either party. Otherwise, pickle it."

The other dominant figure was Alex Rose, the party's master strategist and, in Kennedy's judgment, the canniest politician in the state. He was president of the United Hatters and Milliners Union, and every politician seeking his favors was careful to come to him, hat in hand. His power was dependent on his acumen. Although circumstances forced him at times to endorse candidates who subsequently lost, he himself was never wrong in predicting the outcome of an election. Rose was a man who recognized power and dealt with it directly and without sentiment. When President Kennedy was in the White House, Rose and the Attorney General were in frequent contact. When Johnson succeeded to the presidency, Robert Kennedy did not hear from Rose again until the Senate race became a possibility, and then their conversations dealt solely with New York political questions.

Although the New York reform-liberal community supported Kennedy for senator, its suspicions and doubts of him were carried well past the election. His attacks on the Vietnam war did more than anything else to soften their attitudes. "I really hated him during that campaign," one woman told columnist Wechsler. "Now I write him letters once a week telling him he's the man who can save the world." But for the most part this alliance on issues only slightly improved his personal rapport with this powerful group of opinion-makers. Kennedy recognized that part of their wariness and hostility lay in his investigative career during the 1950s; but he believed that a larger part was their inevitable reaction to any Irish-Catholic politician, a reaction based on their traditional differences with Catholic leaders over the issues of authority, dissent and civil liberties. Kennedy's reluctance to enter into philosophical and self-analytical discourse, and his way of acting quickly and moving directly also made them uncomfortable. He was equally uncomfortable with them. He did not look upon politics as therapy, and he had little patience for those who fought ideological conflicts with no real intention of winning the power to make things happen.

Kennedy's growing collaboration with liberals and reformers could have been expected to weaken him with the more conservative wing of the party. His position on issues made it increasingly difficult for many Irish-Americans to believe that Kennedy was still "one of their own." But among the Catholic voters, sympathy for the martyred President and admiration for the Kennedys as a symbol of Catholic success in American politics ran too deep to be overturned. Although they may have shaken their heads at some of the things he said about accommodation with the Vietcong, they still mobbed him at St. Patrick's Day parades and cheered him at Communion breakfasts. The New York *Daily News,* the great reflector of political conservatism, blistered him for his opinions but still found it useful to put the christening of his latest child on the front page. His name and his family were shields that allowed many who disagreed with his policies to give his views a hearing, and gain a better understanding of the new forces loose in their nation.

Kennedy's most significant political victory in New York State was a result of his growing alliance with the Liberals. It came in June 1966, in an election for a judgeship in Manhattan. The contest involved the far larger issue of judicial selection. Most judges in New York are elected, but if the purpose was to give the people a role in choosing their judges, the election process had become a democratic mirage. The average voter had no idea who the candidates were, and since tradition forbade active campaigning, there was very little chance to learn about them. The nomination of the Democratic party in New York City and of the Republican party in the upstate areas, was tantamount to election. By controlling the nominating procedures, the political leaders thereby controlled the selection of judges.

Judicial nominations were the most attractive rewards a party could offer. The prestige and salaries were high.[11] Since most judicial terms ran fourteen years and an incumbent judge was always redesignated without opposition, they were, in effect, lifetime positions. All this made judicial nominations extremely important assets for the regular organization. Lawyers served their party long and faithfully in the hope of wearing judicial robes, and it was common knowledge that, in some areas, they made substantial contributions to the organization

[11] State Supreme Court judges receive $39,100 a year; City Court judges $25,000.

to enhance their prospects for nomination. The peripheral patronage involved in a judge's office—clerks, law secretaries, personal secretaries, even valets—added to its political usefulness.

It was natural that, with such stakes, the politicians wanted to arrange things so the patronage could flow with as much certainty and as little conflict as possible. It was not unusual for Republican and Democratic leaders to negotiate a division of the judicial positions on the ballot in any particular year, roughly according to the relative strength of the parties in the area, and then agree to endorse each others' candidates. Looking at the election machine, voters noticed that the same man was the candidate of all parties. The intended impression was that this was a triumph for judicial non-partisanship and merit selection. Actually, it was plain political dealing.[12]

The system had not been challenged in the voting booth since 1932, when good government groups tried unsuccessfully to elect an independent slate of judicial candidates nominated by the bar associations. Mayor Wagner had tried to dilute the practice by establishing nonpartisan commissions to recommend judges for those city court positions filled by appointment. Governor Rockefeller, on the other hand, treated the question with the same disdain with which he treated lawyers, and almost without exception followed the recommendation of Republican county leaders in making appointments to the Court of Claims or in filling judicial vacancies.

The Surrogate's Court, which supervised the administration of estates, provided the richest vein of political patronage. In Manhattan alone, it was estimated that the Surrogate's Court presided over the disposition of property worth $1 billion a year and generated fees of $500,000 annually. Because the generous fees of its appointees were paid out of the estates, the late Mayor Fiorello La Guardia had called the court "the most expensive undertaking establishment in the world."

In the spring of 1966, an impending vacancy in one of the two

---

[12] Nevertheless, this system produced a judiciary that has probably been as good as any in the country, which included, on New York's highest court, such jurists as Benjamin Cardozo, Irving Lehman, Charles Desmond, and Stanley Fuld. There were obvious deficiencies. The level of judicial competence was very uneven. Eminent judges like Bernard Botein never tired of fighting for reforms that would reduce the political considerations and emphasize individual merits in judicial selection, but for the most part, it was a losing battle.

Surrogate judgeships in Manhattan set the usual political procedure for filling it into motion. The candidate of the Democratic organization was a former Congressman and State Supreme Court Judge, Arthur Klein, who, in his ten years on the Court, had been an able judge. The Democratic leader of New York County, J. Raymond Jones, made an agreement with the Republican leader, whereby Klein would also receive Republican endorsement. This was an unusual departure from the tradition of different designations by the major parties where a new judge (as differentiated from an incumbent judge) was being elected. But in this case, Jones agreed to give the Democratic endorsement to a Republican judge who was the GOP candidate for State Supreme Court.[13]

In selecting the candidates for the Supreme Court vacancies that year, Jones had disregarded the recommendations of the reform leaders. Some of them wanted to retaliate by challenging the choice of Klein in a primary contest. But Jones, knowing the personal ambitions of key reform leaders, divided their ranks by promising judicial promotions and support for other future candidacies. The discontent was contained, and Klein was endorsed by the county executive committee with several reformers abstaining. The anticipated newspaper criticism came with clockwork regularity and was dismissed by the politicians, who understand that the active life of such stories rarely survives twenty-four hours. This time they were wrong, and a newspaper column played a crucial role in transforming an election for an obscure office into a contest of national significance.

On Thursday, May 19, 1966, Kennedy was in New York to attend the Kings County Democratic Dinner. As part of his effort to stay in touch with political leaders, he scheduled a meeting with Alex Rose at the Prince George Hotel in Manhattan. Neither man had any pressing problem to discuss with the other. Rose, with no specific purpose other than offering more evidence of the venality of Democratic leaders, gave Kennedy a column by James Wechsler that was appearing in that day's New York *Post*, detailing the double designation of Klein and calling it a "crass, old fashioned political trade." Rose

[13] The arrangement also involved joint party endorsement of candidates for four vacancies that were coming up later on the State Supreme Court. Two of the candidates were to be chosen by Jones, one by Vincent Albano, and one by the Buckley organization in the Bronx.

was indignant about the deal, which had also excluded any member of the Liberal Party from judicial consideration.

"Can we do something about this?" Kennedy questioned.

"You can," said Rose.

"Do you think we can win?" Kennedy asked, and Rose answered: "You can't ever lose if you do the right thing—you know what I mean?"

Kennedy's intervention in the Surrogate's race was a sudden, essentially instinctive decision. It was an opportunity to uphold an important principle of judicial integrity, challenge political enemies, and gain significant allies, but in no small part he did it because it was a chance for a good fight, which tempted a politician already restless with the mediocre maneuvering of a party he presumably was directing. He asked an associate to canvass the field, but the most obvious prospects, incumbent judges Owen McGovern and Arthur Markewich, wanted no part of such a battle. On Friday Kennedy went back to Washington, still anxious to make the challenge but with no candidate and no reliable commitment of reform support.

By late afternoon of that Friday, two names were under consideration. One was Civil Court Judge Edward Greenfield, the first successful judicial candidate to emerge from the reform Lexington Democratic Club. Greenfield's real aspiration was the State Supreme Court but he understood the power of the Surrogate's office and the meaning of Kennedy's intervention. Though reluctant to commit himself, he finally agreed to run, if Kennedy asked him and if the reform leaders supported him.

But Kennedy was hopeful that the other prospect would materialize. The name of Supreme Court Judge Samuel J. Silverman was proposed from many quarters, including former county leader Edward Costikyan and Justin Feldman, a Manhattan lawyer whose judgment and assistance Kennedy always valued. Silverman was the ideal candidate. A mild-mannered, almost diffident lawyer known for his brilliant mind and subtle wit, he had been born in Odessa, Russia, and had added his own chapter to the saga of the Lower East Side by an eminent career as a trial attorney, including a major role in the defense of J. Robert Oppenheimer in his "security" trial in the mid-1950s, and as the instructor of a generation of young law students taking "cram" courses for the New York bar examination. Elected to the bench in

1962, Silverman was known as non-political, and as a prodigious worker who welcomed the most complicated cases. His decisions were marked by a superior literary style that had won him a large audience of admirers. Kennedy did not know Silverman personally at the time, but when he heard the judge described over the phone, his only response was: "Habemus papem."

When Silverman was approached by a Kennedy adviser, he was astonished at the idea, but agreed to consider it. He consulted with several colleagues on the bench and former law partners, and failed to find the opposition he thought they would express. Silverman recognized the political implications of the contest, but he admired Kennedy and was deeply concerned about judicial reform. The Surrogates Court had no intellectual appeal for him. He enjoyed the trial aspect of the State Supreme Court and had every reason to believe that he would be promoted to the Appellate Division in the normal course of events. If he challenged the system, he would isolate himself from many of his colleagues who had reached the judicial sanctuary by the same political ladder. With many misgivings, but no illusions, Silverman spoke to Kennedy by phone early Sunday afternoon, May 22, and told him: "If you are willing to get into this, so am I." Kennedy said he would fly to New York immediately, and would not ask Silverman to run unless he could assure him of a Democratic-Liberal coalition that gave him a real chance of victory.

Kennedy met that night at the Commodore Hotel with the reform district leaders. He told them he would not undertake the fight without their support, since only a few days remained for the filing of nominating petitions and the reform clubs were essential to gather the 2500 valid signatures required by law. He spoke of the contest in terms of its significance for the city and the reform of the Democratic party. But many of the leaders were reluctant. Some felt it could not be won. Some felt the fight would drain manpower from other primaries where they had a more direct interest. A few had had their own conversations with Jones about political offices and patronage for themselves, and clearly a Surrogate's campaign would destroy those possibilities.

When, after ninety minutes' debate, one participant questioned Kennedy's own motives in backing the insurgency, the senator stood up and put the challenge directly to them:

"Look," he said, "I am not committed to this. This is not my personal fight. I have much less at stake in it than you do. But I am willing to do it because the way judges are chosen in the State of New York is wrong—and this one is totally wrong. If there is going to be a fight, it will have to be *our* fight. You people are supposed to be the leaders of reform in New York. This is your chance. If you don't make this fight, in my judgment, you are finished as a reform movement in this city."

He sat down amid cheers and stunned surprise. A motion was made to adjourn for ten minutes. When the leaders reassembled, the vote to back Silverman was unanimous. Two days later, Silverman received the endorsement of the Liberal Party, assuring him a place on the November ballot even if he lost the Democratic primary.

For the first time in New York politics, a nomination for judicial office had been the major focus of a primary election. The campaign was quickly billed as a showdown between Kennedy and Tammany Hall. The campaign chairman was Adrian DeWind, a former law partner of Silverman's, but the campaign was managed in fact by Stephen Smith, who moved quickly down the now familiar path of securing a headquarters, setting up store fronts around Manhattan, and mobilizing the writers, advertising men, advance men and organizers who comprised Kennedy's personal political shock troops. Murray Kempton wrote: "What is extraordinary in this performance is the artistry of the management. Kennedy is splendid enough as a horse, but he is a thing apart as a jockey."

Silverman himself broke precedent by issuing a campaign statement. He recommended that the Surrogate's Court be merged with the Supreme Court, and its work performed by lawyers appointed on a basis of merit. The campaign drew the main issue very simply as the integrity of the judiciary. The idea that voters elected judges was an illusion. In fact they were chosen by deals. If this particular deal was not canceled by the voters, the political bosses would control the Surrogate's Court.

Unaccustomed to primary challenge for judicial offices, the organization reacted sluggishly. Klein made the traditional rounds of the clubhouses. James A. Farley, former Police Commissioner Francis W. H. Adams, and former Mayor Vincent Impellitteri endorsed him. The chief factor working in favor of Klein was the offbeat time of the election. A normal primary in early June in Manhattan for local office draws fewer than fifteen per cent of the registered Democrats in Manhattan. The hard core of party regulars could be depended upon to vote for Klein. Only one other contest could be expected to draw a large vote—a congressional primary in the nineteenth Congressional District, which included the area Klein had represented in Congress and where he was personally known.

The organization charged Kennedy was using the primary to take over the county organization for himself. "Kennedy did not get into this to reform the Surrogate's Court," Klein said. "I don't even think he knows where the Surrogate's Court is!" But the only group who might have been influenced by this, the liberals, were unconvinced. All the leaders and journals of opinion they trusted were supporting Silverman, something they knew would not be so if this were solely a "Kennedy power play."

On June 1, Kennedy left for a visit to South Africa. He considered changing his travel plans because of the primary, but too many were relying on the trip, and any postponement would allow the South African government to discredit his intentions. He rationalized his departure to the campaign staff by saying his presence in Africa would offset the attacks on him by Jones, who, as the first Negro leader of Tammany Hall, was trying to turn the primary into a civil rights contest. In any event, he allotted the ten days after his return to the Silverman effort and thought this would be enough.[14]

When Kennedy returned he began a press conference at the airport with the observation that "everybody in Africa is interested in Sam Silverman." But when he arrived at campaign headquarters, the fun was over. The reports were gloomy. The Republican County organization was working among its Democratic friends to gain support for Klein. The public was not aroused. Telephone sampling showed few people realized that there was an election on June 28. Researchers had been rebuffed in efforts to find evidence of politically-connected lawyers

[14] While in Kenya, Sander Vanocur interviewed Kennedy for NBC television. It came at the end of a hot, grueling day. The interview ended with a long question about Kennedy's travels and what the senator regarded "as the most important issue of the day." Without hesitation, Kennedy replied, "The election of Sam Silverman," thereby breaking up the show. From remote villages along the African trail, postcards would be sent to Silverman campaign headquarters telling how all of Kenya or Tanzania or Ethiopia was awaiting word of Sam Silverman's success.

getting Surrogate's fees. Expensive commitments had been made for advertising and staff, but no funds had been raised. Lawyers, the logical group to finance a campaign to improve the judicial system, were reluctant to help. Some did business at the Surrogate's Court and did not want to take sides; others were nervous about the propriety of their contributing to a judicial contest.

Kennedy had more confidence in the outcome. On review, he felt the groundwork had been laid for an effective campaign. He needled the reform leaders to greater activity: "You don't want me to think my father was right about you, do you?" he asked.

Kennedy took to the streets for Silverman in the same manner he had campaigned for himself two years before. Waving a copy of an old *Harper's* magazine article on Surrogate's Court corruption, he shouted to a Puerto Rican crowd on Fourteenth Street, "Don't die in the city of New York. Don't die—if you want to leave anything to your wives and children." The Surrogate's Court, he said, was "shot through with scandal" and the manner of Judge Klein's selection had about it "an aura of corruption or a deal." Pointing to Silverman smiling benignly at his side, he said "he is an honest man, he will protect you."

At first Silverman was not quite sure how to go about campaigning. But he learned quickly, and in his own quiet and cultured way, he was very effective: "I am not a politician" he said (shouts of "hurray"). "But I want to say just one thing: I promise you simple justice." Then Kennedy talked to the children in the crowd: "How many of you have heard of Surrogates? Raise your hands . . . okay, how many of you are going to go home tonight and tell your mothers and fathers to vote for Silverman for Surrogate?" (A forest of hands.) "Silverman, Silverman, remember that name," Kennedy shouted. (More cheers.) "Let's go over it now, what are you going to tell your mothers and fathers when you get home?" "Vote" the children shouted. "And vote for whom?" "Kennedy," they shouted. The marimba band played as the motorcade sped off to another rally.

The campaign picked up speed. In a loft in mid-Manhattan, Albert Blumenthal supervised a large group of girls who went down the lists calling voters ("I am calling for Judge Silverman. Have you heard about the deal to give the bosses control of the courts?") Kennedy was having a marvelous time. He received a letter that Vincent Albano, the Manhattan Republican leader had sent Republican workers telling them to work for Klein. Before reading it at street rallies he urged the children present to shut their ears because it was so evil. (Kennedy: "Are you too young to hear this?" Children: "No.") His enthusiasm overflowed to Silverman, who emerged as an engaging, effective campaigner in his own right. "I've heard it said we have to win this because Kennedys don't finish second," he said to the crowds. "Well, Silvermans don't finish second either."

The final impetus came when the New York *Post* revealed, the weekend before the election, the names of lawyers who had been getting fees from the Surrogate's Court. Through detective work by persons associated with the reform movement, *Post* reporters had obtained documentation of what the newspaper called "a pattern of political patronage in which a big share of the plums go to jurists' relatives, politically connected lawyers and former officeholders." The recipients protested. The son of one judge said the Surrogate had appointed him "because he had confidence in my ability to protect the interests of my wards." The net effect was to confirm the worst fears that had been raised about the extent of the patronage.

The election was a landslide. Of 465,000 registered Democrats in Manhattan as of 1966, 127,000 came out, a record for such a primary, and gave Silverman a majority of 23,000 votes. Silverman narrowly lost Harlem, but only 15 per cent of the vote was cast there. In the reform areas, he won by as much as five to one. In a victory appearance, Kennedy thanked the workers and said the result "showed how sophisticated the voters in New York are." Photographers asked Silverman to raise both arms in a victory gesture. He refused. "You know, I am not exactly a prizefighter," he said, "I am a judge."

The Silverman campaign was Kennedy's high point in New York politics. He had forged a coalition with both reformers and liberals in the crucible of a campaign struggle. He had expanded his personal organization with effective New York political operators. His influence was greatly enhanced. The lesson was not lost on the organization leaders: If Kennedy could win a primary for an obscure office on short notice and with a jerry-built organization, he could, if he desired, threaten any Democratic leader in the state by running primaries against him. That ability, which he alone possessed, made him the unchallenged leader of the party and redoubled the pressure upon him to reform and redirect the political energies of the entire state.

The broader purposes of the campaign, reform of the Surrogate's Court and of the judicial selection process, did not fare so well. In 1967, Kennedy followers in the legislature introduced Judge Silverman's reform proposals. Kennedy told the legislature's Joint Committee on Court Reorganization that special guardians should be abolished and their work transferred to full-time state employees. But the Surrogates from other counties, with their political sponsors and legal allies, defended the existing system and criticized Kennedy's attacks as irresponsible. When reform plans were defeated in the legislature, the fight was carried to the floor of the 1967 constitutional convention, but forces in both parties beat it down again.

Kennedy knew the Surrogate's Court was not a sufficient challenge to a man of Silverman's abundant energy and intellectual capacity. In early 1968, he decided to recommend Silverman for the next federal court vacancy, satisfied that at least a model for administering a Surrogate's Court had been established. But the events of June came before such a vacancy developed.

Judge Silverman is still Surrogate of New York County. In February 1969, Edward Katcher of the New York *Post,* who had broken the initial Surrogate scandals, took another look at the court. He reported that Silverman had removed politics from the administration of his court, but that among the other Surrogates "nepotism, cronyism and political connections are still the prime factors behind appointments of special guardians." Katcher cited as proof appointments (none made by Silverman) worth $345,000 in legal fees to forty-two lawyers including a former Surrogate and two former judges. Ironically, all of the Supreme Court nominees involved in the second part of the Jones-Albano-Buckley deal were nominated in September 1968 and were elected. At that point, there was no longer anyone left with both the power and the will to use it in the cause of judicial reform.[15]

15 The Silverman campaign was not the only case in which Kennedy intervened successfully in a local race. In 1967, he succeeded in deposing Rufus Elephante, the Democratic leader of Oneida County by defeating his candidate for mayor for the city of Utica. For almost forty years, Elephante's control had made the Utica Democratic Party the political arm of the Mafia. In 1967, independent Democrats supported by Kennedy nominated an insurgent candidate, Dominic Assaro. Jerry Bruno stepped out of his role as political liaison and advance man for the senator, and in that heavily Italian city made campaign speeches and helped organize the election operations. Near the end of the primary, Kennedy himself went to Utica to speak for Assaro, who won the primary and was later elected.

8

SOUTH AFRICA:
JOURNEY INTO CONTROVERSY

Throughout his career in the Senate, Robert Kennedy was impelled to the extraordinary course, the neglected problem, to fields of action remote from the path of contemporary liberal politicians. Because whatever he did attracted attention, he was able to dramatize obscure but significant problems. His trip to South Africa was one of the best examples of how he was able to do this.

He had traveled to black Africa in 1962. It would have been simple for him to visit again, and comment knowledgeably on the problems of underdeveloped nations and their struggle for national identity. Africa was on the periphery of the struggles which engaged the world's powers,—important, but not crucial, to the peace and security of the world. But when Kennedy visited that continent in 1966, he did so in a way that illuminated one of the fundamental causes of international tension, the problem of race. It was a journey into controversy, and it became one of the most important journeys of his life.

Kennedy did not seek an invitation to visit South Africa. It came unexpectedly, in the autumn of 1965, in the form of an invitation to be the main speaker at the annual Day of Affirmation celebration at the University of Cape Town, sponsored by the National Union of South African Students (NUSAS), whose membership included al-most all of the country's English-speaking students.

The Day of Affirmation was a protest meeting, a symbolic event affirming the sponsors' commitment to human liberty and academic freedom in the face of governmental oppression. The invitation was signed by Ian Robertson, a twenty-one-year-old medical student who was president of the organization. NUSAS was identified with the viewpoint of the Progressive Party in South Africa, a beleaguered minority which accepted the concept of a multi-racial state and the eventual enfranchisement of the black majority. For years, the South African government had harassed NUSAS and its leadership, considering it a reprehensible, communistic, unpatriotic organization. Kennedy's appearance at the event would undercut the government's attacks and give new stature to NUSAS in the country.

Kennedy instinctively welcomed the invitation. Having in mind the success of his Polish trip, he saw another opportunity to reach the people of an oppressed land despite the barrier of their government. There were many uncertain implications in such a trip so Kennedy consulted Wayne Fredericks, then Deputy Assistant Secretary of State for African Affairs, who was regarded by both President Kennedy and Robert Kennedy as one of the ablest and most effective advisers on African problems. Fredericks urged him to accept the invitation. He told Kennedy that because of his name and his experience with racial conflicts in the United States, he could be an important spokesman for the values of American democracy. His visit would help establish contact with South Africa's youth and give encouragement to the forces that believed in racial accommodation. His confrontation with racism would help America's standing with the rest of the peoples of Africa, to whom South Africa represented the final outrage of colonialism. Frederick's arguments confirmed Kennedy's initial reaction, and he applied for a visa to visit the country.

In South Africa, spokesmen for *apartheid* dismissed his request as politically inspired. Their American counterparts, such as William Loeb of the Manchester, New Hampshire, *Union Leader,* urged South Africa to reject Kennedy's request, describing him as "the most vicious and dangerous leader in the United States today." The government of Prime Minister Hendrik Verwoerd was perplexed. It did not want to do anything to draw attention to the Day of Affirmation, and Kennedy's presence would greatly magnify the occasion. The emotional reactions to his visit were unpredictable and could become uncontrollable. To bar him, however, would give credence to everything the opponents of the Verwoerd regime were saying about its oppressiveness.

The government also recognized the power realities of the situation. Kennedy was a major political figure in the United States who well might become its President. America was an important trading partner, and, furthermore, South Africa liked to style itself as an ally in the fight against Communism. The insult implicit in the denial of a visa could carry serious consequences in the years ahead. Verwoerd chose the lesser risk. On March 22, 1966, five months after Senator Kennedy had publicly accepted the NUSAS invitation, the South African Minister to Washington, Johan Botha, went to Capitol Hill and personally delivered the visa.

Kennedy knew that the liberals and the blacks of South Africa would welcome him, but he hoped his trip would have an additional dimension. He wanted to exchange views with the leaders of the government who had created and believed in the *apartheid* policies. Botha informed him, however, that the government intended to regard his visit as "purely private" and that none of its leaders would meet him. In addition, the government "banned" Ian Robertson under its "Suppression of Communism" law, which meant he was put under house arrest and he could not attend the occasion to which he had invited Kennedy. Finally, on May 25th, just six days before the trip was to begin, a spokesman for Verwoerd announced that there would be no visas for members of the press accompanying the Kennedy party. An official statement said: "South Africa is not prepared to allow such a visit to be transformed into a publicity stunt, whether as a build-up for a future Presidential election or for other reasons." Arthur Krock, writing in the New York *Times,* described the ban on foreign reporters as a "stupid error." If by barring them Verwoerd hoped to limit publicity of the trip, Krock said, he had already lost his chance when he granted the senator his visa; for Kennedy, in Krock's words, was "one of the most skillful and industrious harvesters of publicity in politics, and a pretty good newsman on the side."

The senator briefed himself carefully for the trip.[1] He followed the

[1] Among the books that he read were Leo Marquard's *Peoples and Policies of South Africa* and Cornelius de Kiewiet's *A History of South Africa: Social and Economic.* In addition to Fredericks, he consulted Lady Jackson (Barbara Ward), Waldemar Nielsen, and Lawrence Ralston, all longtime observers of South Africa.

hearings on United States-South African relations which the Subcommittee on Africa of the House Foreign Affairs Committee held in the spring of 1966. He scheduled weekly sessions at Hickory Hill which Professor Vernon McKay of Johns Hopkins University helped organize. Professor Fred Burke, then of Syracuse University, brought together another group of experts for special briefings. The preparation for the trip typified the Kennedy style: seek out expert opinions, gather the facts, trust no single channel of information, form your own conclusions.

The complexities and paradoxes of South Africa absorbed him. A nation of 17 million people, with only 3.25 million whites, it was a microcosm of the world's ethnic order. The whites maintained their privileged status by undisguised oppression of a black and "colored" population that outnumbered them five to one.

The classic conflicts of European imperialism were woven into the country's history. The Afrikaners were the proud descendants of Dutch, French Huguenot, and German settlers who came there in the seventeenth century and struggled for generations against the black African tribes of the East and the Northeast for control of the grasslands and sources of water. The nineteenth century saw the establishment of British control, beginning with the military occupation of the coastal areas in 1806. In 1835, the Afrikaners began their "Great Trek" to the interior of the country, where they sought to live beyond the control of the British authorities, whose policies toward the black natives they considered altogether too lenient. The Boer Republics, established by these Afrikaners, survived the harassment of British authority until the diamond and gold resources of the country were discovered in Kimberley and on the Rand.

The development of these incredible mineral deposits transformed the relationship between whites and the blacks. Large numbers of British colonists and other "outsiders" arrived to lay claim to the new riches. The mines needed labor. Blacks were wrenched from their tribal society and emerged as an exploited proletariat group, enslaved rather than liberated by the resources of their own land.

In the Boer War at the turn of the century, British imperial power prevailed. The little Afrikaner Republics lost their independence, and their remnants were welded together into a Dominion. Afrikaner nationalism survived the painful defeat of the War. Although a large segment of the Afrikaner people, led by Jan Botha and Jan Christiaan Smuts, were convinced that the best future for South Africa lay in a working coalition with their English-speaking countrymen, the African nationalists disagreed. Their cause was strengthened by the bitterness engendered by defeat in the Boer War and the feeling of being second-class citizens in a country where the British "overlord" dominated business, society, and cultural life.

The Afrikaners kept their language and culture, and helped one another gain economic security and power. They were not "colonials" in the classic sense. They were not representing an absent imperial power, nor working for a foreign king or country. This was their land, hewn out of the bush by their ancestors. They despised the British so much that their leadership associated sympathetically with Hitler. Many were arrested and detained for pro-Nazi activities during World War II. They admired the structure of National Socialist Germany and hoped to emulate it in South Africa. Out of their defeats and bitterness was forged a bond of nationalist feeling that resented any "outsider," built power out of fear of the black majority, and isolated its own children from the currents of change that were transforming race relationships in the rest of the world. At the same time, by applying their own great energies to the magnificent resources of the land, they created, at least for the white people, one of the most modern nations in the world. Any fair-minded observer had to be impressed by the heroic, pioneering struggle of the Afrikaner population which had helped to transform this remote country into a modern industrial state.

In the election of 1948, the nationalists, under Dr. Daniel Malan, finally won control of the government and embarked on a policy of complete separation of the races—*apartheid*—which included harrassing the opposition and gradually suppressing both the dissent and the conscience of their white countrymen. A white South African theological student, Reverend Kenneth Carstens, described in the House hearings the circumstances in which most of his black countrymen lived under *apartheid:*

> Completely disenfranchised . . . kept in perpetual poverty by the color bar and the laws against collective bargaining and strikes . . . deprived of freedom of speech, movement and assembly in over

87% of the country . . . in urban areas at the mercy of a government labor bureau . . . in constant fear of being classified as "surplus labor" or "politically suspect" by an administrative officer, robbed of job and livelihood and transported to some impoverished "tribal homeland" . . . in rural areas reduced to serfdom by laws which make it a criminal offense to have employment without permission . . . even robbed of the right to live with wife and family in an urban area.

The Nationalists' retort to this kind of attack was to point out that the Bantu standard of living, in terms of per capita income, was far and away the highest for colored men anywhere in Africa. They also argued that the political stability and military power of their government were solid barriers to the unrest and revolution the Communists were spreading in the rest of Africa.

But the transcendent issue was the conflict between the races. How South Africa would resolve this profoundly difficult problem was what gave that country special meaning for the world, in Kennedy's opinion. He did not believe a white tyranny on a black continent could survive the twentieth century.

The official policy of the United States condemned *apartheid* and forbade the sale of military equipment to South Africa but regarded economic sanctions as both unpromising and counterproductive. In other ways, it tried to maintain as normal a relationship as possible, hoping that world opinion could eventually change the direction of race policies in South Africa toward an open society with majority rule and minority rights. One reason why American policy was not more militant was the presence of major American corporations doing almost $700 million a year in business in South Africa.

As Kennedy completed his briefing, the themes he would strike in his visit began to emerge. He would try to bring hope and comfort to the blacks by reminding them there were nations and individuals in the world beyond, for whom freedom and human rights were the supreme values of civilization. He would tell the leaders and white citizens of South Africa that the United States shared the problems of race and understood their anguish and difficulty; but he would warn them not to isolate themselves by their actions from the world community. He would tell them South Africa was no longer a bulwark against Communism, and in fact had become a liability in Western efforts to gain the support of the nations of Asia and Africa. He would warn that South Africa's advancing technology would require the educating of black people, and once touched by enlightenment, they would surely challenge the repression that permitted the whites to live in privilege and false security.

The scene at Johannesburg airport at midnight of June 4, 1966, as Robert and Ethel Kennedy landed, was in the pattern of a hundred such airport stops in the course of his Senate career. The planning was done with political style: the crowd, the noise, the acclaim, the excitement, the placards of the "airport rally" were there, along with the tension of having friend and foe in the same surging crowd. Since the government curfew kept the blacks away, the welcoming crowd of 1500 was predominantly white, English-speaking—mostly students, with some Indians risking the racial barriers of the terminal to join the reception. The senator's first words were in Afrikaans— "Gooinaand" ("Good Evening"). A local reporter muttered, "Well, there's his first mistake. I suppose someone told him that there would be lots of Afrikaners here to greet him." Actually Kennedy wanted the story of his arrival to report that his first words were in Afrikaans. If those most hostile to him could feel he was making an effort to talk with them, in some small way a barrier might be broken.

With that very first audience, he struck one of the major themes of his visit: "We Americans are, like you, people of diverse origins. And we have a problem, though less difficult than yours, of learning to live together in mutual respect for the rights and well being of all of our people." Picking out an angry "Yankee Go Home" sign, he used it to advantage: "We will not always agree, as we in the United States do not always agree among ourselves. But what is important is that we frankly discuss the problems and prospects of the future, the hopes and the hazards, which we share as inhabitants of the globe."

The visit was to last only four days, but he had scheduled a whirl-wind: five major speeches, countless impromptu statements, discussions with the politicians of the Progressive and United Parties, meetings with editors of English and Afrikaans newspapers, appearances at every major university in the country, dinners with businessmen, clergy, labor and community leaders, meetings with leaders like Zulu Chief Luthuli, author Alan Paton, and liberal member of parliament

Helen Suzman, and an appearance in Soweto, a black "compound" established under *apartheid*. An Afrikaans newspaper said Kennedy's visit "seemed more like four years than four days."

The first day, Kennedy used the residence of his host, American Ambassador William Roundtree, in Pretoria, for private discussions. The closest he came to meeting with government spokesmen was his session with editors of Afrikaans newspapers. The discussion was stiff. He knew that some cabinet ministers were willing to see him but that Prime Minister Verwoerd, contrary to the tradition of Afrikaner hospitality, had sternly forbidden them. He let the editors know he was irritated at this discourtesy. Kennedy understood that the editors regarded him with hostility, but that did not dissuade him from asking some pointed questions. He asked how they defined the word "colored," which was fundamental to their system of segregation. One of the editors defined it as a "bastard." The senator pressed his point. Would a child born out of wedlock to a white man and a white woman be considered "colored?" How would you categorize a South American? An Indian? A Chinese? A Japanese? That was his point—the Indian and the Chinese were "colored," but not the Japanese. Why? Because South Africa trades heavily with Japan, and it was more profitable to call them white.

One of the editors wrote later that "there was no contact between him and ourselves." They saw him as an adversary. All the vocabulary of his political enemies found its way into their stories, "cold," "tough," "ruthless."

That evening, he dined in Pretoria with the directors of the South African Foundation, an organization of business leaders devoted to promoting foreign investment and tourism in the country. They represented the ethnic and political diversity of white South Africa. His hosts expressed their belief that South Africa was entitled to the support of Western nations, regardless of what they felt about its racial policies, because it was so staunchly anti-Communist. To Kennedy, this was a false issue no longer plausible enough to forge an alliance between countries. "What does it mean," he asked, "to be against Communism if one's own system denies the value of the individual and gives all power to the government, just as the Communists do?" When the businessmen described their country as "beleaguered," Kennedy made clear that he thought the term could more appropriately be applied to men like Ian Robertson, Alan Paton, or Albert Luthuli, whose freedom had been taken away. If stability was important to business, Kennedy argued, a national commitment to social justice was essential to stability. He emphasized the fact that leaders of American industry had been prominent in the fight for civil rights and against poverty.

He ended his first day frustrated and depressed by what he had heard, and increasingly convinced that those who talked about the virtues of "separate development" for the blacks were not prepared to share the opportunities and wealth of their country in any meaningful way.

The next day, on the way to Cape Town to deliver the Day of Affirmation speech, he made an unplanned forty-minute stop in Kimberley to meet with C. Edward Crowther, a thirty-nine-year-old American Anglican bishop, who had been a chaplain for seven years at the University of California at Los Angeles and who now administered the remote diocese of Kimberley. Bishop Crowther was one of the small but significant number of Christian churchmen in the country who preached opposition to *apartheid*. He had also welcomed blacks into his church and his communion. Because of this, the government had attacked him as a foreign agitator and a fanatic, and kept him almost totally isolated from all but his black parishioners. Kennedy was aware of these attacks and made his visit in symbolic appreciation of the bishop's courage.[2]

As he stepped from the plane and was greeted by Crowther, Kennedy said, "For God's sake, don't ask me why I've come. I just thought I might help." They talked on the airport runway, to avoid the terminal office, which was bugged. They discussed *apartheid* and the work of the Kimberley diocese.

When Kennedy arrived in Cape Town to deliver the Day of Affirmation speech, he went first to see Ian Robertson, in the house where he was confined. His first question to Robertson was, "Is this place bugged too?" Robertson said he thought it was, so Kennedy told

---

[2] A year later, Bishop Crowther was expelled. Returning to California, he stopped in Washington to discuss with Kennedy the possibility of his running for the Senate. Kennedy encouraged him to look for local support—and also told him to keep his deportation order framed. "It might be a very good credential in the days to come," he said.

him to turn on the phonograph. He also thumped the floor boards with his foot, knowing that this would upset any listening devices for at least fifteen minutes.

Kennedy told Robertson that he felt reponsible for the fact that he had been "banned" and the possibility he would be exiled, but Robertson assured him that he had decided to leave his native land when he was only eleven, after reading Alan Paton's book, *Cry the Beloved Country*. Before Kennedy left, he gave Robertson a copy of *Profiles in Courage,* autographed by both himself and Mrs. John F. Kennedy.

Robertson watched from his window as Kennedy departed his house and was startled as a throng of his white, middle-class neighbors, most of them Afrikaners, jammed the narrow street and applauded the senator as he walked among them. In a country where political leaders were treated with distant respect and where television was banned by the government, such a crowd reaction was unprecedented. Robertson reflected that there was probably no other political person-ality who could evoke such spontaneous enthusiasm from white South Africans, even though presumably they opposed everything Kennedy represented. Later that evening, Ethel Kennedy, knowing how much Robertson wanted to hear the senator's speech, visited him to describe in detail the scene his invitation had made possible.

Pandemonium and 18,000 people greeted Kennedy as he arrived at the University of Cape Town for the speech. It took half an hour to get him into the hall. His arrival reminded a retired English Army officer on the scene of the exhilaration of the allied prisoners in a prison camp he had liberated in Burma in 1945. An unlighted Grecian torch, carried at the head of the procession, symbolized the fate of academic freedom in South Africa. An empty chair was reserved on the platform for Ian Robertson.

The Day of Affirmation address was probably Robert Kennedy's finest speech. It came closer to expressing his fundamental public philosophy than any other. In Cape Town that evening, Kennedy spoke not only to the young people in front of him, but to the con-cerned all over the world:

> If you fly in a plane over Europe, toward Africa or Asia, in a few hours you will come over oceans and countries that have been a

crucible of human history. In minutes you will trace the migration of men over thousands of years; seconds, the briefest glimpse, and you will pass battlefields on which millions of men once struggled and died. You will see no national boundaries, no vast gulfs or high walls dividing people from people: only nature and the works of man—homes and factories and farms—everywhere reflecting man's common effort to enrich his life, everywhere new technology and communications bring men and nations closer together, the concerns of one more and more becoming the concerns of all. And our new closeness is stripping away the false masks, the illusion of difference that is at the root of injustice and hate and war. Only earthbound man still clings to the dark and poisoning superstition that his world is bounded by the nearest hill, his universe ended at river shore, his common humanity enclosed in the tight circle of those who share his town and view and the color of his skin.

Each nation has different obstacles and different goals, shaped by the vagaries of history and experience. Yet as I talk to young people around the world I am impressed not by the diversity but by the closeness of their goals, their desires and concerns and hope for the future. There is discrimination in New York, apartheid in South Africa, and serfdom in the mountains of Peru. People starve in the streets of India; intellectuals go to jail in Russia; thousands are slaughtered in Indonesia; wealth is lavished on armaments everywhere. These are differing evils, but they are the common works of man. They reflect the imperfection of human justice, the inadequacy of human compassion, the defectiveness of our sensibility toward the sufferings of our fellows; they mark the limit of our ability to use knowledge for the well-being of others. And therefore, they call upon common qualities of conscience and of indignation, a shared determination to wipe away the unnecessary sufferings of our fellow human beings at home and around the world.

He had little faith this could be done by the generation presently holding political power. He looked instead to the youth of the world— not alone because they were his constituency, but because they were not mortgaged by fear and the dreadful experiences of depression and war.

He saw the world in a state of revolution, and he welcomed it. It suited his temperament, his judgment, and his vision. He spoke of what President Kennedy symbolized in phrases that also expressed his own deepest convictions:

. . . the belief that idealism, high aspirations and convictions are not incompatible with the most practical and efficient of programs —that there is no basic inconsistency between ideals and realistic possibility—no separation between the deepest desires of heart and mind and the rational application of human problems.

He spoke of racism in the world in the same moral terms he had applied to the civil rights struggle in America:

We must recognize the full human equality of all our people—before God, before the law, and in the councils of government. We must do this, not because it is economically advantageous—although it is; not because the laws of God and man command it—although they do command it; not because people in other lands wish it so. We must do it for the single and fundamental reason that it is the right thing to do. And this must be our commitment outside our borders as it is within . . .

The response was a wild, sustained ovation.

The next day Kennedy went to Stellenbosch University, an intellectual center of Afrikaner students, to try to carry the dialogue to the group which would be taking over the leadership of the white majority. He had been invited by the Current Affairs Club, but after public intimidation, the invitation had been rescinded. A considerable part of the student body refused to accept this discourtesy, and by majority vote, one of the men's residence halls invited Kennedy to lunch.

His speech was an exhortation to put aside prejudice and myth, to welcome instead the light of reason, and the opportunity to work with fact and logic. A long and lively question period followed in which some students defended *apartheid,* saying it would eventually produce two nations, one black and one white. Had not India been divided into Hindus and Moslems? "Are you really facing up to the situation in an honest, candid way?" Kennedy replied. "Do the black people have a choice? Why aren't they or the 'colored' people consulted? The black Africans are 70 per cent of the population but they would receive only 12 per cent of the land, with no seaport or major city. How would they live in areas whose soil is already exhausted and which had no industry?"

"Pour on the holy water," a heckler shouted.

[157]

Kennedy kept on. "You say your policy does not treat nonwhites as inferior. Why don't you allow them to worship in your churches? What would you do if you found God was black?"

Another student asked: "Do you think you can make a worthwhile assessment of a country on such a brief trip?" It was a valid question, and Kennedy had given it some thought. "I don't say I am going to leave here an expert. But I have been here in good faith and I have —as much as possible in view of the government's refusal to meet me —made a conscientious effort to know as much about South Africa as I can."

This free discussion was a new experience for Stellenbosch students. They gave Kennedy an ovation. He felt he had accomplished a major purpose of his trip. He had met young Afrikaners, they had listened, expressed their differences and exchanged views. In fact, the later results of the meeting were even more profound. The Stellenbosch students later disaffiliated from the National Afrikaners Student Union; rival student newspapers sprang up; and for the first time, Stellenbosch students publicly demanded reasons rather than blind dogma from government spokesmen to justify *apartheid.* A wave of widespread dissatisfaction had begun.

The next stop that day was Durban, where he had dinner with some distinguished opponents of *apartheid,* including Alan Paton; Archbishop Denis Hurley; an opposition leader in the government-dominated Xhosa Bantustan, Knowledge Guzana; a Zulu notable, Paramount Chief Gatsha Buthulezi; Dr. I. D. Lazarus, a leader of the Indian community; and Edgar Brookes, historian and frequent President of the South African Institute of Race Relations. "Having dinner with so many people in trouble reminds me of the days when I was Attorney General," he joked. At the University of Natal, in Durban, Kennedy assailed the government's contention that its opponents were Communists. "Reform is not Communism," he said. He urged the young people to "keep challenging, to keep looking for solutions —that's what youth is and that's the challenge of youth." A white man shouted from the gallery, "Can you tell me what President of the United States said in 1885, 'there is an undeniable difference between the white man and black man'?"

Without hesitation, Kennedy replied: "The one who was beaten in 1888." Someone asked him to lead the singing of "We Shall Overcome," and he did. For the thousands who crowded around him, whistling, shouting, singing, it expressed the hope and endurance the years ahead would require.

In the early morning of June 8, a surprise decision by the South African government allowed Robert and Ethel Kennedy to visit the farm of Chief Albert John Luthuli, spiritual leader of the South African blacks. The government had deprived Luthuli of his Zulu tribal leadership in 1952. Since that time, except for a trip to Norway in 1961 to receive the Nobel Peace Prize, he had been "banned" to his township of Groutville.

Kennedy gave him a portable record player and they listened together to excerpts from President Kennedy's civil rights speech of June 1963. South African secret service agents hovered about so that any kind of private conversation was impossible in the small house. The agents were flustered when Kennedy and Luthuli chose to go out and walk along the paths of the farm, where they discussed the racial problems of their countries and the possibilities of non-violent political change. Despite the grimness of his captive life, Luthuli was not embittered. He believed that the exploitation of black labor was the real basis of *apartheid*. He feared that the policies of the government would drive the African people to such despair that they would turn to violence to gain their liberty. His expressive face, with its warm, generous smile; the grim hurt in his eyes as he spoke of the evils of *apartheid;* the tremendous restraint he imposed upon himself in the face of violence; the gentle eloquence of his conversation—all these, combined with his courage, caused Kennedy to describe him later as "one of the most impressive men I have ever met."

The last day of the journey was spent in Johannesburg. The senator and Mrs. Kennedy were taken on a tour of Soweto, a vast township complex outside the white city, which housed more than 600,000 black Africans. Soweto was the best-managed of the "native" communities because Johannesburg was governed by the United Party which was committed to "discrimination with justice." It was willing to spend a larger portion of its wealth than many other South African cities for the municipal needs of its black satellite. Later, Kennedy was to describe it this way:

"Many of the homes there are pleasant, far more attractive than those in Harlem or South Side Chicago. But Soweto is a dreary concentration camp, with a curfew, limited recreation, no home ownership, and a long list of regulations whose violation could cause eviction."

Seeing Soweto, Kennedy understood what Chief Luthuli meant by "exploitation." In South Africa, every black had to have a passbook at all times and in all places. Without it, he was subject to immediate arrest and imprisonment, heavy fines and banishment to the "tribal area" from which he presumably came. Because most laborers had to travel long distances to the mines or other places of employment, they could not live with their wives or families. The shame of pre-Civil War America lived again in this deliberate destruction of family stability.

For the black Africans in Soweto, Kennedy's visit was an incredible event. Their welcome was emotional and joyous. They jammed around the Kennedy car, shouting, "Master, Master." "Please don't use that word," he asked, embarrassed, but the chant continued. He talked to them about a world moving away from racism, and pleaded for non-violent change. The pro-government newspapers faithfully reported the reception given him by the blacks, which prompted raging letters to the editor about the "western leader who wants a mongrel world."

The final public event was at the University of Witwatersrand, another liberal stronghold. A student asked, "How do you keep up a dialogue with people who change the rules of debate to suit themselves, tell you what you can talk about, insist upon being judge and referee, and ban you when you say too much for their liking?" Kennedy had no ready answer. "The only alternative," he said, "is to give up, to admit that you are beaten. I don't know about that. I have never admitted that I am beaten."

On June 8, the journey ended, leaving behind hope and hostility that would long be remembered. In *Contact*, a Liberal Party periodical. Alan Paton said of the visit:

"White South Africa has been likened to a room full of men and women smoking and drinking with doors and windows closed, and when a stranger came in and exclaimed, 'My, what a fog in here!'

They cried out at him—'how do you know? You've only just come in.' Kennedy was like a fresh wind from the outer world reassuring those who said there was a fog—they were right after all. The Kennedy visit can only be described as a phenomenon. It was exhilarating to hear again that totalitarianism cannot be fought by totalitarianism, that independence of thought is not a curse, that security and self preservation are not the supreme goals of life, that to work for change is not a species of treachery . . . It was to feel part of the world again."

In other cities, there was passionate approval and disapproval of what Kennedy had done. Opinion in other nations was generally favorable. Some thought his Cape Town speech the most significant statement made in South Africa since Prime Minister Harold Mac-Millan's "winds of change" speech there five years before. The London *Daily Telegraph* described it as "perhaps the most fluent and inspiring address ever delivered in South Africa by a foreigner." The Johannesburg *Star* wrote of his visit as "unquestionably one of the most important political events in South Africa for many years." The Washington *Post* said Kennedy "had an unnerving compulsion to seek out the excitement of danger . . ." and that his trip was ". . . serious, free of self-righteousness and finally, revolutionary."

But Afrikaans papers, like *Die Vaterland* said: "His visit has not made us wiser . . ." *Die Burger* wrote: "His speeches, technically smooth and well-rounded, do not give the impression that they derive from internal, personal struggle and the wisdom of experience. In all that show of zeal for changing things for the better, there was no shaft of lightening which struck the heart of South Africa."

To a regime which lived with the haunting fear that the black masses might one day find white leadership, the Kennedy visit was ominous. When he left, Kennedy had promised to return. Within hours of his departure, the government made it clear he would never again be permitted to enter.

Kennedy himself regretted that his visit had not been longer. He felt he had begun to establish contact with the whites, that they were beginning to listen to his words, that the first step of shaking old dogmas had taken hold. He had no illusions about what could be done. As he toured East Africa over the next ten days, he resisted the argument of black government leaders that the United States should boycott South African products and broaden its embargo. He felt the real victims of such a policy would be the blacks and the colored. He believed private steps would be more effective. One of the first things he did when he returned to Washington was to send a letter to American firms doing business in South Africa, pointing out that there were many things they could do, within the legal framework of the country, to help ameliorate economic and racial conditions. Some companies sent representatives to discuss his suggestions and made a real effort to follow up. Most did nothing. In the process, Kennedy learned that some American companies send our own breed of southern racist to represent them in South Africa, and these men are not interested in racial accommodation.

Apartheid had left its mark on him. In an article in *Look* magazine, he called South Africa "a land of sadness, humanity hiding behind color." He deeply regretted that the people of this talented, beautiful, wealthy country should be on such a dangerous course, and that its national life should be so corroded by fear, hatred, and suspicion. A friend who spent the final day in Johannesburg with him felt that when Kennedy came to South Africa, he knew the situation was bad, but when he left he sensed it was impossible.

But Kennedy had met an extraordinary group of people, white and black, who were heroic in their resistance to oppression, and intent on pursuing their ideals even though they knew the years ahead would be bleak and that the world at large found it hard to sustain interest in their plight. For Kennedy, who believed personal courage the highest of virtues, no praise was enough for the brave citizens he had met. His final message was addressed to them: "I believe that in this generation those with the courage to enter the moral conflict will find themselves with companions in every corner of the world."

In 1968, a South African was to send a contribution to the New York *Times* Christmas appeal for the neediest in memory of Robert Kennedy. In his note, he said: "I have always hoped to be able to tell him what his visit did to my failing spirits . . . If he did nothing else, he showed me that I was not alone in my convictions, and for that I am more grateful than I can say."

9

LATIN AMERICA:
THE ALLIANCE REVISITED

In the autumn of his first year as United States senator, Robert Kennedy spent three weeks in Latin America, visiting Peru, Chile, Argentina, Brazil, and Venezuela. It was his first trip there since 1962, when he made a twenty-four-hour trip for urgent discussions with the President of Brazil during one of that nation's financial crises. Most of his recollections of Latin America went back to 1946, when he had toured the continent after finishing his enlistment with the U. S. Navy.

The impact of John Kennedy's assassination had been as profound in Latin America as anywhere in the world. Peace Corps volunteers in a remote village of northeastern Brazil told Robert Kennedy how they had talked together for hours in disbelief the day the news came, and then heard quiet clapping outside their hut. The villagers had come to the only Americans they knew to express their sorrow. The senator had his own sense of why his brother's memory brought out such affectionate response in Latin America. His youth, style, and Catholicism were part of it, but most important was the fact that he had convinced these nations, which live in the shadow of American power, that his decisions were made with an awareness of their interests and sensitivities.

One of the first and most important programs of the New Frontier had been the Alliance for Progress, a commitment to plan massive economic aid in support of objectives of social justice. In the three years of the Kennedy administration, Latin America had received ten times as much economic aid as it had in all sixteen years since World War II, and the aid was channeled in a way that tried to encourage democratic political development. Robert Kennedy believed the policies of the Johnson administration were endangering the Alliance. At the same time that Johnson had appointed Thomas Mann as Assistant Secretary of State for Inter-American Affairs, Johnson had recognized the military junta that had overthrown the elected government of Juan Bosch. Those identified with President Kennedy's policies in Latin America saw this as the beginning of a return to the old policy of working with the traditional coalition of oligarchic-military power in South America, instead of with democratic forces seeking constitutional government, land reform, and economic liberation. They feared the Alliance for Progress would continue as a lending program only.

The unilateral intervention by American military forces in the Dominican Republic in April 1965 had confirmed the critics in this judgment. President Johnson justified the intervention in terms of protecting American lives and property and preventing a Communist takeover. Senators Morse, Fulbright, and Clark spoke forcefully against it, and Kennedy had joined them. Shortly thereafter, he began planning his trip to South America to learn what was happening to the Alliance, and to identify himself with its original purposes.

In preparation, Kennedy spent many useful hours with expert scholars, business leaders, South American diplomats, and students. The official State Department briefings, however, were stormy and unproductive. Part of the reason related to Kennedy's previous criticism of the Dominican intervention. Jack Vaughn, then Assistant Secretary of State and later Director of the Peace Corps, argued that the American action had general support in Latin America and was not a matter of extended controversy and debate. He predicted Kennedy would get no questions about the intervention during his trip. The senator was incredulous. His own private briefings had convinced him our action had raised deep doubts in Latin America, even among our friends. It was one thing for the State Department to defend and support the President's decision to intervene; it was another thing to be blind to the anger and suspicion the intervention had aroused. He bet Vaughn five dollars the Dominican problem would be among the first five questions asked him after arriving in South America. Kennedy won the bet at his first meeting in Lima and cabled Vaughn to collect the wager. In fact, the question was raised in almost every session he had with Latin Americans.

On November 10, 1965, Kennedy arrived in Peru. A wild public reception awaited him, as it would in every country; but it masked much discontent with U.S. policy. The chief issue for months had been the status of the International Petroleum Company (IPC), a subsidiary of the Standard Oil Company of New Jersey. Peru's agreement with IPC had been structured decades ago, and all sides agreed that a new contract governing royalties, ownership, and new oil exploration had to be negotiated. IPC was not a significant asset to the Standard Oil Company, but the contract terms would have broad implications in areas such as Venezuela and the Middle East where holdings were substantial. In August 1965, the United States had announced that it would delay economic aid to Peru because of this dispute.

Latin Americans were very sensitive to the fact that for centuries their mineral wealth had been sent abroad, to the coffers of Spanish kings and then to the banks of Europe. Peru's President, Juan Belaunde-Terry, knew that his political opponents, including certain military elements, would attack any agreement short of expropriation. He delayed a final confrontation but resented the insensitive attitude of the United States Government.

During the briefings at the State Department, Kennedy had objected to the use of Alliance programs as a means of economic and political pressure to protect American firms. He argued it was counterproductive to both private and national interests. A few days later, McGeorge Bundy, President Johnson's adviser on National Security Affairs, talked with Kennedy about his objections. As the senator related it, Bundy agreed that these pressure tactics were a misuse of the Alliance, but said that any changes in these policies and problems were the special province of Thomas Mann, who was jealous of his prerogatives. Bundy said if Kennedy were to criticize the policies publicly, any possible improvement would be delayed for at least an additional three months.

While in Peru, Senator Kennedy did not discuss the IPC controversy publicly, but he listened to President Belaunde and others privately castigate the attitude of both the IPC and the United States Government. When he returned to the United States, he talked to representatives of the Standard Oil Company and warned them that Belaunde was walking a tightrope that would snap if the negotiated agreement could reasonably be interpreted as anything less than a victory for Peruvian nationalism.[1]

Anti-Americanism had traditionally been strong in Latin universities, so Kennedy wanted to meet with a representative group of intellectuals in each country. In Lima, Fernando Seizlo, Peru's leading artist, hosted the occasion at his home. His Peruvian guests attacked American policy as being dominated by private economic considerations. They charged that David Rockefeller, on a recent visit, had said American aid would be cut off until the Peruvian government reassured the oil companies that their interests would not be jeopardized. Various guests joined in, claiming that the American government was the handmaiden of the Rockefeller interests, that the Rockefellers dictated policy in South America. Kennedy countered, "We Kennedys eat Rockefellers for breakfast."

Unknown to Kennedy, a tape recorder had been placed under a couch by an enterprising journalist who was also a guest. Several days later, while Kennedy was in Santiago, Chile, an embassy official showed him a popular magazine headlining the senator's remark. Kennedy laughed when he thought what Nelson Rockefeller's reaction would be when the article was delivered some morning on his desk. When he reached Buenos Aires, a reporter asked him whether it was true that he had breakfast every morning with one of the Rockefellers.

In every country Kennedy met with students. He found they were inclined to blame their nation's problems on the United States as a substitute for organizing themselves to solve them. When Peruvian students called the Alliance for Progress a tool of imperialism, Kennedy suggested they lead a movement against it: "If you feel the Alliance or any other program is not in your best interests, then oppose them. Whether our governments agree or disagree, we Americans

[1] Within six months of the senator's death, President Belaunde was deposed by a military coup following the announcement of an agreement with IPC, and the hostility of the new Peruvian government toward the United States created the worst hemispheric political crisis since the advent of Castro in Cuba.

are interested in your welfare. But it is *your* welfare—and you have to define it. You have to decide what is in your interests. If you object to American aid, have the courage to say so. But you are not going to solve your problems by blaming the United States and avoiding your own personal responsibility to do something about them." The students seemed to appreciate this, and it became part of his repertory of answers.

The next stop was Chile, where the Dominican intervention had inflamed anti-American feeling among students and where the only organized attempts to disrupt his reception occurred. The most violent confrontation took place in Concepción, Chile's third largest city, where Communist strength was at its greatest. In the city itself he was greeted by crowds lining the entire route from the airport. Children threw flowers and functionaries stopped the motorcade to present gifts and bouquets. But Chilean security police warned that trouble was being organized at the university, where Kennedy was scheduled to speak in the evening. A meeting was arranged with about thirty student leaders for the afternoon. For almost two hours Kennedy answered their questions, hoping to defuse the threatened demonstrations. Many of the students were Communists, divided into Soviet and Maoist factions which bitterly resented each other. In the course of the exchange, he tried to get them to concede that there was another side to the issues they had raised against U.S. policy. "Why do I give a damn about your opinions," he said. "Why do I sit here and listen to you? There are a lot more pleasant things to do in Concepción. But I'm here because I am interested in the revolution in Chile. Certainly we have differences, and our countries have differences. Yet Chile gets more assistance per capita than any other Latin nation. Do you ever think about that? No, because it doesn't fit your position. I'm not here to fool you. We've had a candid discussion. I doubt we could have had this meeting in Havana, Peking or Moscow. I'm delighted we could in Chile. That's why I'm against Communism."

When he asked whether they would like him to come to the university, one of the student leaders, speaking in English, said, "No, not me. We do not condemn you personally, but we oppose you as a representative of a government whose hands are stained with blood. If it is up to me, I would not let you speak." Kennedy suggested that the real indictment of their position was the refusal to allow those who disagreed with them to speak. He even offered them equal time, but the student leader refused, and the meeting broke up.

Kennedy had several hours to decide whether to go to the university. He knew the Communists were sufficiently organized to prevent him from speaking. Fifty or sixty determined demonstrators could stop anyone. The rector of the university came to see him, suggesting it would be inadvisable to keep the speaking engagement because he could not be responsible for the senator's safety. (Chile's tradition barred police and military forces from entering university property.) Kennedy listened to the various arguments. Any doubts he may have had were resolved by two Christian Democratic students, who told him that his failure to appear would be a great Communist victory and would mean that no reputable democratic spokesman would again accept an invitation to the university.

The appearance was scheduled that night for the gymnasium, converted to a meeting hall for the occasion. About a hundred Communist students were in one section of the balcony, thirty yards from the speaker's platform. The scene had all the tension and excitement of the bullring. When he entered, Kennedy slowly circled the hall. As he walked beneath the Communist section, he was met with a fusillade of eggs and garbage, all of which missed its target. He stood before the lectern while song and countersong, yell and counteryell boomed across the room. The Communists sang the Cuban national anthem. The Christian Democrats sang the anthem of their own country. The Communists shouted "Kennedy—*paredón* (Kennedy —to the wall)." From across the way came the cry of "Hungary, Hungary." Kennedy began speaking. The Communists shouted so loudly he could not be heard. He challenged them to debate him. They cursed him, refused to come to the lectern, dared him to come to their area. And he did, standing on a chair below their section. As Kennedy reached out to shake the hand of a Communist student, another leaned over and spat in his face. The student was pulled away by his Communist associates, but the chanting and shouting continued. The senator decided to leave. As he walked slowly to his car, he received a thunderous ovation.

Subsequent reports from students vindicated his judgment in going to the university. The incidents had divided the Communist ranks and reassured the anti-Communist students in their commitment. But throughout the world, newspapers headlined the Communist demonstrations against Kennedy, obscuring the friendly receptions he was receiving everywhere.

Kennedy asked Chilean officials why the Communists were so strong in the Concepción area. They described the working conditions at the nearby coal mines. The miners earned $1.25 a day. The work was dirty, hard, and dangerous, and in their despair, the miners had long provided a strong base to the Communist movement.

The embassy had not included the mines on the schedule, but after his experience at the university, Kennedy determined to go there to try to show the men that the United States was interested in their welfare. The Chilean police were appalled by the decision, but worked through the night to establish security precautions. When Kennedy started out at 5 A.M. in the fog, along the road to the mines, soldiers were stationed every hundred yards.

The managers of the mine, taken by surprise, were unhappy when the senator insisted on going down into the mines. It is hard to imagine anyone welcoming such an intrusion of foreigners, newspapermen, photographers, and dignitaries. In addition, for someone unused to mining conditions, it could be a dangerous excursion. The mines burrowed under the Pacific Ocean. To get to where the miners were, it was necessary to go down 1500 feet in an elevator, take a coal train underground for three miles, through low-hanging high-voltage wires, and then another two miles farther. But Kennedy insisted, walking along in the near blackness, introducing himself to some very surprised miners as "Senator Kennedy of the United States." At one point, he turned to a superintendent, a Welshman, and asked: "If you worked here as a miner, would you be a Communist?" "I'm afraid I would," the superintendent replied. "We breed them here."

His next stop was Brazil, where he spent most of his time in the poverty-stricken Northeast, where the need for agrarian reform was the major national issue. The large landowners could tolerate antiquated methods of farming with obsolete equipment because the low wages they paid allowed them substantial profits. The minimum wage in Brazil for sugar-cane cutters was established by law at approximately $1.25 per day, but a kilo of dried meat cost more than that, and the prices charged by the company stores inflated the cost of living even further. The workers were left politically impotent by laws permitting only the literate to vote. Only 8 per cent of the peasants in the Northeast could read and write. The young generation had little hope of breaking out of this cycle of deprivation. Only 10 per cent of the 250,000 children under age sixteen in the Northeast's "sugar zone" attended school.

Kennedy was impressed by the progressive leadership of the Catholic Church in northeast Brazil, led by Archbishop Camara of Recife and supported by local priests who were constantly threatened with imprisonment because of their commitment to the workers. One of them, a Father Crespu, told Kennedy that the illiterate should be entitled to vote, and Kennedy recalled how he had argued to abolish the literacy requirement for voting in the United States, on the grounds that a system which permitted illiteracy should be challenged by those it permitted to remain illiterate.

As Kennedy toured several sugar-cane fields in the Northeast, he found that four out of every five workers he talked to were getting less than the minimum wage. At one stop, an outdoor picnic celebrating the opening of a new building for an agricultural cooperative, he brought the landowners together with the workers and union officials for a frank discussion of working conditions. He was told that the pollution of the local rivers by the sugar-cane mills was one of the principal causes of the epidemics that ravaged the area and killed seven out of every ten children before they reached the age of one.

Kennedy's approach was not sophisticated. Some embassy personnel were embarrassed by his "interference" in the affairs of a foreign country. But he had found injustice, especially grave because it affected children and others without power to protect themselves. If the minimum wage was $1.25 per day, the least the Brazilian government could do was to enforce it. Its failure to do so was, he felt, symptomatic of its remoteness from the people. Brazil had much social legislation on the books, land reform, union organization as well as minimum wage, but the laws were frequently unenforced. This was the soil in which violence and revolution flourished.

The Senator celebrated his fortieth birthday in São Paulo on November 20. The date was difficult for him. It was on his birthday two years before that he had last seen his brother alive. On that occasion there had been a reception at the White House in honor of the Supreme Court. Kennedy had arrived late from the Justice Department, and the President had wished him a happy birthday in his remarks. Reliving those moments and events sent him back to the pensive, brooding mood he had experienced in the months after Dallas. The trip to South America had been planned so he would be out of the country on November 22, free of the publicity that would attend the remembrances at Arlington Cemetery. But there was really no escape for him. Even at the surprise birthday party Mrs. Kennedy arranged in São Paulo, there was a moment of horror. A guest set off some firecrackers which sounded like three quick reports from a gun, and Kennedy sunk his head in his hands, saying, "Oh, no, no."

On November 22, he and Mrs. Kennedy went to an eight o'clock mass in Salvador's São Francisco Church. His face was sorrow itself. His aides had scheduled a particularly heavy day, so he would be too busy for painful memories. First he toured an orphanage, then a seaside shanty slum, where the open sewers and humid heat combined to create a stench so foul that the Brazilian security policy deserted Kennedy to find sanctuary in their closed cars. In Natal that afternoon, 100,000 came out to cheer him in a four-hour motorcade. He spoke as though he were on the stump again in New York, exhorting for the universal right to housing, jobs and education. He singled out the children and pleaded with them to stay in school "as a favor to President Kennedy." As he stood atop a truck in the principal square of the city near the end of the motorcade, it was already evening. Only flashlights in the pressing crowd allowed him to be seen. The generous welcome of the people of Natal had freed him from his grief. He ended by saying: "As long as there is a Kennedy in public life in the United States, there will be a friend of northeast Brazil."

Toward the end of the trip, Kennedy said he wanted to see the Amazon River. Richard Goodwin, who was with him, solved the logistical problem by arranging a special charter from Varig Airlines to fly to Manaus, the port where the river begins its thousand-mile course to the Atlantic Ocean. The party hired a paddle-wheeler which, at a speed of ten knots against a strong current, made its way up the Solimões, a main tributary of the Amazon. It landed at Manacapuru, where hundreds of children rushed forward to meet the first senator of any nationality ever to visit their town.

Andrew Glass, writing for the *Saturday Evening Post,* caught the spirit of the trip in his later report:

> "Soon we were headed inland toward what we were told was a lake quite suitable for swimming . . . A wide, low wagon was hitched to a tractor, and we hopped aboard. Kennedy invited dozens of children running beside and behind the already overloaded flatbed to climb on . . . The tractor at one point swerved suddenly to avoid a deep hole in the jungle track. Kennedy was hurled off the flatbed and landed in the bushes on his back. He sprang to his feet, borrowed a bicycle from a boy riding behind the tractor and pedaled the two remaining miles to the lake while carrying two children on the bike's rear fender. At the lake, still surrounded by curious children, Kennedy swam out to a large log bobbing thirty yards off shore and tossed a football back and forth with Goodwin. Not until we left did the local officials tell us that the lake was really a branch of the Solimões and consequently infested with flesh-eating piranha fish . . ."

After dinner, Kennedy returned to the lake for a fishing trip by canoe. Just as he was about to shove off, a tropical deluge began. The local guides turned back. With Tom Johnston bailing amidship and Goodwin in the forward seat, Kennedy pulled away, with neither a light nor a guide in the middle of the jungle. The rain was so heavy he could not even see his companions. Forty-five minutes later, without having seen another boat or landmark, the trio returned triumphantly carrying four fish. The native guides said that they had not expected them to come back alive.

To keep to his schedule for flying to Venezuela the next day, Kennedy had to wake at 3:30 A.M., and with the help of four village guides, make his way in a dugout canoe downriver for fifteen miles to where the water was deep enough for the plane to take off. When the canoe foundered in the rapids, Kennedy jumped overboard and pushed the boat forward. Splashing along in the river, he mimicked Walter Cronkite in declaring: "It was impossible to pinpoint the exact time and place where he decided to run for President. But the idea seemed to take hold as he was swimming in the Amazonian river of Nhamunda, keeping a sharp eye peeled for man-eating piranhas. Piranhas have never been known to bite a U. S. Senator."

Kennedy waited six months after his return from South America to report his observations and recommendations to the Senate. One reason for the delay was his major involvement in the Vietnam debate, beginning with his statement in February 1966. But primarily he wanted time to discuss his conclusions with experts and to speak in detail rather than generalities.

Kennedy's report to the Senate on his trip was the longest speech of his career. It required two sessions of the Senate for the full text to be read, May 9 and 10, 1966. It began with the recognition that the United States had taken Latin America for granted. In the fifteen years following World War II, for example, that continent had received less than one fifth the amount of aid that had gone to Asia and one twelfth of what had gone to Europe. "We were content," he said, "to accept, and even support, whatever governments were in power—asking only that they did not disturb the surface calm of the hemisphere. We gave medals to dictators; praised backward regimes; and became steadily identified with institutions and men who held their lands in poverty and fear." Then came the Alliance. The difference, Kennedy said, from what had gone before was "not the statistics of economic development, but the human and spiritual reality behind them." The Alliance would identify itself, wherever possible, with progressive forces and continually press Latin nations to strengthen democratic processes and institutions internally. But it would not try to dictate the nations' policies externally. (Chilean president Eduardo Frei had commented to Kennedy on the pressure Washington was exerting to make him go along with the policies of isolating Cuba. "If you want a government that says 'Yes, yes, yes' to everything you do," Frei said, "you will soon have a government that says 'no, no, no' to everything you need.")

Kennedy urged Americans to see the United States as others saw it. "The United States can never seem neutral to Latin Americans," he said. "Our power is too great, our wealth too overwhelming, our shadow over events too dominant. The Bay of Pigs invasion, the intervention in the Dominican Republic, the battle between Peru and the International Petroleum Company, the price of coffee—each of these is only one of many crises the government of the United States must confront every year, but to the South American nation directly affected, the event is one of crucial importance resurrecting with it age-old fears and suspicions." Kennedy urged the United States to deal with the Latin nations in a way which accepted *their* conception of the importance of the issues. This would not assure agreement on every decision, or success on every issue, but at least the disagreements and failures would not be the result of carelessness or lack of effort.

As to military governments, whose numbers were increasing steadily, he suggested a case-by-case approach. He did not favor cutting off aid to Brazil, for example, even though its government came to power through a military coup and was sustained by the armed forces. "The Alliance for Progress was not meant to be—and could not be—a means for the United States to determine the government of every American nation." There may be some governments we would have to endure, but this did not mean we had to praise them or identify with them. In the case of Brazil and its President, Castelo Branco, whose integrity and motivation he respected, Kennedy urged strong support for those forces working for the return of representative democracy, and maintenance of a relationship with the students, labor, clergy, progressive businessmen and other forces of reform. Our identification with the government would be confined to those of its acts which were in accord with the ideals of the Alliance. There were times, he said, when more drastic steps might be proper to confront the overthrow of democratic governments—such as the withdrawal of aid or even collective action by the Organization of American States, "but in the overwhelming majority of cases, we must rely on the people of the Americas themselves, supported by our political action to move toward the goals of the Alliance."[2] As to the "leftists," whose actions and strength had afforded the rationale for all-out support of the military dictatorships, Kennedy urged that the real source

[2] In part, Kennedy's attitude toward military governments in Latin America was conditioned by his observation that the military, once the preserve of the oligarchy, was increasingly dominated by the sons of the middle class. He recognized that in some countries, the military sought to play a modernizing—even democratizing—role. The oligarchy remained the only force that was politically powerful and at the same time faithfully willing to protect American property interests, at least as long as their own interests were protected.

of left-wing strength be recognized. "There is a village in the Andes where only one person has ever come to say that he believed in land for the peasants. That one man was a Communist, and now many of these villagers call themselves Communists, too, since they are in favor of land reform. Here is the great danger of subversion in Latin America: If we allow Communism to carry the banner and promise of reform, then the ignored and the dispossessed, the insulted and injured, will turn to it as the only way out of their misery."

Kennedy believed the so-called "anti-American" forces would reject foreign-supported Communism, which was as great a threat to their independence as the dominance of American political and economic power. "Communism is not a native growth in Latin America. Given any meaningful alternative, the people will reject it and follow the path of democratic reform. But if we allow ourselves to become allied with those to whom the cry of Communism is only an excuse for the perpetuation of privilege then we do much to ensure that reform, when it comes, will bear the Communist label."

Kennedy saw poverty as the powder keg which could destroy democracy in Latin America. Only a drastic realignment of priorities would save the nations from violent upheaval. He had said in Natal, Brazil, on November 22, 1965: "The responsibility of our time is nothing less than to lead a revolution, a revolution which will be peaceful if we are wise enough, humane if we care, successful if we are fortunate enough, but a revolution which will come whether we will it or not."

The Senate speech discussed economic problems in depth. Kennedy suggested doubling the amount of capital aid to Latin America over the next several years as the individual countries showed the capacity to absorb it, "an equivalent for all Latin America of the cost of approximately 4 weeks of the struggle in Vietnam." He emphasized the need to assure sound and expanding export earnings which would liberate the various economies from the domination of single commodities such as coffee, oil, or bananas. He recognized the critical importance of private enterprise, but argued that foreign investment is best encouraged by countries which are confident of full control over their own economies. In an obvious reference to the IPC controversy and others that were looming, he opposed the inflexible withdrawal of economic aid as a means of coercing Latin Americans to negotiate "prompt, adequate and effective" compensation for expropriated property.

He also took up the sensitive issue, for a Catholic, of birth control. It was obvious that the population explosion was wiping out the gains in economic growth and threatening the hope for any substantial, material progress. The United Nations survey estimated that by 1980, Latin America would have a population of 363 million, an increase of more than 50 per cent in fifteen years. While in Lima, he met privately with a group of Peruvian senators. His first question to them was "what are you doing about birth control in South America?" They were surprised that this young, wealthy, Catholic father of nine children would ask such a question. Kennedy cited their answer in his speech: "The rich nations who worry about population growth are concerned about reducing the number of Puerto Ricans, Hindus, Negroes, Chinese and Mexicans; or else, of certain classes and social groups, like the poor, the working class, or the Catholics. But they do not worry, for example, about the increase of Aryans, of Protestants or of Rotarians." He considered the argument unsound, but indicative of the strong emotional feeling that surrounded the question. He recommended that the U.S. provide assistance to nations which decided that family planning and population control were in their national interest, but only in response to their initiative.

Kennedy's speech was given close attention in the Latin and U.S. press, but it was to have little impact on his own country. It was the last time he was to direct major attention to Latin America. The Administration continued in the path that it had chosen. None of the recommendations he made were implemented. The fire of the Alliance gradually died out, as the Mann policies were continued and the government's preoccupation with Southeast Asia resulted in increasingly less attention to Latin problems. The conditions Kennedy had observed on his trip worsened. Enmity toward the United States grew. Less than four years after Kennedy's visit, Nelson Rockefeller visited Latin America and was met by violence, in places where Kennedy had drawn cheers and affection. It was not that the Latin people had a personal hostility toward Nelson Rockefeller, but the hope people had for the United States had been allowed to die out, and Rockefeller became the target of the resentment that replaced it.

During Kennedy's trip, incredulous reporters asked him why he was making the effort to visit a remote village or distant sugar-cane planta-tion. Kennedy answered in mock seriousness that he had to because he was "running for President of the world." He had gone to South America already committed to the Alliance for Progress be-cause it was President Kennedy's program. But in his "campaign tour" of the world, he saw suffering, hunger, hope and hopelessness that he believed were related to America's power and responsibilities. He re-turned to the Senate with his own ideas of how to carry out his brother's programs. Apart from suggesting how the Alliance should respond to new problems, Robert Kennedy had little influence on his nation's Latin policy. In this important area, there was little a senator could do. It was clear, however, that if Kennedy were ever to win the presidency the enormous needs of Latin America would be the subject of new policies and different approaches.

10

FAMILY AND FRIENDS

Kennedy did not draw a sharp distinction between his social and professional acquaintances. Most of his friends were people who, during various periods of his life, shared his interests and ambitions. There were his friends from school who had moved to Washington with the New Frontier, men like David Hackett from Milton Academy and the late Dean Markham from Harvard. Their bond to him was marked by unquestioning loyalty. They understood his moods and his purposes and he could totally relax with them. Another group, like John Siegenthaler, Edwin Guthman, Burke Marshall, and Kenneth O'Donnell were men with whom he had worked closely in the Rackets Committee and the Justice Department. They, too, were his contemporaries and he continued to seek their advice and judgment in all of the significant personal and public decisions he had to make.

There were two other groups of friends who did not fit into the traditional categories. The first, considerably older than he, were men he had come to know and admire while they served as his colleagues in his brother's administration: Robert McNamara, Maxwell Taylor, Douglas Dillon, Averell Harriman, men of substantial public reputation before Kennedy met them. Having worked with him as Attorney General they admired his talents, respected his judgment, enjoyed his company and did everything possible to encourage his career. Thomas L. Watson, chairman of the Board of IBM, although he had not worked officially for President Kennedy, was also in this group.

Among other men who became his close friends were John Glenn, first American to orbit the earth; James Whittaker, first American to climb Mount Everest; Roosevelt Grier, football star of the Los Angeles Rams; and Rafer Johnson, Olympic Decathlon Champion. In the final months, they would set aside their own public careers and private business to travel and campaign with him. What attracted him to them initially was not their fame. It was the fact that each of them, in his own way, had survived personal tests involving supreme physical effort, often the danger of death. Courage was the virtue he admired in men over any other, regarding it, as Winston Churchill did, as "the first of human qualities because it is the quality which guarantees all others."

Kennedy's family always remained the most important part of his life. It was not a matter of "finding time" for his children. They were an ever-present part of him. His father had shown him how to be both a busy man and a family man. Following that example, he managed to be with his family constantly, if not in person, then by telephone, from wherever he was.

One of Kennedy's regrets about his heavy schedule was that it separated him for long periods of time from his family. He often spoke of the need for young children to be with their father and insisted on returning to Hickory Hill whenever possible. He did not like Washington in the summer with his family away. "Sometimes," he said, "people think that because you have money and position you are immune from the human experience. But I can feel as lonesome and lost as the next man when I turn the key in the door and go into an empty house that is usually full of kids and dogs."

Home for the Kennedys was Hickory Hill, a large white mansion which had been the headquarters of the Union Army during the Civil War. It stood in the verdant, rolling country of McLean, Virginia, rural, horse-riding country when the Kennedys moved to it in 1955, but steadily suburbanized in more recent years by the encroachment of the huge, hidden headquarters of the Central Intelligence Agency and the increasing population pressure of metropolitan Washington. The house, a large and graceful structure originally built in 1810, was situated on a modest hill with sloping lawns and landscaped grounds surrounding it. A tennis court, almost always in use by family and friends on seasonal days, was in the far corner of the property. In back was a pool, and a bath house that also provided shelter for weekend movies.

A sense of personalized history filled the house. Near the entry was a letter from Franklin Delano Roosevelt written in 1939 to fourteen-year-old Robert Kennedy, commending him on his hobby of stamp collecting and inviting him to see the presidential collection at the White House. On the tables were autographed pictures of Winston Churchill, Konrad Adenauer, and Herbert Hoover, whom Kennedy had worked for as a young lawyer on the Government Reorganization Commission. Lincoln's Emancipation Proclamation, mounted on an easel, dominated the den. On one wall was a copy of President Kennedy's Inaugural Address inscribed "to Bobby from Jack—Christmas, 1961." To a guest, the house was a wild, informal mixture of a children's playground, menagerie, upbeat discotheque, and a humming political headquarters.

Home in the summers was a smaller white clapboard Cape Codder in Hyannis Port, the place where the deepest roots were planted. All the summers of his life were spent there. Ambassador and Mrs. Joseph P. Kennedy lived in the sprawling house next door, where their children had grown up, and all the brothers and sisters had homes within a mile. The profusion of children, cousins, friends and animals gave the "compound" the atmosphere of a happy summer camp. Whatever separate ways careers led them, the summer brought the family together for weeks of sailing, tennis, water skiing, the perennial touch football, and long picnics aboard the Marlin.

The center of the home, and of his life, was Ethel Skakel Kennedy. It is impossible to overestimate her meaning to him. She shared his energy, his humor, his interests, his enthusiasms, his friends and, zestfully, his enemies. She mothered eleven children, managed one of the most complicated households in the nation, and made the success of her marriage the most important purpose of her life. She succeeded to such an extent that after seventeen years of marriage her husband sought her company above all others. In 1951, while at Sun Valley, he had sent her a note which she kept and gave to herself as a Christmas present in 1968. Quoting from the Bible, he wrote: "And Ruth said: Entreat me not to leave Thee, or to return from following after Thee, for whither Thou goeth I will go; and where Thou lodgest I will lodge; Thy people shall be my people and Thy God my God. When Thou diest then will I die and we will be together forever."[1]

Ethel Kennedy is a person of profound faith and strong opinions who encouraged and strengthened her husband's feeling about injustice. The suffering of others became her anguish too. Once in 1965, he visited the Willowbrook Hospital for retarded children on Staten Island and was appalled at the conditions of filth, carelessness, and over-crowding that surrounded them. Without notice, Ethel Kennedy visited Willowbrook six months later to see if promised improvements had been made—and responsible state officials are still hearing from her. On another occasion, while riding near Hickory Hill, she came across an emaciated horse whose owner had starved and neglected it. Without hesitation, she led it to her own stable for care. When the owner brought a lawsuit accusing her of theft, she prepared for that trial as though facing life imprisonment, absolutely determined that the owner be compelled to accept responsibility for the animal's condition. There may have been a moment when she feared the newspaper publicity would harm her husband, but he was unconcerned. He was proud of the risk she had taken and joked about being "married to a horse thief." Ethel won the case.

The Kennedys had seven children in the first eight years of their marriage and four more later on. For weekend guests, it was an awesome sight to see the table set for family breakfast on a Sunday morning. Kennedy occasionally had trouble keeping the children's names straight, especially when all the boys were dressed up in identical blue blazers and gray pants. Making his election eve television show in New York in 1964, he failed twice to list his children in the order of their birth.

He knew that having so many children ran counter to the accepted American fashion, but he felt the size of a family should be an individual decision, and he and Ethel wanted to have as many children

[1] Kennedy's memory of the biblical quotation was essentially accurate. The Douay version of the book of Ruth, published in 1949 by the Catholic Book Publishing Co. reads: "Be not against me, to desire that I should leave Thee and depart; for whithersoever Thou shalt go, I will go; and where thou shalt dwell, I also will dwell. Thy people shall be my people, and thy God my God. The land that shall receive Thee dying, in the same will I die; and There will I be buried."

as they could. The size of his family was a favorite subject of his public humor. "I took a vote among my family to see their preference for President," he would say in the 1968 campaign. "Three are for me, two are for McCarthy, two are leaning to Humphrey, two are undecided and the youngest is sticking with Dr. Spock."

Although zealots for birth control shuddered every time he appeared with his brood, the Kennedys' attitude was completely favorable to the idea of family planning. When Patrick Cardinal O'Boyle of the diocese of Washington announced his intention to read a pastoral letter sternly denouncing the critics of the Papal encyclical on birth control, Ethel Kennedy was prepared to join the dissenters in walking out of the Sunday service, but the letter was not read in her McLean parish church. The Kennedys loved children and could afford to have eleven of them without concern about their financial security. Each child received a generous trust fund from grandfather Kennedy at birth. But the Kennedys had no intention to force their example on families where poverty and ill health distorted the possibilities of family happiness. Both parents guided the children's daily lives, and found time for each one. Growing up in such a large family was in many ways beneficial. Children who could have easily been spoiled learned the requirements of cooperation. The older ones helped care for the younger. Discipline was often better enforced by their peers than by their parents.

Kennedy tried to recreate in his home the family activities that had meant so much to him as a boy. His children participated in touch football games almost as soon as they could walk. His staff would arrive for a morning meeting at Hickory Hill to find him conducting a breakfast classroom, asking his children, as his mother had asked him, what they had read in the newspapers, and what they thought about it. He discouraged them from feeling sorry for themselves by making light of their falls, bumps and bruises. The Kennedy household had the same petty fights, competitions and jealousies that any home experiences. Douglas Harriman Kennedy was born shortly after the christening of the aircraft carrier *John F. Kennedy* in 1967. After Douglas' christening, Christopher, age four, who was already outspoken and fearless, asked, "Daddy, why didn't they hit him with a champagne bottle like they did the ship?" On another occasion, at supper, Kennedy asked Bobby, Jr., if he had "done anything kind this week."

"I put a coat over a puddle so that Courtney wouldn't step in the water."

"Whose coat?" Kennedy asked.

"It was Courtney's coat."

Each child was encouraged to develop his own interests. Joe, Jr., the oldest boy, became proficient at sports. Courtney developed a skill at painting. One of her oils was hung in the Washington Gallery of Art. Bobby, Jr.'s specialty was animals, so he was allowed to keep a small zoo in the basement complete with snakes, monkeys, an anteater and a falcon; but to purchase them, he had to earn his own money. The eldest child, Kathleen, was educated in the strict atmosphere of a Catholic convent school but when she chose to finish high school at Putney, one of the most progressive schools in the country, her parents made no attempt to dissuade her.

If Kennedy had an exceptional gentleness and perception about children, part of the reason was that he had as much experience in loving children as any man. If he developed a special sensitivity toward youthful suffering in the ghetto and the rural slum, it was partly because he saw there the contrast between what others lacked and what his children had. The Kennedys had special obligations, not just because they were wealthy or because their uncle had been President of the United States, but because they meant something to one another.

The other important members of the Kennedy household were the dogs. There were four, perhaps five; no one was quite sure. The children liked them to participate in their activities. Kennedy liked to have a couple with him when he walked off alone in thought. The most noticeable was Brumus, a huge, black Newfoundland who looked ferocious and sometimes was. Like Lennie in *Of Mice and Men,* he wanted to be friendly, but his size was an obstacle to his wish. At buffet dinners, Brumus would sample the food and sometimes the guests. Once, when he took Art Buchwald's leg in his mouth, Buchwald "retained" a prominent Washington attorney to bring suit, alleging Brumus had caused Buchwald traumatic shock necessitating an extended stay at Martha's Vineyard at a $2000 a month rent.

In his years in the Senate, Robert Kennedy probably spent a third of his working hours as President Kennedy's public legatee. With Jacqueline Kennedy in partial seclusion, he took on most of the burden created by the flood of requests and obligations that poured in. He was the one who had to approve the arrangements by which the X-rays, clothing, and other evidence of the events in Dallas were to be made available to specialists, and later to scholars. He attended the masses and memorial tributes. His permission was sought by those wishing to rename things in memory of President Kennedy.

Many of those who had helped his brother on the road to the Presidency had scattered, but he felt a special obligation to them also. If a man who had helped win a critical primary went broke, Kennedy loaned him money. If another could not hold a job, he put him on his own payroll. He was forever recommending Kennedy stalwarts for employment or intervening to keep them from being fired. He listened to their woes, shared their joys, and consoled them in their personal grief. When a campaign acquaintance was indicted, Kennedy helped him retain the best criminal lawyer in Arizona for his defense, and he was acquitted.

If a serious book or film was in preparation on the Kennedy presidency, and many were, the producer sought his imprimatur. He had no illusions about rewriting history. His interest was in seeing to it that historians would know the President and what he had tried to do, as those who worked with him had observed it.

To Kennedy, these were not just obligations. They were a vital part of his life. He defended his brother's reputation against exploitation and error as fiercely as he had defended him in life against political attacks. He read every word written about his brother's life and sent personal notes of appreciation to all who treated him generously.

Out of these feelings and responsibilities came the celebrated controversy with William Manchester over the book *Death of a President*. In retrospect, the Manchester incident was an extension of the Dallas tragedy. The basic decisions related to the writing of the book were made in March, 1964, at a time when Robert Kennedy could not think about the events of November without anguished effort. There were a number of conflicting realities that prompted the decision. Clearly, the detailed account of those four days would have historical importance as well as compelling contemporary interest. As memories fade, there was some urgency in having the participants tell their stories at the earliest possible time. Mrs. Jacqueline Kennedy was isolated by loneliness, but at the same time she was the most publicized woman in the world. Factual inaccuracies were appearing in news stories and were leading to serious and unnecessary misunderstandings.

Robert Kennedy was not interested in an authorized history of the events; but he was anxious to have an authentic history, authentic at least from the point of view of those who shared those grim hours with the Kennedy family. In accepting the recommendation that Manchester be asked to undertake the project, Kennedy chose a man whose previous work had shown an uncritical admiration of the President. He should have entrusted the decision and the details of the contract to associates and attorneys expert in literary law. Instead, he personally approved the selection of Manchester and the agreement, confident that the express language empowering Jacqueline Kennedy and himself to have final text approval was sufficient to avoid any future disagreements. With this power in mind, it was not necessary, in his judgment, to have another detailed agreement about the use of the tape transcripts of the interview of Mrs. Kennedy by Manchester. She gave the interview as part of the oral history for the Kennedy library, and presumably she could control its use by Manchester through the power of final editing given by the agreement.

As the book neared completion two years later, misunderstandings escalated. Kennedy did not want to read the Manchester work himself. The wounds of the Dallas events were still too raw. He asked four friends with editorial and journalistic experience to review it. Goodwin, Guthman, Schlesinger, and Siegenthaler made some important editorial suggestions, particularly tempering the author's hostility to Lyndon Johnson. When the "final" text was submitted to Jacqueline Kennedy, she was distressed by the personal references, especially as they affected her children. Efforts were made to reconcile the differences, but they foundered on the iron will of a protective mother and the growing exhaustion of a proud writer. The problems were further complicated by an unprecedented offer from *Look* magazine to Manchester of $650,000 for the serial rights to the book. The tangled facts may be long debated, but the realities Robert Kennedy faced were clear; his first obligation, in his mind, was to support Jacqueline Kennedy's position regardless of the political and public consequences to himself. He saw the agreement simply as giving the right of final consent to him and Mrs. Kennedy. They were not interested in editing what other people had told Manchester or the author's own impressions, but they were determined to have the final judgment on matters of taste and privacy related to what the two of them had told Manchester.

Legal counsel advised that the agreement did give Mrs. Kennedy such a right and that a lawsuit was the only means of enforcing it. When both Manchester and representatives of *Look* refused to make any further deletions, the decision was made to go ahead with litigation. The result was harmful to everyone. Given the subject matter of the book and the public identification of the Kennedys, a lawsuit could only bring resentment, not satisfaction.[2] He made the fight because of his sense of obligation to the President's widow and children. It was a battle that could not be won and the scars were deep and damaging.

By the time Kennedy was elected to the Senate, his father, the late Joseph P. Kennedy, was seventy-six years old and in the fourth year of severe physical handicap resulting from a stroke he had suffered shortly after his son's inauguration as President. He spent his winters in Palm Beach, and the rest of the year in Hyannis Port, with infrequent trips to his office in New York. He was confined to a wheelchair and his speech was seriously impaired, but his mind was active and he followed everything his children did. Joseph Kennedy's health was frail enough to be always of concern and several times he suffered temporary cerebral incidents. Kennedy would marvel at his father's strength, fighting his way back after every reverse. It was almost a miracle of will.

Robert Kennedy was deeply devoted to his father, and keenly aware

[2] A solution might have been to submit the deletions suggested by Mrs. Kennedy to an objective panel of editors, approved by all parties, with the understanding that they would have the final decision as to what was personal, private, and a matter of taste, as opposed to what changes were being asked for political reasons—which only the author should control. Such an effort was agreed upon with the German magazine publishers, who were intensely hostile to the family efforts to edit the manuscript. The German panel agreed to 95 per cent of the suggested changes, agreeing that they were tasteless intrusions on the privacy of Mrs. Kennedy and her family. The remaining 5 per cent, which were considered to have political overtones, had actually been suggested by the editors of *Look*, not by the Kennedy family.

of the upbringing and the advantages he had received from him. The Ambassador had made each of his children independently wealthy, using his resources to free his sons rather than hold them. Kennedy called his father regularly to report on his activities and made special trips to New York to have dinner with him. When on the Cape, he saw his father every day, always bringing some of his own children with him to visit. He was struck by the loyalty some of the older political leaders in New York still showed "the Ambassador."

In a book of essays compiled by Edward Kennedy, Robert expressed his feelings about his father this way:

> I don't believe he is without faults. But when we were young, perhaps because of the strength of his character or the massiveness of his personality, they were unobserved or at least, unimportant. When we grew a little older we realized he wasn't perfect; that he made mistakes, but by that time we realized everyone did. In many, many ways, to us he is something special.
>
> He has called on the best that was in us. There was no such thing as half-trying. Whether it was running a race or catching a football, competing in school—we were to try. And we were to try harder than anyone else. We might not be the best, and none us were, but we were to make the effort to be the best. "After you have done the best you can," he used to say, "the hell with it." What it really all adds up to is love—not love as it is described with such facility in popular magazines, but the kind of love that is affection and respect, order, encouragement and support.
>
> He knew if he insisted on remaining in the center of national affairs, we would continue to be known as his children. He would be the dominating figure, the personality, the spokesman for the family. And in how many other families have the young been stultified. Again and again, young men with ability and talent have been kept from taking their places in the affairs of business or on the national stage because an older figure refused to make room and insisted on the glory and attention until the very end. He decided, I believe consciously, this would not happen in our family. The most important thing to him was the advancement of his children. His sole concern was to contribute to that advancement. After the end of World War II, he decided this aim could best be accomplished by doing what, for a strong figure, is probably the most difficult thing to do—to submerge his own personality. This is what he did.

My father has believed we could think and decide things for ourselves. There have been disagreements, sometimes violent, on politics, economics, the future of the country, the world. But he has stimulated them. If his sons had a different philosophy, were more optimistic about the future of life on this planet, then in a more mellow mood he would say, "If I were your age I would hold those views also."

His interest in life has been his children—not his business, not his accomplishments, not his friends, but his children. Any lasting contributions we might have made have been in a large part due to the effect he had in our lives.[3]

Robert Kennedy's mother, Rose Fitzgerald Kennedy, also in her seventies, enjoyed good health and was extremely active. Her deep religious faith helped her overcome the tragedies of the family. She kept a brisk schedule of her own, traveling alone between Cape Cod, New York, Paris, and Palm Beach. She amazed everyone with the youthfulness of her appearance. In her younger days she had been a schoolteacher, and she retained a zest for teaching. She wrote out her own speeches and carried on a lively correspondence with her children about thrift and other virtues. She kept a card file on each of her children, going back to when they had been inoculated against childhood diseases, and kept up an active and critical interest in their activities. The interest of President Kennedy and his wife in culture was highly publicized, but they and the other members of the family would have agreed that Mrs. Joseph Kennedy was the prime patron of the arts in the family. She spoke German and French, and could enjoy both music and art from a background of many years of experience and personal acquaintance with artists of all kinds on both sides of the Atlantic.

Robert Kennedy and his brothers acquired their zest for campaigning from their mother's side of the family. Her father, John F. (Honey Fitz) Fitzgerald, had been mayor of Boston in the glory days of Irish ascendency in that city. She campaigned for her father, and later for all her own sons. At teas and on television, she was tireless and charming. Although Kennedy treated her with affectionate respect and gen-

[3] From *The Fruitful Bough*, edited by Edward M. Kennedy. Privately printed, 1966. Reproduced by permission of the editor.

tleness, even she was not safe from his banter. "Now I would like to introduce my mother," he would say at rallies. "Mother has been campaigning for the Democratic Party since Grover Cleveland."

"Why, Bobby—I have not," she would reply firmly, with a smile.

The relationship Robert Kennedy had with his older brother could not be re-established with anyone. But with his brother Edward, he developed another relationship equally as strong and significant in their mutual careers. They confided intimately in one another and consulted each other on every important decision. In the Senate they had special telephone numbers so they could communicate quickly and privately. They spent long periods discussing political and family problems, in that conversational shorthand used by people who understand each other perfectly.

Six years separated them in age, a sufficient gulf of time and experience to allow the older to be the mentor of the younger. Their strengths complemented each other. Robert regarded his younger brother as having a brilliant political instinct and trusted it above all others. In describing the senator from Massachusetts, the senator from New York would say he was more congenial, more relaxed, more patient, more tolerant of imperfection, more gracious than himself. Edward Kennedy depended on his brother, for advice, example and strength, more than on any other man.

When Edward Kennedy, not quite thirty, decided to run for the Senate, Robert was one of those around the President who encouraged his decision. Then Attorney General, he personally flew to Massachusetts to brief his brother before his crucial debates with Edward McCormack, the most critical confrontations of the campaign. The day after Robert's victory in New York in November 1965, he visited his brother, who was still recuperating from his airplane crash in a Boston hospital. As they posed for pictures together, a photographer asked Robert to move over because his brother was in his shadow. "That's the way it's going to be from now on," Edward joked.

They were totally devoted to each other's careers. Whatever problems they faced, they faced them together. When Senator Everett Dirksen threatened to release material wrongly relating Frank Morrissey to Mafia figures, it was Robert Kennedy who faced him down, even though Morrissey was Edward Kennedy's recommendation for the federal judicial appointment in 1965.

Their relationship in the Senate was one of competition, not rivalry. Their recorded votes were usually the same because their viewpoints and constituencies were similar, but they deliberately concentrated on different activities. Robert Kennedy declined an invitation to join the Judiciary Committee, offered him as a former Attorney General, because Edward Kennedy was on it already. While they served together on the Labor and Public Welfare Committee, Robert concentrated on educational problems, Edward on matters relating to health and medical research.

In their family's tradition, they used each other as an object of public humor. Edward Kennedy began almost every public speech with what he called "Bobby jokes." He would refer to his brother's relations with the President—"Bobby and President Johnson are enjoying their annual lunar New Year's truce"; or to the size of his family—"every time the President announces a new cabinet member, Bobby announces a new baby"; or to his presidential ambitions— "Bobby is house hunting. There's a house he's interested in on Pennsylvania Avenue, but it is already occupied and the present owners give no intention that they want to move out." To the baseball writers dinner, he told how "when I turned thirty and was about to announce for the Senate I was offered a $75,000 bonus to choose baseball instead of politics. The offer came from my brother Bobby." At the time of the controversy over Governor George Romney's charge that on his trip to Vietnam he had been "brainwashed," Edward Kennedy said "a lot of people have tried to brainwash Bobby, but they decided all he really needs is a hair wash."

In turn, Robert Kennedy did not spare his brother. Speaking in Massachusetts prior to the 1966 State Convention, he said:

"I want to assure all Massachusetts Democratic candidates that my brother Ted favors an open convention. That's a convention where the delegates fully consider all the possibilities, debate all their merits and then pick whomever Teddy selects . . ."

And there would be laughs about their supposed competing ambitions:

"Teddy's going to Buffalo tomorrow night to speak at a county dinner isn't he?"

"Yes," a friend replied.

"And isn't he in Delaware today?"

"Yes."

"And didn't he see the Pope last week and also go to Geneva?"

"Yes."

"Do you know something I don't know about his plans?"

But in fact, they were not rivals for public honors. It was accepted as a reality, beyond discussion within the family circle, that Robert would be the one to seek the Presidency. No one was a greater champion of his brother's aspiration than Edward Kennedy. He understood that he was spared much criticism because Robert was the candidate for higher office and therefore the lightning rod for political attack. They were "Robbie" and "Eddie" to each other. Together they were inseparable in their trust, confidence and affection.

They came from a family where brothers always relied on one another. When President Kennedy was killed, Robert could turn to his younger brother to share the grief, and together hope for brighter days. After June 1968, Edward Kennedy was alone. The obligations of his family and its reputation were his alone to bear, and the man to whom he always turned for guidance was not there to help. Few had ever been burdened so suddenly with so heavy a load.

11

NEW YORK:
THE CONTEST FOR GOVERNOR, 1966

All of the pitfalls New York politics held for Robert Kennedy showed up in the shattered expectations of the Democratic party in the election for Governor in 1966. The gubernatorial contest, the major political struggle in New York that year, had begun several months prior to the Surrogate's primary, but that victory placed Kennedy in a key position to influence the selection of the Democratic nominee. Before, it would have been difficult for the Democratic Convention to nominate anyone Kennedy opposed. Now, it appeared that the Convention might nominate the candidate he preferred.

There was little participation by party members in the selection process. Candidates for all state offices, including governor and senator, were selected at conventions, attended by delegates chosen and controlled for the most part by the county leaders. Since the New York City leaders controlled a majority of the delegates, they in effect chose the candidates, if they could agree among themselves. The process lent itself to classical smoke-filled-room bargaining and a certain remoteness on the part of the delegates. The idea that five men who were more concerned about their political power than their party's appeal could pick the Democratic candidate for what was probably the most important governorship in the United States, and that this procedure was accepted by the delegates practically without question,

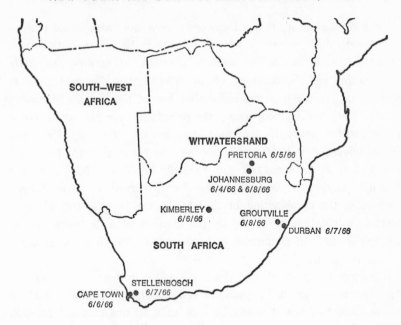

SOUTH AFRICAN ITINERARY—1966

illustrated the remoteness of the Democratic party from its own grass roots and the difficulty it would have in regaining power in New York.

Nevertheless, by the summer of 1966, it was generally agreed that the Democrats, by default, had an excellent opportunity to regain the governorship they had lost to Nelson Rockefeller eight years before. Rockefeller's decline—far greater than the normal attrition of eight years in office—was in part related to his broken promise, made in the previous gubernatorial campaign, not to raise taxes. Even with spiraling taxes, the quality of state services was declining. Each day citizens were reminded of the new levies as merchants, making change, took their "two cents for Rocky" for the sales tax levy enacted in 1965.

Rockefeller's own opinion polls showed him losing to every antici- pated Democratic candidate. The situation caused such alarms within the Republican party that an effort was begun to have Senator Jacob Javits challenge Rockefeller for the nomination. It would have been one of the colossal confrontations of New York Republican politics, but Javits resisted the pressures.

Kennedy was aware that a Democratic governor, with broad patronage powers and an ability to move around the state continuously, would be in a far better position than he to control the party organization, and the make-up of the delegation to the next national convention. He was also reminded that five of the last six governors of New York had actively sought the presidency. He did not welcome a competitive figure in the state, but he felt that any Democrat elected governor in 1966 would not become his rival, since he would have to run on the same ticket as Kennedy in 1970. While Kennedy's personal political interest might be better served by Rockefeller's re-election, the combination of the state's, the party's, and his own interests would best be served by the election of a Democrat whose nomination he had sponsored and who would therefore be indebted to him politically.

If Kennedy tried to dictate the nomination, however, and failed at the convention, or if his hand-picked candidate were defeated in the election, he knew it would be seen as a serious personal setback. He therefore set two tests for his active participation on behalf of a candidate for the nomination: confidence in the personal loyalty of the candidate and a good expectation of victory.

None of the men who sought the Democratic nomination met Kennedy's double test. The leading candidate was Frank O'Connor, a product of the Queens County organization, who had been elected president of the New York City Council the previous year by a large margin as Beame was losing to Lindsay. A former criminal defense lawyer, O'Connor had made a notable record in fifteen years as Queens district attorney, where he had been especially solicitous of civil liberties. But his political sponsorship, and his earlier conservative record in the state Senate, made him suspect in liberal circles.

Another candidate was the former Undersecretary of Commerce, Franklin D. Roosevelt, Jr., who had launched his own political career as a reform Democrat, beating the Tammany candidate for Congress in New York City in 1949. Roosevelt sought his party's designation for governor in 1954 but lost out to Averell Harriman. He then accepted the nomination for Attorney General, but while Harriman was winning by a minuscule margin, Roosevelt was defeated by Jacob Javits, in part, he felt, because Carmine DeSapio ordered leaders in

Catholic areas not to work in his behalf. Roosevelt still bore the most revered name in New York politics and ran well in the 1966 polls.[1]

Less known at this stage of the campaign were Eugene Nickerson, Nassau County Executive, a handsome, patrician and earnest man, who for five years had run one of the nation's largest suburban governments and drew well in a strongly Republican area; and Howard Samuels, the only active upstate candidate, who had made money in plastics in the Rochester area and was running as a successful business-man. Samuels was an indefatigable campaigner, but he had no previous experience in public affairs and was unacceptable to labor leaders and the Liberal Party because of alleged anti-union practices in his factory.

Roosevelt, Jr., presented a complex and difficult problem. Kennedy knew him well and liked him personally. He was the most forthright on the issues; of the four, only he had risked the displeasure of the county leaders by endorsing Silverman. He had won the loyalty of the Kennedy family with his crucial support in the 1960 West Virginia primary, and Kennedy's father, in gratitude, had made a contribution to his gubernatorial campaign. The pressures on Kennedy were somewhat relieved by Roosevelt's supreme confidence that he would garner the necessary support on his own. Reports of conversations would come back to Kennedy where Roosevelt was telling mutual friends, months before the convention, that the senator had better climb aboard the bandwagon or risk being left behind. Kennedy could hardly believe Roosevelt's estimate of his strength, but was quite content to withhold his own attitude until evidence of that strength was made public.

Of the four candidates, Kennedy felt Roosevelt would be the hardest for him to sell to the convention. But O'Connor, the only one who

[1] Kennedy occasionally mused about how Roosevelt's career illustrated the vagaries of politics. Had Roosevelt won the Democratic nomination for governor in 1954, Kennedy felt he probably would have been elected President in 1960, instead of his brother. Charles Buckley had told him how Roosevelt had thrown away the possibility of Buckley's support at the 1954 convention. Buckley had been leaning toward Roosevelt as a far better speaker and campaigner than his rival for the nomination, Averell Harriman. But when Buckley accepted an invitation to lunch with Roosevelt for the purpose of negotiating the terms of his support, Roosevelt's first words to him were: "I've got twenty county leaders with me, and you had better get on the bandwagon."

"I didn't know that was why you invited me to lunch," Buckley said rising from the table without eating. Whereupon he called Harriman to assure him of his support.

could win the convention without his help was, because of his weakness with the liberals, potentially the most difficult to elect. Nickerson had no chance to be nominated without an all-out Kennedy effort, and even then the result was far from certain. Unlike the Surrogate's race, which the voters decided, this nomination was in the hands of the party organizations, many of which would be hostile to an attempt by Kennedy to impose his choice over their desires.

Weighing these considerations prior to the Silverman campaign, Kennedy decided not to back a candidate at that time. He felt the best thing he could do was to open up the nominating process as much as possible so that the eventual candidate could lay claim to grass-roots support and avoid the stigma of "boss selection." In March 1966, with this in mind, he wrote a public letter to John Burns, urging that the state committee sponsor a series of forums at which all potential candidates could appear. At the same time he tried to interest prominent New Yorkers not identified with partisan politics to become candidates for the governorship.[2] With Kennedy fully committed to such a person, the convention might have nominated a candidate whose non-political status would have helped win the necessary independent support in the general election.

The forums, which began in May, proved a breakthrough for no one. Only Roosevelt, O'Connor, Nickerson, and Samuels participated. Since they disagreed on almost nothing, little interest was stirred, the occasions serving primarily for mass denunciation of Rockefeller.

In the flush of the Silverman victory, it was widely assumed that Kennedy could pick the Democratic nominee for governor if he wished to do so. In fact, the day after the primary, a New York City radio station reported he was about to endorse Nickerson. If Kennedy were going to impose his personal choice, this would have been the best time to do it. Numerous Democratic leaders were urging him to state a preference. But though he wanted the Democrats to pick someone who could win the election and use the governor's power to begin a basic reform of the party, he was unwilling to make the

[2] Approaches were made, through intermediaries, to the president of Cornell University, Dr. James Perkins and John Gardner, at that time Secretary of the Department of Health, Education and Welfare. Perkins was ineligible because he had not been a resident of the state for five years. Gardner turned out to be a registered New York Republican.

personal commitment of time, energy, and resources that were required if a candidate were to run under his banner. By the summer of 1966, he was becoming increasingly involved with Vietnam and the urban problems which were part of his growing commitments in the Senate. He had also agreed to campaign in the fall for Democratic candidates around the country, and this would consume a major part of his time. If he chose one candidate over another, he would also have to assume the major burden of getting him elected, including the financing of the campaign (he had personally been left with 85 per cent of the deficit of the Silverman campaign). The more he thought about it, the more he believed his Silverman success had been, as columnist James Wechsler wrote, a "perverse entrapment, wiping out his original strategy of staying above his Party's divisions, raising expectations he was not prepared to fulfill."

Kennedy often said Nickerson "would be a fine governor if he could get elected," and there was no question of his loyal support of Kennedy on the national scene. But Nickerson was not a forceful campaigner and the polls showed he was neither well known state-wide nor favored among most Democratic voters. In fact, two weeks before the state convention he had fewer delegate commitments than he had when he announced in February. This meant that Kennedy would have to force the convention to nominate Nickerson, thereby assuming full political responsibility for the election result.

O'Connor's position regarding a political alliance with Kennedy was at best unreliable. Kennedy could never understand why O'Connor and his associates made such an effort to see and be seen with Vice President Hubert Humphrey. If O'Connor wanted to be governor, he observed, Humphrey could not help him and certainly the Kennedy forces would be less than enthusiastic about electing a Democrat as governor who might well favor Humphrey over Kennedy in 1972. While Kennedy liked O'Connor and considered him an able and decent man, he recognized that O'Connor came out of the same mold as the disastrous organization candidates of the past, who were singularly unsuccessful in winning the independent-liberal support that was essential for victory.

On July 8, O'Connor formally announced his candidacy. In a month he had become the front runner for the nomination, with 200 committed delegates and another 200 upstate delegates, who told him they would back him if he was not unacceptable to Kennedy (573 votes were needed to nominate). A poll taken for Kennedy showed O'Connor was the first choice among Democratic voters, with Roosevelt a close second and Nickerson and Samuels far behind. It soon became apparent that the large, controlled delegations of Brooklyn and the Bronx would back O'Connor, assuring his nomination.

But on July 23, the race was rocked by a charge, made by Roosevelt, that Buckley and Steingut had secretly committed their support to O'Connor over a year before, at a meeting in Buckley's home, in return for O'Connor's agreement to withdraw from the primary for the Democratic nomination for mayor, leaving their organizations free to support Beame. This agreement had been generally assumed among Democratic politicians. To the professionals, it was an appropriate and shrewd arrangement. Roosevelt, about to be denied a second time by the system of "boss control," decided to risk everything and make the charges publicly, arguing that if he did not do it the Republicans would, once the campaign was underway.

The controversy blazed and generated more and more heat as the media welcomed some excitement during the pre-convention doldrums. The New York *Times* said, "The nomination process has been compromised and predetermined by the Democratic bosses, reducing the forums and elections of convention delegates in the June primary to a farce." O'Connor steadfastly denied any such deal existed. His forces countercharged that Roosevelt had offered to support him for mayor in 1965 if O'Connor would promise to support him for governor. George Daly, the public relations director of the Beame campaign, alleged that Roosevelt had made a similar offer to Wagner in 1965 (prior to his announcement he would not run) if Wagner promised to support him for governor. Columnist Murray Kempton commented that Roosevelt's charge reminded him of "a man who tried to buy liquor from a respectable bootlegger and was turned back as already drunk enough and forthwith began screaming that the country was controlled by bootleggers."

On August 11, the Liberal party indicated that because of the Buckley-Steingut deal, they would "under no circumstances" be able to back O'Connor, and if he were nominated, would run a third-party candidate for Governor. O'Connor, who was an unusually candid politician, was quoted as saying in reply: "There is a strange suspicion among many of the leaders of the Liberal party concerning an Irishman. And to have an Irish-Catholic District Attorney—no matter what your record, no matter what your promise—it's hard to convince them you are really a liberal." The comment was artless. On hearing it, Alex Rose immediately named off a long list of Irish Catholics his party had supported and accused O'Connor of raising "an ugly religious issue."[3]

In the fusillade, the Democratic party in New York slumped to the ground, gravely wounded once more by its own adherents. Damaged by the controversy, O'Connor moved to line up sufficient delegates outside New York City to be nominated without the benefit of the votes involved in the alleged "deal." The charges created a backlash against Roosevelt among regular Democratic leaders around the state, making it easier for O'Connor to gain their endorsements. On August 13, O'Connor won 27 of the 34 votes of Suffolk County, forcing Nickerson to withdraw from the race. The last obstacle to O'Connor's nomination was now Robert Kennedy.

Kennedy's conversations with Rose and Dubinsky convinced him that the Liberal party would offer Roosevelt their party's nomination, and that Roosevelt would accept it. Although the latest polls still showed any Democrat defeating Rockefeller, Kennedy foresaw the charges of "bossism" and the Liberal defection exacting their usual toll. When pro-Kennedy county chairmen called to say they were under heavy pressure to endorse O'Connor because he was so close to the votes needed for the nomination, Kennedy said, "I understand your problems, but with O'Connor and Roosevelt running against each other I think we are going to take a bath in the fall."

His judgment that O'Connor would lose led Kennedy to make a last attempt to promote a new candidate. He looked to Sol M. Linowitz, an attorney from Rochester, New York, who had gained public attention and a considerable fortune as an executive of the Xerox Corporation. Linowitz had an attractive television presence, having moderated a local television panel show for many years—and to Kennedy, this was an important asset in modern politics. Objectively, a Linowitz candidacy had much to recommend it: he was an upstater,

[3] The party's decision was not entirely unselfish. In order to retain its third line (Row C) on the state ballot, it had to have a greater vote than the Conservative Party in the upcoming election. The Conservatives had been steadily increasing their vote. The Liberal leaders feared a poor showing would drop them to Row D and diminish the Liberal party as a political force. O'Connor, running against Rockefeller, would get a minimum of votes on their line. An independent candidate would certainly do better.

a liberal respected in the business community, able to finance his own campaign, not identified with political partisanship, prominent in Jewish circles, capable of understanding political intrigue. But he lacked the indispensable trait, "the gut to run," that obsessive commitment to win elective office that makes a man subject himself to the brutal punishment of exhaustion, boredom and impersonal living involved in modern American politics.

Linowitz was interested, but he insisted on being drafted, feeling that the act of seeking the nomination would diminish his appeal as an independent. That meant Kennedy would have to deliver the nomination, probably an impossible task in any event, and in the process alienate a major part of the party apparatus.

Kennedy would not go that far. He did not know Linowitz that well, had never really worked with him, and had no reason to suppose he would return the kind of loyalty that so great an investment of political muscle deserved. This last opinion was reinforced by the knowledge that Linowitz was, in Kennedy's words, "playing games" by holding himself available for the gubernatorial nomination while at the same time negotiating an appointment in the Johnson administration.[4] Relations between Kennedy and Johnson being what they were, any attempt to curry the favor of both was bound to result in losing some standing with each.

Despite all this, unhappy with the prospect of another Democratic defeat, Kennedy decided to make a last try for Linowitz. On August 12, three weeks before the opening of the Democratic Convention, he met with him at National Airport in Washington. "If you announce your candidacy," he said, "I'm willing to go to every caucus and fight it out with every county leader. I think you can win the nomination, but I can't guarantee it. If you are nominated, I think you'll win the election. I'll make this fight with you. But I can't do it alone."

Linowitz replied that he was flattered but he could not actively seek the nomination. If he were nominated, he would accept and campaign hard.

"It doesn't happen that way anymore," said Kennedy, and that

---

[4] An appointment came through, several months later: United States Ambassador to the Organization of American States. It was not the one Linowitz wanted, but he accepted it.

ended the matter. He was not about to fight to nominate a man who would not fight for the nomination himself.

A few days later, Kennedy invited O'Connor to Washington and told him he would not stand in his way. He asked only two things: O'Connor's assurance that he would keep John Burns as state chairman, and that he would allow Kennedy to control the selection of the delegates to the 1968 Democratic Convention. O'Connor agreed happily. On August 16, Kennedy announced that he "did not plan to support or oppose any individual candidate prior to the Convention." O'Connor's nomination was assured.

On September 8, Senator and Mrs. Kennedy flew to Buffalo to attend their first and only New York State Convention. He went out of obligation and expected to remain aloof from the proceedings, but the atmosphere aroused his instincts as a veteran political manager; and the confusion, division and plain unprofessionalism of the Convention goaded him to action. The O'Connor nomination was a foregone conclusion, but there were two other nominations, for lieutenant governor and attorney general, that were not yet decided. Traditionally, these were postponed until the day after the selection of the gubernatorial candidate. The decision would then be made at a meeting of the nominee and the major political leaders and later ratified obediently by the delegates. Kennedy had no personal stake in the ticket, believing that only Arthur Levitt, the state comptroller, would survive the election in any event. When O'Connor asked Kennedy for his recommendations, he said he had none, and asked the O'Connor forces to work it out and call him back. By 2 A.M., having heard nothing, he went to bed and left word he would meet O'Connor for breakfast in the Senator's suite at the Statler-Hilton hotel.

That evening, O'Connor and Lawrence Pierez, his campaign manager, went over the list of possibilities with Stephen Smith. The merit or ability of the candidates were not discussed, only political considerations such as the ethnic balance of the ticket. "It seems a shame we have to think in terms of an Italian and a Jew," said O'Connor, "but I suppose we must."[5] O'Connor then went down the list of eligibles, giv-

[5] With characteristic frankness, O'Connor had told reporters he supposed his ideal running mate would be a "black Jewish nun who spoke Spanish", but none could be found.

ing his impression of each man. When they reached Howard Samuels' name, Smith said that while Samuels was not Kennedy's choice, if O'Connor wanted him, he would go along. O'Connor then left Smith and continued his conferences with the county leaders through the night.

At breakfast the next morning, O'Connor told Kennedy that the professionals preferred Samuels for lieutenant governor. O'Connor said Samuels was not his personal choice. He was not sure he could work with him, and he was angry because Samuels, knowing the contest was over, had insisted on a roll-call vote for the gubernatorial nomination, delaying almost until midnight O'Connor's acceptance speech and thereby losing him valuable free prime time on state-wide television.

Asked for alternatives, Kennedy suggested consideration of Professor Jack Weinstein of Columbia Law School, who had also been county attorney of Nassau County. Weinstein was the kind of political intellectual Kennedy admired, brilliant, tough, and a man of action. He thought Weinstein would make a good candidate for attorney general, adding ability and liberal appeal to the ticket. Weinstein was summoned to Kennedy's suite where, after a brief discussion, O'Connor offered him the attorney general nomination. Weinstein agreed, and immediately went to work composing his acceptance speech.

Meanwhile the county leaders were meeting in the suite of the state chairman, John Burns. They were told O'Connor had accepted Weinstein for attorney general. The Erie County leaders were insisting on a place on the ticket. Their candidate was the mayor of Buffalo, Frank Sedita. Although the O'Connor forces were willing to accept Sedita for attorney general, they did not want him for lieutenant governor. Marvin Rosenberg, a friend of Vice President Humphrey's who was sitting in the leaders' meeting, changed the ethnic signals by suggesting Orin Lehman for lieutenant governor, with Sedita for attorney general. Lehman, the talented and public-spirited nephew of the former governor, had been narrowly defeated earlier that year in the election to fill the vacancy in the Seventeenth District, where Lindsay had been congressman. In 1965, he had run for comptroller of New York City on Paul Screvane's ticket, and had lost, in a very close count, to Mario Procaccino. Rosenberg argued that Lehman's name on the ticket would help offset Roosevelt's on the Liberal ticket.

PLATE 1 – Kennedy on the rostrum of the Democratic Convention in August, 1964, during a twenty-three minute ovation in honor of his slain brother.

PLATE 2 – At Hickory Hill in spring, 1965, with Edward Kennedy, who was still recovering from a broken back sustained in a near-fatal air crash the previous June.

PLATE 3— At the helm off the coast of Maine in September, 1966.

PLATE 4 – Touring the Watts section of Los Angeles in October, 1965, two
months after the riots.

PLATE 5 – With a new-found friend near Stockton, California in 1967.

PLATE 6 – With Mexican-American Union leader César Chávez in March, 1968. "What do you say to a man who's on a fast?" "Just say 'hello, César.' "

PLATE 7 – Kennedy at the grapepickers Communion: Delano, California, March, 1968.

PLATE 8 – The dramatic high point of the 1964 Senate campaign. Senator
AND 9   Kenneth B. Keating debates "empty chair" while Kennedy tries
         to get into the television studio.

PLATE 10 – With Chief Albert Luthuli at his home near Durban, South Africa, where Luthuli lived under house arrest. Kennedy said of Luthuli, "he is one of the most impressive men I have met."

PLATE 11 – Kennedy extends a hand of friendship to Communist students at the University of Concepción, Peru, in November, 1965. The Communist leaders were surprised by the gesture. Some reached out to greet him, others tried to kick his hand.

PLATE 12 – Brazil, November, 1965. With the help of a native guide, Robert Kennedy launches a boat before joining friends for a swim in the piranha-infested Nhamunda River.

PLATE 13 – At Hickory Hill, 1967: Matthew Maxwell Taylor Kennedy looks
for a receiver as brother, Christopher, and sister, Mary Kerry,
try to decide what the play is all about.

PLATE 14 – Paris, January, 1967. Senator Kennedy and William vanden Heuvel walking along the Seine immediately after meeting with President Charles De Gaulle at the Elysée Palace.

PLATE 15 — Lyndon Johnson and Robert Kennedy were powerful men with many parallel interests but their personal and policy disagreements prevailed and their conflicts made the news.

PLATE 16 – Kennedy and McCarthy at a Democratic dinner in New York City in December, 1967, shortly after McCarthy had announced for the Presidency.

PLATE 17 – A family advisory council aboard the campaign plane.

PLATE 18 – In Oregon, aboard the "Beaver State Express" May, 1968.

The other county leaders agreed. O'Connor acceded, and the ticket was to be Lehman for lieutenant governor and Sedita for attorney general.

Kennedy was astounded that O'Connor could have been so cavalier about the offer he had made to Weinstein, but at that point he had ceased to care. He said good-by to O'Connor and the political leaders gathered with their nominee, wished them well, and left for New York City on the *Caroline*. As he left his suite, Lehman came in, exhilarated by the turn of events.

"Is there an acceptance speech around?" he asked.

"Yes," said a Kennedy friend. "See Jack Weinstein. But don't lose it, because you can't tell who might end up needing it."

The remark was prophetic. The nominating session had begun at 11:00 A.M. but was recessed until the leaders had settled on their recommendations. As the day passed, the delegates became increasingly restive. Rumors floated through the hotel lobbies that Kennedy was dictating the rest of the ticket, and that he had vetoed Samuels. O'Connor lieutenants did nothing to deny the reports. At midday, a large number of upstate county chairmen sent a telegram to O'Connor saying selection of Samuels as lieutenant governor was indispensable to party victory.

When word of the Lehman-Sedita ticket came out, resentment against Kennedy flared on the floor of the Convention. A coalition quickly formed behind the leadership of J. Raymond Jones, the Tammany leader, who was angry at not being included in the bosses' meeting, and was seeking a measure of revenge against Kennedy for the Silverman campaign. When the Convention reconvened, O'Connor quickly understood that it was out of control and opened further nominations to the delegates' choice. Lehman withdrew before the balloting, and Samuels was nominated.

Kennedy had disregarded the lesson learned in Los Angeles in 1960: that a convention choice cannot be created in a day because loyalties and commitments are built up over a period of months or years by candidates who go out and work for them. Having held aloof for months to avoid the impression of dictating to the party, he had created it anyway. The experience of that Convention confirmed his earlier assessment that he would not have been able to impose a gubernatorial nominee on the Convention.

A few days after the Convention, Kennedy received a form letter from State Chairman Burns, thanking him for "all you did to help at the Convention in Buffalo."

"You can say that again," he wrote back.

The campaign itself bore out his forebodings. Ten days before the Convention, a poll released by the Liberal party gave O'Connor a 600,000-vote margin over Rockefeller. But upstate, the "deal" charges revived the old fears that the New York City bosses would run the state government for their own benefit. This, combined with an offhand remark of O'Connor that the New York subways should be free (from which upstate papers assumed that their citizens would have to pick up the deficit), caused his campaign in that area to falter. Newspaper opposition and an early surge of Roosevelt support had the same effect in the city. From a 20 per cent deficit in the pre-convention polls, Rockefeller quickly pulled even with O'Connor. By the end of October he was the favorite.[6]

Preoccupied with winning the nomination, O'Connor had made almost no plans for the campaign itself. Assailed on both right and left, he had only eight weeks to heal the party's wounds and campaign across the state. Roosevelt's third-party candidacy started strong, drawing most of its support from nominal Democrats. O'Connor's campaign appearances suffered from poor advance work and drew no crowds. Although his managers had assured Kennedy they had access to $2 million, they ended up raising less than $500,000, making it impossible to mount the television campaign necessary in a state like New York.

Meanwhile Rockefeller, aided by months of advance planning and the most expensive campaign operation on record,[7] moved to correct what his public opinion research showed to be a lack of public appreciation of his accomplishments. He created front page news events every day, using his power as an incumbent to announce new crime,

[6] There was a suspicion among Democrats that the earlier poll was more Liberal fantasy than Democratic fact, fabricated so that the actual decline in O'Connor's standing would be more dramatic.

[7] The Rockefeller campaign reported spending $11 million, the largest political expenditure ever made outside the presidency. By contrast, the Nixon *national* campaign in 1968 reported less than $20 million. The actual Rockefeller expenditures (there are many ways to spend that do not have to be reported) will never be known.

housing, and transit programs and such politically appealing projects as a new State Office Building in Harlem.[8] He demoralized O'Connor by picking up endorsements from labor unions which he had been carefully cultivating for years. Rockefeller's own personality was carefully de-emphasized. The television commercial touting accomplishments in the field of health showed only his fingertips touching each other, with his voice over. O'Connor, whose major strength at the Convention had been his reputation as a good campaigner, seemed almost uninvolved in the effort. Rockefeller privately expressed amazement that a man who had sought the governorship in 1962, had worked hard toward that goal for four years afterward, and knew for at least a year that he was his party's most likely candidate, would be so unprepared on the issues of state government.

On October 22, O'Connor got his first and only break of the campaign. The *Daily News* poll, with its awesome reputation for accuracy, showed him leading Rockefeller by a slight margin. His lead increased fractionally each day until the election. For the last two weeks, the O'Connor campaign floated on that poll. There was no effective grass-roots organization, little television, poor crowds, little content, but inside the headquarters the air of victory was strong and attention had already turned to selecting jobs in Albany.[9]

On election day, the voters handed the Democrats their fifth gubernatorial defeat in the last six tries (and *The Daily News* poll its first). Rockefeller won by almost 400,000 votes, doing poorly upstate for a Republican but carrying the suburbs by a large majority and doing well in the city.[10] The debilitating effect of Roosevelt's candidacy was far greater than the 507,000 votes he received, as he tagged O'Connor with the boss issue throughout the campaign. The reaction against Rockefeller, so overwhelming just two months before, had been largely offset by O'Connor's weakness and the Roosevelt candidacy. Kennedy's pre-convention activities and his remoteness from the campaign itself shielded him from responsibility for the defeat.

For O'Connor, the campaign was a disillusioning experience. A

8 Which at this writing, three years later, has still not been started.
9 Some believe the *News* poll had the effect of helping Rockefeller by convincing many voters who were prepared to cast a protest ballot for FDR, Jr., to switch to Rockefeller to prevent an O'Connor victory.
10 The anti-Rockefeller revolt, so massive a few months before, did show in places like conservative Onandaga County, home of the tax revolt, which went for O'Connor 80,000 to 57,000.

product of organization politics, he soon learned that the organization that could deliver the nomination was no longer powerful enough to deliver the election. Yet the qualities of kindness and courtesy which distinguished him were never ruffled, and he never had a harsh word for those who had disappointed him so badly. Kennedy, who had campaigned with him the last few days, said that on election night, after the results were in and everyone was about to go home, for the first time in months Frank O'Connor seemed a happy man.

Robert Kennedy's years as a political leader in New York were a mixture of success, disappointment, and anticipation. His immediate, personal goals were attained, but his larger party goals were not. He played a more significant role in party affairs than any national Democrat since Roosevelt. He increased the respect and support for himself among all factions of Democrats, and became indelibly associated with New York State. While he did not try the impossible task of repairing the ideological divisions, he did strengthen the younger, more progressive leaders within both the reform and regular organizations.[11] The Silverman campaign showed that if the issues were right and he had the opportunity to take them to the voters directly, changes could be made in the deepest-rooted institutions. But he could not elect state-wide candidates of his choice, or revise the Constitution, or reform the method of judicial selection. Kennedy was able to dent but not alter the traditional system in New York by which political power is concentrated in small groups and exercised without popular participation. It remained to be seen whether the direct primaries, which were not to go into effect until June 1968, would demolish the system.

Had he become involved in the beginning, had he used his prestige to endorse Screvane, or even Lindsay, or been able to capitalize on the Silverman victory to elect a governor of his choice, he no doubt could have accomplished more than he did. The opponents of party change, however, remained on the scene, working their designs every-

[11] When he ran for the Senate, the Democratic National Committee members from New York were Edwin Weisl, a personal friend and representative of President Johnson, and Congresswoman Edna Kelley, a staunch organization supporter. In 1968 they would yield to Jack English and Shirley Chisholm, now the black congresswoman from Bedford-Stuyvesant.

day. The party procedures, which they had installed, worked in their favor. It was hard to outmaneuver them from Washington.

Given his senatorial and family duties, as well as his national political obligations, he could not give New York politics the time and personal attention it needed. Leaders of all areas and factions complained that they did not see him enough, that he did not consult with them enough. His staff struggled to meet their demands, but the politicians wanted personal contact, not staff assistance. These complaints were a tribute in part to his eminence; but they also reflected his reluctance to be a "professional politician," attending the luncheons, making the phone calls, glad-handing one and all —the things that supposedly are a senator's local homework. Politicians thought him somewhat insulated from their attentions, and he was. There were some leaders in the state like Burns, English, Crotty, and Crangle, who would do anything for him. But the majority of every faction saw him as an independent and remote figure whom they followed because they feared rather than knew him.

Kennedy did not run for the Senate to change the politics of New York. His first priorities were the vital issues of foreign and domestic policy, and New York politics, unrelated to these, was far less significant by comparison. He considered his political work an obligation as much as an opportunity. To contest, in other people's names, with a fickle and demanding electorate in a bear pit of struggling politicians, was not a task that attracted him.

His reluctance to become involved in New York's Democratic politics came partly from the realization that his personal popularity was not transferable to either his party or its candidates. When he went into the streets for Beame and O'Connor, and even Silverman, the crowds came to see him, and the real candidate traveled unnoticed in his wake. In other states where he campaigned, he was greeted with frenzy, but the candidate he went to help often lost the election. He knew that voters assess candidates on their own merits, not those of their endorsers; and that while he could bring workers, attract funds, and gather an audience, the candidate would stand or fall on his own merits and efforts.

Robert Kennedy's more lasting contributions to New York came outside of party politics. The work of the New York office set a model for party organizations and congressional offices throughout the country. The upstate areas gained, through him, a stronger voice than they had before in Washington. The community causes he was interested in would become the agenda for the nation in the years to come. He would have been amused watching old line politicians scrambling to keep up with the New Politics at the Democratic Convention in Chicago, as New York's delegation aligned itself with the youth and dissenters and some of its members even managed to get themselves arrested.

On June 6, 1968, Edward Katcher, chief political reporter of the New York *Post,* who knew every corner of the story, wrote a column which summed it up very well:

> The excitement, the drive and the dream that Senator Robert F. Kennedy brought to Democratic politics in New York are gone today, perhaps never to be recaptured in our time.
>
> Profoundly moral, deeply religious, physically reckless and mentally deliberate, Kennedy sought to give an added dimension to politics here.
>
> If he had lived, he would have had a greater measure of success, but could he have accomplished his real mission in the state? Politics in New York, particularly, and in the nation as a whole, often devours idealists—even when they have a vein of pragmatism.
>
> Kennedy lost every battle within the party except one, and that victory was possible only because he could make a direct appeal to the people.
>
> The state party he leaves behind is no monument to the man. It is a reminder of his limitations. He could not force the party to take that first upward step. But as long as his name will be remembered, Democrats will have a star to reach for.

12

VIETNAM:
THE TORTURED PATH

On the last day of January 1967, Robert Kennedy spent an hour at the Elysée Palace with the President of France. The entire discussion concerned Vietnam. As he left, General de Gaulle took him to the door and spoke some emotional words of advice that marked his friendship and paternal concern for his guest. "You are a young man," he said, "with a brilliant future that will affect both your country and the world. I am an old man, who has lived through many battles and bears many scars, so listen closely to what I say to you: Do not become embroiled in this difficulty in Vietnam. Then you can survive its outcome. Those who are involved will be badly hurt. When their effectiveness is destroyed, you will be able to step in at the proper time and help your country regain its proper course."

Right or wrong, the advice came too late. The issue of Vietnam, which had dominated the first ten years of the post-war politics of France, consuming her resources and leaving a residue of bitterness and frustration, was already taking its toll of the life and politics of the United States.

As Attorney General, Robert Kennedy had been more than an observer of the decisions that enlarged the American role in Vietnam. As a Senator, he watched with mounting despair as policies which he had helped conceive, grew like some inhuman fantasy, to monstrous perversions of the principles they were supposedly protecting. He could not stay aloof from the issue, for it was the most debilitating problem of his country. Slowly and painfully, he turned against almost every aspect of his nation's policy, and many of his own earlier conceptions.

When Kennedy finally chose to speak, he did so because he could do nothing else and still retain his constituency and serve his conscience. He was well aware that most of those whose judgment he trusted and who also had access to the confidential intelligence from the war front shared his doubts about the President's course. Their responsibility as part of the Administration and their loyalty to the President silenced their dissent. His independence as a senator freed him from such restraints.

In 1951, Robert F. Kennedy and Congressman John F. Kennedy had visited Asia to inspect the war in Indochina personally. They saw it in the context of the demise of colonial power. A new generation of Foreign Service officers warned them that the French would inevitably lose because France could neither sustain the war nor resist the pressure of Vietnamese nationalism. The brothers were told that this surge to independence might not be won by Communism, but it could no longer be controlled by colonialism. The American interest was to identify with the non-Communist forces of nationalism. It would not be an easy task because the struggle had already been polarized between Ho Chi Minh, an acknowledged Communist, and French colonialism, seeking to maintain itself by playing on the fears in the Western world of Communism and an expanding China.

On April 3, 1954, Secretary of State John Foster Dulles met secretly with congressional leaders to seek their support for a congressional resolution permitting the President to use air and naval power in Indochina. Lyndon B. Johnson, then Democratic Minority Leader of the Senate, argued against the proposed American intervention. John Kennedy was among the senators who supported him. Soon after, the French were defeated at Dien Bien Phu. Confronted by military defeat and domestic revulsion, and notified of forces, France agreed to the Geneva Conference to negotiate an end to the war.

During this period, the French permitted Ngo Dinh Diem to become the Premier of the Vietnam they were about to abandon. Diem was mandarin in attitude, Roman Catholic in religion, ascetic in personal habits, fearless of personal danger, fiercely anti-Communist, and genuine in his devotion to the independence of Vietnam. He was a hero to many of his countrymen because of his long resistance to colonial rule. His personal integrity was beyond reproach.

He assumed power under conditions which few believed he could survive. Against formidable odds, he defeated the local armies of the sects that threatened anarchy, gained control of the police and the armed forces, and established a central government in Saigon strong enough to absorb more than one million refugees who fled from the North in the wake of the Geneva Agreement. Diem's regime offered a nationalist, non-Communist alternative to Ho Chi Minh, an alternative that in the judgment of Dwight Eisenhower, Richard Nixon, John Kennedy, and Lyndon Johnson was worth the investment of American economic and military assistance. But as time passed, Diem began to alienate the groups whose support he needed. Instead of building a democratic coalition with strong Buddhist participation, he isolated himself from his people, retreating more and more to the comfort of the sinister servility of his brother Ngo Dinh Nhu, who increasingly exercised Diem's power for his own corrupt purposes.

In 1960, the National Liberation Front (NLF) was formally established. Both Diem and the State Department labeled the Front as "Hanoi's creation," but in the growing atmosphere of repression directed by Saigon, the NLF prospered. Its guerrilla warfare tactics challenged Diem's control of the countryside and opened the cities to endless incidents of terrorism. By 1961, despite the presence of 3000 American military personnel, there was a real prospect that South Vietnam would collapse.

President Kennedy dispatched General Maxwell Taylor and Walt W. Rostow to Saigon to re-evaluate the situation. As a result of their recommendations, the program of military and economic assistance was increased to an annual level of more than $400 million. Military assistance teams were already in Vietnam, but it was agreed to supply additional support forces to provide training and tactical advice for counterguerrilla operations. Despite the deterioration of Diem's political base, President Kennedy's advisers were optimistic that the Vietcong forces could be contained while the political fabric was being repaired. The Taylor-Rostow team made another recommendation: that a logistical force of engineers be sent to repair the ravages of a devastating Mekong River flood, and that combat ground troops accompany the engineers, ostensibly for protection but with the understanding that their further mission be left open. By the time it reached the President, the recommendation called for the commitment of 10,000–20,000 American combat soldiers, and it carried the approval of the Joint Chiefs of Staff. Secretary McNamara and his deputy, Roswell Gilpatric, opposed it and President Kennedy rejected it.

At this point, Robert Kennedy was already immersed in counterguerrilla strategies, as the most active member of the Counter-Insurgency Committee (CIC), an outgrowth of a special committee to review the decisions and errors which led to the abortive invasion of Cuba at the Bay of Pigs. Kennedy studied the success of Ramon Magsaysay in defeating the Huk rebellion in the Philippines, and the British tactics in Malaysa. But neither area was contiguous to a Communist state which could provide supplies and sanctuary for the insurgents. Vietnam was. Despite this significant difference, Kennedy believed the Vietcong would stand or fall on their political success rather than the outside assistance given them. Their hopes lay in the fact that they, not the government, were identified with the hope of reform.

The CIC agreed to make Vietnam a major testing area for American counterinsurgency strategy. The Special Forces, the Green Berets, were created for this task. Their ranks included medics to fight tropical diseases, engineers to build schools, clinics, and housing, and soldiers schooled in the basic problems of community development. Guerrilla warfare in Vietnam, as elsewhere, was nurtured by political unrest, by dissatisfaction with land reform, by a lack of confidence in the established government's capacity to fulfill the hopes of its people for a better life. Kennedy's hope was that the Special Forces would teach the indigenous troops how to recapture the political initiative essential to any success over the insurgents.[1] He believed that the commitment of American Special Forces to South

[1] Kennedy's commitment to the Special Forces never faltered. He always kept a green beret on his desk. When the commander of the group, General Yarborough, was assigned to Korea in a move that Kennedy and others interpreted as a decision by President Johnson to downgrade the Special Forces program, Kennedy protested vigorously to Defense Secretary McNamara—so vigorously in fact that their relationship was temporarily strained.

Vietnam, in an advisory capacity, could help stop the Communist insurgency.

In February 1962, Kennedy went to the Far East and spoke the same homilies about freedom and victory that others would speak with haunting echo in the years to come. In Hong Kong, he said, "The solution there (in Vietnam) lies in our winning it; this is what the President intends to do." Several days later, during the brief stopover in Saigon, he said:

"Hanoi may deny its responsibility but the guilt is clear. In a flagrant violation of its signed pledge at Geneva in 1954, the North Vietnamese regime has launched a course to destroy the Republic of Vietnam." He concluded his statement by saying: "We will win in Vietnam and we shall remain here until we do."

By the end of 1962, there were 11,000 American military advisers in Vietnam, and Robert Kennedy was saying that "where a year ago the situation in South Vietnam was dark, the forces of national independence now have a fighting chance." But despite these hopeful expressions, the kind others later used to justify military escalation, Kennedy remained firm in the judgment that the military effort was only useful to create conditions of stability, and that political and economic reforms were necessary to permit a successful resolution of the conflict without Communist domination.

In the summer of 1963, after mounting religious and political repression of the Buddhists, Diem and Nhu finally turned against their own people in force. Breaking a pledge given to the United States, they ordered Vietnamese military units to attack the major Buddhist pagodas, shooting the bonzes who resisted and desecrating statues and holy relics. By this act, they destroyed any hope of creating the coalition of domestic support which would be necessary for their survival.

On September 2, in an interview with Walter Cronkite of CBS at Hyannis Port, President Kennedy directly confronted the situation that had developed. "I don't think," the President said, "that unless a greater effort is made to win popular support that the war can be won out there. In the final analysis, it is their war. They are the ones who have to win or lose it. We can help them, we can give them equipment, we can send our men out there as advisers but they have to win it, the people of Vietnam, against the Communists."

As threats of an army coup against Diem mounted, the Kennedy administration felt compelled to pressure Diem to broaden his political base and institute reforms to end the widespread corruption. Almost every alternative involved a deeper American commitment. If Diem took steps to reform his government in response to U.S. pressure, he would have a call on our further support. If he failed to reform, a coup was likely and the new government would look to Washington for immediate assistance. On September 6, 1963, the National Security Council met to discuss the limited options for action. At this meeting, Robert Kennedy questioned for the first time some of the basic assumptions of American involvement in Vietnam. As he understood it, he said, the U.S. was in Vietnam to help the people resist a Communist takeover. If Diem's regime could not do this but another government could, we owed it to the people of Vietnam to help the latter come to power. But if no possible government could successfully resist a Communist takeover, he said, we should pull out of Vietnam now, rather than wait.

It is difficult to tell whether Kennedy's questions at the NSC meeting represented a change in his own thinking or an attempt, by raising issues, to get his colleagues to take a new look at the nation's commitment. At least it can be said that he now seriously questioned whether the conditions necessary to stablize the military situation through a counterinsurgency effort, with its necessary political and economic reform, could be created.

Three weeks later the New Frontier ended in Dallas. At this point there were 16,300 American advisers in Vietnam. The rate of spending for military and economic assistance was $400 million a year. Seventy-eight American lives had been lost. Although commitments had been made, they were strictly defined, and had not been related to the treaty obligations under the SEATO pact. The options open to the President of the United States were largely unexercised. He could still commit American armies or withhold them; he could assume the unilateral responsibility for the outcome, or internationalize it through the United Nations; he could withhold American power to force the Vietnamese to deal with one another; or commit it in limited quantities to encourage them to bargain, with neither side clearly dominant militarily. The options were as broad or as narrow as the new President wished to measure them. It was still a Vietnamese war, between contending forces of the South. Hanoi had less than a regiment of its own troops committed to the struggle, but Ho Chi Minh was manipulating the conflict between the U.S.S.R. and China to make both give greater support to the NLF which was carrying the battle.

Although he remained in the government for another ten months, the death of President Kennedy effectively ended Robert Kennedy's involvement in the formulation and execution of foreign policy. In 1964, Lyndon Johnson began exercising the options of presidential authority. Blanketed with the immense popularity won by his masterful handling of the transition between Presidents, Johnson used the shadowy crisis of the alleged attack on American ships in the Tonkin Gulf to elicit a congressional resolution that would serve as authorization for his future decisions to escalate the conflict.

The successful coup d'etat against Diem on November 1, 1963, had cast South Vietnam into political chaos. Through most of 1964, the Vietcong won significant victories in the countryside, as a succession of governments tried to collect enough authority in Saigon to prosecute the war. In this turmoil, the hopes Kennedy and others had held for the successful training of counterinsurgency forces were shattered. Johnson's top civilian and military advisers agreed that a substantial increase in American forces, and a shift to a combat role, would be essential to prevent a Communist takeover until political stability was restored in Saigon. Only then, they argued, would conditions permit a reversion to the Kennedy administration's more limited policy of training and support. Strengthened by his enormous political victory in November, Johnson accepted this advice, and by doing so changed the nature of the war.

The first move came on February 7, 1965, after Vietcong guerrillas attacked the United States compound at Pleiku. United States bombers retaliated by striking targets in North Vietnam for the first time. Robert Kennedy, now a member of the Senate, did not publicly disagree with the President's decision. Answering questions in Ithaca, New York, on February 23, he opposed the suggestion that the United States pull its forces out of Vietnam. "The United States has made a commitment to help Vietnam," Kennedy said. "I'm in favor of keeping that commitment and taking whatever steps are necessary. If our word means anything, we must remain as long as it is evident that the people favor it."

Kennedy, however, was determined to keep his own options open. In May 1965, when Johnson sought immediate approval of a $700 million supplemental appropriation for the Vietnam effort, Kennedy took the floor of the Senate to warn that congressional approval of this appropriation should not be interpreted by the White House as a "blank check." He urged that Congress, especially its committees, be completely informed and involved before further decisions regarding escalation were taken. Kennedy had doubts whether large scale bombing would prove effective. An old friend, John Kenneth Galbraith, the Harvard economist whose erudite and witty reports as ambassador to India had rankled Dean Rusk and amused John Kennedy, told him of a study he had made of the consequences of the allied bombing of Germany in World War II. The Allies had caused tremendous material damage, but the bombing did little to impede the German war effort. In fact, it had strengthened the fighting spirit of the German people. If this was the impact on Germany, a highly industrialized nation particularly vulnerable to aerial assault, what could be hoped from intensive bombing of North Vietnam, a nation essentially without industry, whose people had already survived a generation of war? The British experience in World War II and our own revolutionary struggle were added reminders that a tenacious national spirit was as important as firepower and could successfully resist even the most powerful military forces in the world.

Of Johnson's three major arguments for the bombing, only one made sense to Kennedy. Johnson said it was needed to sustain the sagging morale of the Saigon government, and to bring about a greater military and political effort by its followers, but this point had been made to validate every increment of aid to South Vietnam over the years. He also said the bombing would interdict the supply of men and material from the North, but in the light of General Matthew Ridgway's experience in Korea, where allied bombing, with far fewer obstacles, had failed to stem the flow of enemy supplies, Kennedy did not think this persuasive. The rationalization that did make sense to him lay in the power the President now had, by offering to end the bombing, to induce the North to negotiate to bring the conflict to an end. It was unthinkable to Kennedy that Johnson would risk his political power, the success of his social programs at home, and the moral leadership of the world in the vain hope of winning military victory in a place where America's vital interests were not involved.

This step of escalation, the bombing of North Vietnam's military installations, could be rationalized as a negotiation tool. To support this interpretation, the President and his spokesmen were publicly committing themselves to peace, speaking of unconditional negotiations, giving eloquent speeches about the need for political and social reform in Vietnam. On April 7, 1965, speaking at Johns Hopkins University, Johnson offered "unconditional" talks and held out the prospect of substantial economic aid to all of Vietnam once the war was ended. Symbolic gestures were in abundance: a cable to Pope Paul VI, a letter to UN Secretary General U Thant; even the appointment of Arthur Goldberg to succeed the late Adlai Stevenson as the U. S. Representative to the United Nations. President Johnson convinced Goldberg that the resolution of the war was the greatest service he could render the nation. With a presidential commitment of support for this objective, Goldberg took the extraordinary step of resigning from the Supreme Court of the United States.

Traveling in South America in the late fall of 1965, Kennedy made it a practice, as he did on all of his foreign trips, to praise Johnson's leadership in Vietnam. And he went to great lengths to explain the difficulties of American responsibility for peace in Southeast Asia. He emphasized that his nation's basic concern was to establish the right of a people to determine its own destiny, and he repeated the President's assurances that we would accept whatever result a free election would bring in Vietnam, including the selection of a Communist government. During these months, Kennedy deliberately edited his statements about Vietnam to avoid any interpretation of personal criticism of the President.

On December 5, 1965, on "Meet the Press," Kennedy was asked directly whether he favored halting the bombing of North Vietnam as a means of bringing about negotiations. He replied that he did. When pressed to amplify his statement, he made it clear that he would not favor a unilateral halt in the bombing unless it could definitely help in bringing about such talks. When asked if he fully supported the present policy in Vietnam, Kennedy said, "I basically support the policy." He expressed reservations that not enough was being done in the economic and political fields and that the military aspects of the struggle were being greatly overemphasized.

As 1965 ended, 184,300 American troops had been committed to the defense of South Vietnam. The cost of the war had escalated geometrically. American bombing of the North had not stopped the flow of supplies from Hanoi. In fact, the infiltration had increased substantially. The struggle which Eisenhower and Kennedy had approved by sending supplies and advisers had now become a conflict to which the power and prestige of the American nation was increasingly committed. But to Kennedy it still appeared that Johnson was trying hard to find some kind of settlement. Moreover, the experience of working with a President had made him especially sensitive to those who criticized the conduct of foreign policy without having all the facts available.

In January 1966, as a debate raged about the continuation of the bombing pause ordered by Johnson during the Christmas holidays, Kennedy sent a private letter to the President expressing sympathetic understanding for the situation he confronted, having to make decisions in the face of so much advice from the Congress and the press. The letter compared Johnson's situation with Lincoln's during the Civil War, and quoted an excerpt from one of Bruce Catton's Civil War histories, *Never Call Retreat,* which ended with this paragraph:

> ". . . Mr. Lincoln . . . had told a friend that all of the responsibilities of the administration 'belong to that unhappy wretch called Abraham Lincoln,' and as he tried to meet those responsibilities the last thing he needed or wanted was a contrived or enforced harmony. Precisely because he was leading a divided country he needed diverse counsels. He had his own grave doubts about the era that lay ahead, so did most of his fellow citizens, and the true strength of his leadership had to arise from his ability to work out his doubts as he went along . . . He listened to everybody and then did what he thought best."

Johnson wrote back a grateful note. "You know better than most the gloom that crowds in on a President," he told Kennedy, "because you were so close to your brother." At a meeting with congressional leaders on January 25, Lyndon Johnson read the passage from the book without identifying who had sent it to him. Five days later, the President ordered the resumption of the bombing.

At this point Kennedy began to see that the President, more ebullient than ever in the glow of unchallenged political power, was accepting the advice that he wanted to hear. The generals were reporting that American military forces could crush the northern aggression and destroy the Vietcong subversion. The legislative legerdemain which had marked Johnson's senatorial leadership had always contained an element of duplicity. Now that duplicity was visible again. If the American expectation was military victory, then the prospect of a negotiated peace in the near future was unrealistic.

In February 1966, the Senate Foreign Relations Committee began two weeks of hearings on Vietnam. Spokesmen for the Administration appeared to defend the President's policies. Kennedy was absorbed by the hearings. He followed them on television and several times went to the hearing room and stood listening among the spectators. In addition to his doubts about the purpose of the bombing, he had become convinced, through his contacts in the State and Defense Departments, that though the Administration said its goal was negotiations to end the war, no real thought had been given to the terms of any settlement. As the hearings neared their end, he decided to address himself in a public statement to this question.

In preparing the statement, and in all of his subsequent major pronouncements on Vietnam, he consulted closely with Richard Goodwin, the brilliant and controversial writer who had served both Presidents Kennedy and Johnson. On his staff, he relied principally on Adam Walinsky, who from the start had both produced and provoked a cascade of ideas, memoranda, and drafts criticizing the Administration's policies. He also sought opinions and advice from General Maxwell Taylor and Secretary McNamara, who had quite different views. The final statement was no one's initial views, only Kennedy's best judgment. He issued it on February 19, 1966, before leaving on a skiing holiday with his family. Before the uproar of the holiday weekend was finished, he had become a rallying point for the growing opposition throughout the nation to the Johnson policies in Vietnam. In the words of Walter Lippmann, he had succeeded in raising "the decisive question about a negotiated settlement, which is whether the Administration is prepared to negotiate with its adversaries in the field."

In the statement, Kennedy said for the first time what he was to say many times thereafter: "There are three routes available to the United States in its involvement in Vietnam—military victory, unilateral withdrawl or a peaceful settlement." He categorically ruled out the possibility of withdrawal, regarding it as a repudiation of the commitments undertaken and confirmed by three administrations. Military victory as a goal was at best uncertain and at worst unattainable. President Johnson had publicly rejected it as an objective of American policy in several statements. To Kennedy, the costs in human, moral, and political terms of such a course were unthinkable. The only satisfactory solution to the war was a negotiated settlement. His crucial disagreement with the Administration at this point was how to bring these negotiations about. Kennedy's basic point was that there was little prospect for successful negotiations unless we were prepared to grant status to the National Liberation Front, accepting "the fact that there are discontented elements in South Vietnam, Communist and non-Communist, who desire to change the existing political and economic system of the country." These elements, he stated, must be admitted "to a share of power and responsibility," and this was central to any hope for a negotiated settlement.

Senator Fulbright had raised essentially the same point in a colloquy with Dean Rusk during the committee hearings. He asked the Secretary of State whether we had left any alternatives for the Vietcong "but surrender or annihilation." Secretary Rusk's response, which deeply disturbed Kennedy was: "They do have an alternative. They are the front of Hanoi. They do have an alternative of quitting, of stopping being an agent of Hanoi and receiving men and arms from the North." This exchange had gone practically unnoticed, but with the Kennedy statement, the issue of NLF participation and the eventual acceptance of a coalition government became the focus of the controversy. As the New York *Times* pointed out, the essence of the Kennedy statement was that "We cannot show all our cards before we get to the bargaining table. But we must have our terms firmly set in our minds. And we must reveal enough of our intentions to Hanoi to eliminate any reasonable fear that we ask them to talk now only to demand their surrender."

Before the week was over, the Administration had clarified its proposal for negotiation: It was contingent upon the acknowledgment that the Vietcong was nothing more than an instrument of the Hanoi government. But if this acknowledgment was a necessary prelude to negotiations, then President Johnson's invitation was not "unconditional," as the President had said. Furthermore, in Kennedy's judgment, such an acknowledgment was neither accurate nor realistic. If the war was to end in negotiation rather than military victory over the Viet Cong, a new government for South Vietnam would undoubtedly arise from the settlement, and it was clear to Kennedy that unless the NLF and other dissident forces were part of that government, there was no inducement to end the fighting.

Thus, for the first time, a significant public disagreement arose between Johnson and Kennedy on the most important issue before the country. The press reports highlighted the difference and added the element of political confrontation. Bill Moyers, the White House press secretary, did everything possible to minimize the difference between the President and Senator Kennedy. Few men in the Administration were held in higher esteem than Moyers, and none was more total in his loyalty to the President. He believed a break between Johnson and Kennedy at this point would cement a tragic division within the Democratic Party, and seriously undermine the President's capacity to deal with the war and its settlement. The day after Kennedy's statement, Moyers said publicly that the nature of an interim government should be a subject for negotiations. Kennedy, anxious to discuss the substance of the issue and avoid political division with the President, quickly accepted the Moyers' remark as a concession by the Administration that NLF participation in an interim government was a possibility, and therefore that the differences between the Administration and himself were semantic rather than substantive. On February 21, General Maxwell Taylor telephoned Kennedy to express his opinion that there were no real differences between what Kennedy had said and what the Administration intended. But either the President thought differently, or he could not control the public disagreement of his advisers. Important presidential lieutenants chose to interpret Kennedy's statement as a challenge. McGeorge Bundy asserted that "the Administration does not take the view that admitting the Communists to a share of power and responsibility would be a useful or helpful step." Bundy attempted to support his opinion by saying that President Kennedy had been opposed to coalition governments. The senator resented the statement, especially its inaccuracy, since Bundy himself had participated in the Laotian settlement in 1962, which involved Communist participation in the newly established government.

Hubert Humphrey, apparently believing that Kennedy's statement had left the senator politically vulnerable, spoke from Australia, where he was visiting en route home from Vietnam. The Vice President argued that permitting a coalition government would be the same as putting "a fox in a chicken coop or an arsonist in a fire department." Upon his return to Washington, Mr. Humphrey spoke more harshly, saying that the Viet Cong "engage in assassination, murder, pillage, conquest, and I can't for the life of me see why the United States of America would want to propose that such an outfit be made part of any government." On February 27, the two men appeared on national television shows separately. Kennedy declared: "I think statements that are made that we will never deal with assassins and we will never deal with murderers makes it difficult for them to believe that they are being asked to come to the negotiating table other than to surrender."

In the days that followed, Kennedy went to great lengths to minimize his differences with the President. He even warned those who welcomed his statement to be careful not to challenge the motives of presidential action. Kennedy had not intended his comments as an attack on Johnson, but the press and most of the country saw the differences between the two men as a "break."

In retrospect, the senator's surprise at the hostility of the Administration's response may seem naïve, but it was genuine. For the first time, Kennedy was an open target for those in the President's entourage who, knowing the personal antagonism and rivalry between the two, welcomed the opportunity to exacerbate it. He felt later that he had made a mistake in participating in the seemingly endless television appearances and press conferences that followed his statement because they left an impression of confusion and ambiguity. "I made the speech because I thought there was something that was worth saying," Kennedy said. "We haven't really discussed with any completeness or thoroughness the heart of what our policy should be. I made some mistakes in handling it. I think it was unpopular politically. But I would do it all over again if I had to."

The conflicting statements in response to his speech convinced him that he was right. The Administration had not defined for itself what its political objectives were. Until it did so, no one could predict how much our military involvement would be escalated. For the moment, Kennedy continued to believe that the domestic political imperatives would compel Johnson to turn away from the advisers who were suggesting the possibility of military victory. But there had been a major evolution in his own position. Kennedy was now committed to negotiation and political resolution of the Vietnam struggle. If the Administration chose a different course, he would oppose it.

As he sought an independent policy on Vietnam, Kennedy had access to much of the same information channeled to the President. Joseph Alsop, for example, sent Kennedy copies of captured enemy documents showing that Hanoi was hurting, and did not want to negotiate. The information that was crucial to his judgments was generally available to the Congress. But he had one advantage that Johnson forfeited once the criticisms of his policies gained momentum—he had frequent access to objective witnesses who had a different viewpoint of what was happening. Kennedy made a point of talking to individuals who had returned from Vietnam and had no domestic political interests to protect, who were eyewitnesses to the war and executors of our policies, and who frequently conveyed a sense of remorse at what was being done in the name of the national interest.

In March 1966, Robert Kennedy had lunch in New York with an old friend, Pierre Mendes-France, whose courage and sagacity had extricated his country from its calamitous involvement with Vietnam a decade earlier. Throughout the three-hour discussion, Kennedy for the most part listened as Mendes-France expressed his opinion in unequivocal terms: "China controls the situation in Vietnam and there is very little that encourages them toward negotiation and settlement. The present war costs them nothing in manpower and very little in resources and matériel compared to the political gain of paralyzing Soviet mobility in the Communist world. The Chinese believe deeply that time is on their side, that the "whites" will tire—maybe not tomorrow but in five years, or ten years—but time and its measure do not weigh heavily on the Chinese. That is one reason why it is so terrible to negotiate with them at a conference—time means nothing. The Americans are losing men, billions of dollars; their political rapprochement with the Russians is stopped, their political position among the Asian peoples is jeopardized because "white" bombs are again killing Asians. There is only one thing," Mendes-France warned, "that the Chinese fear—and only one thing that will bring them or the Viet Cong to the conference table—the fear of an American presence permanently rooted in the Asian mainland. The mobile war of the jungle and the mountains is their war. They know they can beat you at it. You may win the pitched battles, but you will not win the country. The Vietcong will die in the paddies, fade into the jungles, but they or others will return and reclaim what you think you have won. The people are not with you."

Kennedy asked what could be done to win the popular support that was crucial to any kind of stable political settlement. Mendes-France was not encouraging, "I do not disparage American motives," he said. "America is undoubtedly sincere in wishing to build a democratic nation in Vietnam, and you are clearly willing to spend billions for social and economic reform. But it is too late. There is no political alternative among the Vietnamese. Ngo Dinh Diem was a thoroughly honest man, a decent man, but he and his brother systematically destroyed their opposition, and in the process, destroyed the possibilities of a democratic alternative to the Vietcong." Mendes-France dismissed Marshal Ky as a mercenary. "We paid him before you did—and now you want him to lead a political revolution for nationalism and independence in Vietnam! What you Americans think of yourselves is not important. To the Vietnamese you are our successors whether you like it or not. You are 'white imperialists' and, like the French, you are bombing their villages and killing their people, and you are supporting puppets who mean nothing in their own country." Mendes-France advocated identifying the essential parts of Vietnam—the coast, the ports, the main cities—and then letting it be known that these areas would be defended until a meaningful settlement was negotiated. He compared it to Guantanamo Bay in Cuba. "Build your Gibraltars and wait—and wait—and wait. Your interests will be protected, your commitments will be honored and your political costs at home and abroad will be reduced to a level that you can survive. At that point the Chinese will take your presence seriously."

Kennedy sought Mendes-France's opinions about NATO, German reunification, and nuclear-weapons control. In answer to all of them,

Mendes-France replied: "Vietnam. Vietnam. Vietnam. That is the only problem that has meaning for you today. How can you restructure NATO until you know what kind of foe you face in Russia, and how can you know until the Vietnam question is settled. There can be no real negotiation on these fundamental problems until Vietnam is settled. Time is on the side of China. They will grow stronger. The sooner you begin talking the better."

Kennedy disagreed with Mendes-France that Vietnam could be defended by enclaves, but the conversation confirmed many of his own conclusions, especially that Vietnam and its ramifications would be a nightmare in American life, and that every effort must be made, regardless of the domestic political cost, to bring the war to a conclusion through a negotiated settlement.

Kennedy's February 19 statement had made no reference to the bombing, which Johnson had resumed at the end of January 1966, after a thirty-seven-day pause. In June, when Haiphong was added to the list of targets, Kennedy questioned the effectiveness of the step in reducing North Vietnam's capacity to supply the Viet Cong. "Unfortunately, past escalations have often been accompanied by assurances and predictions that this would be the case," said Kennedy's statement. "Those predictions, as most concerning Vietnam in the last twenty years, have been wrong."

The relentless complexity of Vietnam began to take its toll. The credibility of President Johnson himself was the first victim, as hope and illusion were crushed by reality. In 1966, for the first time, American casualties outnumbered those of the South Vietnamese. Escalation invited escalation. As American troops increased, so did Vietcong recruitment and the infiltration of North Vietnamese regulars. As America brought the weapons of modern warfare into combat, so did the enemy, with increasing assistance from the Soviet Union. The ironies became profound, as people whose freedom we were safeguarding found themselves refugees in their own land, their homes and their hopes destroyed around them. The land was governed by a military clique in Saigon, whose senior officers had fought as allies of the French colonial forces and whose spokesman, Air Force Marshal Nguyen Cao Ky, declared war to the death on anyone who favored negotiations.

As a result of his February 1966 statement, Kennedy had been marked as an "opponent" of the Administration's policy in Vietnam. Influential citizens who shared this view urged him to speak up every time a move was made that intensified the war or made peace talks more difficult. Each incident caused him anguish. He was silent far more often than he spoke, for he recognized that coming from him, such criticisms inevitably would be distorted by political interpretations. Although his doubts about American involvement were well known to his associates, he felt that his colleagues in the Senate were making excellent arguments that should have brought a most sympathetic audience from the White House. Two of the President's personal friends, Mike Mansfield and J. William Fulbright, were the principal opponents of Johnson's policies. Yet Kennedy was invariably attacked as having personal and political motivations for making the same criticisms of our Vietnam policy that Mansfield, Fulbright, and a score of other senators were making as a matter of course. He encountered Mike Mansfield at a dinner in Maine while vacationing there in early September 1966, and listened while a mutual friend asked Mansfield how he could maintain a cordial, friendly, personal and working relationship with the President when their views about Vietnam were so opposite. Mansfield replied that he no longer discussed his disagreements with the President. Johnson just was not listening and it served no purpose.

An example of Kennedy's reluctance to engage the President in public combat occurred after President Charles de Gaulle, speaking in Cambodia on September 2, 1966, denounced the American intervention in harsh terms but at the same time offered to mediate between the adversaries. Kennedy worked on a statement as his sailing trip in Maine was ending. It deplored De Gaulle's arbitrary analysis of the U.S. role in Vietnam, but stated that this denunciation at least gave him credibility to the North Vietnamese as an acceptable arbitrator. The important thing to Kennedy was that General de Gaulle had outlined settlement objectives that were compatible with President Johnson's own public declarations. Kennedy's proposed statement said "We owe it to ourselves and the world to give General de Gaulle's offer serious consideration. It is a mistake to reject all of it because we disagree with some of it. I join Senator Mansfield therefore in urging President Johnson to take the initiative in meeting General de Gaulle to explore every possible means toward effecting the negotiations the President himself has already done so much to bring about." But by the time Kennedy had returned from Maine and was ready to release the statement, Johnson had categorically dismissed De Gaulle's suggestion. The President having acted, Kennedy felt that his words could serve no purpose except to separate them even more. He put it aside.

In the autumn of 1966, Janusz Lewandowski, a Polish diplomat in the International Control Commission for Vietnam, told Ambassador Lodge that he believed North Vietnam was prepared to open secret exploratory discussions with the United States. North Vietnam's refusal to acknowledge that its forces were in the South was the major obstacle to the convening of the secret meetings in Warsaw. Before this disagreement could be resolved, United States airplanes bombed Hanoi, and the discussions were broken off by the North. The Foreign Minister of Italy, Amintore Fanfani, later told Kennedy that the bombing had been carried out as part of a long-arranged plan. Apparently no one who was privy to the secret discussions had informed the military of their progress. The scheduled bombing raids were carried out and the political consequences were disregarded.

As 1966 ended, the President had begun another extended bombing halt and hopes for peace were expressed by every world leader. As 1967 began, Robert Kennedy was absorbed in a bitter and damaging dispute with author William Manchester about the book *The Death of a President*. It was a good time to get away. He arranged to attend a parliamentary conference in Ditchly, England, and expanded the trip to include France, Germany, and Italy.

As 1967 began in Europe, the future of NATO was in doubt, Great Britain's entry into the Common Market was a paramount concern, the Kennedy round of tariff negotiations was at a critical stage, the nuclear nonproliferation treaty was being circulated for agreement, and European leaders were increasingly concerned about America's preoccupation with Vietnam.

For Kennedy, his trip to London was a time of relaxation and learning. He stayed at the home of the Radziwills. Prince Stanislaus ("Stas") Radziwill was a son of one of the most distinguished Polish aristocratic families. He had come to London as a refugee and made a huge business success, primarily in land investments. In the campaigns of 1960 and 1964, (and in the primaries of 1968), Radziwill spoke in Polish areas around the country, earning Kennedy's respect and affection. Lee Radziwill, Jacqueline Kennedy's sister, and her children took long walks with the senator and watched on the sidelines as he joined the soccer games in Hyde Park. Great cities give a shelter of anonymity, and Kennedy enjoyed the privacy of London. He saw old friends like Margot Fonteyn and Rudolf Nureyev. At mass at a neighborhood church, he was surprised to find ex-President Janio Quadros of Brazil in the next pew. He visited Blenheim and lunched with the Duke of Marlborough, and stood at the grave of Winston Churchill at Bladen. Nothing was more enjoyable than his afternoon as a guest of the students of the Oxford Union.

His London stay recalled the special meaning of Great Britain for his family, combining as it did so much of their triumph and tragedy. The appointment as Ambassador to the Court of St. James had been the zenith of Joseph Kennedy's public career. With the memory of Ireland's revolution against British rule still fresh, his proud and obvious Irish identification gave the appointment an ironic dimension. Robert Kennedy's sister Kathleen married into one of the noblest families of the realm. She was buried in British soil. His oldest brother had flown off on his fateful mission from an English airfield, a hero in Britain's last great war. President Kennedy had made a memorable presidential trip to London in 1961, and had dined at Buckingham Palace. His cordial relationship with Prime Minister Harold Macmillan personified the highest hopes and best traditions of both countries. In an unprecedented gesture, Great Britain had set aside an acre of its most historic land, Runneymede, as a memorial to President Kennedy.

Evenings after dinner, Robert Kennedy talked passionately to British friends about their passive acceptance of Britain's decline of power and influence. "Your politics are losing interest because you don't stand for anything. Agree or disagree with America's position in Vietnam, but do it because you believe it, not to save the pound." To others he would say: "Your history is your power. The new world that our children will live in will not be interested in your armies and your empire. You have given us the basic social values of the civilization we are defending. You have lost faith in your future because you are forgetting how much your past has meant to all of us."

He believed that Britain, as an integrated part of Europe, would reassert its leadership. For America, a united Europe would be a rival, a competitor and an uncertain force to deal with; but Kennedy regarded it as an inevitable development that the United States should encourage, because of the political and economic stability such a union would give to a crucial part of the world. He interpreted General de Gaulle's opposition to Britain's entry into the Common Market as a means of gaining time for France to build its economic and political base, so that it could lay claim to the leadership of the new Europe. It was a perilous course for De Gaulle. He was taking advantage of the fact that for Germany, the legacy of war had created a political impotence which had neutralized its economic superiority. De Gaulle's opportunity arose because Britain had deliberately refrained from participation in the attempt to unite Europe during the 1950s. Kennedy believed that De Gaulle's reign might give France enough time to become at least equal to Britain's power when the latter's inevitable entry into the Common Market occurred. If Germany then threatened to dominate, it would not be too late to revive the Anglo-French alliance. It was a great gamble for France, and perhaps a historic bluff, but Kennedy did not see anyone among Britain's contemporary leaders with the stature or spirit to call it.

On the evening of January 26, he was received by Prime Minister Harold Wilson. As he waited for Wilson to return from the House of Commons, Kennedy wrote letters on 10 Downing Street stationery to his father, reminding him of the family's time in London a quarter-century before; and to his own sons, to touch them with the history that "Number 10" represented.

Wilson was in an informal mood, serving cocktails in his shirt sleeves, puffing away at his pipe, relaxing with his feet on the conference table in the Cabinet Room and inviting his guest to do the same. There was in the Prime Minister the feeling of a man consumed by politics who calculated his moves, manipulated power adroitly, and found pleasure in the daily combat of his office.

The primary topic was the Common Market and Great Britain's future relationship to Western Europe. Wilson had just returned from a visit to Paris and General de Gaulle. He spoke about the possibility of Britain's entry in very optimistic terms. Kennedy thought the optimism was either naïve or deliberately inflated. The political realities affecting the French veto could not be easily changed, and there was very little Britain could do about it. Knowing Wilson's determined friendship with Lyndon Johnson, Kennedy left the issue of Vietnam alone, except to express hope that the impending visit to London of Premier Kosygin would be productive.

Before leaving Great Britain, Kennedy met with Foreign Minister George Brown and the leaders of the Conservative and Liberal parties, among others. It was clear to him that the country faced several years of economic and political crisis, and he was saddened by it. On his way home after his meetings on the Continent, he began a letter to Wilson expressing the judgment that British hopes for an early entry into the Common Market were more dream than reality. He did not send it because he feared Wilson would have resented such a letter as presumptuous.

France was in the midst of parliamentary elections and preparations for the state funeral of Alphonse Juin, its last surviving Marshal, when Kennedy arrived in Paris on January 29. Henry Kissinger happened to be in Paris at the same time, and Kennedy spent several hours with him in an intense discussion of Vietnam. Together they visited Jean Sainteny, the former French High Commissioner in Indochina, who had just returned from a trip to Hanoi where he had met with his old acquaintance, Ho Chi Minh.

Kennedy met with the leaders of the government and its opposition. He was fascinated by André Malraux, France's Minister of Cultural Affairs, an epic personality in both politics and literature. Malraux had recently returned from China and reported that while Chinese interest in Vietnam was tremendous, its means of implementing that concern were small. Chinese policy, he said, was intended to create an impression of influence and power, but the reality was far different. No Chinese leader believed that the United States would use atomic weapons against them. Mao had asked Malraux why America had committed itself so firmly to Chiang Kai-shek, adding wistfully that if the United States had chosen to support him in the 1940s, it could have meant the alliance of the richest and the poorest nations in the world. Malraux said that Chinese hatred of the United States was fabricated, and like any totalitarian-directed attitude, it could be changed overnight. But in Malraux's opinion, the situation in China would not change in any important respect for the next fifteen years.

In Bonn on February 1, Kennedy met Chancellor Kiesinger for the first time. He was impressed by his intelligence, personality, and candor. One fascinating aspect of the discussion was the Chancellor's description of his recent meeting with President de Gaulle. The general had told him that Germany was too obedient to American interests and influences. By its nature, De Gaulle said (with generous references to American history) that the United States must dominate in all of its relationships, even in Europe. France does not want domination, even friendly domination.

Kiesinger had defended German policy by arguing that American interests were parallel in broad areas to those of both Germany and Europe. De Gaulle smiled at the response, and gently said that some day Germany would agree with him. In eloquent and affectionate terms, Kiesinger described his great esteem for De Gaulle and dismissed the idea that the general's attitude toward the United States was motivated by any personal animosity. Rather, it was romantic nationalism. Quoting De Gaulle, he expressed it by saying: "Frankreich, Frankreich Himmel, Frankreich Boden, Frankreich Meer muss ewig Frankreich bleiben."[2] De Gaulle was seeking a dominant place for France in a world of giants, and he sought this role through a consolidation of continental power under French leadership. Kiesinger recalled De Gaulle's disdain for the American position in Vietnam. His long arms sweeping out, the General had said, "You cannot conquer a swamp." As a divided country itself, the Germans were more willing to accept American involvement in Vietnam; but Kiesinger admitted that the large majority of his countrymen did not understand what the Americans were trying to do.

Kennedy urged the Chancellor to stand with Great Britain in its effort to join the Common Market. He added his own impression that Great Britain, feeling both politically and economically isolated, had unrealistic hopes for the immediate future in terms of joining Europe. Kiesinger said Germany wanted a close alliance with Great Britain and he had told this to De Gaulle as well as to Harold Wilson.

[2] "France, the French heavens, the French ground, the French sea must remain French forever."

When Kennedy met with Willy Brandt, the Foreign Minister in Germany's "Grand Coalition," he concentrated on the nuclear non-proliferation treaty. From his own involvement with the problem of weapons control during the New Frontier, Kennedy had become convinced that this was the single most important problem for every nation. In 1965, seventeen nations began meeting in Geneva to draft an effective nonproliferation treaty. Kennedy argued the necessity of such a treaty in his first major speech in the Senate and in countless speeches, and public statements thereafter.[3]

Kennedy had told Maurice Couve de Murville, then Foreign Minister of France, that he did not understand the French refusal to sign the nuclear non-proliferation treaty. A new generation of Germans would soon emerge who would not accept the responsibility or the guilt for World War II. They would read the speeches of General de Gaulle and they would ask why their country should not have nuclear weapons so it would not have to be dependent on any other country for its security and protection. Couve did not hesitate in his reply. He repeated it twice: "I would tell the Germans that their history does not permit them to have nuclear weapons." Kennedy said he also opposed giving Germany nuclear weapons, but that it would be a profound mistake to think that Germany could be deprived for generations to come of a role of power and responsibility, in a Europe where its economic and political strength would be a dominant force. That, argued Kennedy, is the reason for the urgency in European integration, with Great Britain as a full-fledged partner. Only then could Europe, with its existing nuclear weaponry, be self-secure and part of the control mechanism of the nuclear age.

Kennedy also visited Rome, where he had lengthy meetings with President Giuseppe Saragat, Premier Aldo Moro and Foreign Minister Amintore Fanfani, as well as final sessions with the Pope and Cardinal Cicognani. Saragat emphasized what every European leader had told Kennedy, that America's obsession with Vietnam was causing a deterioration in programs, attitudes, and initiatives in Europe that could only be harmful in the long run. To make his point that

---

[3] Including a discussion carried on the Telstar communications satellite with him in New York, Lord Chalfont in London and Franz-Josef Strauss in Bonn. Kennedy understood that one major hurdle for the treaty was the difficulty of reconciling Soviet fears of German resurgence with West Germany's demand for a significant voice in NATO's nuclear decisions.

the United States was losing interest and contact with European problems, Saragat pointed to President Johnson's State of the Union speech made two weeks before. "There are fifty lines on Latin America," he said, "twenty lines on Africa, and one line—listen carefully to my words, one line—not two—for Europe."

As Kennedy turned toward home, he talked again and again of the opportunity the United States was losing to make a different world. "Civilizations come and go. Great powers used to survive at the crest of their wave for several centuries. Now we will be lucky to have several generations where our power can make the difference in helping the world survive. And here we are—throwing our men, our dreams, our power into the swamps and no one will ever understand why we did it."

For Vietnam in 1967, the Tet holiday season, which begins in late January, was a time of hope. The negotiation brokered by the Polish and Italian governments had aborted just weeks before, but it raised the possibility of bringing the parties to the conference table. Perhaps the most hopeful sign was the announced visit to London of Soviet Premier Alexei Kosygin. It was widely anticipated that the Russians, using the good offices of the British Government, would pressure Hanoi and the NLF leadership to begin negotiations in return for the American concession of an unconditional bombing halt.

When in England, Kennedy had met with some fifty American Rhodes Scholars at Oxford, who two days before had sent a powerful letter to President Johnson raising basic questions about American involvement in Vietnam. They poured out their concern, and he was greatly impressed by their knowledge, courage, and sophistication. In an extemporaneous speech sponsored by the Oxford Student Union, Kennedy tried to avoid going over all his disagreements with the Administration on Vietnam, and said that the next "three to four weeks will be crucial in bringing about negotiations." He was referring to the Kosygin visit, the Tet holiday and the continuing halt in American bombing. Any analyst of foreign affairs could have reached the same conclusion from reading the newspapers, but some newspaper stories in the United States reported that Kennedy was compromising the possibility of negotiations by revealing confidential information made available to him in briefings. He resented the stories and believed they were inspired by White House sources. The truth was that pressure for negotiations to end the war was intense, and every responsible European leader was adding to the pressure.

On January 31, 1967, after two days of meetings with French officials and political leaders, Kennedy called on President de Gaulle. Their entire discussion concerned Vietnam, and the senator remembered it in sharp detail.

"As I told your brother," De Gaulle began, "the United States is involved in a wrong course in Vietnam. The United States should not be there. Vietnam is not America's business. The people of Vietnam should decide how they will live and be governed. There can be no peace in Vietnam until the United States stops the bombing of the North and announces its intention to withdraw its troops." De Gaulle made it clear that he did not mean immediate withdrawal, but rather the announced intention to withdraw within a specific time, perhaps a period of years.

Kennedy questioned how serious negotiations could be possible under that plan. The adversary would only have to wait out the withdrawal time and then occupy the country. The general did not reply directly, but instead spoke obscurely of the basic geographical and political considerations affecting Vietnam. There was a regional rivalry between the North and the South, he said, perhaps more significant than the ideological conflict.[4] The South would not permit either the North or northerners to run their country. Ho Chi Minh realized this and would not attempt it. Kennedy answered by saying that even if this were so, unilateral withdrawal by America would deliver the country to the NLF. In his judgment, the South Vietnamese wanted neither the North nor the Communists nor Marshal Ky as their governors. Our obligation, he continued, was to protect their right to choose their own government. Kennedy said that as a member of his brother's Administration, he felt some responsibility for the situation in Vietnam. Although he was critical of the direction of the policies now, neither he nor any other major political figure in Amer-

---

[4] The French, for purposes of colonial administration, combined three independent states, Tonkin, Annam, and Cochin China, into the territory of Indochina. These states had proud histories, cultural differences, and ancient rivalries, all of which survived the French rule. The "South" is generally Cochin China and most of Annam. The "North" is Tonkin.

ica, nor any substantial number of Americans, would favor unilateral withdrawal and the abandonment of our South Vietnamese allies. The French President replied: "All problems have solutions. You must not become concerned." If American forces were to withdraw, he said, many elements in Vietnam presently underground would emerge. Something quite different than what Kennedy anticipated would result, probably not Communist, nor dominated by Marshal Ky (a name the General sputtered with disdain) but more truly representative of the power elements of the country.

President de Gaulle spoke with passionate eloquence of the larger problem, the morality of the war. "The United States," he said, "has always had a special role in the world which has commanded the respect and admiration of other countries. It has been the symbol of the finest ideals, the highest hopes. This is now being destroyed. The United States is in the process of destroying a country and a people. America says it is fighting Communism, but by what right does it fight Communism in another people's country and against their will?" Kennedy spoke again of South Vietnam's right to self-determination. "I was talking about the world," interrupted the General. "You have returned again to a local matter. History is the force at work in Vietnam and the United States will not prevail against it."

Kennedy regarded President de Gaulle as a person of extraordinary intellect and political genius. He accepted his friendship and admiration for America as genuine. At the same time, he felt the General was primarily interested in the power, prestige, and interests of France, which the overwhelming power of the United States could only submerge as an effective world force. From this point of view, the American involvement in Vietnam was helpful to De Gaulle's purposes. It caused Europeans to believe that American priorities were elsewhere and that the United States, having acted without regard of the consequences to other nations, was not a reliable ally. There was thus a conflict between De Gaulle's friendship and respect for the United States and his commitment to French interests, especially in Europe, which were being served by the American involvement in Southeast Asia. It was possible, in Kennedy's opinion, to force the General into a significant, constructive role in ending the Vietnam War, but Washington's policy of isolating De Gaulle from the conflict, as illustrated by the rejection of his offers of mediation, permitted the General to make majestic criticisms without fear of being asked to share responsibility for settlement.

Earlier in the day, Kennedy had called on Etienne Manac'h, the director of Asian Affairs for the French Foreign Ministry. Kennedy was accompained by John Dean of the American embassy. Manac'h had impressive credentials as an Asian authority and Kennedy listened carefully to his analysis of China, Vietnam and the growing Russian involvement in Asia. Kennedy asked what the United States had to do to bring about negotiations. Manac'h, who was in frequent communication with representatives of Hanoi and the NLF, replied in some detail. North Vietnam is distrustful of American offers of negotiations and peace, he said. With every offer of peace, there has been a parallel action of war. Manac'h suggested solving the problem in slices. In his judgment, Hanoi was ready to negotiate with the United States, leaving aside temporarily the problem of the NLF. The one indispensable condition, he said, was cessation of the bombing. The bombing was based on a miscalculation that it could stop the movement of troops and supplies. This has not happened. The Soviet Union cannot permit the destruction of a Communist country by American bombing. Suspend the bombing unilaterally. A meeting with Hanoi can be arranged where reciprocal concessions can be worked out. Hanoi does not regard the NLF as the only representative of South Vietnam, but its political reality must be recognized. The NLF role is negotiable, Manac'h said.

The State Department official, John Dean, who accompanied Kennedy to the Manac'h interview, thought this appraisal significant, especially the willingness of Hanoi to talk directly to the United States without first resolving the question of the NLF status, certainly significant enough to cable immediately a report on the conference. Several days later, one of Washington's best diplomatic reporters, Edward Weintal of *Newsweek,* was making his rounds at the State Department for news concerning Vietnam. For weeks the papers had been reporting "peace feelers" on an almost daily basis. Harrison Salisbury of the New York *Times* had sent a significant dispatch in January after a meeting with North Vietnam's Premier, indicating that Hanoi had altered its position regarding negotiations. Wilfred Burchett, an Australian Communist reporter, on January 28 confirmed the Salisbury impression that Hanoi was dropping all preconditions for negotiations to begin, except for the cessation of the bombing. United Nations Secretary General U Thant offered the same independent judgment. All of these reports were labeled "peace feelers," so when Weintal asked if there were any new ones, the State Department official replied that they came in every day. "Here's one from Paris connected with the Kennedy visit," he said.

Shortly thereafter, a *Newsweek* story appeared describing a "significant peace signal" which had been "unveiled for the benefit of Robert F. Kennedy for reasons best known to the enemy." The report indicated that the "peace feeler" had been transmitted by Hanoi's Foreign Minister and that it went far beyond anything received so far. Hanoi's "message" was that negotiations could begin as soon as the bombing stopped. The story stated that the French, by relaying the signal through Kennedy, made it "certain that the proposal was not helped at the White House" and added "to the catalog of French sins." Spokesmen for the Administration were quoted as saying that "we will wait until they (Hanoi) spin out their own story in their own way." This reflected the attitude that time was on the American side and that the longer Hanoi waited, the less it would have to negotiate.

When the *Newsweek* story was published, the White House asked the State Department for its source. A search was made of the "limited distribution" cable files for Europe and Asia. Nothing was found and this was reported back to the White House. When the President heard this, he immediately assumed that Kennedy had leaked the story. In fact, the cable was in the State Department, classified for "general distribution," a classification too low to merit inclusion in the department's search.

Newsweek broke the story as Kennedy returned to the United States. When reporters questioned him, he was amused. "I return from Europe, hopeful about peace but without any 'feelers,'" he said. For a while he did not know what the reporters were talking about. When he learned it was related to his conversation with Manac'h, he could hardly believe it. He had thought the discussion interesting and significant, reflecting as it did the judgment of one of the most learned and respected men in Asian affairs of any Foreign Ministry, but it was only a variation on the theme that he had heard in every foreign capital from the highest sources: Hanoi would begin to negotiate if the U.S. stopped the bombing. Manac'h had only been more precise by suggesting the stages of negotiations after discussions began. Kennedy feared that Manac'h might face personal repercussions, so he telephoned the Foreign Ministry to be sure it understood the origins of the story.

The "peace feeler" incident was a political liability for Kennedy. It appeared as though he were upstaging the President at a time when the fragile possibility of negotiations seemed to be gaining strength. It was the kind of story that had its impact on publication, and whose initial impression no amount of clarification could change.

Nor was the incident over. On February 6, Kennedy called President Johnson's appointment secretary, Marvin Watson, to request an appointment. Those who knew of his conversations in Europe had urged Kennedy to see the President to report on his trip. While the appointment was under discussion, the White House had Undersecretary of State Nicholas Katzenbach visit Kennedy in his Senate office. While they talked a call told them to go to the White House.

There were four men at the meeting: President Johnson, Kennedy, Katzenbach, and Presidential Assistant Walt Rostow. None would forget the occasion. President Johnson was in a rage. He believed that a Kennedy associate had leaked the "peace feeler" story in a deliberate attempt to embarrass him. Kennedy replied firmly, "Your own State Department leaked the story." "It's your State Department," the President shot back.

The exchange continued, with Kennedy talking about Europe's concern that the United States had failed to follow up peace overtures, and the President insisting that every hint had been pursued. When Kennedy offered his suggestions for negotiations—a bombing halt in the North, a reduction of the violence in the South and an internationally supervised cease-fire—Johnson lashed out at all the senators who were urging de-escalation. He predicted that in six months, they would be badly hurt politically because the voters would realize they had been engaging in cheap politics which could only prolong the war and increase the casualties. After every point, he turned to his associates. "Isn't that right, Nick?" or "Right, Walt?" he asked, and they nodded agreement.

The discussion degenerated into an argument over who had requested the meeting. The President said that he had not invited

Kennedy—Kennedy had asked to come. The senator said it would not happen again. Before Kennedy left, Johnson urged him to tell waiting reporters that every possibility for peace talks was being pursued. Kennedy said he could not do so because he knew it was not true.

The newspaper stories that appeared later indicated that Kennedy had called Johnson an "S.O.B." Kennedy had not used offensive language, but the heat of the meeting was too intense to contain behind the closed doors of the White House, and rumors about the confrontation were widely reported. As far as Kennedy was concerned, he had learned one thing—the prospects for peace talks were dim and the President was committed to a course that made them even dimmer.

The emotion of February overflowed into March. Soviet Premier Kosygin, during his London visit, stated that the U.S. should stop bombing "to enable talks." To Kennedy, the United States was willing to do this in 1966, why not in 1967? In the second week of February, there had been an exchange of letters between President Johnson and Ho Chi Minh. This correspondence was released on March 21, and strengthened Kennedy's judgment that the United States had escalated its demands and in the process had diminished the possibilities of negotiations. Kennedy issued a short statement pointing out that Johnson not only required a military de-escalation in return for a cessation of the bombing but that the President's letter also imposed "the further condition that we have evidence that Hanoi has *already* ceased infiltration before we stop the bombing." A further disturbing point was that the President had ordered the resumption of the bombing before any response had been received from Hanoi to his letter. As Kennedy saw it, important advisers to the President felt that the U.S. was on the brink of a military victory and could afford to stiffen its position.

Meanwhile, the mood of many Americans was turning from frustration to anger. A series of eyewitness articles by Harrison Salisbury of the New York *Times* from North Vietnam revealed that U.S. government spokesmen had spread gross misinformation, if not deceit, about the bombing. Americans had been assured that only military targets were being bombed; in fact, as Salisbury's articles and photographs proved, civilian centers were being systematically destroyed and the bombing had hardly disrupted Hanoi's military effort.

As chances for negotiations died, and new escalations began, Kennedy decided to speak out in a major statement for the first time in over a year. Close advisers warned Kennedy that another statement criticizing the Administration would subject him to new torrents of personal abuse. The senator had no illusions. According to the Harris Poll at this time, 70 per cent of the American people supported the involvement in Vietnam. Analyzing this poll in *The New Yorker*, Richard Rovere wrote: ". . . Those opponents of the President who favor de-escalation and could therefore be counted upon to approve the application of the Kennedy proposals even if they did not bring early and entirely satisfactory results amount to only twelve per cent . . ." The problem in speaking out at this time was not related to Johnson's strength. The same Harris Poll showed only 43 per cent of the country approving the President as a war leader. Major New York politicians identified with Lyndon Johnson had confided that the President was in trouble politically. The real problem in speaking out now was the backlash of the Manchester controversy that made Kennedy vulnerable, and the related danger in what appeared to be Kennedy's interference, while in Europe, with the President's conduct of foreign affairs. But Kennedy's anger at what Johnson was doing overcame these personal considerations. Predicting to friends that within six months the country would agree with him, Kennedy spoke to the Senate on March 2. For the first time publicly, he raised doubts about the war's morality:

". . . although the world's imperfections may call forth the acts of war, righteousness cannot obscure the agony and pain those acts bring to a single child . . ." He described the horror and terror and the endless nightmare of bombing, murder, violence, and destruction. ". . . a country where young men have never lived a day in peace and where families have never known a time when it was not necessary to be afraid." Then he posed the question of moral responsibility:

> ". . . All we say and all we do must be informed by our awareness that this horror is partly our responsibility; not just a nation's responsibility, but yours and mine. It is we who live in abundance and send our young men out to die. It is our chemicals that scorch the

children and our bombs that level the villages. We are all participants . . . Even though we must know as a nation what it is necessary to do, we must also feel as men the anguish of what it is we are doing . . ."

The speech placed part of the blame for the failure to find peace on the Viet Cong and the North Vietnamese, but its main thrust was a call for the unconditional cessation of the bombing of North Vietnam by the United States:

". . . I propose that we test the sincerity of the statements by Premier Kosygin and others asserting that if the bombardment of the North is halted, negotiations would begin—by halting the bombardment and saying we are ready to negotiate within the week; making it clear that discussions cannot continue for a prolonged period without an agreement that neither side will substantially increase the size of the war in South Vietnam by infiltration or reinforcement. An international group should be asked to inspect the borders and ports of the country to report any further escalation. And under the direction of the United Nations, and with an international presence gradually replacing American forces, we should move toward a final settlement which allows all major political elements in South Vietnam to participate in the choice of leadership and shape their future direction as a people . . .

With his recommendations now before the country, no matter how delicately his thoughts were cushioned by words, Robert Kennedy had finally broken with the Administration.

Vietnam for most Americans was a series of shattered hopes, as all the lessons of past wars and all the statement of trusted leaders had proved to be misleading. In the summer of 1967, there was still the hope that the general election scheduled for South Vietnam would produce a government capable of fighting the war by attracting the willing allegiance and support of the people. With its own solid political base to support it, perhaps such a government could negotiate a settlement. At a minimum, the elections gave the United States an opportunity to validate its presence as a shield, permitting the people of South Vietnam to choose their own government freely. Instead, as Kennedy saw it, the hopeful possibilities of the election were destroyed before a ballot was cast. The elections were not "free" and the government was not representative. Not only Communists but "neutralists" were barred from participation. No candidate representing militant Buddhism was allowed. Non-Communist candidates, barred from the ballot because their views were "unacceptable," included General Duong Van Minh, the man with the broadest popularity and support in all of South Vietnam. The military junta won the election, but their manipulation of the electoral machinery deprived their victory of any meaning. Kennedy commented:

> With all the advantages of incumbency, with the support and votes of the armed forces, with their strongest rivals excluded from the contest, running against candidates who themselves did not represent social change or identification with the peasantry—with all this, the military ticket could still win only 35% of the vote of ⅗ of the nation.

Increasingly Kennedy was becoming concerned about the war's effect on the soul and spirit of his own country. The picture of the world's greatest military power locked in a ferocious struggle with a primitive land, without industry to arm itself or an air force to defend itself, disturbed him deeply. In his March 2 speech, he said that "freedom and security must at times be paid for in blood," but increasingly he came to believe that the violence, the brutality, and destruction in Vietnam were for no purpose. Perhaps, if Vietnam were lost, Communism would be a thousand miles closer to America; but this was no justification for destroying a country and a people. The war had been justified as a way to contain China. But perhaps the historical animosity of the Vietnamese to China would be a better counter to Chinese belligerency than a government that could not survive without the presence of American armies. In balancing the hopes, illusions, and human costs of Vietnam, Kennedy saw the escalating destruction as a burden to the national conscience.

In his March 1967 speech, Kennedy had invoked the prophecy of Saint John the Divine to describe how the war must appear to the Vietnamese: "And I looked, and beheld a pale horse: and his name that sat on him was Death, and hell followed with him. And power was given unto them over the fourth part of the earth, to kill with sword, and with hunger, and with death . . ." By November, he had concluded that continuing escalation was immoral, not because all military action is immoral, but because this escalation far exceeded our vital interests, and destroyed the purposes that justified our original involvement. At this time Kennedy was writing his memoir of the Cuban missile crisis. Explaining his opposition to a surprise air attack on Cuba, his own words had present meaning: ". . . our struggle against Communism throughout the world was far more than physical survival—it has as its essence our heritage and our ideals and these we must not destroy." He believed that that destruction was going on in Vietnam.

By November 1967, the State Department had come to the conclusion that North Vietnam would not seriously negotiate until the American presidential elections were over. William Bundy, Assistant Secretary of State for the Far East, spoke of stalemate, saying "things will just have to rock on." At this point, a former aide to Secretary McNamara who was writing about the history of the American involvement in Vietnam asked Kennedy whether his brother would have made the commitment of American combat troops. It was the kind of question Robert Kennedy disliked, but on this occasion he answered it. The senator said: "Never. The President would never have done it. He was determined not to send troops." He cited President Kennedy's rejection of the Taylor-Rostow recommendation for combat troops in 1961. "If the South Vietnamese could not do it," he continued, "the United States could not win it for them. The President had in mind a Laos-type solution."

The writer asked how come the brothers had understood this fact, which seemed more crucial with each passing year of bloody struggle. *"We were there,"* Kennedy said. He referred to the trip he and his brother had made to Indochina in 1951. They had seen the political dimensions of the struggle and understood the limited possibilities of military involvement.

President Johnson's decision on March 31, 1968, to stop the bombing and not to seek re-election muted Vietnam as an issue in the presidential primaries. No one is sure what political and personal calculations Lyndon Johnson had in mind in this decision, but the concessions he made were the same that Kennedy had advocated at least a year earlier. Negotiations began in Paris on May 10, 1968. In the last hours of the Johnson administration, substantive discussions were begun. Richard Nixon, elected President in good part because of the political havoc caused by the war issue, chose as his special assistant for National Security Affairs and his principal personal foreign-policy adviser a man who had consulted closely with Robert Kennedy, who had agreed with Kennedy's analysis of the Vietnam conflict, and who had hoped to see Robert Kennedy President of the United States.

New hopes rose for peace, but by the end of Nixon's first ten months in office, it was clear that the "plan" he had promised for ending the war was a sham, and he was no more willing than Johnson to force a more representative regime in Saigon. In Vietnam, the killing continued. In Paris, the negotiations foundered amidst mutual recrimination. In the United States, the focus of debate shifted from how to negotiate a mutual withdrawal of foreign forces, to how and when to achieve the unilateral withdrawal of American troops.[5] The Nixon administration held to the hope that the South Vietnamese, trained and equipped by the United States, could take over the burden of the fighting—a hope that had proven so hollow since first attempted in 1961. The new President tried to invoke the "silent majority" of the public, as his predecessor had invoked his "consensus" in support of his view toward the war.

The war in Vietnam had become almost a condition of life. Many of those who thought they had helped create a new direction, in the political upheavals of 1968, were angered and despairing at the continuation of a conflict that presidents could not justify, generals could not win, statesmen could not negotiate, and that millions of men, women, and children would not survive.

[5] At no time did Kennedy favor unilateral withdrawal that would amount to abandoning the commitment in Vietnam. He was for a negotiated settlement and believed that a continued American military presence was necessary to achieve that result. In his book, *To Seek a Newer World,* he discussed the problem: "Withdrawal is now impossible. American intervention has created its own reality . . . These people (the Vietnamese who staked their lives on the American presence and protection) cannot suddenly be abandoned to the forcible conquest of a minority . . ." He also said: "I believe defeat or precipitous withdrawal from Vietnam (would) damage our position in the world. We would not suddenly collapse; Communist fleets would not suddenly appear in the harbors of Honolulu or San Francisco Bay. But there would be serious effects, especially in Southeast Asia itself."

13

KENNEDY AND JOHNSON

From 1964 to 1968, Robert Kennedy and Lyndon Johnson dominated the politics of the Democratic party. To the public, the two were brooding generals of hostile armies camped in the same city, skirmishing on occasion, making sporadic attempts at negotiation, while each prepared for the ultimate clash in which one would emerge the victor. Their feud had its stormy and quiescent stages, its periods of sharp confrontation and attempted accommodation; but the over-all trend was toward gradual breakdown. To both men, it was a frustrating relationship that neither considered to be in his interest, but neither could seem to change. In the end Kennedy did set out to topple Johnson from his office, the first time any man with a chance to succeed has tried to unseat an incumbent president of his own party.

The relationship between Kennedy and Johnson was much more complex than that portrayed to the public. It grew out of the nature of the men and the nature of the presidential office. It involved elements of respect as well as antagonism. They could have made the most effective team of their time, but they were too entwined in bitter memory to cooperate in any meaningful way.

They were different men in almost every way. Kennedy was shy; Johnson was expansive. When Johnson talked to a man, he stroked his shoulder, pumped his arm, and talked point blank into his face. Kennedy kept a distance between himself and others. Johnson was mercurial, subject to wide swings of mood. He could curse and bully a man in the most brutal manner, and then charm him in a way that was both patronizing and effective. Kennedy's moods were private matters, hard to ascertain by any but his closest friends. Johnson took himself very seriously. He was the kind of man who could name his children, his ranch, and his dog after himself. Kennedy took his power, his work, and his problems seriously, but never himself. These personal differences made communication difficult and friendship impossible.

So did their differing styles. To Johnson, Kennedy and his circle were part of the urbane, educated, Eastern establishment he felt had always snubbed and belittled him. To Kennedy, Johnson and many of his intimates were bad-mannered and crude. On one occasion, after John Kennedy's election, Robert Kennedy had gone deer hunting on Johnson's ranch. Johnson took him to an elevated concrete structure from which they awaited in comfort the appearance of deer to be shot, much as a sultan shoots game from his balcony as bushwhackers push the animals toward him. Kennedy was disgusted. "This isn't hunting," he said, "it's slaughter."

Another vital difference was in age. The two were eighteen years apart, but Johnson had been in public life for thirty years. Molded by the New Deal, Johnson turned instinctively to federal programs as the answer to public problems, while Kennedy was receptive to evidence that the federal approach was not working. Johnson regarded Kennedy's criticism of his policies as the result of inexperience as well as ambition. In private, he sometimes referred to him as "that boy."

But these feelings did not prevent a certain kind of admiration. Both men had won success in politics, and they respected each other's abilities in this field. Had they been able to trade insights they would have enjoyed it, for each was a consummate politician. Johnson envied the way Kennedy could project on television, and he told him so when they campaigned together in New York in 1964. Kennedy believed Johnson was sincere in what he tried to do for the poor, and that some of his civil rights stands had been taken at considerable political risk. He was also sympathetic to the responsibilities Johnson had, as was so obvious in the letter Kennedy wrote citing the dilemma of Lincoln, at the time of the bombing pause in 1966. Kennedy and Johnson were among the handful of men who had lived with the awesome burdens of the presidency, a fact which created, amidst all their difficulties with one another, an indiscernible bond.

But while they both relished politics, they approached it in a different way. Kennedy sought confrontation. Johnson sought consensus. Kennedy was at his best leading a crusade. Johnson was at his best negotiating the terms of settlement after the test of strength had taken place. Johnson had come out of the legislative process where a premium is put on moderating differences to achieve compromise. Important achievements in his career as Senate leader, the Civil Rights Act of 1958, the National Defense Education Act, and statehood for Alaska and Hawaii, had been accomplished through these personal skills. Kennedy could and did moderate differences among opposing groups, but his puritanical emphasis on right and wrong made him more comfortable as an advocate for what he believed in strongly.

The unique historical setting of their relationship also fed the conflict. A President of the United States has to be the sole preeminent personality within his party. When competing for the nomination he is treated as one among equals; but once he is elected he cannot afford to have rivals for power. All party members, regardless of individual differences must acknowledge his leadership.[1] If he cannot command this support, and if the party that is his base of support is divided by his policies, he cannot hope to have a majority behind him in the country at large, and eventually the authority of the presidency itself is undermined.

This is part of the reason why the pull of party loyalty is so strong on politicians. Men who seek their party's presidential nomination and are defeated at the convention can only be effective within their party if they subordinate themselves to the President. In the history of the American presidency, at least until Lyndon Johnson succeeded John F. Kennedy, all the men in the President's party who had challenged him for the nomination had either been absorbed into the presidential orbit or had decided to stay out of public life.[2]

[1] The monopoly of attention the President holds is one reason why the political party in power has such difficulty building up and electing a successor to an incumbent President—as Richard Nixon discovered in 1960 and Hubert Humphrey in 1968.

[2] Presidents Lincoln, Wilson, Harrison, and Kennedy took challengers Seward, Bryan, Blaine, and Stevenson into their cabinets, on the logical premise that their prestige and participation would broaden the appeal of the administrations. President Harding sent Charles Evans Hughes to the Supreme Court. President Truman took a somewhat different tack. He accepted the resignation of all the men who had been national figures in the Roosevelt Administration, except for Henry Wallace. Wallace later rose to challenge him.

Generally the range of appointments a President can make is broad enough to encompass the disappointments of his competitors and the aspirations of his challengers. Since their power and tenure depends on presidential good will, he can generally control their public attitudes and maintain his pre-eminence in the country.

Robert Kennedy's position was unparalleled. No other assassinated President had left a political heir.[3] No other President had died in office leaving a lieutenant with a political base that could stand independently of his constitutional successor. Other families had a continuing identity with the presidential office, such as the Adamses, the Harrisons, the Roosevelts, but their future claim was exercised by descendants, not brothers.

By winning election to the Senate, Robert Kennedy became constitutionally independent of the presidency and liberated from White House control and direction. At the same time, his election gave plausibility to the view that he regarded the Johnson incumbency as an interregnum, and that the energies of the Kennedy "organization" were singularly directed to a restoration of the office which brutal fate had taken away.

It is easy to say, but also true, that the Kennedy-Johnson feud might have been avoided. Faced with similar circumstances, different men could have maintained an effective working relationship, if only in recognition of their mutual interests. But the possibilities of a working relationship between Kennedy and Johnson had been impaired at an early date. Johnson's personal feelings were shaped by events well before he became President. "John Kennedy," Johnson would say to intimates, "did nothing against me except beat me at Los Angeles— and I deserved to be beaten." But Robert Kennedy, he felt, had tried to prevent his nomination as Vice President. Johnson would not have been Robert Kennedy's first choice as his brother's running mate, but he went along with his brother's desire to offer him the place. He saw the political logic of the selection, in terms of Johnson's ability to help carry southern states where John Kennedy was weak. But

---

[3] Of America's assassinated Presidents, Abraham Lincoln had one brother who died in infancy and four sons, none of whom ever ran for office (Robert Todd Lincoln held appointive posts). James Garfield had three brothers and four sons. Only one son went into public life, and he was Secretary of the Interior. William McKinley's brothers remained in private life. Both his children died in infancy.

when opposition among labor and liberal elements posed the possibility of a floor fight against Johnson, it was Robert Kennedy whom his brother dispatched as his sole emissary to warn Johnson of what might happen. Twice, Robert Kennedy came to Johnson's hotel suite for this purpose. The second time, after Johnson had already prepared his acceptance statement, he suggested that Johnson withdraw. Johnson went into the next room, telephoned John Kennedy, and made it clear that he had accepted the offer to run for Vice President. John Kennedy immediately confirmed the arrangement, leaving Robert to face Johnson's embarrassed wrath.

Afterward, Johnson rationalized the situation by implying that Robert had gone beyond his brother's directions. In fact, Kennedy felt he had followed those instructions explicitly. In later years, when he was asked, Kennedy would say: "Would I do something on a major matter like that contrary to my brother's wishes?" But even he had to admit the circumstances were such that Johnson could reasonably have believed Robert Kennedy, on his own initiative, was trying to unmake an understanding he had with the presidential nominee which Johnson felt was firm.

After the election, John Kennedy was especially careful to seek the advice and assistance of his Vice President and make sure he was included in important discussions. Johnson appreciated this. "The vice presidency is the most miserable, forlorn job in the world," he would say later. "Jack knew it. He was good to me." But Robert Kennedy, he believed, did his best to exclude him from the councils of the Administration, and took upon himself many of the important projects Johnson felt he should have done.[4] When *Life* magazine, in January 1962, carried a prominent article on Robert Kennedy as the "number two man in Washington," Johnson, who felt he deserved the title, went so far as to suggest Kennedy had planted the story. Johnson also resented the way Kennedy acted at meetings of the President's Equal Employment Opportunity Commission, of which the Vice President was Chairman. Kennedy asked questions indicating his belief that the committee was not operating effectively. He felt the Committee

---

[4] In fact, however, Robert Kennedy, knowing his brother's preoccupation, was frequently the one who reminded the White House staff to involve the Vice President in public, political, and social activities. But as his brother's closest associate, he was the target for those who felt affronted by the President's inattention but did not wish to criticize him directly.

was dominated by "Uncle Tom" attitudes and was not doing the aggressive job that had to be done.

John Kennedy's assassination turned everything around in the harshest way. The public wondered how these two would act toward one another. Kennedy, numbed by grief, had little time to think of this. Not so Johnson. He knew the greatest need at the time was to give the appearance of smooth transition and confident continuity of power, and this necessarily meant avoiding any hint of a split with Kennedy. The impression Johnson gave in the days following the funeral was of an exceedingly considerate and thoughtful man sharing a shattered family's sorrow. He stayed out of the family quarters at the White House for two weeks until Mrs. Kennedy could establish a new residence in comfort and convenience. He took a personal interest in the planning of the Kennedy Library in Massachusetts, the family's chief project at that time, attending an organizational meeting at Edward Kennedy's home and making a generous financial contribution.[5]

As the Johnson era began, however, the tensions seemed unavoidable. A proud and vain man, Johnson had trained and planned for the presidency as much as any man in modern times. He would have wished to come to the office through a victory of his own making but, acknowledging the fateful circumstances that brought him to the White House, he welcomed the panoply of presidential duties with unconcealed enthusiasm. Johnson had ideas of his own for the country and for winning a place in history. He hated being thought of as an "accidental" President or as a pause between two Kennedy administrations. Yet even his successes were shadowed at every turn by the growing legend of a Camelot that preceded him. President Kennedy was being lionized in Europe while Johnson was ignored; John Kennedy was the hero of the liberal and intellectual communities where Johnson was reviled; and Robert Kennedy, as his brother's heir, was receiving much of the affection so pointedly denied Lyndon Johnson.

The sense of national guilt over the assassination survived the sorrow and contributed to the legend. So deep and pervasive was the national sense of loss that, at the pinnacle of Johnson's popularity,

---

[5] Kennedy would acknowledge these actions five years later, when he included in his announcement of his candidacy for the presidency recognition of the fact that Johnson had been "extremely kind to me and members of my family in the difficult months which followed the events of November of 1963."

he was still compared unfavorably with President Kennedy. *Time* magazine, no partisan of John Kennedy, compared Lyndon Johnson to him on November 26, 1965, in these words:

> He impresses people, but he does not touch them; he persuades them, but he does not gladden them. His creased face, with its oddly forced smile, cannot displace the memory of Kennedy's youthful radiance, and his unctuous prosiness cannot match Kennedy's eloquence. Compared with Kennedy's graceful dignity Johnson's homely touch can be embarrassing.

Even the television coverage of Johnson's Inauguration in 1965 kept juxtaposing the flame burning at Arlington Cemetery to the ceremonies at the Capitol, as if to say that this dead man was the man who should be taking the oath. Johnson's sensitivity to any comparisons seemed to encourage the press to make more of them, almost as though they were tempting his temper.

Kennedy's interest in the 1964 vice-presidential nomination, so strange yet so strong, caused additional ill-feeling. Johnson wanted to be completely free in making his choice, and he believed Kennedy was trying to force his hand. In March, for example, Kennedy received 25,000 vice-presidential write-in votes in the New Hampshire primary, just 3000 fewer than Johnson received for President. When Johnson learned that a staff member of the Democratic National Committee, known as "a Bobby man," had visited New Hampshire before the primary, he concluded it was to encourage a pro-Kennedy campaign. Johnson called Kennedy to the White House and told him to fire the staff member from the committee. Kennedy implied that the hiring and firing of personnel at the committee was no longer his responsibility. Besides, he observed of the staffer, "President Kennedy thought he was a good man."

This angered Johnson: "President Kennedy isn't President anymore. I am," he said. "I did you a favor," he said irrelevantly. "I sent you on that trip to Asia."

Kennedy was furious. "A favor?" he said sarcastically. "I don't want you to do any more favors for me."

Later, Kennedy was insulted by the graceless way Johnson eliminated him from consideration for the vice presidency. To give the impression that he was not ruling out Kennedy alone, Johnson contrived to eliminate the entire Cabinet and those who sat with them. He took the precaution of recording, on a tape machine Kennedy observed, the meeting at which he told Kennedy of his decision. Although such meetings are traditionally confidential, Johnson unburdened himself of its details in a lunch with three newsmen the next day, including his own impersonations of Kennedy's reactions. Johnson's breach of their confidential conversation and his obvious enjoyment of Kennedy's discomfort were not easily forgotten. His elaborate machinations to make it look like Kennedy was withdrawing from consideration encouraged Kennedy's judgment that Johnson was the kind of person who had dealt cavalierly with the truth for so long that he could no longer tell when he was engaging in falsehood.

Despite this legacy of bitterness, an open feud made no sense to either man. There was no basic policy difference to justify a public collision. Johnson, anticipating a two-term administration, did not want to alienate Kennedy's large and loyal following. Kennedy recognized that Johnson's massive victory of 1964 made him invulnerable as well as insensitive to criticism. Peace and cooperation, at least in public, prevailed throughout Kennedy's first year in the Senate, during which time he often spoke publicly of "the policies of President Kennedy being continued by President Johnson." In a memorandum to Kennedy early in the first year, Adam Walinsky said it was possible to introduce a legislative program independent of Johnson's, but advised: "I think the role of lonely spokesman would probably have serious adverse effects on your ability to do more for New York." In Latin America, despite his disagreement with the President's handling of the Dominican crisis and his concern about his attitude toward the Alliance for Progress, Kennedy deliberately praised Johnson and avoided any criticism, hoping to give the President whatever strength his support could mean.

Incidents inevitably arose during this period, but both men attempted to de-fuse them. In August 1965, for example, a *Life* magazine excerpt from *A Thousand Days* by Arthur Schlesinger, Jr., implied President Kennedy had expected Johnson to turn down the vice-presidential nomination when he offered it to him. Schlesinger quoted President Kennedy as being surprised Johnson accepted it and saying: "I held it like this—close to my chest—and he took it!"

When the publicity over the excerpt threatened to revive the bitterness about Los Angeles, Kennedy used the occasion of his next speech[6] to remove any doubt about his brother's intentions. Reviewing the accomplishments of the New Frontier, the senator said:

> "All of this had happened because men had a dream—and were willing to go to the people and ask for their support on the basis of these programs. They were willing to win a mandate, take it to the halls of Congress, reason and persuade and marshal their efforts. President Kennedy knew that Lyndon Johnson was such a man, that he was committed to these programs, that he shared their dreams, that he was the best man to carry on this fight. It was for this reason that President Kennedy wanted Lyndon Johnson to run with him for Vice President in 1960."

But, as always in politics, the evidence of personal conflict was considered far more newsworthy than any attempts at conciliation. Hints of a Kennedy-Johnson split became one of the most sought-after news items in Washington. The media did not create the tension and distrust between Kennedy and Johnson, but they did magnify it into something with a life of its own, beyond the acts of the two men. When Kennedy made a policy statement that differed in any respect from the Administration's line, reporters immediately contacted the White House to get an adverse reaction, often inflating Kennedy's remarks to provoke one. If they succeeded, they would go back to the Kennedy office for his reaction, trying to enlarge the conflict even more. Both camps realized this, and after a few experiences, they passed up the reportorial bait more often than not. Kennedy seemed always to be deleting criticism of Johnson from drafts written by his more combative staff. Johnson also was restrained. At the time Kennedy was deep in controversy over William Manchester's *Death of a President,* Johnson ordered his staff "not to raise an eyebrow about anything in that book" in their talks with reporters. His orders were followed. Nevertheless, the media had a true sense of the antagonism between the two men. In provoking the stories, they were frequently dismissing the façade of cooperation for the reality of disagreement.

In truth, Kennedy did little to prevent the growth of an anti-Johnson climate around him. His private comments encouraged it. In his Senate office, "the President" referred to John F. Kennedy.

---

[6] A testimonial dinner for Patrick Lucey, then seeking the Democratic nomination for Governor of Wisconsin.

The incumbent President was called "Johnson." The Kennedy staff helped circulate all the latest anti-Johnson gossip, savoring reports of his latest outbursts. And when Johnson wished to hear the latest jibe about Kennedy, he had only to listen to some of his close friends from Texas. Men who worked for Johnson swore that all of Kennedy's actions were motivated by a desire to weaken Johnson. Men who worked for Kennedy felt the same about many of Johnson's activities. With all this happening in private, some of it inevitably became public.

When Johnson received notice Kennedy was about to criticize his policies, he would go to great lengths to create a diversion. On the day of the speech proposing an end to the bombing of North Vietnam (March 2, 1967), Johnson made two unscheduled speeches in Washington, held an unscheduled news conference to announce that Russian Premier Kosygin had agreed to talks on reducing the stockpile of nuclear weapons, announced he was inviting all the nation's governors to the White House, had Senator Henry Jackson of Washington read on the floor of the Senate a predated letter from him, explaining why the bombing was necessary, and confirmed the rumor that his daughter Lucy was pregnant. Washington reporters regarded Johnson's effort as "publicity overkill," and despite his exertions, Kennedy's speech was still the lead item of the day.

Johnson believed Kennedy's criticisms reflected only personal antagonism. With his intimates, he never discussed the merits of Kennedy's criticisms, only their motivation. In his darker moments, he would lash out at Kennedy and look suspiciously at those around him who were known to be friendly with Kennedy, even if they had served Johnson loyally for many years. Despite Johnson's admiration for Robert McNamara and his great dependence on him, he suspected McNamara's closeness to Kennedy and thought some of the arguments Kennedy was presenting came from McNamara's men in the Pentagon.

In his more amiable moments Johnson viewed his rival philosophically. "I don't know," he would say, "why this boy and I have to destroy our party by fighting with each other. I'm too old for that. He's too young. This party has been good to me, it was good to his brother, and good to him—and the party is the only thing that can really be hurt." Kennedy also cared about the Democratic Party, but he blamed its difficulties on Johnson—especially his inattention to political matters and his lack of rapport with urban Democratic leaders.

To the outside observer, Kennedy's criticisms were often self-defeating. It sometimes seemed that the surest way to prevent policy changes by the Administration was for Kennedy to suggest them. Actually, Johnson frequently responded to such suggestions privately while belittling them publicly. The day after Kennedy spoke in the Senate about rats biting children in New York City, Johnson devoted a large segment of his cabinet meeting to the subject of rodent control. The result was a federal rat-control program. When Kennedy proposed his program of tax incentives to encourage more housing in ghetto areas, Johnson shortly thereafter came forward with his own housing plan. When an agreement was under discussion with major financial institutions to provide a mortgage pool for residents of Bedford-Stuyvesant, to encourage private home ownership, there was a scramble at the White House to put together a vast mortgage pool for the ghettos financed by the major insurance companies, so that the President's announcement could precede and overshadow whatever Kennedy was trying to do. After Johnson learned Kennedy was planning his trip to Africa, the President scheduled a major speech on African policy which he delivered before Kennedy departed. It was the only African speech made during his presidency.

But on the issue of Vietnam, the arguments for de-escalation and accommodation were weakened inside the White House by the fact that Kennedy supported them. Kennedy too tried to keep up an appearance of party unity. In one instance, his personal intervention prevented the New York State Democratic Convention from inserting a critical plank on Vietnam in its 1966 platform.

Had it not been for Vietnam, they could have maintained a strained but bearable truce until the lines were drawn over the presidential succession, which both men believed would not be until 1972. But Vietnam ultimately divided them beyond accommodation. Robert Kennedy did not seek a political quarrel over Vietnam with President Johnson, nor were his political purposes served by having one. He had favored American involvement in Vietnam, and he saw the larger implications of Communist success in that struggle. It is easy enough to say that Lyndon Johnson's popularity during this period made any criticism politically unwise, but those who knew Robert Kennedy best believed that his special sympathy for the problems of any President, and his own feeling of responsibility for the commitments Lyndon Johnson inherited, imposed a restraint on his growing uneasiness about the course the Administration was taking. In the ensuing years of their tragic disagreement, Lyndon Johnson assumed that Robert Kennedy had chosen to oppose him about Vietnam because it was the only major area of his Administration where Kennedy could find a large base of support within the Democratic Party for his position. In private conversations, he would cite Kennedy's letter to him in the spring of 1964, offering to serve as ambassador to South Vietnam as compelling evidence of a shared conviction that the war was crucial to America's security.[7] Having sat with Kennedy in National Security Council meetings during his predecessor's administration, Johnson knew that Robert Kennedy was tough and realistic about the nature of the Communist challenge. Therefore, Johnson reasoned, since I am opposing Communism in a rough and realistic manner, Robert Kennedy's opposition to my policies must be political rather than substantive. But political logic did not sustain President Johnson's conclusion about Kennedy's disaffection over Vietnam. A divided Democratic party would be no one's springboard to the presidency.

With Kennedy's criticism on Vietman creating growing opposition to the war, Johnson looked for ways to contain it. He sent Averell Harriman to try to persuade Kennedy not to give the March 1967 speech. Attorney General Nicholas Katzenbach was transferred to the State Department as Undersecretary partly because Johnson felt he could be a restraining influence on Kennedy in this area. Although Kennedy consulted Katzenbach frequently on Vietnam, their close friendship and ease of communication did not retard his criticism. Kennedy was bitter about the way Johnson had used Katzenbach as a foil at the meeting at the White House in February 1967 after the "peace feeler" incident. Eventually, disagreements over Vietnam and the actions Katzenbach had to take on behalf of the State Department were to strain the close friendship between the two men.

[7] Johnson turned down Kennedy's offer politely, noting the danger of sending a man with eight children into a war zone. He told intimates that he did not want the responsibility and the blame "for the killing of a second Kennedy brother."

On June 3, 1967, the President was to speak at the New York State Democratic Committee's annual dinner. A group of reform Democrats had announced their intention to boycott the dinner and demonstrate outside the banquet hall. These fund-raising events were always matters of delicate negotiation between the State Committee and the White House. Johnson's aides insisted that the President would not appear unless Kennedy were prominently identified with the program, and furthermore, that the senator had to agree to be a sponsor of the private President's Club fund-raising event scheduled later in the evening. The financial needs of the State Committee and the constant pressure he was receiving from organization politicians in New York to give evidence of party unity, made Kennedy accept these conditions, even though, as he expressed it, "most of my real friends will be outside picketing." He agreed to introduce the President, and searched for a way to be courteous and show support for the leader of his party without appearing hypocritical.

His problem was compounded by the crisis atmosphere in the Middle East where the Six-Day War was about to begin. The President's actions made him a very sympathetic figure to the largely Jewish audience, which was emotionally involved with Israel's fate and desperately anxious that the United States support its stand against the Arab states. This was not a moment to do anything but support the President as he faced perilous international crisis. Kennedy accepted some language suggested by Theodore Sorensen which structured praise without compromising the disagreements. As 1400 demonstrators chanted anti-war and anti-Johnson slogans outside, Kennedy said of the President:

> He has led us to build schools, homes, clinics, hospitals, to rebuild the cities, to clean water, to reclaim the beauty of the countryside, to educate children, to comfort the oppressed on a scale unmatched in history. He has poured out his own strength to renew the strength of the country . . . he has sought consensus, but has never shrunk from controversy . . . he has gained huge popularity but never hesitated to spend it on what he thought important.

As Kennedy spoke, the President, chin in hand, sat staring at him, enraptured by the pleasant melody of the words. Mrs. Johnson kissed Kennedy gratefully as he concluded. Afterward, many of Kennedy's friends told him the introduction was out of character, and he agreed.

But he was caught between his feelings and the traditions of politics, and it was a taste of the conflict that would face him increasingly in the months to follow.

Could the feud have been avoided? Perhaps by making Kennedy his Vice President, Johnson might have absorbed him into the Administration, as former Presidents had done with their rivals, enhancing Kennedy's chance to become his successor while eliminating him as a competitor. Certainly the nation's politics would have been different had Kennedy and Johnson found it possible to be allies, but not necessarily its policies. It is doubtful that Kennedy alone could have added enough weight to the forces of de-escalation and domestic priority within the Administration. And if he could not, what would he have done? The Johnson administration itself came apart over Vietnam and its consequences. John Gardner, George Ball, and eventually Robert McNamara left; Adlai Stevenson was seriously considering doing so just before his death. If these men felt they had to resign, who is to say a man of Kennedy's strong views might not have joined them, upholding the view of de-escalation within the Administration, then expressing his dissent forcefully and publicly.

But this is speculation. All that can be said with certainty is that at no time did Kennedy seek to undermine the President's capacity to execute the powers of his office or enforce the decisions he made. Kennedy's policy differences with Johnson were no greater, his criticisms no more fierce, than those of a dozen other Democratic senators. It was the wide attention they received that gave them their power.

In the end, Kennedy ran against the President, just as Johnson had feared would happen and, in a sense, had always expected. When the 1968 New Hampshire primary results were reported to Johnson, his reaction totally ignored Senator McCarthy. Johnson understood immediately that the real meaning of the primary was that Kennedy would run.

On April 2, 1968, two days after Johnson announced he would not seek re-election, Kennedy visited him in the White House for the last time. By contrast to others, this meeting was calm and pleasant. Johnson briefed him on the prospects of peace negotiations resulting from his order to halt the bombing of North Vietnam. He introduced him to his grandson, Lyn. There was no pretense at new-found friendship, but the rivalry was over. Facing the prospects of a fight at the National

Convention, Kennedy never doubted that Johnson would use whatever power he had left to deny Kennedy the nomination. But Johnson no longer had to fear that Kennedy would take away his office. He had surrendered it. They parted cordially.

In the nostalgia of his last night as President, January 19, 1969, Lyndon Johnson, speaking to friends, recalled the words Kennedy had used in the speech he had made at the New York dinner on June 3, 1967: ". . . He has sought consensus, but has never shrunk from controversy . . . he has gained huge popularity but never hesitated to spend it on what he thought important." He said Kennedy was the only one who could understand something that he, Lyndon Johnson, hoped everyone would understand, but no one else did—that Johnson had been willing to expend the enormous popularity reflected in the 1964 election in order to do what the nation required, because it was less important to be popular than to be President. "Perhaps," Johnson said, "Kennedy could understand it because he was the same kind of person as I am."

The minds of men work in strange ways. Ironically, as the curtain was closing on the drama of his public life, Lyndon Johnson managed to find a grand and almost predetermined design, justifying all that had befallen him, in the words of his greatest rival.

14

DECISION TO RUN

On March 13, 1968, the day after the New Hampshire primary, and three days before he announced his candidacy for the presidency, Robert Kennedy wrote a private letter which expressed the doubts and the anxieties that had consumed him for the last four months. The letter was to Anthony Lewis, chief of the New York *Times* London bureau. Lewis, a friend of twenty years, had been a classmate at Harvard and a neighbor in McLean, and he was one of the few with whom Kennedy always talked frankly about personal political problems. The letter read:

Dear Tony:

I don't quite know what to write you. The country is in such difficulty and I believe headed for more that it almost fills one with despair. I just don't know what Johnson is thinking, but then when I realize all of that I wonder what I should be doing. Most everyone whom I respect with the exception of Dick Goodwin and Arthur Schlesinger have been against my running. My basic inclination and reaction was to try; and let the future take care of itself. However the prophesies of future doom, if I took the course, made to me by Bob McNamara, and to a lesser extent Bill Moyers plus the politicians' almost unanimous feeling that my running would bring about the election of Richard Nixon and many other Republican right-wingers because I would so divide and split the party, and that I could not possibly win—all this made me hesitate—I suppose even more than that.

But the last two days have seen Rusk before the Foreign Relations Committee, the New Hampshire primary—and in the last week, it has been made clear that Johnson is going to do nothing about the Riot panel report.

So, once again—what should I do.

By the time you receive this letter, both of us will know.

If I am not off to the California primary, Ethel and I will be coming to Ireland in the end of May. Why don't you join us. The Irish Government is dedicating a memorial to President Kennedy on his birthday, May 29—you look a little Irish and it would be good for your black soul—and maybe mine also.

Much has been written and more will be about Robert Kennedy's challenge to Lyndon Johnson for the presidential nomination in the extraordinary political year of 1968. It was Kennedy's most dramatic campaign, his ultimate personal effort, and it influenced both the election and the Administration that followed. But despite its drama and its tragedy, it was not a test of Kennedy at his best. Kennedy's insights and his passion about America's difficulties, his themes and his program, had all been developed before the campaign. The campaign and the agony of indecision that preceded it took up the last seven months of his life. It was a period of strain and exhaustion, in which he drew heavily on both his physical and political capital.

Robert Kennedy ran for the presidency not because he wanted to, but because he felt he had to. If he could have avoided the race and kept peace with his conscience and his constituency, he would have done so gladly. He ran an impressive race, but by the morning of June 5, he was decidedly the underdog for his party's nomination; and had he announced sooner or run in another manner, he would not have been closer to his goal. In fact, had Kennedy yielded to those who urged him to become the first to run against Lyndon Johnson, it is probable that Johnson would have been not only the Democratic nominee in 1968 but would have been elected President for four more years.

These conclusions derive from the mood of the nation as it developed during Kennedy's Senate years; from the nature of the Democratic Party; from the political power of the presidency; and from the political position of Robert Kennedy himself. It is perhaps best to take the last first.

Although Kennedy had a large and devoted following in the United

States when he was in the Senate, he was a far more controversial figure than those to whom the major political parties have always given their presidential nomination. By the end of 1967, he could count very few important labor leaders among his supporters, and practically none of the business establishment. He was unacceptable in most of the southern states, which sent one fifth of the delegates to the Democratic convention. Among Republicans, he provoked somewhat the same reaction that Richard Nixon did among Democrats.

Mixed in with the adulation he received was a significant degree of hostility. As early as November 1965, 46 per cent of those responding to a Gallup poll of a cross-section of American voters said they did not wish to see him become President; only 40 per cent said they did. Among independent voters, whose views decide presidential elections, the feeling against him was even higher, 52 per cent to 30 per cent. His standing with the American public waxed and waned during the following three and a half years, but always as a function of the public support for Lyndon Johnson. The basic feelings toward Kennedy himself remained unchanged. The 1965 poll had asked people what it was about Robert Kennedy that bothered them. The most frequently cited criticism was that he was "capitalizing on his family name"; followed (in descending order) by comments that he was "too young and inexperienced to be President"; too "forceful," "pushy," "aggressive," and too "opportunistic." Polls taken by Oliver Quayle for the National Broadcasting System in Indiana, Oregon, and California during the 1968 primaries provoked the same criticisms, in the same order. The only addition was that "his hair is too long."

If Kennedy had continued to seek the presidency on a graduated, four-year timetable, he would have tried and might have succeeded, in moderating this antagonism. As early as 1966, Richard Goodwin, who wanted Kennedy to be at least in a position of availability for the nomination in 1968, advised that some of his activities were making him seem to the public like the very kind of ideological liberal Kennedy himself had always disliked. "It is not good," advised Goodwin, "to be regarded as an ideological *anything*. It is better to leave an area of uncertainty, leaving room for wishful thinking on the part of many groups that you may be the man for them." Referring to the growing antagonism of establishment groups, Goodwin said, "If they just prefer someone else, it does little damage. If they are really afraid and look on you as the enemy, in a curious, diffuse way this transfers itself to the public, which is adversely affected." But until March 1968, Robert Kennedy could disregard these cautions, and enjoy the luxury of pursuing the causes that interested him with their political consequences only a secondary consideration. He was not challenging Lyndon Johnson for the presidential nomination. This is not to say that he did not want to become President. But in his calculations, the time to seek the presidency was 1972. In that year the Democratic Party would have to select a new leader, either because a re-elected Lyndon Johnson was facing mandatory retirement, or because the party would be out of office and its leadership would be in open contest. At that point, Kennedy would be forty-seven years old, a full eight years younger than the average American President on the day he took office.

But in 1968, a conservative tide was running. The nomination for the presidency would not go to the hero of the liberals. The path to victory that November did not lie through the Delta of the Mississippi, or in the ghettos, or on the college campuses. The dominant force in American politics were those voters—"unblack, unpoor and unyoung" in Richard Scammon's description—who provided Richard Nixon and George Wallace with 57 per cent of the ballots in 1968.

Even had he retired to private life after President Kennedy's death, his experience in government, his political contacts and the power of the Kennedy name would have made him a contender in 1972. By remaining independent of the Administration, he would be free of the antagonisms which were certain to develop against the Democrats over nine years of a Johnson administration. There would be other contenders: certainly Hubert Humphrey, probably a candidate from the South, and perhaps a new figure who would emerge victorious from an election in a major state in 1970. But Humphrey would carry the burden of the Johnson administration's liabilities; any southern candidate would be encumbered by his views, and whoever emerged in 1970 would, as Ronald Reagon discovered in 1968, lack sufficient time on the national stage to become a major rival.

Waiting until 1972 did involve risks. Overexposure was one; with the continuing glare of the spotlight on him, Kennedy's popularity might be preceding his opportunity. The public might be tired of him by 1972. But the spotlight had been focused on him for several years without letup, and his popular strength as a leading contender for the presidency had been sustained.

There was the far greater risk that, by continuing to involve himself in current issues, he would make so many powerful enemies that his party would turn to a less controversial candidate. Kennedy felt, however, that by 1972, his controversial views would have been absorbed by a changed and restructured society. By then, he might be even considered a moderate. Six years is a long time in politics. Memories fade as though a century had passed, something Hubert Humphrey, long the whipping boy of the South, discovered happily as he traveled through that area garnering delegates in 1968. By 1972, the general public would have very different impressions of Kennedy's present challenge to the established order. But the people directly affected, the minorities, the young, and their liberal supporters, would remember what he had done for them.

But these considerations, which Kennedy took for granted, were not shared by the electorate. The political environment in which Kennedy had to operate was shaped by the fact the great numbers of Americans, probably a majority, believed from what they read in the papers and saw on television that he *was* running for the presidency in 1968. In this sense they were the victims of the media habit of magnifying political conflict when it exists, and assuming it when it does not. On November 18, 1964, for example, the Houston *Chronicle* ran an eight-column, banner headline: KENNEDY WILL NOT OPPOSE JOHNSON IN '68.[1] That a major newspaper, twelve days after Lyndon Johnson had been elected by a margin of 16 million votes, felt such a denial rated major news play, seems incredible; but it was not atypical. On countless occasions over the next three years, Kennedy would give the same answer to the same question and each time the disclaimer was considered an important news event.[2]

Every time Kennedy made a political move, it was interpreted as laying the foundation for a challenge to the President. Unlike other Democratic senators, he could not criticize administration policy without its being portrayed as an "open break" with Johnson. Nor could anyone associated with Kennedy, or Johnson, decide on his own to

[1] The story concerned a routine answer to a question Kennedy had been asked by a student while in Mexico City dedicating a memorial to his brother.
[2] Often it was a case of the media making news out of denials of a story they had created themselves. They were thus able to make two news events out of none.

run for elective office without drawing speculation that he was a stalking horse. When Tom Braden ran against Lloyd Hand in California for lieutenant governor in 1966, when John Hooker and Buford Ellington contested for the governorship of Tennessee, when Patrick Lucey ran against David Carley for the governorship of Wisconsin, the press said they were doing it at the behest of Kennedy or Johnson to improve positions for 1968. When Matthew Reese, who had worked in voter registration for John Kennedy, went to Kansas to help Governor Docking, Docking's opponent said "he is associated with the Bobby Kennedy organization and he is here to consolidate Democratic support for Kennedy in future political efforts." When William Haddad went to Florida to assist Mayor Robert King High of Miami, it was also alleged to be "a Bobby Kennedy takeover."

The more sophisticated political writers downgraded this speculation. Alan Otten in the *Wall Street Journal* concluded in August 1966 that "chances are overwhelming that Kennedy will make no challenge." Hugh Sidey, in his *Life* magazine column in March 1967, said "the evidence available suggests that about the last thing Kennedy wants to do is run in 1968." Bruce Biossat, writing for the Newspaper Enterprise Association, said that "the notion that Kennedy has a fairly sturdy political establishment around the nation, a well-knit structure holding the allegiance of many political professionals is wholly fanciful." These opinions may have been accurate, but they were not as interesting as stories about Robert Kennedy that embroidered the impression of a personal feud, fed by restoration politics, with Kennedy determined to defeat or dislodge the man he had opposed for Vice President and whom fate had put in the White House.

The constant speculation affected both Kennedy's standing and his actions. If he received the coverage normally reserved for a President or presidential candidate, he also received the abuse. One reason he remained controversial was precisely *because* it was believed that he was reaching for the presidency. Directors of the national opinion polls, responding to requests from their newspaper clients, began in early 1966 to rate Kennedy and Johnson against each other. By giving the impression that voters were already choosing sides, the polls strengthened the feeling that a contest was inevitable.

Kennedy often remarked how he wished he could diminish his presidential boom, but he did little about it. He neither slowed the pace of his activities nor tried to discourage his heavy press coverage, even though much of the latter obviously came from interest in the confrontation with Johnson. He could have anticipated this problem in 1964 and decided not to run for public office at all, since basically what exposed him was the fact he was in public life. Yet to be silent or inactive for fear of this speculation would be to allow himself to be immobilized as a public figure, and to Kennedy, this was unthinkable.

Since Kennedy found it impossible to persuade the public he was not running for the presidency in 1968, why, then, did he not just decide to do so? The answers involve Lyndon Johnson and the nature of the presidential office, as well as Kennedy himself. No one in public life, including Kennedy, or in journalism, ever seriously believed that the President would decide not to seek re-election in 1968. For thirty years, Lyndon Johnson had been consumed by politics. He had overcome poverty, learned the labyrinthine ways of Texas politics, mastered the intricacies of congressional procedures, survived a serious heart attack—all the time directing his formidable energy toward a single objective: the power, panoply, and prestige of the White House. Having gained it by fateful tragedy, having maintained it by the largest vote in modern history, none could believe that he would voluntarily surrender it.

The real test of political men is how they react when their own political survival is at stake. Harry Truman, with popularity ratings far below any ascribed to Johnson, stood practically alone in 1948, defying his enemies, and defeated them. In 1966, the midsummer polls in New York State showed that any Democrat would defeat Nelson Rockefeller for governor if he sought re-election, but Rockefeller accepted the challenge and won. Incumbents have power that belies temporary weakness in the polls. It was inconceivable that Lyndon Johnson, who had fought so hard and achieved so much, would quit rather than defend the policies that were making him vulnerable.

That being so, the rest followed easily. There is a rule in American politics that has never been broken: a President can ensure his own renomination; and if he chooses to retire, he can dictate his party's choice of his successor. The only President ever denied renomination was Chester Arthur in 1884, whose mediocre experience as Port Collector of the City of New York was not sufficient to protect his accidental ascendancy to the presidency from powerful predators like James G. Blaine. Even the most legitimate draft of this century, the nomination of Adlai E. Stevenson by the Democratic Convention in 1952, was encouraged and probably engineered by President Truman, who did not attend the convention but gave his alternate delegate instructions to announce he would vote for Stevenson. It is said that nothing is certain in politics, and that any political rule is nothing more than a summary of what has happened before. Yet to plan future action without considering past analogies is to sail without a compass, and Kennedy was an excellent sailor.

At the 1968 Democratic convention, 20 per cent of the delegates would be from southern states, 30 per cent would be inclined to follow the lead of labor, which was friendly to Johnson, and a good share of the rest would be controlled by party leaders with ties to the President. Such a convention would not be friendly territory for a challenger. Even one who had won all the primaries (as Kefauver had done in 1952) would not be strong in the Convention against a President who had managed to stay out of the primaries and avoid direct confrontation and defeat.

There was one circumstance in which a convention could reject an incumbent President: if he had so weakened his public standing that his running would surely lead to the party's defeat throughout the nation. But to Kennedy, the only national problems that had the remote potential of creating this situation were the war in Vietnam, which the President, as Commander in Chief, could control as an issue; and racial violence, which could be controlled, if necessary, by force.

Vietnam was the most difficult kind of issue to debate successfully with a President. Not only did he have the patriotic side of the issue, but he had the initiative and the exclusive possession of current military and diplomatic intelligence.[3] Moreover, the public tended to approve any presidential action in foreign affairs.[4]

[3] For example, Kennedy was completely frustrated by Johnson's argument that if the bombing of the North were suspended, war material would come South that would "find its way into the hips and bellies of American soldiers." "How can you argue with that?" he would say.

[4] On each occasion that President Johnson resumed or continued the bombing of North Vietnam, the Gallup and Harris polls showed heavy public support for his action. On March 31, 1968, when he restricted this bombing, the public approved that too, according to the polls. Similarly, once U.S. troop withdrawals began in Vietnam, poll support shifted from strong disapproval of withdrawal to strong approval.

As early as the spring of 1965, Kennedy had expressed to Burke Marshall his belief that if the involvement of American combat troops in Vietnam continued over the next four years, the Democratic Party would be defeated. But just as Johnson had the power to escalate, so he had the power, almost at will, to de-escalate or negotiate and thereby transform the political climate. Kennedy could not believe these powers would not be used. The national interest and the President's political position both seemed to call for an expeditious end to the war. He knew Vietnam was politically damaging to Johnson, but he felt it could be damaging only as long as Johnson allowed it to be.

For all these reasons—the political strength of the presidency, the universal assumption Johnson would seek a second term, and the President's control of the key issue—it made little sense for Kennedy to seek the nomination before 1972. If he challenged Johnson in 1968, Kennedy believed he would lose. In doing so, he would permanently be branded as one who put personal ambition over principle. The fight between them would rage with rancor and bitterness for weeks and months, with every Democratic leader compelled to choose sides. His losing challenge would divide and weaken the Democratic Party. "Lyndon can be renominated," Kennedy said to friends in February 1967, "but if I really challenge him, he cannot win the election."

Thus, Kennedy felt he would be blamed for Johnson's defeat, and many Democratic leaders, on whose good will he depended for 1972, would charge him not only with losing the presidency but with defeating the scores of other Democratic officeholders who would go down with the head of the ticket. He had only to look at Nelson Rockefeller's pitiful prospects of winning the Republican presidential nomination after refusing to endorse Goldwater, to see how damaging such a charge could be. Helping to elect a Republican President and a conservative Congress was not Kennedy's idea of using his political power in the nation's interests. Thus, Kennedy's political strategy was to preserve his political independence of the Johnson administration, and remain a Democratic alternative within the party framework.

Beginning in 1966, Kennedy watched the slow unraveling of Lyndon Johnson's support among the American people. Johnson had always been a President whose standing derived from the success of his program and the favorable tide of events rather than from any personal affection. Although his handling of the transition had been masterly, the size of his victory in 1964 was due as much to Goldwater's weakness among normally Republican voters as to his own personal strength. As long as Vietnam was obscure and his legislative program was being implemented, Johnson was triumphant; but once events began to turn against him, he had no reservoir of public good will to ward off the rising ill feeling against him.

By the middle of 1966, Johnson's job rating in the Gallup poll had dropped from the 79 per cent he enjoyed at the beginning of 1965 to 48 per cent.[5] As this occurred, Kennedy's standing, always reciprocal to Johnson's, boomed. In March 1966 the Gallup poll showed that if the election were held then, Kennedy would defeat Richard Nixon, the top Republican contender, 54 per cent to 41 per cent. In June, the Los Angeles *Times* state-wide poll indicated that if the California primary were to be held at that time, Kennedy would defeat Johnson by a margin of 2 to 1. By August, Romney had replaced Nixon as the leading Republican, but polls conducted by the largest newspapers in Iowa and Michigan showed Kennedy beating Romney, and Johnson losing to Romney badly.

Kennedy's seeming position as an alternative to Johnson was underscored by the campaigns each carried on for Democratic candidates in 1966. Listing the legislation he had signed and the economic well-being of the country, Johnson called for a vote of gratitude. His theme was "you never had it so good." Kennedy took the opposite approach. At a testimonial dinner for Senator Paul Douglas, he complained about the deteriorating quality of medical care. At a Democratic dinner in Maine, he criticized the Administration for sending warships to Peru. On October 8, 1966, in Columbus, Ohio, he answered the President's theme directly:

> We have deep and difficult problems—decay in the cities, pollution in the air, inflation in the economy, crime and danger in the streets —and above all, the problem of relations between the races . . . What we as Democrats do is at the heart of the matter. We can treat this as just another political question . . . Or we can assume

[5] Another comparison, made in the states of the deep South, showed that while two thirds of the people thought President Kennedy had done a good job, only one third believed the same of Johnson.

the burden and responsibility of leadership—which is above all to tell the truth . . .

(The American people) are not going to vote for the Democratic party because things are fine or because 'they never had it so good' . . . No, they will vote for us only if they want to keep America moving.

Wherever he campaigned in 1966, Democratic leaders told him of the malaise in the party and their lack of communication with the White House. The normal relationships between Democratic Party leaders and the White House were either strained or non-existent. Johnson's ties were with the members of Congress, who rarely hold key political power in their states. Because he had never run a national campaign for the presidential nomination, Johnson had never had to build personal relationships with the governors and local politicians who controlled what remained of party organizations. In his preoccupation with "consensus government," he chose to ignore the leaders of his own party in order to establish an association with industrial, financial and other non-political leaders of the country. A week before the 1966 election, Johnson flew to Asia and then, deciding to rest in preparation for minor surgery, canceled scheduled campaign speeches in ten states, demoralizing the Democrats' congressional campaign.

Most of the Democrats Kennedy campaigned for that fall were defeated. All of the "peace" candidates, running independent campaigns against organization Democrats, lost badly. The impression Kennedy brought back from campaigning was that the people were prosperous and not personally concerned about the mounting problems he was talking about, but were nevertheless dissatisfied with the performance of the national government.

It was during this campaign tour that Kennedy first began to believe that the Democratic party was in danger of losing the election of 1968. The situation was salvageable, he felt, if the organizational deficiencies could be healed, the situation in Vietnam improved, or the Republican candidate (at that time he thought it would be Romney) proved inept. But the seeds of defeat were in the ground and growing. The senator had spent two days in October with Harold Hughes, who was running for re-election as governor of Iowa, a state where Kennedy was unusually popular for the Midwest. Kennedy and Hughes discussed national problems and the political situation, and found themselves in agreement. Hughes expressed his strong feeling that Johnson and some of his advisers were incapable of governing, and that the President was taking dangerous risks in Vietnam. It was the first time a major Democratic leader had indicated he might not prefer Johnson as the Party's presidential candidate in 1968. Two months later, Hughes would criticize Johnson publicly at the Governors' Conference for giving insufficient help to state Democratic candidates. "If he had a respectable opponent who was acceptable to the American people, the President would have a very tough race in 1968," said Hughes.

During the last half of 1966, the escalation in Vietnam continued. The President had dropped his earlier emphasis on negotiations, and was stressing the belligerent nature of the enemy. The Secretary of State even raised the threat of the Chinese "yellow peril" as the real reason for our presence in Vietnam. Domestically, the forward movement of 1961 to 1965 had been stopped. The recommendations of the White House Conference on Civil Rights were ignored. In the budget presented in January 1967, the President asked for less than $2 billion in new domestic programs, but $22 billion for Vietnam. Despite his statements that the country could have both guns and butter, Johnson had opted for guns. Of the total new government spending in 1966 and 1967, 93 per cent was going to the military. First priority went to a tax increase to finance the war and stem its inflationary consequences, rather than the domestic programs Kennedy felt were necessary for the country. As these events unfolded, Kennedy's mood shifted even further. He wondered not only if Johnson *could* win re-election, but whether it would be best for the country if he did.

By January 1967, the growing support of liberals and the exposure of the 1966 campaign, along with the decline in Johnson's popularity, had installed Kennedy as the first choice of Democratic voters for the presidential nomination. Democrats told the Gallup poll they preferred him over Johnson by the amazing margin of 48 per cent to 39 per cent.

A few days after this poll appeared, the news broke that the Kennedy family might sue to prevent publication of William Manchester's book *The Death of a President*. That controversy, with the enormous publicity and resentments it engendered, damaged his popularity severely. At the height of the dispute a Harris poll showed

Johnson now was preferred over Kennedy by Democrats, 56 per cent to 44 percent.[6]

Kennedy was besieged with advice to lay low, avoid anything controversial for several months, and stop criticizing the President. It was even suggested he concentrate on family and athletic activities that could keep him on public view in a non-political way. Fred Dutton, for example, a former State Department official and a prolific adviser to prominent politicians, wrote him "not to reach for anything in 1968. Your even obliquely flirting with the possibility could severely damage your long-term prospects through the personal qualities it would appear to bring out."

In line with this advice, Kennedy pursued a policy of personal and political retrenchment through the summer of 1967. He did not change his views, but refrained from major speeches and prefaced any criticism of the Administration with the words "as I have said previously," a signal to reporters that what he was about to say was not news. In May 1967, he made a point of dropping by a meeting of Democratic state chairmen in Washington, reassuring them privately of his support for Johnson's re-election and saying publicly, "We are brothers together in this effort." In June he made the flattering and sympathetic introduction of Johnson at the New York Democratic dinner previously described.

Some of Kennedy's friends felt this posture was out of character. They wanted him to remain uncommitted regarding the President's re-election, but Kennedy interpreted the polls, and other political reports he received from around the country, as a sign that his continued opposition to Johnson's policies was being taken as political sniping. He reaffirmed his support of the President for re-election, in the hope that by clearly renouncing any personal claim for 1968 he could once again make policy statements and get some attention for their substance.

Kennedy did not, however, read the poll results to indicate that Johnson had cured his own political problems. He noted Johnson's popularity would rise at a time of international crisis, such as the Middle East war, or of international hope, such as the Glassboro

[6] By May, the Gallup standings of January were almost reversed, Johnson leading Kennedy 49 per cent to 37 per cent.

Conference with Premier Kosygin in September 1967. Glassboro, especially, he considered powerful evidence of a President's ability to create international events for short-term political advantage.

As the war continued, the hopes for agreements with the Soviets dimmed, and as the racial disorders entered their fourth and most violent summer, Johnson's position again deteriorated sharply. As he had a year before, Kennedy expressed the opinion that the Republicans could win the presidency in 1968. In late July 1967, he conversed with Goodwin about the issues he would stress if he were campaign manager for the Republican nominee. Goodwin was later to use the essence of Kennedy's remarks in a mock interview with Democratic strategist "Bailey Laird," that appeared in *The New Yorker.* Said the fictional political boss:

> Here we are the most powerful nation in the world and once the most respected. Now the President of the United States can't visit Latin America, or Asia or Africa for fear of violent demonstrations. Hell, he can't even go to Paris. The European alliance is falling apart. NATO is dying. Hardly a single one of our traditional allies supports our policies or sympathizes with our objectives. We are losing influence and prestige in every part of the world. It's never been lower. We're involved in endless costly war that no one knows how to end. Our cities are filled with violence and revolution. We are failing to meet almost all our domestic problems from poverty to education. Taxes are going up. Young people, the hope of the future, are turning away from the ideal of public service. Five years ago, the biggest things in colleges were the Peace Corps and civil rights. Now it's smoking marijuana. America is adrift and purposeless —filled with an aimless discontent. The country destined to be the hope of the world hardly knows what it stands for anymore.

Then he added: "It is getting so bad that the President cannot be seen by his own people. He can only travel around the country by going from one military base to another. What an opportunity for a Republican."

With so many issues, Kennedy felt the Republicans' only real problem was in choosing a candidate who could distinguish himself sharply enough from Johnson. The President's best hope for re-election, Kennedy believed, lay in the caliber of the Republicans in the field. California governor Ronald Reagan was both a parochial and a factional personality. Illinois Senator Charles Percy was not yet a national figure, and as a freshman senator had no way to become one in only one year. Richard Nixon, Kennedy felt, had solid support within his party, but, like Johnson, little personal appeal. This was a greater disadvantage for a man out of office, since he could do nothing to make people respect him for his effectiveness. Ironically, the strongest Republican candidate in Kennedy's view seemed to be a man who could not possibly win the nomination of his party, Nelson Rockefeller. The basic reason for Rockefeller's unacceptability—his refusal to support the party's nominee in 1964—was very much on Kennedy's mind as he pursued his own course within the Democratic party. Despite the growing problems facing the President and the country, Kennedy did not think Johnson's cause was lost, and was certainly not about to offer himself as an alternative.

The first clear call for Robert Kennedy to run for the presidency came from those who were organizing to change American policy in Vietnam. The original peace movement was small. It consisted of organizations like the Committee for a Sane Nuclear Policy (SANE), the Fellowship of Reconciliation, and Women's Strike for Peace, which had been originally organized around such causes as control of nuclear weapons. Gradually, they were joined by the older liberal organizations, a handful of black leaders such as Martin Luther King, and students. The latter conducted discussions on their campuses, but did not organize for political action until 1967. All these groups were politically impotent and inexperienced, and they badly needed elected officials to take the leadership of their movement.

The first approach to Kennedy from this source came late in 1965, from Dr. Benjamin Spock, who at that time was head of SANE. He told Kennedy he thought he was the only person who could save the country from the disastrous course Johnson had chosen in Vietnam. In the fall of 1966, Spock contacted Kennedy again, explaining that while the peace movement was growing, the candidates it was running in the congressional elections that year were amateurs who did not have the ability to convert public feeling into votes. Spock feared that Johnson, despite his protestations of peace and his desire for negotiation, was determined on a course of further escalation. He asked Kennedy to lead a nationwide movement in opposition to the war, and offered to line up prominent members of the intellectual and religious communities to urge Kennedy to do so, if Kennedy would give him the green light. Kennedy, Spock felt, could give the peace movement a new hope and a new standard. Prophetically, he cautioned Kennedy that if such a move were delayed until the last moment, it would be considered opportunism on his part rather than statesmanship.

Kennedy did not want to accept Spock's offer, but he did not want to reject him out of hand. He asked Goodwin to meet with Spock and explain that while he had grave doubts about the war, if he were to lead a nationwide campaign at that point, his political influence would drop and he would forfeit the ability he had to work for change within the Democratic party. Spock said he understood Kennedy's position, and the matter was not pursued.

At about the same time, an organization was formed in New York to urge the nomination of Kennedy and Senator J. William Fulbright as the Democratic ticket in 1968. "Citizens for Kennedy-Fulbright" was originally organized by a Manhattan psychiatrist, Dr. Martin Shepard, as a grass-roots reaction against Johnson's Vietnam policy. Shepard's organization found stray supporters in other states —political mavericks such as former Congressman Charles Porter of Oregon and Eugene Daniell, a former mayor of a small New Hampshire city. Even at its height the organization had fewer than 2000 members, none with political standing; but the dramatic nature of its purpose gave it considerable publicity. Informed of the group's activities, Kennedy wrote its leaders several times asking them to desist, but without success.

In the autumn of 1967, the most subsequently publicized approach to Kennedy came from Allard K. Lowenstein, an organizer of the peace movement, which by this time had been strengthened by important clergymen, students and prominent public figures and was actively seeking an alternative to Johnson. Kennedy had been introduced to Lowenstein by Ronnie Eldridge in the spring of 1966, when Lowenstein was competing with three other Kennedy friends for the reform Democratic nomination in the West Side Manhattan congressional district where Leonard Farbstein was the incumbent. Lowenstein, a rational evangelist with the charm of the Pied Piper, had been involved in every liberal and humanitarian cause for a generation. Because Lowenstein had been to Southwest Africa and written a book on it, Kennedy asked him to discuss the area with him before going on his trip to South Africa. Now Lowenstein came to ask Kennedy to run for President. Kennedy responded to the Lowenstein proposal as he had to Spock's and the others: he, too, was interested in changing the party's policies, but if he were to run, it would have to be as a serious candidate for the presidency, which was not then a likely prospect. Kennedy felt he had already done much to give the peace forces both legitimacy and support by his own strong statements on Vietnam, and by his firm defense of the right and obligation of dissent.

The reason Kennedy gave the peace movement so little encouragement was because their real goal was different from the one they asked him to pursue. Theirs was not primarily a political movement aimed at electing a President, but a protest movement aimed at changing policy. If the peace movement could have attained its goal by means short of running a candidate for President, it would have done so. It had spent most of the past two years trying, through peaceful demonstrations, teach-ins at universities, and nationwide appeals to the public conscience. As these instruments of protest had failed, the approaching national election offered another vehicle to accomplish the same goal. A threat to his political survival might compel the President to make accommodations where lesser measures had failed.

For this challenge, they wanted Kennedy because he was the strongest, most visible public figure. Where they and Kennedy differed was in his certainty that his relationship to Johnson, constantly described by the media in terms of rivalry, bitterness, and personal ambition, made him an unsuitable vehicle for their purpose. If Johnson were to be challenged, it would have to be by someone who could make the President and his policies the issue without becoming the issue himself.

When Kennedy turned them down, the peace leaders approached George McGovern of South Dakota, who had warned the Senate of the quicksand of Vietnam as early as September 1963. McGovern declined because he was a candidate for re-election in 1968. In his opinion, there were a number of senators who could begin the challenge, such as Ernest Gruening of Alaska, Vance Hartke of Indiana,

Joseph Clark of Pennsylvania—but Kennedy could not do so personally. Once, however, Johnson had been discredited politically, only Kennedy could command the political power to complete the challenge successfully at the Convention. McGovern also suggested that the Coalition leaders see Eugene McCarthy of Minnesota.

The next call for Kennedy to run came from members of his office staff, and some of his brother's former advisers, who were more in tune with politics than with protest. Walinsky, who after the 1966 election declared Johnson to be "a lame duck," began advocating Kennedy's candidacy at that time. From California, Pierre Salinger urged Kennedy to give serious thought to the possibility. From Italy, where he was working on his biography of Adlai Stevenson, John Bartlow Martin, former ambassador to the Dominican Republic and speech writer for several Democratic presidential nominees, wrote Kennedy in October 1967 that "for the first time I am beginning to think that Johnson cannot be elected." If the President himself came to that conclusion, Martin calculated, he would not announce it immediately, but would wait until shortly before the Convention, so he could use his power to ensure the nomination of someone like Humphrey. "I hope," Martin told Kennedy, "you will be trying to get contingency delegate strength. I previously subscribed to the 1972 theory for you, but I'm switching to 1968."

A few weeks later, Fred Dutton wrote Kennedy of his feeling that Johnson would not run in 1968: "He will not want to risk a major debacle at the end of a 35-year public career. After New Hampshire will be a moment of truth for him. He will make his announcement then or wait until after the Republicans nominate." At the same time, the polls, so unfavorable to Kennedy the previous spring, began to come around again. His lead over Johnson among Democrats polled by Gallup was greater than ever, 51 per cent to 36 per cent.

Kennedy absorbed this advice and followed developments, treating the latest "groundswell" lightly. He had been through enough ebbs and flows in his popularity to see it was in direct proportion to Johnson's and that the polls, while accurate indicators at the time they are taken, change with the popular mood, are overtaken by events, and are hardly reliable foundations on which to premise momentous decisions. Receiving a report from a friend about a meeting of a "Draft RFK" Committee, in which participants had called him "a gift from the gods," Kennedy told the sender: "You had better get aboard—there is only one Cabinet vacancy and four Ambassadorships left."

By the middle of the fall of 1967, however, enough stray pieces and possibilities were floating around to lead Senator Edward Kennedy to decide that some of the people concerned with his brother's future should get together to exchange views. The meeting, which Robert Kennedy did not attend, took place at the urging of Pierre Salinger. Of the old White House group, he had been the most vociferous advocate of a Kennedy race.

The meeting took place in Salinger's suite in the Regency Hotel in New York City on October 8.[7] Edward Kennedy began it by saying there were three possible developments that could require some change in his brother's present political posture. He might decide to oppose Johnson openly for the nomination; he might wish to be in a position to move if Johnson decided not to be a candidate; or Johnson might find himself in such difficult straits come August 1968 that he might open up the nomination for Vice President at the Convention, in an effort to restore a coalition that could assure his victory. Edward Kennedy said he wanted the group's opinions as to what action his brother might take in the light of these possibilities.

First, he asked whether his brother should disassociate himself from the peace groups that were using his name to build opposition to the war in Vietnam and were talking about running slates in the presidential primaries. The general opinion of the meeting was that the political embarrassment these groups might be causing was far outweighed by the importance of their work in regard to the war, and that Kennedy should not prohibit the use of his name at this time.

Ted Sorensen went further, and suggested that instead of repudiating these groups, friends of Robert Kennedy in the primary states should covertly support them, and even join the delegations, while Kennedy himself maintained his attitude of aloofness. If the groups were successful, the voters would then have an alternative to re-

[7] Present were Senator Edward Kennedy, Stephen Smith, Dutton, Kenneth O'Donnell, Sorensen, Charles Daly, John Burns, vanden Heuvel, Richard Goodman, Ivan Nestigen, Tom Johnston, and of course, Salinger.

nominating Johnson, and Kennedy would be sure to have friends on these delegations in Chicago. The meeting felt this was a good plan in theory, but that such an effort, in a state like New Hampshire, for example, would undoubtedly be discovered. The marginal benefits from such a plan were small compared to the risk involved in offering proof that Kennedy was trying to undercut Johnson for the nomination.

Dutton argued that the recent dramatic improvement in Kennedy's standing in the polls was more a sign of dissatisfaction with Johnson than an indication that the public wanted Kennedy to be President. He felt any movement by Kennedy would produce antagonism to him and sympathy for Johnson.

Those who advanced the idea that Kennedy "run" for Vice President offered essentially the same reasons Kennedy himself had accepted in 1964: It would permit him to travel the country and identify with the broad field of executive responsibility without having to vote on compromises and controversies in the Senate; he could preclude any real challenge for the presidential nomination in 1972; and he could overcome the innocuous character of the office because of his own independent political power. But the example of what the office had done to Hubert Humphrey led the proposal to be promptly put aside. In fact, most present believed Kennedy should decline the vice presidency if Johnson offered it to him.

The consensus of the meeting was not to challenge Johnson unless his political position became much weaker than it seemed to be at the time.[8] However, a few more activist recommendations were made, which Kennedy later approved. A poll would be taken in · New Hampshire and Kennedy would be urged to step up his political operation in general, by visiting with congressmen and state political figures who came to Washington. He would no longer make the blanket public endorsements of Johnson which were causing so much dismay among the anti-Vietnam legions. Finally, his staff political operators would increase their contacts with Democratic leaders around the country to elicit their thinking about 1968.

The responsibility for implementing this last directive fell to Joseph

---

[8] Salinger dissented. It was useless to wait until 1972, he argued. If Johnson were re-elected he would use all the powers of the office to block Kennedy's nomination. Ivan Nestigen, the former mayor of Madison, Wisconsin, also favored an immediate contest for the nomination.

Dolan, Kennedy's administrative assistant. He had already made a list of the leaders of the Democratic party whom he believed could deliver a sizable bloc of votes at the Convention.[9] He also attempted a rough count of Kennedy delegates on the first ballot (assuming victories in all the primaries), even though he realized the lack of hard political information made it seem like picking numbers out of the air.

To improve the information available to him, Dolan drew up a list of people in each state whose discretion could be relied on. They were sent pro-Kennedy newspaper articles and polls, and asked to draw up lists in their states of persons to whom copies of Kennedy's recently published book *To Seek a Newer World* could appropriately be sent. They were also asked to gauge the reactions to the possibility of a Kennedy candidacy. Studies of state primary laws and filing dates were also undertaken in the Kennedy office beginning in late October.

This small effort toward movement proved an exercise in frustration. Dolan received little help from the politicians he contacted. Except for a handful who were strongly pro-Kennedy, they made him feel as though he was engaged in a secret conspiracy to overthrow the government—which, in a certain sense, he was.[10] These were veteran politicians, who had been trying to keep a foot on each side of the Kennedy-Johnson feud for three years. They knew that an inquiry from Kennedy's administrative assistant about political condi-

[9] He could think of only nine—Mayor Richard Daley of Chicago, Mayor James Tate of Philadelphia, and Governor Hughes of New Jersey, all of whom controlled large blocs of delegates in large states; Walter Reuther and George Meany, who could swing union members who were delegates; Governor Harold Hughes of Iowa and Senator Stuart Symington, who were influential in the Middle West; Anthony Dechant, head of the National Farm Unions, and P. W. Hunter, head of the National Rural Electric Cooperatives Association, both of whom could number thirty to forty members of their organization among the delegates.

[10] At this point, only two Democratic leaders of consequence were encouraging Kennedy to oppose Lyndon Johnson: Governor Hughes of Iowa, who was reiterating the arguments he had made the year before, and Jesse Unruh, speaker of the California Assembly. Kennedy ascribed Unruh's interest to his situation in California. Because he was labeled as a close political associate of the Kennedys, he had been cut off from any contact with Johnson. His political enemies, with support from the White House, were moving to circumscribe his power. In 1968, he might want to run for the Senate. Meanwhile, he wanted to maintain a Democratic majority in the Assembly so he could remain as speaker. He needed, therefore, a presidential candidate at the head of the ticket who was popular in California, and Kennedy was the man.

tions in their state was not just an idle phone call. They were not going to give Dolan their assessment of Kennedy vs. Johnson, or commit themselves in any way, unless they knew whether Kennedy was going to run. Kennedy was not going to make that decision unless he knew how much support he would have. It turned into an elaborate feinting ritual. Edward Kennedy's administrative assistant, David Burke, who helped Dolan make some of the contacts, said later that it all had to be done with eye movements. "They ask is Bobby running? I say 'no,' and wink a couple of times. I wait for them to wink back. If they do, I mark them down as a friend."

The modest plan for immediate action received little help from Kennedy. He was reluctant to engage in conversations with political implications and was uncomfortable about socializing with the Democratic congressmen, particularly when it involved political discussions where the implications were clear, but his own attitude could not be candid. When Edward Kennedy persuaded him to join him on the floor of the House of Representatives at 12:30 to meet members, he arrived at 1:15, saying he had been tied up. He balked at the suggestion that he autograph 3000 copies of his book for mailing to key Democratic political leaders: "Every time I sit down to sign these books, I say to myself, why am I doing this? The answer has to be because I am running for President. But I'm not running for President."

By November 1967, Kennedy's attitude began to change markedly. Until then, he had read the polls with interest, listened to the advice of others with patience, but had not seriously considered altering his presidential timetable. In that month he began to feel the personal and political pressures that were finally to propel him into an open challenge. The continued deterioration of the American position in Vietnam had enlarged anti-war sentiment into a broadly based protest. The 50,000 who marched on the Pentagon that month and the students who defied and disrupted the draft represented the more militant portion. More significant were the millions who were slowly and reluctantly coming to the conclusion that, whatever the justification for the initial American presence in Vietnam, the war was not working, and further escalation, far from bringing victory, would only make it worse. In November, Johnson dropped behind Nixon in the

Gallup Poll for the first time, and for the first time in ten years, a majority of the voters preferred Republicans to Democrats as the party "best able to handle the most serious problems of the country."

Until November, Kennedy, as other Democrats, could criticize the President while supporting him for re-election. Now it became more difficult. Ever since his March 1967 speech on Vietnam, Kennedy had been framing his arguments less in terms of diplomatic alternatives and more in terms of moral responsibilities. He was deeply disturbed by the apparent indifference of many Americans to the suffering and killing that were being inflicted on the Vietnamese. He began to speak about this with eloquence; hearing him, students, clergymen, and anti-war citizens began to ask how, if he felt so strongly about the immorality of the war, he could continue to support the man responsible for its course. It became an increasingly hard question for him to answer.

At Marymount, a Catholic woman's college in New York, on November 18, he severely chastised the majority of students present who had indicated by a show of hands that they favored escalation of the war: "All of you who put your hands up—what are you doing to a lot of innocent people?" he asked. "Hundreds and thousands of people in Vietnam are being killed on our responsibility. You must think of the implications to your own conscience." The *National Catholic Reporter* defended the students by criticizing Kennedy: "Given his views of the war and the political following he has in part inherited, in part created, he bears a great deal more responsibility for the good name of the United States and for the innocent lives being taken in the war than do any of the students and teachers at Marymount whom he chastised . . ."

The inconsistency surfaced again on November 27, when he appeared on the television panel show "Face the Nation." Before the program, Kennedy had decided to make one modification when asked about his support of Johnson. Instead of offering his usual unqualified endorsement, he would say that he "expected President Johnson to be the Democratic nominee, and if so he would support him." This raised the possibility Johnson might not run, and, more important, left open the question of whether Kennedy would support him in the primaries.

To the "Face the Nation" audience he gave his most impassioned statement yet on the immorality of the Administration's conduct of the war. Referring to General Westmoreland's statement that "we were now fighting in Vietnam to prevent Communism from moving closer to the United States," Kennedy said this represented a fundamental change from the rationale of the American commitment undertaken by President Kennedy. "We've changed—we switched," he said. "And the result is that we have badly undermined our whole moral situation." His reaction to the destruction he had witnessed on the television overflowed as he said:

> Do we have the right here in the United States to say that we're going to kill tens of thousands, make millions of people, as we have, refugees, kill women and children, as we have? . . . Do we have that right here in the United States to perform these acts because we want to protect ourselves so that we don't have—so it is not a greater problem for us here in the United States. I very seriously question whether we have that right . . . when we use napalm, when a village is destroyed and civilians are killed . . . This is also our responsibility. This is a moral obligation and a moral responsibility for us here in the United States. And I think we have forgotten about that . . . when we say we love our country, we love our country for what it can be and for the justice it stands for and what we are going to mean to the next generation. It is not just the land, it is not just the mountains, it is what this country stands for. And that is what I think is being seriously undermined in Vietnam and the effect of it has to be felt by our people.

The newsmen on the panel were impressed by the passion of the statement. Then came the question which exposed the moral ambiguity of Kennedy's position, as his friend Sander Vanocur asked, "If you feel so strongly about the war in Vietnam, do you really feel that President Johnson should run?" And Kennedy said he would not stand in Johnson's way.

"Face the Nation" was the first time Kennedy had spoken so emotionally about the war on national television, and it had an electric effect. Hundreds of letters poured into his office urging him to run. Many criticized his support of Johnson. "Entering the race," said liberal columnist I. F. Stone, "might mean political suicide, but the alternative is the risk of national suicide."

The ambiguity of his position made Kennedy very uncomfortable because it compromised the standard of candor he had always tried to apply to his public utterances. He had tried to explain his position on the program:

> If I ran for President of the United States, [he said] I would not strengthen the question of these issues or the dialogue that is taking place in connection with these issues, but in fact I would weaken it. It would immediately become a personality struggle. It would immediately become a struggle between me, as an overly ambitious figure trying to take the nomination away from President Johnson, who deserves it because of the fact that he is not only President but served the Democratic party and the country as President for four or five years.

In other words, it was still Kennedy's view that if he became a candidate, the personal struggle between him and Johnson would overshadow the issues. But if he failed to win the nomination, as he expected, this would be interpreted as a vote of confidence in the President's policies, which would injure the peace movement. President Kennedy had quoted Dante as saying that "the hottest places in hell were reserved for those who in times of moral crisis did nothing." But Dante also reserved a hot place in hell for suicides, even political suicides.

Those who opposed the war were, with good reason, not as concerned with Kennedy's political future as he was. Nor did they care about the political realities of a Democratic convention. They wanted the strongest possible man to make the most dramatic case—now. They felt Kennedy's name and reputation made him their best advocate, but he believed it exposed both him and the issue to a greater risk than necessary. "Why is it," he would say, "that Bill Fulbright and Vance Hartke can speak out against the war and no one criticizes them because they don't run for President." The answer came back very simply: "They are not Robert Kennedy. They do not have a majority in the polls against Lyndon Johnson."

The survival of the two-party system in an increasingly large and diverse nation has meant that, in the preliminary stages of a presidential campaign, each major segment of each party produces its own preference for President. Conversely, each major candidate has a base from which to reach for the nomination. Republican conventions, for example, have produced at least one "liberal" and "conservative" candidate since the days of Theodore Roosevelt; both the South and the liberals have had their own candidates in the Democratic pre-convention contests as did forces pro and anti Prohibition in the 1920s. Kennedy's reluctance to run, combined with the growing anti-war sentiment, thus created a political vacuum. On November 30, 1967, Senator Eugene McCarthy stepped forward to fill it.

McCarthy's sixteen years in Congress had been marked by traces of both independence and expediency. He had spoken out against Senator Joseph McCarthy much earlier than most Democrats had deemed prudent. In 1958, he had upset Minnesota's Democratic-Farmer-Labor party organization led by Hubert Humphrey by winning the Senate nomination. After nine years in the Senate, however, McCarthy had not distinguished himself from the thirteen other Democrats who had been elected to the Senate for the first time in 1958.

At the time of McCarthy's announcement, the New York *Times* called him "much more a Johnson Democrat than a Kennedy Democrat." Actually, he was close to neither. He resented the success of John Kennedy, feeling that he was more qualified by experience and intellect to be the first Catholic President of the United States. He had gone to the 1960 Convention pledged to Lyndon Johnson, and at the last minute, agreed to nominate Adlai Stevenson, serving the stop-Kennedy movement which hoped to see Johnson emerge as the presidential nominee. If Kennedy were stopped, McCarthy presumed Johnson would salve the feelings of Catholic voters by picking him as his running mate.

McCarthy's attitude toward Johnson changed abruptly in 1964. All during the first months of that year, Johnson led McCarthy to believe he was at the top of the list for the vice presidency. Support for McCarthy came from top members of the White House staff, and several Southern governors, including Texas' John Connally, who felt the nomination of an attractive, mildly liberal Catholic would assuage any bitterness about not choosing Kennedy. But Hubert Humphrey was also a contender, and key supporters in Minnesota were urging McCarthy to withdraw in Humphrey's favor.

On the day before the President was to come to Atlantic City to announce his choice to the Convention, McCarthy sent a telegram to

Johnson endorsing Humphrey. At three o'clock the following morning, McCarthy received a frantic call from White House aide Walter Jenkins urging him not to release the telegram to the press. (It had already been released.) The next afternoon Johnson called McCarthy from the White House and told him Humphrey was his choice.

Later that day, White House aides called McCarthy again with a request from the President to nominate Humphrey. At first, McCarthy refused. "Get Walter Reuther to do it," he said, referring to Humphrey's broad support for the nomination among labor leaders. The next morning, McCarthy, somewhat tempered, had breakfast with Jenkins and said that the only thing he could not understand was why, if Johnson had decided on Humphrey, he had been reluctant to see McCarthy's telegram in the newspapers.

"The President wanted it to look like you were still under consideration," Jenkins said. "He had planned to call you and Humphrey to the White House, fly with both of you to the Convention, walk into the Convention and onto the rostrum with both of you and *then* have you step forward and nominate Humphrey."

McCarthy could only reply: "What a sadistic son of a bitch."

McCarthy met the peace movement's needs, in that he was much more a candidate of protest than a serious seeker after the Presidency. He made it clear, in the first months of his campaign, that he was challenging only "the President's position," as he put it, not the President himself. His purpose, he said, was not to deprive Johnson of the nomination, but to provide a vehicle by which Democratic voters might participate in a meaningful debate on Southeast Asian policy and persuade the President to move toward a negotiated settlement in Vietnam.

Even those who did not think this would succeed saw another benefit in McCarthy's move. As Walter Lippmann put it:

> . . . The most serious accusation that can be laid against the Johnson Administration is that it has corrupted and undermined the faith of our people in their political system . . . It is not small service on (McCarthy's) part to have raised a flag to which the dissenting and despairing can repair because they see again a way to express themselves. They do not have to win. In a democratic country everybody can believe, even when he loses, that he has been honestly heard,

has made himself felt, has had a fair chance to take part in the give-and-take of debate and voting . . . I do not expect to see him unhorse Lyndon Johnson. I do not expect him to force a change in the policies to which President Johnson has now so irretrievably committed the Democratic party. But Eugene McCarthy will have spoken out and there will have been close to him some men who will in time pull the Democratic party out of the disaster into which it has been led.

A few days before his announcement, McCarthy paid a courtesy call on Kennedy to tell him his intentions. The meeting, which lasted only seven minutes, confirmed Kennedy's impression that McCarthy was not a serious candidate. He did not, for example, even discuss any of the problems of the primaries he was entering. "I've had some experience in running primaries," Kennedy said later, "I've managed them in New Hampshire, Wisconsin, and Oregon, the states where he may be running. My experience might be of some help." But McCarthy only wanted to make sure Kennedy himself was not going to run.

At that meeting, Kennedy did not promise McCarthy he would stay out of the race. He said only that if he had to give an answer at that time, it would have to be no. McCarthy confirmed this in his press conference on November 30, when he said "Senator Kennedy has made no commitment to stand aside all the way" and "there would surely be nothing illegal or contrary to American politics if he or someone else were to take advantage of what I am doing." In fact, on the day he announced, McCarthy made a bid for the support of pro-Kennedy Democrats by making it clear, as Warren Weaver of the New York *Times* reported, that "it would not disturb him if his campaign against Mr. Johnson in the primaries resulted in making Senator Robert F. Kennedy the Democratic candidate next year."

From the beginning McCarthy's manner and tactics made Kennedy uncomfortable. The two men were colleagues but not friends; they were Democrats but not political allies. Kennedy was not unhappy with McCarthy's announcement at the time because it relieved him of some of the pressure. "McCarthy's entrance is useful," Dutton told him. "He loosens the situation up." Those around Kennedy who wanted him to run also welcomed McCarthy's announcement. Here was a chance to isolate and test Johnson's vulnerability without giving the

White House an opportunity to dismiss the challenge as an example of Kennedy's ambition and antagonism. On the day he announced, Mc-Carthy buttons appeared on the insides of the lapels of the Kennedy staff.

The announcement was followed by a flurry of activity by and on behalf of Johnson. In the first two weeks of December, a large number of Democratic governors and state political organizations, in a show of loyalty, endorsed him for the nomination. In the Gallup Poll, Johnson moved into an eight-point lead over Nixon among all voters, and into a 63 per cent to 17 per cent lead over McCarthy among Democratic voters. Stung by an open challenge, the bulk of the Democratic party seemed to be moving into position behind their President. On January 3, 1968, the *New Republic* could report "President Johnson is running hard for re-election. Speeches, interviews and a wild dash around the world from the antipodes to the Pope show what a tough campaigner he is."

But as the pressure on him eased in late November and December 1967, Kennedy was again considering the question of running. The event that touched this off was the summary dismissal of his friend Robert McNamara as Secretary of Defense. For all his participation in the decisions to enlarge the war, McNamara had been a leading advocate within the Administration of de-escalation and the cessation of bombing as a way to end it. It was the Defense Department, rather than the State Department, which took the lead in proposing ideas for new initiatives toward peace.[11]

In the early years of his Administration, Johnson made no secret of the fact that McNamara was the most admired member of his Cabinet. The first indication that he was placing less reliance on his recommendations was the announcement in the summer of 1967 that the Chairman of the Joint Chiefs of Staff would begin to sit in on the weekly luncheon strategy meetings on Vietnam, which until then had been limited to the President, McNamara, and Rusk.

In the spring of 1967, George Wood, then President of the World

[11] Within Defense, this work was led by the International Security Affairs staff, headed by the late John McNaughton and later by Paul Warnke, both assisted by Morton Halperin.

Bank, had discussed with McNamara the possibility of heading the Bank after his term at the Department of Defense ended. McNamara expressed some interest, but no timetable was discussed. No one was more surprised than he to learn, on Decemeber 1, that his "request" to direct the World Bank had been "honored" by the President. It was a classic example of Johnson's elaborate secret manipulations of personnel.

The day McNamara's "resignation" was accepted, Kennedy went to see him at the Pentagon and urged him not to let Johnson's device obscure the real issues involved. "Tell him," Kennedy said, "that as Commander in Chief he has the right to have whomever he wants as Secretary of Defense; but you will not, under these circumstances, accept the position at the World Bank." But McNamara, his sense of loyalty to superiors deeply ingrained by experiences in the business world, declined to do something that hinted so broadly at the real reasons for his dismissal.

To Kennedy, McNamara's dismissal made it clear that Johnson was not about to pursue a more conciliatory course in Vietnam, and did not even wish that alternative to be pressed upon him. This fact made him once again begin to consider a political challenge. On December 10, Kennedy met for lunch in New York with his brother and a small number of political advisers.[12] There were two issues on his mind: whether if he announced his candidacy now, it was possible for him to be nominated and elected; and whether the prospect of four more years of a Johnson presidency was so ominous and dangerous to the country that he had an obligation to make the fight, even though he would lose it.

He asked Goodwin, who was an advocate of his running, to summarize the arguments in favor. Goodwin ran through the deterioration of the national mood, the profound hostility to Johnson in the country, the catastrophic consequences of the Vietnam war, the racial strife that threatened every city in America, and the national yearning for a leader. These factors, added to Kennedy's own powerful charisma, would win for him in the primaries. The Convention would be much more difficult, but if, having won the primaries, he were denied the

[12] Including Goodwin, Schlesinger, Sorensen, Dutton, Salinger and vanden Heuvel.

nomination, he could approach the 1972 Convention, his real goal, as a man who had been selected by the people but rejected by the bosses.

As to splitting the party, Goodwin asked what there was to be split. The loose confederation of state organizations existed, as it always had, but Johnson had let the national party machinery atrophy. As for McCarthy, Goodwin (who had no contact with him at the time) felt he would probably defer to Kennedy at this point, but even if he did not, he would be ignored in the drama of Kennedy's entry. Dutton, who had not yet come over to Kennedy's running, nevertheless felt that the longer Kennedy waited, the less he could count on McCarthy's bowing out. McCarthy supporters, he predicted, would resent Kennedy's entry, since McCarthy had paved the way. Arthur Schlesinger also urged Kennedy to become a candidate. He recognized the risks but felt that the plight of the country demanded his running. "If Johnson is the nominee in 1968," he added, "the Democratic party will be ruined permanently."

Edward Kennedy summarized the case for not running. Johnson, he said, was stronger than many people assumed. As the incumbent, he could command the issues, taking them away from any opponent if the political cost made it necessary. The political opposition to the Johnson policies in Vietnam, for example, could be shattered if the President ordered a bombing halt, and he could do it on his own initiative. The polls also were indicating a resurgence of the President's popularity, again, a matter substantially within his control, as the Glassboro conference with Kosygin had shown. He listed the familiar considerations of the difficulty of winning in 1968 as compared to the bright prospects for 1972, when the leadership of the Democratic party would be open. He ventured that Robert Kennedy would be able to have a far greater voice in the determination of the policies of the next four years if he stood as the heir to the next nomination, rather than the cause of the party's defeat.

Edward Kennedy's view was generally shared by all present except Goodwin and Schlesinger. After further discussion of delegate numbers and of the possibility of losing liberal and youth support, the group recommended that Kennedy delay any action, stay in touch with party leaders, and take another look in January, both at how McCarthy was progressing and at whether the considerations under discussion had changed. At another meeting later that afternoon, at Forrest D. Murden's office on East Fifty-first Street, with an enlarged group of associates but Robert Kennedy absent, the same consensus was reached. It was agreed that two or three Democratic leaders, prominent enough to talk frankly to other leaders but not closely tied with the Kennedys, should be asked to travel to various states to take soundings on how a Kennedy candidacy would be received, and what his chances for the nomination would be were he to win the primaries. The names of Jesse Unruh, former Governor Terry Sanford of North Carolina, and former Governor Edward Breathitt of Kentucky were recommended. None of them was ever approached because Kennedy rejected this suggestion on the grounds that such conversations could not be kept private. It was unworkable in any event. Two days later, Breathitt accepted an appointment from President Johnson, and within five months Sanford was serving as chairman of Citizens for Humphrey.

Thus, three months before the first primary, the Kennedy "organization" had only one political leader of substance (Unruh) to undertake this kind of assignment. Smith and Edward Kennedy did take some cautious soundings of their own, but their reports were uniformly negative. All the politicians Smith consulted advised Kennedy against contesting Johnson, fearing it would tear apart their local organizations. Every one of Kennedy's fellow senators who opposed the war also warned him against running and splitting the party. Senators Joseph Clark and Wayne Morse added that it would jeopardize their own chances for re-election. The poll Kennedy had commissioned in New Hampshire showed that Johnson would beat him, 60 per cent to 28 per cent, with 12 per cent undecided if the primary were held at that time.

With the decision made not to become a candidate at this time, Kennedy turned to other matters. He finished work on the manuscript of his book on the Cuban missile crisis. He told Tom Johnston to arrange a three-week trip through New York State in January, and asked Peter Edelman to prepare a summary of his activities on issues affecting New York.

Meanwhile, McCarthy's campaign was in the doldrums. His announcement had stirred hope, but the first forays on the campaign trail provided little evidence that a major protest was stirring in the country. In Wisconsin, even outspoken opponents of the Vietnam policy, such as Senator William Proxmire and Congressman Robert Kastenmeier, refused to break with Johnson. The earliest, most bitter critic of the Vietnam policy, Senator Wayne Morse of Oregon, merely declared his neutrality. McCarthy spent almost two weeks in January in a running battle with the Federal Communications Commission, which had refused his demand for equal time after Johnson, in a television interview, had spoken of a "Kennedy-McCarthy movement," implying that McCarthy was a stalking horse for Kennedy. Six days of campaigning in California added no support beyond what McCarthy already had through the endorsement of the policy-oriented California Democratic Council. When he spoke at the University of California at Los Angeles, the student newspaper, the *Daily Bruin,* charged that McCarthy was really a front for Lyndon Johnson. By entering the race, said the *Bruin,* he made it difficult for Kennedy to do so and therefore ensured Johnson's nomination. By the end of January, the Gallup Poll showed that after two months of campaigning, McCarthy had actually fallen further behind the President. The margin favoring Johnson was now 4–1, instead of 3–1. Even Dr. Spock concluded publicly on January 6, that there was little chance to deny Johnson renomination.

Logically, McCarthy's apparent failure should have lessened the pressure on Kennedy by showing the futility of opposing an incumbent President. It had the opposite effect. Those who opposed the conduct of the war concluded it was not the cause but the candidate that lacked appeal. McCarthy's difficulties reinforced their view that Kennedy was the only person who could seriously challenge the President. The pressures on him to run increased dramatically, especially from Democratic liberals. As Kennedy persisted in his refusal, many charged him with being more interested in protecting his political career than in saving the country. Kennedy found himself in a position where, if he ran against the President, he would bring about the seemingly conflicting result of consolidating the Johnson forces against him and being the cause of the division that could defeat the Democrats in the November election. If he did not run, he risked the present alienation of many of his new allies, and the anger of some of the most influential opinion makers in his own state. McCarthy exploited Kennedy's vulnerability with statements like:

> There are some Americans, including some at the highest levels of government and politics, who have not yet spoken as their minds and consciences dictate. In some cases they have done so for reasons of personal or political convenience. They are a few who are waiting, I suspect, for a kind of latter day salvation. Four years are too long to wait. Judgment and action are needed now.

Kennedy spoke frankly about his dilemma. Asked on January 8, at Manhattan Community College, why he was remaining neutral in the primaries, he answered: "I must examine the issue in relation to my concern about my own future, my own conscience, and my judgment on what can be most useful. My feeling at the moment is that what I am doing is the most useful, but perhaps not accomplishing a great deal."

By the end of January, he was almost totally preoccupied with the question of whether to become a candidate. He would sit at his desk for long periods, his fingers touching, a study in contemplation. He could not keep his thoughts to himself. He talked with staff members at length about the details of the problem. He widened his circle of advice, calling scores of friends and friendly political leaders. Inevitably, speculation about his plans intensified. In California, Unruh was telling Democratic leaders that Kennedy "had not made up his mind" and that it was "not inconceivable" that Unruh himself might head up a slate of pro-Kennedy delegates in June's California primary. Coming from one of the most prominent Democratic politicians in the country, this touched off yet another round of speculation in the press. Kennedy felt it was time for yet another disclaimer. On January 31, he was scheduled to breakfast with a group of Washington reporters who regularly hold off-the-record discussions with prominent political personalities. On the way to the meeting, he asked his press secretary, Frank Mankiewicz, what he should say about the possibility of his running. Mankiewicz, whose feeling for months had been that Kennedy would eventually become a candidate, suggested saying that he was not one at this time, would not enter the primaries, but would reserve any decision beyond that. Kennedy chose his own course. When asked the inevitable question, he said he would not become a candidate for the presidency "under any conceivable circumstances" and had so advised those friends who were urging him to run. Reporters asked permission to write this as a story and Kennedy granted it. Mankiewicz succeeded however, in diluting the statement to read "under any *foreseeable* circumstances."

Because the hour was late (the deadline for entering the New Hampshire primary had already passed) this statement had an air of finality. His younger staff members, who had sensed the possibility of a positive decision, were demoralized. When Walinsky told him that he would probably have to leave the staff, Kennedy matter-of-factly replied that while he understood the disappointment, Walinsky should feel free to do whatever he wished. Arthur Schlesinger chose to interpret the statement as a tentative one. He urged Kennedy to adopt a more flexible position, since events were occurring so fast that by spring he might regret any unconditional statement of non-candidacy.

The liberals treated his decision with disdain. Touring New York in early February, he was asked everywhere why he would not run, or at least support McCarthy. His "reassessment" was ridiculed on television's Rowan and Martin's "Laugh-In" and the Smothers Brothers Show. Fred Dutton warned that "the present picture of your seemingly backing off for reasons of expediency (rather than the real problem of effectiveness) is a new public view of you, and like most first impressions or suddenly changed ones, can have a lasting residual effect if not wiped out fairly quickly."

No sooner had Kennedy made his January 31 statement than he began to have deep reservations about it. It was not the public reaction. He had been through that before. The critical thing was that a climactic event had taken place which was of a kind that could justify a change in his position. The Vietcong Tet offensive had begun, ironically, on the very day Kennedy announced he was not running. As the offensive unfolded, the Administration's assurances and credibility were swept away. The enemy was attacking and occupying areas supposedly secure—Vietnamese cities, American air bases and even the U. S. Embassy building in Saigon. They easily overpowered South Vietnamese forces, who apparently were unprepared for the assaults. The Vietcong obviously were getting information and cooperation from civilians who were presumed friendly to the government or at least unfriendly to the Communists. The White House and General

Westmoreland depicted the Tet offensive as a Viet Cong defeat. "Body counts" revealed enormous enemy casualties. The areas occupied by the attackers were regained, although the ancient city of Hue was essentially destroyed in prolonged battles. But the statistics of victory were as hollow as the hopes that preceded them. The Tet offensive was a disaster for Lyndon Johnson. Instead of fulfilling a promise to reduce American combat forces, he was faced with a recommendation from the Joint Chiefs of Staff for a major escalation involving 207,000 more troops. Despite the most prolonged, intensive bombing in history, a guerrilla army had not only survived but had managed a maneuver that reasserted its military and political power. Embarrassment, anger, frustration, and disbelief combined to make the national mood. At best, Tet meant that the war and its drain on American life could drag on for years unless the policies were changed. At worst, there was the possibility that the country, faced with a major defeat, might rally behind a presidential decision for major escalation.

There was a sense among those who had faithfully supported the Administration that they had been duped. Men like General David Sarnoff, a strong-minded advocate of American military power and a supporter of the intervention in Vietnam, came to see Kennedy to express the opinion that the nation was in danger, that Kennedy had been right in his criticisms, and to offer his help to bring about a change in policy. More than any single person, more than any political movement, the Tet offensive changed the politics of 1968. It was the event that gave Kennedy an impersonal justification for reconsidering his position and becoming a candidate for the presidency.

On February 8, 1968, a week after Tet began, Kennedy delivered a bitter blast against the Administration's Vietnam policy to an author's luncheon in Chicago. A year before he had carefully chosen his words and qualified his criticisms, concerned about their political consequences. Now all restraint was gone; he spoke as a vindicated man:

> Our enemy, savagely striking at will across all of South Vietnam, [he said] has finally shattered the mask of official illusion with which we have concealed our true circumstances even from ourselves. . . . they have demonstrated that no part or person of South Vietnam is secure from their attacks; neither district capitals nor American bases, neither the peasant in his rice paddy nor the commanding general of our own great forces . . . the first and necessary step

is to face the facts. It is to seek out the austere and painful reality of Vietnam, freed from wishful thinking, false hopes and sentimental dreams . . . We have misconceived the nature of the war . . . We have sought to resolve by military might a conflict whose issue depends upon the will and conviction of the South Vietnamese people . . . the war cannot be settled in our own way on our own terms . . . we must actively seek a peaceful settlement that will give the Vietcong a chance to participate in the political life of the country.

While in Chicago, he met with Mayor Daley. He talked to him as an old friend of his father, an ally of his brother, and as the single most powerful municipal politician in the Democratic Party. He told Daley that there were mounting pressures on him to run for President and that he expected he would become a candidate, because the consequences of continuing a policy of escalation in Vietnam would be disastrous for everyone. Daley replied that the war was of equally great concern to him. In fact, Daley said, he had told President Johnson that the issue was so damaging politically that unless the policies were changed, he could not hope to be re-elected. Kennedy told Daley he doubted Johnson would change policies because his personal identification had made them a matter of honor. "There comes a time," replied Daley, "when you must put honor in your back pocket and face realities."

Daley said he had suggested to the President that a blue ribbon commission be appointed to make a full review of Vietnam policies and propose changes. The commission would be a gesture to party unity, a demonstration of presidential leadership, and a victory for the dissenters on the prime issue of national protest. Would Kennedy, Daley asked, be chairman of such a commission? Kennedy declined, believing the President should have a chairman who had his personal confidence. But he would be willing to be a member of such a commission if the President wanted him and if there was a clear prior understanding that the recommendations of the commission would be followed. Kennedy added "I want to change the policies, not split the party."

Kennedy heard no more about the commission for the next six weeks. In the days after his trip to Chicago, he seemed settled in his posture of accelerated criticism and non-candidacy. On February 10, he reaffirmed that his Chicago speech did not mean he had changed his mind about running. On February 11, Pierre Salinger said flatly that Johnson would be renominated. On February 14, faced with a deadline, Kennedy notified the Secretary of State of Nebraska not to enter his name in that state's primary.

Throughout February and into March, he kept reaching out for advice and ideas, but took no definitive action. He seemed to be helpless in the grip of events. The disadvantages of the alternatives available to him made indecision preferable to final choice. On February 18, he met informally with several close associates who agreed that the political situation had not changed substantially enough to warrant recommendation of his decision not to enter the primaries. He let the March 3 filing deadline for the Massachusetts primary pass by, allowing McCarthy to win its seventy-two delegates on the first ballot by default, without asking his brother Edward to enter as a favorite son to keep the option open.

He almost failed to qualify for the primary in California, where, under a law designed to discourage fringe candidates, if a group is going to file nominating petitions it must officially indicate its intention to do so ninety days before the filing deadline.[13] It looked as if the passage of time and his own inaction would keep Kennedy out of the primaries. Those who spoke to him about it found he knew every argument, and in his mind the pros and cons divided about evenly.

"It breaks down this way," he said on March 10, in his office. "All of my sisters are for it, Teddy is against it. All the smart people we have listened to are against it except for Dutton, Schlesinger, and Goodwin. All the politicians are against it except Jesse. It will put every political leader in the Democratic party on the spot. They all think Nixon will be the Republican nominee and they think they can beat him with Johnson." In the middle of the same conversation, he would switch to the other side: "Can I wait until 1972? Won't I just keep getting

[13] Kennedy wanted Unruh to set up the declaration of intention, but the assistant to whom Unruh instructed the arrangements dragged his feet, and the last-minute filing was not in order. A valid filing in his behalf was ultimately made, on their own initiative, by members of the Citizens for Kennedy-Fulbright group in California.

into more controversies? In just three years, I've had Hoffa, Hoover, and Johnson. I really can't afford many more."

A few who favored his candidacy addressed themselves to the feeling that Kennedy could not win the nomination. They took another tack: Suppose he lost? Would that really upset the timetable for 1972? In a lengthy memo, Walinsky threw all the opposition's arguments back in their teeth:

> "I believe you need not lose; that you can win, in any of a number of ways; that you can affect policy, win the nomination and election, or make a substantial and enduring contribution to the politics and history of this nation. Perhaps—though I agree that the odds are heavily against it—you can do all three this year."

Continuing, Walinsky agreed with the point about the President's power to shape the issues. The moderate response to the North Korean capture of the ship *Pueblo* indicated to him that Johnson would not escalate in Vietnam. But if Johnson tried to negotiate in Vietnam, he said,

> "the mere agreement to negotiations would release tremendous pressure to make them successful; thousands of politicians would rush to support them, and thus would create a huge newly legitimized constituency for peace . . .
>
> "If Johnson does in fact make peace, you can—in one of the great self-abnegating acts of American history—bow out, having made your point, saved the country, and shown that it is not personal power which motivates you."

Walinsky estimated that Kennedy had only one chance in four of winning the nomination, but argued that

> ". . . a defeat at the Democratic Convention may yet be a victory in other ways . . . For the country, I personally believe that [Johnson's] defeat is necessary almost whoever his opponent. Even Nixon, the most likely opponent, is at least a weaker man, less likely to manipulate the public and the Congress as Johnson has done so cutely.
>
> "For you personally, a Nixon victory would be no blessing. But a Johnson re-election, *whether you oppose him or not*, would be an unqualified disaster . . . it is not opposing Johnson, but remaining inactive, which is really the terrible gamble. It is to bet the future, perhaps the nation's future, on Nixon's ability to capture enough of

the discontent to beat him. The safer course is to ensure that he is beaten. Once he is down, you can take your chances with the bosses, who after all will all be dead or finished within eight years. . . .

"I need not dwell on the effects of a Nixon-Johnson race for the country: but I wonder if you have adequately assessed its impact on you. Your own strength, of course, rests primarily on dreams—that politics can be a noble and honorable adventure, that idealism pays, that character and intellect are more important than the shady deals of the manipulators. Kill that belief, cripple those dreams, and your own greatest assets may vanish like those of a bank when all the notes are called at once."

In an emotional climax, Walinsky said:

"Senator, you are on the fourth floor, and I am saying 'jump.' Others say that you will, or may, break a leg; some say it will be your back. But I tell you that the building is on fire—and I think you smell the smoke . . . There are no rules. It is impossible with any certainty to say what comes next. Much of what I present as sure is of course speculation, instinct, hunch. I know only this: that if you opt not to try, you give up the unknown possibilities of the next few months. But if you do try, you preserve a variety of options limited only by the fantastic chances of the incredible times we live in. You are a man who does, you are the active principal; if you try and fail, others may reproach you; but if you do not try, you may always reproach yourself."

With Kennedy still vacillating, attention turned to the first test between Johnson and McCarthy. At the outset, McCarthy wanted to avoid the New Hampshire primary. The state was considered the least anti-war of all the primary states. It had no indigenous peace movement and the only statewide newspaper was the Manchester *Union Leader,* which at the time was leading a crusade for sending armed forces into North Korea to force the return of the *Pueblo.* On December 28, McCarthy had said the New Hampshire primary was "not particularly significant" for the purposes of his campaign. He changed his mind only after leaders of Americans for Democratic Action told him he would have to enter New Hampshire if he wanted their organization's endorsement.

Kennedy had a different view of New Hampshire. He felt its

voters would be receptive to a person like McCarthy. At dinner with Arthur Schlesinger and others, shortly after McCarthy announced, he ventured that McCarthy could do even better than he could:

"If I go in, it will be an overwhelming operation. The first day I go into a store or a barber shop to shake hands, 60 reporters will be with me. It can only be counter-productive. That's not the kind of campaign people in New Hampshire go for. I'll be charged with spending all kinds of money. Loeb (publisher of the *Union Leader*) will be as mean as he can be. The issue in New Hampshire will not be Lyndon Johnson or Vietnam—it will be me."

McCarthy, on the other hand—non-controversial, low-key, not regarded as a serious contender for President—was the ideal protest candidate. "All he has to do," Kennedy said, "is to drive around those little towns alone, talking to people about Vietnam. He needs only one piece of literature: It should have a picture of John Kennedy on it, and say, "This is the state that launched John Kennedy's movement toward the presidency. This is what we hoped for—and this is what we got."

McCarthy did campaign in a low key, but it did not work at first. By January 15, the Johnson forces in New Hampshire were predicting that McCarthy would get a maximum of 7500 votes out of a probable 55,000 cast. Expanding his campaign, McCarthy assembled a small group of skilled student organizers. He asked Goodwin, and others he knew were ardent opponents of Johnson and the war, to come to New Hampshire to give the professional help the campaign so badly needed. Before accepting, Goodwin checked Kennedy's plans once more. Assured that Kennedy had not changed his mind, Goodwin went to New Hampshire in the last week of February to help McCarthy's effort to get a referendum on the war.

The McCarthy campaign began to move. Although he had run because of the war, his criticism of domestic policies such as the 10 per cent surtax were getting a much better popular response. The biggest issue in New Hampshire, he discovered, was not the war but Lyndon Johnson. Even the majority which supported the war did not like the way the President was handling it.

Goodwin composed the kind of pamphlet Kennedy had suggested, containing material from the interview with "Bailey Laird" from the summer before. Under a picture of McCarthy and John F. Kennedy standing together, it said:

> In 1960, we started to get America moving again. Today, five years later, the fabric of that great achievement is unraveling.
>
> In 1963 the economy was booming, taxes were being lowered, prices were stable. Today our prosperity is slowing down, prices are going up and we are being asked to pay higher taxes.
>
> In 1963 our great cities were relatively tranquil. Today we look back on a period of virtual civil war.
>
> In 1963 our children in colleges and universities were concerned with the Peace Corps and Civil Rights. Today it is marijuana and draft protests.
>
> In 1963 we were at peace, today we are at war.

Goodwin sent a copy to Kennedy, whose only comment was "Gene must have plenty of money. He's only using one side of the sheet."

As the impact of the Tet offensive became apparent, McCarthy's prospects began to rise rapidly. As late as February 21, a Manchester *Union-Leader* poll showed Johnson leading six to one, but eight days later the leaders of the Johnson campaign were predicting a McCarthy vote of 25–30 per cent. They began to broadcast commercials implying a vote for McCarthy would be disloyal to the country and would undermine the soldiers in Vietnam. Kennedy immediately denounced this tactic as a smear. A week before the primary, William Dunfy, a manager of John Kennedy's campaign in New Hampshire in 1960, reported McCarthy would get 30 per cent of the vote. Goodwin, in a conversation with Edward Kennedy, said: "It's going up so fast you can feel it. If we had ten more days we would win."

During the last three weekends, hundreds of students, in an outpouring which was to shape the primary politics of 1968, knocked on the doors of New Hampshire homes and farms appealing for McCarthy votes on the basis of the issues. On radio and television, a New Hampshire accent said simply: "Think of how you would feel if you woke up on Wednesday morning and realized Eugene McCarthy had won the New Hampshire primary and New Hampshire had changed the course of American politics?"

By March, Kennedy believed that McCarthy would do well in New Hampshire, but not well enough. If Johnson, who was eligible only for write-in votes, won two-thirds of the ballots, the pressure would again be on Kennedy. The second week in March, Kennedy received a California poll that had been commissioned by Jesse Unruh for use in measuring his chance to win a Senate primary. Among Democratic voters, Johnson edged out Kennedy 34 per cent to 33 per cent, with 13 per cent for McCarthy and 20 per cent undecided. But this was not the form the California primary would take, for Johnson had already deputized California Attorney General Thomas Lynch to run as his stand-in. The more significant finding showed that a slate of delegates pledged to Kennedy would easily defeat a slate pledged to Lynch, 48 per cent to 27 per cent, with only 9 per cent for McCarthy. If Kennedy could do this well in the largest and most important state, it meant he could do equally well in the other states where Johnson would be running stand-ins, and in Oregon and Nebraska where, by law, Johnson had to be on the ballot. Once again, Kennedy made a tentative decision to announce his candidacy. On March 7 he met with Dutton, O'Donnell, and Edward Kennedy and told them he felt he had to run even if he could not win. But Dutton urged him to hold off his announcement. "You clearly seem to want to do it before New Hampshire," he said, "but this would touch off some write-in votes for you, and you would end up far behind McCarthy and Johnson in the actual results. This would be a minor put down for your campaign just as it was trying to show real authority." In addition, Dutton felt his announcement could cut down McCarthy's vote.

Kennedy took this advice, but five days before the primary, he decided he should tell McCarthy he planned to become a candidate. He asked his brother to pass the message, but McCarthy had left Washington for New Hampshire and could not be reached. Kennedy called Goodwin. "I'd like to get a message to McCarthy that I am going to run," he said. "I'd like to get it to him before the primary, so it does not look like I'm doing it because he did so well. Is there anyone he's close to I could ask to do this for me?"

"He's not close to anybody," Goodwin said.

"Why don't you tell him?" Kennedy asked.

"I can't. I'm working for him," Goodwin replied. He hoped Kennedy would understand that the experience of working in New Hampshire, against formidable odds and with such idealistic young people, made him reluctant to compromise his own commitment in their eyes. He

finally agreed to relay the message, but he waited until the Sunday
before the primary to do so. McCarthy was not as much surprised
as annoyed. "Tell him to support me. I only want one term as
President. After that, he can take it over."

"You don't mean that," Goodwin said.

"I do," said McCarthy. "I've thought about it. The presidency should
be a one-term office. Then the power would be in the institution.
It would not be so dependent upon the person."

The night of the New Hampshire primary, Kennedy was scheduled
to speak at a United Jewish Appeal dinner in the Bronx. He was
still thinking in terms of an announcement in about a week. The
latest predictions from New Hampshire had McCarthy getting about
35 per cent of the vote. Kennedy's assessment was as follows: Less
than that 35 per cent would be interpreted as a loss for McCarthy.
He would have fallen short—not of the original expectation, but,
more significantly, of the expectation as of that time. If this happened,
it would be clear Kennedy was the only one that could carry on the
effort. With this much opposition to Johnson within the party, there
was a chance he could win the nomination. Between 35 per cent
and 40 per cent would pose a more difficult choice. This would
be considered a good showing for McCarthy, preserving his position
for later primaries. Over 40 per cent for McCarthy would make
things very difficult.

The returns later that evening sustained Goodwin's optimism.
McCarthy was getting over 40 per cent. Because the Johnson delegates
were split, he was also winning the separate delegate elections.[14]
McCarthy was getting votes from Democratic "hawks" who felt Johnson
was not doing enough to win the war as well as from "doves" who felt
he was not doing enough to stop it. If Kennedy had been on the
ballot, and campaigned, and had only received 42 per cent against

[14] The Johnson supporters in New Hampshire, believing that the primary
would be uncontested, had designated twice as many candidates as there were
places on the delegation. They did this as a harmless method to give every
regional and ethnic group some kind of recognition, and to reward good friends
of the Democratic party with delegate seats. Since the votes were divided
among all the candidates on a slate, this decision cost the Johnson supporters
all but two of the delegate designations, even though their slate received over
half the votes cast.

Johnson, running on write-ins, it would have been interpreted as a stunning defeat. For McCarthy, it was a great victory.

At the White House, the assessment ran as follows: The President had not campaigned personally. McCarthy's name was on the ballot and he had campaigned exhaustively. If over 50 per cent of the voters nevertheless wrote in Johnson's name, it meant McCarthy was no threat. The real significance of the primary, the President felt, was that it would bring Robert Kennedy openly into the running.

As the extent of McCarthy's showing unfolded, Kennedy called the Wayfarer Inn in Manchester and spoke to Goodwin. "We're going to bring Johnson down," he exulted, exhausted but flushed with victory. "It looks like you made a mistake not to come in. If you had, we could have won it all."

"What should I do now?" Kennedy asked.

"Your only options are to run yourself or support McCarthy."

"What will happen if I support McCarthy?"

"He will be our next President."

Kennedy put down the phone and turned to his companion. "I think I blew it," he said wearily.

From the Bronx, he went to a restaurant in Manhattan, for a late dinner with friends. Arthur Schlesinger joined them. Schlesinger already sensed McCarthy's showing would create hostility to Kennedy's candidacy which had not been there before New Hampshire. Kennedy felt that if he were going to run he must announce quickly. Primary filing deadlines were slipping by each week. The options were thoroughly reviewed. When his dinner companions left him, they did not know what he would do. They assumed he would reflect for several days before acting.

The following afternoon, Wednesday, March 13, eighteen of Kennedy's friends and advisers convened in Steve Smith's apartment in New York City for a meeting to discuss the situation in the light of the election results.[15] The meeting had been arranged three days prior to the New Hampshire primary. Kennedy was due to arrive for dinner, and they expected to have some recommendations by that

[15] Present were Edward Kennedy, Stephen Smith, John Burns, Jack English, Jerry Bruno, Tom Johnston, John Nolan, Burke Marshall, Barrett Prettyman, Pierre Salinger, David Burke, Arthur Schlesinger, Jr., Joe Dolan, Fred Dutton, Kenneth O'Donnell, Theodore Sorensen, and the authors.

time. Edward Kennedy asked each participant whether his brother should run.

Ted Sorensen repeated arguments he had made in December: "Everyone here is agreed on one thing," he said, "we all want Robert Kennedy to be President of the United States. The only question is whether running this year will help achieve that goal." Referring to his delegate lists, he argued: "We can't count on anything significant from the South. This means that even if Robert Kennedy wins every primary he can enter, he will need to get three out of every four of the delegates from the non-primary states outside the South to win the nomination."

Sorensen's message was clear: Even Lyndon Johnson, with all his difficulties, would be able to hold on to the one in four he would need to get a majority. The majority of Convention delegates, Sorensen believed, was as elusive after New Hampshire as before.

Arthur Schlesinger spoke next. Of all those at the meeting, he had the best sense of liberal opinion, having created much of it in the past and having spoken that day to many of its other leaders. McCarthy's showing in the New Hampshire primary, he felt, had produced a fantastic current of exhilaration among liberals. McCarthy was now *the* candidate of the anti-Vietnam Democrats. If Kennedy entered the primaries against McCarthy, he would damage himself with these people and it would dramatically revive the image of the ruthless opportunist. Schlesinger felt Kennedy should announce his availability for the nomination, but say he was staying out of the primaries himself and supporting McCarthy, in an effort to change the present policies of the Administration. If the policies were changed, Johnson would be unbeatable at the convention and Kennedy could support him in good conscience. If the policies were not changed, as the year wore on, Schlesinger was convinced it would become obvious that McCarthy would not be able to come anywhere near the necessary convention majority. Recognizing this, McCarthy's delegates, if not McCarthy himself, would end up supporting Kennedy. For now, Schlesinger concluded, all efforts should go into building the strongest possible coalition of opposition against a Johnson renomination.

Sorensen and other veterans of the 1960 experience could not conceive of Kennedy getting the nomination if he did not go into the primaries. As with his brother, Kennedy's strength was with the public, not the leaders, and the primaries were the only way of forcing the leaders to respond to public demand. Nor did they share Schlesinger's belief that as the Convention approached McCarthy would put political reality ahead of his own ambition and withdraw. If Kennedy announced he was supporting McCarthy in the primaries, they felt it would divide the party as deeply as if he ran himself.

An hour into the meeting, Edward Kennedy was handed a note saying that at that moment Robert Kennedy was meeting with McCarthy in Senator Edward Kennedy's office. This was the first indication most of the men at the meeting had of what Robert Kennedy himself had been up to that day. What he had been doing made much of their discussion moot.

He had spent a sleepless night thinking through the implications of the primary results. On an early morning shuttle flight to Washington, he talked casually to passengers and friends about the New Hampshire vote. He had decided to make a strong move in the direction of running without delay. Otherwise, the buildup that was starting around McCarthy would grow to where it would become unchallengeable. If he moved now, people would resent it; but if he waited a few days, he felt they would resent it even more.

Arriving at Washington Airport, he was met by newsmen. In response to a question about the New Hampshire primary, he said that he was "reassessing" his earlier decision not to run. Arriving at the Senate he told Mankiewicz, who was unaware of the statement, that he had said something at the airport that Mankiewicz should know about to brief reporters. He wrote his letter to Tony Lewis. He then recorded an interview for the Walter Cronkite news show that night. In the interview he gave substance to his reassessment:

> I was reluctant to become involved in the struggle because I thought it might turn into a personal conflict between President Johnson and myself and that the issues I believed in so strongly and which I think are being ignored at the moment would be passed over.
>
> But I think that the New Hampshire primary, in which Senator McCarthy did such a brilliant job and those young men and women who feel so strongly about the future of the United States did so well and showed their devotion to their country and their concern about its future—this primary has demonstrated that there is a deep division within the Democratic party that has nothing to do with me.

I'm concerned also about the fact that in Secretary Rusk's testimony yesterday before the Foreign Relations Committee it was indicated quite clearly that in Vietnam we are going to continue the same policies and the same programs that we followed over the period of the last few years, which I think, can lead to catastrophic ending.

I'm concerned that the Riot Commission which was appointed by President Johnson last summer and which came in with recommendations on the subject they and I have described as most dangerous situation—the gravest crisis that has faced this country internally in over one hundred years—several weeks after their recommendations the President of the United States has not approved the report or its findings nor has there been any approval voiced by any member of the Cabinet.

I think in addition that the primary indicated Richard Nixon is going very likely to be the Republican nominee for President of the United States and it is quite clear from the statements he has made that there will be no difference in attitude in either domestic or in our foreign relations if he is President.

Asked whether he might end up supporting McCarthy, he said, "I just don't know. I want to decide that and what I will do after I have had a chance to assess it all."

The meeting with McCarthy in Edward Kennedy's office had produced nothing except a reiteration by McCarthy of what he had told Goodwin, that the Minnesota senator only wanted one term in the White House.

Watching Kennedy on the Cronkite television news, the participants at the meeting at Smith's home knew their discussions were academic. This was reaffirmed when they heard that in California that afternoon, Jesse Unruh had issued a statement saying Kennedy "has almost a duty at this point to offer himself as a candidate for the presidency." They felt Unruh would not have done this without Kennedy's approval. Robert and Ethel Kennedy arrived at the Smith's apartment in the middle of dinner and were greeted with the first cheer of the new campaign. The indecisiveness of the past six months at last was over. Kennedy was a candidate, and now, no matter what they had urged before, all of them were ready to join him for the battle.

But even as Kennedy rallied his associates for the campaign effort, an unexpected development took place that compelled another hesitation. A phone call to Sorensen at the Smith apartment from the White House said the President was actively interested in a blue-ribbon commission to review, at the highest level, the policies in Vietnam. It was the same plan Kennedy had discussed with Mayor Daley a month before.

The idea of the commission had come to the President from two independent sources. Mayor Daley had suggested it to him as well as to Kennedy. On Monday, March 11, Sorensen had been asked to meet with the President. In the course of an unexpectedly prolonged conversation they talked about changes in the policies in Vietnam. The President said he had always been open to suggestions from all sources. He had, for example, talked to Edward Kennedy on his return from Vietnam, and ordered the State Department to look carefully into the recommendations he had made on refugee problems. Sorensen suggested that an independent commission might be established to review the Vietnam commitment. As the President well knew, this was a standard device administrations used to make important changes of policy without having the action look precipitous. The phone call to Sorensen on March 11 from the White House expressed the President's interest in the commission proposal.

No matter what the President's motives in suggesting it, the proposal had to command Kennedy's earnest attention, promising as it did an honorable opportunity to bring an end to the Vietnam conflict while avoiding what otherwise was inevitable, a destructive schism in the Democratic party. If Kennedy served on it, or even supported it, he could not announce his candidacy, since de-escalation in Vietnam, with all it would make possible in meeting domestic needs, was his basic reason for running. If the policy could in fact be changed as the price of keeping him out of the race, he would have accomplished what he wanted without splitting the party. If he did not take it seriously, he could be accused of putting ambition ahead of politics.

Sorensen had left the meeting shortly after receiving the phone call to keep a speaking engagement in Rochester. A few associates to whom Kennedy mentioned the proposal that evening scorned it. Basically, they did not trust Johnson. Dutton put this and a barrage of other reasons in a hastily prepared memorandum:

> The frustrations, restiveness and sickness of this country at present are not just over the war but go much deeper. Much of the malaise

results, I believe, from the human qualities which Johnson personally projects. To interpret the New Hampshire results just in terms of the war is to miss the depth of the opposition, even revulsion, to the man . . . Even if you got concessions on the war, the foot-dragging remains on the problems of the cities, the alienation of the young and so many other basic problems with which he is unable or unwilling to cope. Not much can be done about those matters until there is fresh leadership for the country . . ."

The young people and liberal wing of the Democratic party will be aghast and embittered at you and our political processes if such a deal were made . . . At the political level, such an arrangement could strengthen McCarthy in the short run and probably permanently rupture the Democratic party. . . . Johnson is and has to remain Commander in Chief. Any concession by him could be undone six months later in another country or crisis . . . I do not believe anyone can really do business with Lyndon Johnson. What you get can be taken away as he will still be President and have all the levers . . . For you to be one member of a commission, or even chairman of it, is to use and isolate you. The President cannot and should not turn over his Presidential responsibilities of decision and action to a commission. Equally important, such a commission would merely complicate and compete with the Foreign Relations Committee and other congressional groups . . . At a psychological level, is the Clifford offer really just an escape hatch to avoid your having to choose between running and not running—or find a safe haven for awhile? The commission would be a disservice, I believe, to all those who feel the nation is headed in the wrong direction and has the wrong leadership. It would be better just to decide not to run and let those deeper impulses find their level through the political processes now started.

The meeting at Smith's became a campaign planning session. In the dining room, Edward Kennedy reviewed the list of non-primary states, discussing which party leaders could be persuaded to lead the Kennedy campaign. In the living room, O'Donnell, Dolan, and Smith drew up preliminary plans for the primaries themselves. Burke Marshall drew up a list of high government officials of the Kennedy and Johnson administrations who might be asked to endorse Kennedy when he announced. Another group talked about organizational problems in California, which clearly appeared to be the crucial primary contest.

Kennedy wandered from group to group, listening, offering suggestions, taking time to telephone. He tried unsuccessfully to reach Mayor Daley on the telephone. He talked with Walter Reuther. A staffer called from Washington, brimming with excitement about people who had offered their support. Kennedy cautioned him to stay loose.

The next morning, the action shifted to Smith's office at 200 Park Avenue, home of the business enterprises of Joseph P. Kennedy. Once again, the family's financial staff had to broker their real estate, analyze the market and do their accounting amid a frenzy of political activity. Joe Dolan, seeking support and advice from politicians in the primary states, found himself seated at a desk next to a lady who was making reservations for the Smiths to fly to France for a skiing holiday.

"She and I are working at cross purposes," he complained to Smith.

"Both of you keep going," Smith replied.

Smith was also phoning state politicians. Kennedy had asked him to find out what certain leaders thought and would do, now that his candidacy seemed imminent. Indications of support from Iowa, Washington, Utah, Rhode Island, and Maryland were generally encouraging. In Ohio, Howard Metzenbaum, a prominent Cleveland lawyer who had been campaign manager for Senator Stephen Young, expressed confidence to Smith that half the delegation (which had already been selected) could be won over to Kennedy.

The most disconcerting news came from Kennedy's supporters in the New York reform movement. They believed an announcement at that point would be a disaster. The New Hampshire results had placed their reform followers firmly in the McCarthy camp. Some feared their own leadership would be challenged if they stayed with Kennedy. "See these calls," said Allard Lowenstein, holding a five-inch sheaf of telephone slips. "All of them say please tell Bobby not to do it—and there are fifty more back in the office—all since this morning. He can't do it—he can't." Leaders of the Committee for a Democratic Alternative, meeting with Smith, did not welcome the idea of formulating joint Kennedy-McCarthy slates in choosing New York delegates.

That afternoon, the lead editorial in the New York *Post,* until that time Kennedy's strongest newspaper supporter in the state, made it clear it would not be with him. "In both New Hampshire and Minnesota (the editorial said), McCarthy has confounded the defeatists and cynics. Whether Senator Kennedy would have done better had he chosen to lead is academic. Kennedy should urge his supporters to rally wholeheartedly behind McCarthy's drive. The man from Minnesota has plainly earned the right to carry the banner for concerned, progressive Americans."

Murray Kempton, who had expressed disappointment at the January 31 statement, showed utter disgust now that Kennedy seemed to have changed his mind. Declining an invitation to a cocktail party given that night by the publishers of Senator Edward Kennedy's new book, he said, in a telegram, "Sorry I can't join you. Your brother's announcement makes clear that St. Patrick did not drive all the snakes from Ireland."

In Washington, Kennedy explored the commission proposal. The President wanted Kennedy as a member and also wanted him to suggest a chairman for the group. On Thursday afternoon, he and Sorensen went to the Pentagon to meet with Clark Clifford. Kennedy suggested a list of names whom the President might consider for commission membership.

At the end of the day, Smith called Kennedy to summarize the political information he had collected. He reported that his sources in Wisconsin believed McCarthy would get a minimum of 50 per cent of the vote in the April 2 primary. Kennedy was surprised. Just weeks before, these same sources had told Smith that Johnson was a sure winner in Wisconsin. But the dikes against the Johnson opposition had been broken in New Hampshire, and the President was caught in an outpouring of discontent which none of the forces at his command could control. Kennedy asked Smith's opinion about his running. Smith answered: "If you believe that you have to do it, in terms of that little fellow inside of you, I think we can put something together. I can't say if you do it you'll win. The decision has to be in your gut."

Thursday night, March 14, Kennedy was at home entertaining a group of editors of weekly newspapers from upstate New York. Most of the talk was about his own prospects, but the editors were also interested in the speculation on who would be the Democratic candidate for Senate in New York. Jack Newfield, a writer for *The Village Voice*, said the strongest possibility at that point was Percy Sutton, an eminent Negro leader who was serving as Borough President of Manhattan. The editors did not know him. Newfield spelled out his credentials. Can he beat Javits, they asked? "Yes," said Newfield, "if the Jews riot all summer."

As he walked among his guests, Kennedy encountered Holly Mankiewicz, his press secretary's wife, who encouraged him by dismissing the wrath of the McCarthy supporters. "It's not like you're running for president of your junior class," said Mrs. Mankiewicz. "This is not a popularity contest. If you are the person who can best make the fight, it doesn't matter that the other person is a good guy." Then she pleaded, "But whatever you do, decide soon. All this uncertainty is hurting my stomach."

"I think your stomach will feel better tomorrow," Kennedy said.

Later that night, he received word through Clark Clifford that President Johnson had rejected the idea of a Vietnam Commission. The last barrier was gone. At 6 A.M. on Friday, March 15, he called Goodwin at the Mayflower Hotel and told him that he would announce at a press conference on Monday. Goodwin suggested that with things the way they were, the longer he waited, the stronger the pressure would be from both liberals and organization Democrats not to run. "If you are going to announce, don't delay," Goodwin cautioned, and Kennedy agreed. He told Mankiewicz to arrange a press conference in the Senate Caucus Room for Saturday morning at 10 A.M.

On Friday, Edward Kennedy was still saying that his brother had "grave doubts" about running. Robert Kennedy himself was on Long Island, keeping a schedule of appearances, including a coffee hour with Nassau County Democratic women. He left no doubt, in his off the record comments to them, that he would be a candidate within twenty-four hours. The afternoon Washington *Star* bannered front page headlines confirming his intention to run, based on remarks overheard by reporters. When Kennedy saw the newspaper, he laughed and said he was probably the first person who had announced his candidacy for President of the United States at a coffee klatch in the living room of Mrs. Anita Richmond of Kings Point, Nassau County, New York.[16]

---

[16] As Kennedy toured suburban New York, with only a few hours separating him from the press conference where he would announce his candidacy, there were those who reviewed his options and refused to believe he would do it. In the new CBS building on East Fifty-second Street in New York, top newsmen dined with the chief executive of the network. An informal poll revealed that not one of them believed Kennedy would accept what they considered the insuperable, almost reckless odds of becoming a candidate.

He returned to Hickory Hill early Friday evening. A dinner party for old friends had been arranged weeks before. In the midst of it, Sorensen called from the Senate office where he was working on a draft of the announcement. The statement pledged a coalition effort with Senator McCarthy. This was clearly dependent on McCarthy accepting the offer of cooperation which Edward Kennedy was, at that very hour, flying to communicate to him in Green Bay, Wisconsin. A variation of the statement could serve the occasion if McCarthy rejected the joint effort.

The dinner party and the preparations for the press conference fused. The room was filled with the counterpoint of earnest political discussion, the laughter of friends and family, and the familiar ritual of children saying good night and preparing for sleep. Mrs. Kennedy quieted the group at one point to listen to Jim Whittaker's impromptu suggestions for the statement. The first American to climb Mount Everest, Whittaker spoke in the vernacular of his profession and talked of Kennedy "taking America to the peak where the vista of a world of peace and plenty would be unfolded." The one concession to the political turbulence of the evening was an early end to the dinner party. The senator settled down to two hours of final discussion with his staff and political associates, concentrating on the questions that might be asked him at the morning conference. The expected telephone message had not yet come from his brother, so the final text of his statement would have to wait until morning. As he went to his bedroom at 2 A.M., he asked a friend to wait up for the phone call from Green Bay.

15

THE LAST CAMPAIGN

Robert Kennedy began his campaign for the presidency at least fifteen months behind the standard timetable.[1] The time and effort a candidate normally puts into organizing a campaign was used up deciding whether to run. By waiting until the middle of March, he had only twelve weeks to organize six primaries, four of them major contests. He would have to spread himself and his campaign staff over several states simultaneously. Beyond the New York contest on June 18 stretched a more placid period of ten weeks until the National Convention in Chicago.

At the time of his announcement, Kennedy had conceived his strategy only in its broadest outlines. Victory depended on his winning the primaries, and then using their mandate to convince the other delegates that he was the only candidate who could keep the Democratic party in control of the White House.[2] He would have to defeat

[1] For most candidates, the first stirrings of activity take place after the preceding mid-term Congressional election, by which time the shape of the competition can be discerned. The following twelve months are spent in subdued traveling and discreet probes for support in the various states, with the official announcement coming in the December or January preceding the election.

[2] In this sense, his prospects resembled those of his brother in 1960. John Kennedy also could not have won the support of the large states had he not won the primaries. He had proven his appeal to the voters by the end of the West Virginia primary in May, and the rest of the support he needed came in shortly after.

President Johnson's proxy in California, and the President himself in Oregon, South Dakota, and Nebraska where state laws required him to be on the ballot. New York was crucial. He had to make a very strong showing in his home state to make his battle convincing. These victories would give him a base of over 400 delegates from which to seek the additional 900 plus he needed.

In the non-primary states, citizens organizations would be formed, but only as a show of strength to the political leaders and a nucleus for a campaign organization if he won the nomination. During the primaries, he would stay in close touch with the organization leaders. They knew from past experience that he could deal with them. He would then ask their support not only because he could win, but because they knew he could rebuild the party after years of neglect. It was not a revolutionary strategy. In an early memo, Dutton advised him to "establish at the outset that you are addressing yourself to the middle-class and middle-aged voter at least as much as to young people and concerned Democrats."

A nationwide political apparatus had to be created overnight. One by one, Kennedy's friends made peace with their employers and came to work. A *Life* magazine memorandum said of Don Wilson, who would work on television and radio advertising: "Don Wilson has asked for a leave of absence for the next several months to work on the Robert Kennedy campaign and it has been granted. Politics in 1968 being what it is, Mr. Wilson has already left."

The late entry also intensified the usual chaotic frenzy of the opening of a political campaign. Headquarters space was rented at the Dodge Hotel near Capitol Hill and a long lease signed, but it quickly proved too small. For several days, the campaign stumbled as its workers tried to find one another. Important staffers received assignments in the midst of a collection of the curious and oddballs, drawn by the publicity. Important bits of political intelligence floated in the air with no one to correlate them. Arthur Schlesinger, Jr., tried vainly to operate in this atmosphere for a day, then fired off a memo to everyone he thought might have some authority. It read:

HELP! HELP! HELP!
AM I SUPPOSED TO GO TO CALIFORNIA THIS WEEK? I told Unruh, Dutton, Salinger, and RFK that I could go out on Tuesday

night, returning Thursday night. I have heard nothing from anybody since. If I am to go, someone should be getting reservations. (I do not want to stand all the way to California) . . .

Professor Lawrence Fuchs of Brandeis, former head of the Peace Corps in the Philippines and author of an excellent book on JFK and Catholicism, has been the most active figure in the McCarthy movement in Massachusetts. He is for RFK and hopes to bring along a good part of the McCarthy people in due course. HE WANTS SOMEONE TO TALK TO HIM. His phone numbers are 889-4998 (home); TW 4-6000 (Tues-Thurs); 868-5800 (MWF) . . .

Dick Wade[3] tells me that there is considerable movement among younger Democrats in Louisville, including a fellow named Grafton, son of Wilson Wyatt's law partner, who thinks we stand a chance of getting 20 out of 44 Kentucky delegates. Dick says that SOMEONE SHOULD TALK TO WYATT.

What do I do about letters from friends in Westchester County, in Pennsylvania, in Connecticut who want to go to work for RFK? IS ANYONE IN CHARGE OF ANYTHING, ANYWHERE?

The first tentative answers were given at an organizing meeting held in Edward Kennedy's office the afternoon of March 16. Dolan would handle where the candidate would go hour by hour. Advance arrangements for the trips were to be run by Jerry Bruno and Kennedy's cousin Joseph Gargan, both of whom had done this for the President. Servicing the candidate and the campaign organization with research material fell to his legislative assistant, Peter Edelman, who knew Kennedy's stand on every issue. Until Goodwin felt he could join up, Kennedy's speeches would be written by Walinsky, assisted by Jeff Greenfield, the best of the law school interns who had worked in the Kennedy office. Greenfield was a merry young man with a sparkling mind, a thoroughly capable speech writer at the age of twenty-four.

John Nolan, Kennedy's former Executive Assistant at the Justice Department, would go to California, establish contact with Unruh, and look out for Kennedy's interests as that primary was being organized. Barrett Prettyman, another Washington attorney, would do the same in Oregon. Salinger and Mankiewicz would divide the press relations between them. A national headquarters would be established in Washington under the supervision of Helen Keyes, a former school-

---

[3] Professor of History at the University of Chicago, who ran Kennedy's campaign in Monroe County, New York in 1964.

teacher, who had worked in every Kennedy campaign since 1946; Dun Gifford, Edward Kennedy's legislative assistant, and Carmine Bellino, Kennedy's personal accountant, would control the spending of the money.

Robert Troutman of Atlanta would begin to work on arrangements for the Convention, and also advise on strategy for the southern states. His advice that afternoon was to stay out of those states and let events take their course. "Bobby is not liked in the South," he said. "In fact there's only one politician the South likes less—and that is Lyndon Johnson. Since he's the man we're running against, let's just take it easy for a while." David Hackett would establish a political intelligence operation, staying in contact with friends and delegates in each state. Kenneth O'Donnell would maintain ties with the large-state leaders, urging them to withhold commitments while the primary contests were underway. Edward Kennedy would be the prime contact with political leaders and interest groups, supervising activities in the non-primary states, and substituting for his brother at important occasions he could not attend. With practically everyone on the campaign trail, Sorensen would be the headquarters anchor man, concerned with both delegates and substantive problems. Smith would trouble-shoot the primary states and raise the funds.

It was understood that all the assignments were fluid. No formal structure was possible in the opening chaos. Hopefully, others, like Larry O'Brien, could be recruited, and the preliminary organization charts left plenty of room for their experience. At dinner that night at Hickory Hill, Kennedy, who had been marching in the St. Patrick's Day Parade in New York, agreed to these assignments and added one more: Fred Dutton was to travel with him, performing the same role O'Donnell had played for John Kennedy in 1960, acting as his buffer, agent, and the funnel for communications between himself and others.

Faced with the need for an "instant" national campaign, Kennedy understandably looked to men with whom he had worked at that level of politics. For the most part, they had been associated with President Kennedy. There was a sense that he sought their association partly for his own emotional security, that he was reaching out for the presence of his brother.

These men, anonymous in 1960, had since gained a measure of fame. Their presence was bound to strengthen the charge that Kennedy was once again running on his brother's name. The problems this created were stated by Arthur Schlesinger in a memorandum to his former White House colleagues:

"There is tremendous nostalgia for John F. Kennedy. There is also great potential resentment against anything which might appear an exploitation or manipulation of that nostalgia for political purposes. Obviously putting a campaign together from scratch in a short time requires people with previous experience, and I think everyone from the past should make every contribution that he can. But all of us—Schlesinger, Sorensen, Salinger, O'Brien, O'Donnell—should stay in the background and work behind the scenes (except in specific contexts where any of us may retain a particular connection or appeal). RFK must run on his own record and character. He must run as a contemporary figure. He must not appear to be surrounded by figures from the past, even from the comparatively recent past . . ."

The Kennedy White House staff inevitably had developed personal strains and animosities, which their public responsibilities and their intense loyalty to President Kennedy had concealed. There they worked as independent spokes out of one hub. Now there was no hub. The only man to whom they would all subordinate themselves was Robert Kennedy, and he just could not take enough time from campaigning to mediate their differences of personality or advice.

The arrival of John Kennedy's men also caused conflict with a few key members of Kennedy's Senate staff. "The worst problem I am going to have," Kennedy predicted, "is putting together the men who were with my brother with the men who have been with me." The latter did not appreciate being relegated to seemingly subordinate roles, especially since they felt that the ultimate decision to run had indicated the superiority of their political judgment over those who had initially argued against it. The Senate staff had worked closely with Kennedy on a day-to-day basis. It had made the most significant contribution to the changes in his thinking and his image since 1964. Interpreting McCarthy's success, the more radical of them felt the nomination could only be won "on the streets," through stirring up the public discontent. They feared that the "John Kennedy men," who belonged, they believed, to an outworn day in politics, would steer their candidate toward a more traditional posture. Yet only one of Kennedy's staff had had experience in a presidential campaign, and the senator was not prepared to follow their advice now, any more than in January.

Despite all these difficulties—of strategy, lack of time, personal feuding and organization—the first days of Kennedy's campaign were a time of optimism. It was obvious that his vast personal following had survived the unprecedented nature of his challenge and the awkward manner of his announcement. His first tour, though scheduled hastily, was a triumph.[4] At Kansas State University, 200 miles from the nearest big city, a lecture in honor of former Governor Alfred Landon drew 15,000 people.[5] In California local reporters considered the crowds there the most frenzied in the history of that frenzied state.

There was an important difference in the crowd reactions, as compared to the 1964 New York campaign, when large masses of people cheered Kennedy as a gesture of feeling toward the dead President. The crowds of 1968 roared their welcome as if trying, through his presence, to vent their rage at what had been going on in the country. Their frenzy was an awesome experience. One man at his side had been enough to help Kennedy keep his balance as he stood atop his car in 1964. Now he needed two, often three. One of them, Dutton, had all his suits ripped after one week in California.

Kennedy reached for themes, testing for reactions. The greatest response came when he spoke on the futility of the war and its effects at home:

> But I am concerned [he said in Kansas] that the course we are following at the present time is deeply wrong . . . I am concerned that at the end of it all, there will only be more Americans killed, more of our treasure spilled out, and more bitterness and hatred on

[4] Kennedy called Siegenthaler in Nashville. "I'd like you to get a few of your friends together for me."
"How many?"
"About six thousand."
"When?"
"Tomorrow night."

[5] The lecture had been scheduled long before Kennedy's announcement. Although on the surface, no two men seemed farther apart than Kennedy and the man who, as the Republican nominee in 1936, campaigned against Social Security and the New Deal, they were friendly. In recent years, Landon had been a Republican voice against the war in Vietnam and in favor of recognizing Communist China.

every side of this war . . . Our country is in danger; not just from foreign enemies; but above all, from our own misguided policies . . . I ask you, as tens of thousands of young men and women are doing all over this land, to organize yourselves and then go forth and work for new politics."

Looking up and around the huge field-house, Kennedy reached out with upturned hand and drove the message home: ". . . not just in Southeast Asia, but here at home as well, so that we have a new birth for this country; a new light to guide us."

The first days of the campaign released Kennedy's emotion, as well as the crowds'. He was happy to be on the road. It was a welcome change from the tension and indecision of the weeks before. "I'm sleeping well for the first time in months," he told Pierre Salinger's wife, Nicole. "I don't know what is going to happen but at least I'm at peace with myself."

Kennedy spent himself completely in this first tour. The fatigue, the speaking, the tension, and the changes in climate made him hoarse. By the time he reached Denver, Dr. Gould had to fly out to treat him. He told Kennedy that if he did not let up he would lose his voice permanently, and he put him on another regimen of vitamins and antibiotics.

Once the initial frenzy ended, Kennedy settled down for two months of intensive campaigning. His speaking style, which had been improving each year, was far more assured than when he ran for the Senate. His voice had better resonance, and he conveyed a greater sense of urgency in his message. Making eight or ten speeches a day, mostly off the cuff, he fell back on the things he had already said about Vietnam, race and the needs of the nation. Walinsky and Greenfield worked hard to give him fresh material, but after several weeks, the strain caught up with them. Some new programs were presented: welfare reform, a farm program, and the general outlines of a foreign policy whose goal was "no more Vietnams." But Kennedy felt more knowledgeable and comfortable with the programs he had worked on in the Senate.

Each speech, even the short stops, received all his energy. He was carried away delivering his message, and when he finished he was drained. Other candidates that year made their impact through news conferences or friendly audiences bused into auditoriums. The hard, grueling way was the only way he knew.

His hands were scarred and bleeding from the pull of the crowds. His face was burnt from exposure, his eyes were hollow with fatigue. He tried to rest. Except in the last weeks in the West, Sundays were almost always reserved for Hickory Hill. But relaxation became conferences and phone calls. Invariably, he seemed more tired after a day of rest because the fatigue had had a chance to catch up with him. He kept going through nervous energy and fierce determination.

The strain did not blunt his sense of humor. He enjoyed the banter with the crowds, especially the young people who pushed up front.

"Are you going to help me?" he would ask.

"Yes," they shouted.

"Are you going to vote for me?"

"Yes," again.

"Have you read my book?"

"Yes."

"You lie."

Missing his family and wanting a part of Hickory Hill with him, Kennedy made Freckles, a black and white springer spaniel with wise eyes and serene disposition, the companion of his campaign. Freckles was accustomed to political life. Two years before, Kennedy noted the late Senator Harry Byrd bringing his cocker spaniel to the office, so Kennedy brought Freckles to work with him. He would walk with Freckles to the entrance to the Senate floor, then hand his leash to whatever staff member happened to be with him. The Senate Chamber was the only place Freckles had not been allowed.

The large press and television contingent following him filled most of the jet he had chartered. The Kennedy plane on tour was a happy place. As soon as it took off, everyone was in the aisles chatting. The television camera crews, who hung from the lead car to film the motorcades, were especially gregarious. They stole a key from every hotel they stayed at and displayed them on the plane to mark the progress of the tour. In 1964, Kennedy had kept his distance from reporters. When one correspondent had asked him questions he considered an infringement on his privacy, he balked, and ordered a second plane, so he would not have to travel with the press. Now he was almost always accessible and frank with them. Together, day after day, the reporters developed a camaraderie with each other and an almost protective feeling toward him. Reporters who went out on the assignment cynical toward him came back devoted friends.

The euphoria of the initial tour hid the many difficulties building up for his candidacy. Kennedy's announcement had produced no rush of support beyond the expected centers of strength in New England and California. There were stirrings in places like Iowa and Washington, but southern leaders showed no enthusiasm and, more important, the power brokers in the big industrial states, where John Kennedy had been so strong, offered no significant commitments. In Ohio, Metzenbaum's optimism about winning a clear majority of the delegates seemed justified if he did well in the primaries in the other states. The important leaders in Pennsylvania seemed much cooler, and in Maryland, they told his agents that commitments had already been made to the President.

The most difficult and persistent problem was the candidacy of Senator McCarthy. At every stage of his campaign, Kennedy was to underestimate McCarthy's strength. Kennedy saw the McCarthy effort as something that would never be a serious threat to Johnson, but in itself, could forestall the serious challenge he could mount. Although a coalition of the Kennedy and McCarthy forces would be necessary to deny Johnson renomination, only one man could emerge at the Convention. With his broader and deeper sources of political strength, Kennedy felt he was the logical one for this role. He believed that by the time the campaign reached the California primary, his earlier victories would have made this clear, and leave him as the only challenger to Johnson.

Kennedy interpreted the New Hampshire vote not as an endorsement of McCarthy but a repudiation of Johnson. But he did not immediately perceive, as Goodwin had, how the mystique of the New Hampshire triumph had transformed McCarthy from the political gadfly of January to a fresh, attractive figure with a powerful hold on the imagination of the electorate. To his Senate colleagues, McCarthy was an aloof, laconic figure. If those who worked with him on the Hill were asked to describe McCarthy, almost invariably one of the adjectives used would be "lazy." But politics is replete with sudden transformations of image, and now McCarthy had become

Don Quixote, dreaming the impossible dream, fighting courageously and alone.

McCarthy's rejection of Edward Kennedy's proposal in Green Bay had made it impossible for Robert Kennedy to announce a coalition effort in the Senate Caucus Room. Nevertheless, in his statement Kennedy urged his supporters in Wisconsin, Massachusetts, and New Hampshire to support McCarthy with their "help and their vote," and he expressed the hope that he and McCarthy would be "able to work together in one form or another." This was not intended as a snare. McCarthy had said many times that he wanted support from his Senate colleagues. Interviewed on television immediately after Kennedy's announcement, he said he would welcome Kennedy's campaigning for him in the upcoming primary in Wisconsin. Hearing this, Kennedy asked Dolan to check if any invitations had been received from Wisconsin that could be used as the keystone of a campaign tour. There were a few, but over the next three days McCarthy changed his mind. The new polls from Wisconsin showed him with a substantial lead over Johnson. He decided to campaign alone so that he would not have to share the victory. Kennedy considered going to Madison and campaigning door-to-door in a university dormitory, but he was persuaded that such a move, after McCarthy had pointedly requested him to stay away, could only add to their conflict.

McCarthy's supporters contended it was Kennedy who was splitting the anti-Johnson vote. If only one man could make the challenge, they said, it should be McCarthy because he had shown the courage to start first. The Reverend Richard J. Neuhaus, co-founder of Clergy and Laymen Concerned about Vietnam, repudiated this view in a letter to the New York *Times* on March 19:

> Far from being a latecomer to the peace effort, Senator Kennedy's incisive criticism of Administration policy dates from at least as far back as does Senator McCarthy's . . . Courage is intimately related to risk, and there can be little doubt but that Senator Kennedy has a great deal more to risk politically than does Senator McCarthy.
>
> Senator McCarthy is a potential Presidential candidate by virtue of his challenge to Mr. Johnson at this time. Senator Kennedy had been a potential Presidential candidate for several years. This distinction seems to be lost on some who speak lightly of courage.

At first Kennedy likened the hostility exploding around him to the anger he had to face in New York in 1964 when he announced for the Senate. He expected the opposition would subside as it had then. He began to realize the depth of the commitments involved when he saw how difficult it was to persuade Goodwin, one of his most intimate advisers, to leave McCarthy's campaign. Goodwin had been a key architect in the New Hampshire victory. Kennedy credited 10 per cent of McCarthy's vote to the publicity and strategy Goodwin had developed. He had become a hero to the students in the McCarthy campaign, a struggle which had created a special bond between all its participants. Although he had no doubt about supporting Kennedy, Goodwin wanted to postpone his departure until he could train people within McCarthy's organization to take over his work. Kennedy was annoyed at the hesitation. Had it been anyone but Goodwin, with his awesome gifts as a publicist and political analyst, Kennedy would have written him off. But he had to wait while "His Nibs," as Kennedy called him during this period, followed his own timetable.

The alienation of McCarthy supporters created a serious problem for Kennedy's organization. With most of the regular party leaders holding firm for Johnson, and the most active insurgents committed to McCarthy, he had to rely on second-level Democrats in many states to support his campaign. Even more difficult was the absence of personal friends, like the poet, Robert Lowell, and the novelist, William Styron, who typified those who had urged Kennedy to run, felt so strongly about Vietnam that they supported McCarthy in New Hampshire, and who now felt committed to continue that support until McCarthy released them.[6]

Like the Stevenson effort in 1952, the McCarthy movement brought forward thousands of independent Democrats who enjoyed political work and had signed on when McCarthy seemed a lost cause. Suddenly, after New Hampshire, they were part of a significant movement, and they were not about to relinquish their new power and prestige. In New York, unknown reformers who had linked themselves to the McCarthy candidacy balked at Kennedy efforts to work out joint

[6] But William Manchester, whose respect for Kennedy had survived their epic battle, was happy to become chairman of Citizens for Kennedy in Connecticut.

delegate slates for the June primary. Stephen Smith found himself negotiating with a new breed of political leader to whom the old relationships did not apply. The Kennedy forces found themselves at odds with recent allies. Reform leaders who wanted to support Kennedy found themselves facing constituencies that were passionately involved in the McCarthy drive. On the other hand, reform leaders like John Shea, Russell Hemenway, and Sara Kovner, who had opposed him for the Senate nomination, found new outlets for old antagonisms.

In the letters columns of liberal magazines and newspapers, Kennedy supporters were hard pressed by onslaughts from academic leaders and Pulitzer Prize winners supporting McCarthy. In a particularly bitter column entitled "Robert Kennedy, Farewell," Murray Kempton wrote: "He has, in the naked display of his rage at Eugene McCarthy for having survived on the lonely road he dared not walk himself, done with a single great gesture something very few public men have ever been able to do: In one day, he managed to confirm the worst things his enemies have ever said about him . . . I blame myself, not him, for all the years he fooled me."[7] In general reply to these critics, Arthur Schlesinger wrote an article for the *New Republic* which began: "I must confess a certain sense of *déjà vu* in sitting down to do this piece. Eight years ago this month, many Americans were persuaded that John F. Kennedy was a ruthless political opportunist, shouldering aside more deserving and principled men in his driving ambition for the Presidency."

The McCarthy movement also made it much more difficult for Kennedy to get volunteer help for his campaign. In New Hampshire and Wisconsin, young people gave new life to political canvassing, a technique supposed to be outmoded in the age of media politics. Clean-cut, sincere, and intelligent, these students refined the technique of "issue canvassing," drawing voters into relevant conversations on their doorsteps, and giving them a personalized reason to support their candidate.

Kennedy thought he saw, in the thousands of students who turned out to cheer him, a vast untapped resource for his campaign. He

[7] In an article in the *Saturday Evening Post* in December 1968, Kempton was to look back and say his judgments about Kennedy during this period were "correct but not right—and there is a profound difference."

drove his associates to "get the student thing going." The plan that developed was to solicit names at the rallies and follow up with organization meetings to get the students working. But the enthusiastic crowds at the universities were deceiving. They were spectators; most of them also gave warm receptions to McCarthy and even Rockefeller. It takes a highly motivated student to like the hard work of politics, and most of these were for McCarthy. Kennedy was distressed at the sight of the young people he admired most working so hard to defeat him. But he hoped it would work out in time.

After March 16, McCarthy stepped up his attacks on Kennedy, but Kennedy did not reply in kind. He told his speech writers that the most effective contrast he could make with McCarthy was in the quality of the proposals he would advocate. Kennedy understood that ultimately, among liberal voters in the primary states, the question would come down to why vote for Kennedy instead of McCarthy. These voters did not look at things the way delegates do. The fact that Kennedy could win and McCarthy could not was relatively unimportant. They wanted substantive reasons to support their decisions. There were excellent arguments available if the voters wanted them: Kennedy's experience in the Executive Branch made him better prepared for the presidency. His acknowledged role in the Cuban missile crisis proved him capable of the patience, endurance and flexibility that would be needed to end the war in Vietnam. Unlike McCarthy, he believed in a strong presidency which committed the force and power of that office to the struggle for social justice, as Franklin Roosevelt had done in his New Deal. And alone of the candidates available to the Democratic party, he both understood the social forces threatening the stability of the nation and had rapport with them. When he reflected on the positions he had taken in his Senate years, frequently alone and often at real political cost, he would say: "If this campaign is going to be fought on the basis of what happened in New Hampshire, I can't win. But if it is fought on who did what for the two years before New Hampshire, I think I have a chance."

The comparative voting records of the candidates was not an important factor to these Democrats, certainly not a decisive one. Schlesinger's *New Republic* article, the best statement of why Kennedy should be preferred, hardly criticized McCarthy's record except to say he had little rapport with the poor. Congressional voting records are slippery things. It is difficult enough to find one's way through the maze of votes and motions which often allow a member of Congress to appear as a supporter of a program while actually working to defeat it. It is especially hard when two men like McCarthy and Kennedy have taken essentially the same voting positions, at least on the most significant issues. McCarthy's record was not like Senator Keating's, where hidden but significant votes showed basic opposition to important liberal programs. McCarthy's questionable votes went to issues of good government and ethics rather than political philosophy.

Nevertheless, to satisfy those circles where absolute fidelity to the liberal line is insisted upon and where voting records are a standard campaign tool, Kennedy field workers, fighting a difficult battle anyway, badgered national headquarters for material on McCarthy's record. Meetings of Manhattan reform clubs were being held at that moment for the purposes of endorsement. In the absence of documentation from the campaign headquarters, some of the clubs were compiling material on their own, some of it inaccurate. Finally, the Washington research staff compiled a list of a dozen votes on which the two men had differed[8] and showed them to Kennedy. He was surprised at many of them, and thought they showed an important difference in attitudes on crucial issues, at least for a small segment of sophisticated voters who understood their significance. The material was made available to Kennedy workers in the various states.

The selectivity of the voting record study angered McCarthy's advocates and deeply offended him personally. His supporters refused to consider the selected votes as relevant. It was as if McCarthy had been born again in New Hampshire, free of previous faults or political history. When the old Citizens for Kennedy group of Dr. Shepard circulated, entirely on its own, a hastily compiled and inaccurate version of McCarthy's voting record, it was widely, although

[8] The roll calls on which McCarthy cast negative votes included such issues as abolition of the poll tax in state and federal elections (1965); removal of limitations on length of coverage and deductible amount for recipients of Medicare (1965); minimum wage of $1.60 for farm workers by 1971 (1967); eighteen-year-old vote for the District of Columbia, (1961); national standards for deferment in administration of the draft law to replace the discretion of local draft boards (1967); public disclosure of finances and sources of income by members of Congress (1967); draft deferments for Peace Corps and VISTA volunteers (1967); limitation on foreign aid to Latin American countries that spend a disproportionately large share of their budget on defense instead of social programs (1966); and reduction of the 27½ per cent depletion allowance for oil companies (1964).

erroneously, ascribed to the Kennedy organization. This helped undermine the entire issue of the comparable voting records, and in the
end, the effort could only be described as an embarrassment for the
Kennedy campaign.

Another problem flowed from the intensity of the public response.
The large crowds were an important part of Kennedy's strategy. They
evidenced support for the man and his cause and could show the
leaders of non-primary states that he could pull votes. They provided
a vivid contrast with Johnson, who had been forced to seal himself
off from the people. But the reaction of the crowds was so emotional
and so physical that it had other consequences. In the minds of the
millions who followed Kennedy only on television, the crowds *became*
the campaign, as they had in 1964. But what had happened each
summer since 1964 in the cities of America, and what was to happen
after the death of Martin Luther King, changed the nature of the
impact of the crowd scenes. The daily picture of Kennedy being
mobbed and mauled, with police clearing the way and fending off
admirers, looked dangerously like the urban and student riots which
had caused so much public fear. The emphasis on crowds made it
impossible to draw attention to the substantive superiority of Kennedy's
programs. Brilliant speeches were buried beneath the details of Kennedy
losing his shoes to fans. Ironically, Kennedy's crowds emphasized the
appeal of McCarthy—that he was an underdog, walking alone, stressing
coolness and reason amidst the disorder of the times. The very size
and frenzy of the crowds threatened to be self-defeating, not only in
the place where Kennedy was campaigning, but in the primary election
states, where telecasts of the tumultuous scenes were being shown
every day.

His advisers pleaded with him and his advance men to limit the
crowds. "You have made your point about nomination and razzle-
dazzle," observed Schlesinger. "Now I think it is time to slow down."
But Kennedy believed that the excitement stirred by his presence was
necessary to bring out the important vote in those areas. Perhaps
more basic were his need for the crowds and what they represented to
him. Bone-weary with fatigue, depressed at the opposition building
against him, he experienced days when the chemistry of the crowd
was the only thing which carried him through the exhausting schedule.

The crowds made him believe that what he was fighting for was worthwhile. This was especially true in the black neighborhoods, where his presence meant so much.

Realizing the problem, Dutton, who had taken on over-all responsibility for the schedule, tried to balance the crowd scenes with a major news event or a unique appearance that lent itself to television coverage—in Indiana, for example, a trip down the Lincoln trail; in California a boat tour of San Francisco Bay to dramatize conservation. He hoped in this way to steer the coverage away from the frenzy without isolating Kennedy from the large numbers of people who wanted to see him. The effort failed. The crowds intruded on the news events. The advance men, encouraged by Kennedy himself, measured their success by the size of the crowds he drew. To the television public, Kennedy's campaign continued to look like a mobile riot.

As March drew to a close, the liabilities of the campaign were clear, difficult, and surmountable. Whatever his opponents might say, there was a basic political reality that none could honestly deny. Only Robert Kennedy had a chance to stop the renomination of Lyndon Johnson; and since most of the rebellion in the country was aimed at Johnson and the policies he symbolized, the opposition forces would have to coalesce around Kennedy if they really wanted to achieve their objective. At this point in time and logic, the White House announced that the President would make an important speech to the nation.

The speech would presumably deal with Vietnam. The Joint Chiefs of Staff had requested another 207,000 troops, while the civilian officials of the Department of Defense had recommended the bombing of the North be curtailed in another attempt to begin negotiations. On March 30, 1968, the day before the scheduled speech, Kennedy had learned the President would probably announce cessation of the bombing north of the 20th Parallel, which runs close to the North Vietnamese city of Vinh. Believing such an initiative would have an important effect on the campaign, he scheduled a press conference at the Overseas Press Club in New York City for the morning after the President's speech, Monday, April 1. Meanwhile, researchers were digging out examples of previous conciliatory statements by Johnson which were followed by more acts of escalation. They were also instructed to research the occasions on which President Johnson said a cutback in the bombing, without an agreement on infiltration, would be an unacceptable risk.

Kennedy, en route to New York from Oklahoma by plane, did not see the telecast of the President's speech. On his arrival at the airport, he was told that Johnson had not only stopped the bombing of North Vietnam and offered to begin negotiations. He had also taken himself out of consideration for renomination.

President Johnson may claim, in his history of the period, that his mind had been made up well in advance and that hints had been carefully dropped along the way—to McNamara in the summer of 1967; to General Westmoreland on his trip to the United States in December of that year; to his son-in-law, Pat Nugent, who passed them on to business associates, including political friends of Kennedy. McNamara, in his long discussions with Kennedy during the first weeks in March 1968, used the possibility of Johnson's withdrawal to oppose Kennedy's announcing for the presidency, arguing that Johnson could not be defeated, but that he was going to retire, and when he did retire, Kennedy could enter the race without being accused of splitting the party. The argument was not new to Kennedy's staff, but in anticipating it, they argued that if Johnson did withdraw, he would wait to announce it until the eve of the Convention when it would be practically impossible to prevent the nomination of Johnson's choice, presumably Hubert Humphrey.

The fact is that no one in politics or government believed that Johnson would quit. Why would he have insisted on a Convention date built around his birthday in late August, a time so late that only an incumbent could benefit by it? Why had the White House directly intervened in the New Hampshire primary, financing and organizing the campaign for a pro-Johnson slate, and thereby staking the President's prestige on the outcome? Why were cabinet members criss-crossing Wisconsin a week before its primary, pleading for an endorsement by the voters of LBJ and his Great Society? For every hint of withdrawal, there were a hundred sure signs that Johnson would run again. In the authors' view, President Johnson did intend to run again. His replacement of Defense Secretary McNamara was done as insurance to protect his political flanks in an election year. He deliberately tried to keep the situation ambiguous by talking of his return to the Pedernales, just as FDR talked in 1939 of returning to his home "on the banks of the Hudson," so that his friends would not take him for granted and his opponents would be kept off balance. Johnson was confident that he could win renomination because the White House controlled the levers of the Convention.

Two things happened in March 1968 that forced Johnson to change his decision. The first involved Vietnam. General Westmoreland and the Joint Chiefs of Staff were requesting more men and an indefinite commitment of national resources to bring a successful conclusion to the war. The credibility of the Administration, and particularly of the Pentagon, had been rocked by the impact of the Tet offensive. Now the President was being asked to make an even greater commitment to an effort that had already deeply divided the nation. He assigned his new Secretary of Defense, Clark Clifford, a trusted friend generally identified as a "hawk," to conduct the policy review. It began in earnest on March 10. Within two weeks, Clifford had reversed his own position, advised rejection of the major military requests, and urged the President to negotiate an end to the war, both in the national interest and his own. Lyndon Johnson was now being told of impending disaster by his most trusted adviser, who was using the same arguments Robert Kennedy had used for over two years. He had to reverse his position, and his obsession with his niche in history influenced him to gloss his reversal with an act of heroic self-abnegation.

He might still have fought it out, but the second event of March forced his hand. He understood immediately the results of the New Hampshire primary and the apparent trend in Wisconsin. As far as Lyndon Johnson was concerned, Eugene McCarthy did not win in New Hampshire, but his strong showing and its electric impact around the country would force Robert Kennedy to become a candidate, and what would follow from that meant that Johnson could not be re-elected as President.

The majority of the aides who assembled in Kennedy's apartment the night of March 31 had a sense of being part of an historic event. They felt Johnson's withdrawal had assured both Kennedy's nomination and election to the presidency. But Kennedy was much more cautious. Noting newsmen were camping outside the building, he told his aides to make sure they did "not appear too happy about this thing." He discussed the statement he wanted prepared for the press conference the next morning. Sorensen observed that the bombing halt would be greeted with almost universal acclaim. "That was a very damaging speech for us—until the last paragraph," he said. He suggested Kennedy send a telegram to Johnson associating himself with the initiative for peace and requesting a meeting at the White House to discuss how they could "work together in the interest of national unity during the coming months." In the dramatic uncertainty of those moments, even the prospect of a helpful relationship between old adversaries seemed possible.

Most disturbed by the announcement were those who had been anxious for Kennedy to run early. For them, the removal of Johnson as a target eliminated the possibility of accomplishing any significant change in the structure of American life by means of the campaign. The "revolution" had lost its target.

To Kennedy, the President's decision broke open the political situation and gave him a chance to ask commitments from leaders who had held aloof, out of loyalty to the incumbent President and fear of his retaliation. He tried that night to contact some of the leaders who would be major forces at the Democratic Convention. "We can sew it up tonight," said Dolan, excitedly placing the calls. But Kennedy was reserved and restrained in his conversations. To Mayor Joseph Barr of Pittsburgh and Governor Richard Hughes of New Jersey, he said only that he knew the presidential announcement created a new kind of situation, that he hoped they would consider his position, and that he would see them soon. To Governor Miles Godwin of Virginia, whom he reached at 1 A.M., he said, "I know I have a lot of problems in Virginia and I don't want to underestimate them; but I just want to stay in touch with you and I hope that later on, you will let me make my case to the people of your state."

Some of the leaders were asleep; others were unavailable. Four attempts to reach Mayor Daley were in vain. Johnson was going to be speaking in Chicago the next day and Daley obviously did not want to talk to Kennedy before that meeting. Those he did reach were polite, and just as surprised at Johnson's decision as Kennedy was, but they gave no commitments that night.

Kennedy also used the opportunity to complete his recruitment. He talked to Larry O'Brien about leaving the Cabinet to work with him, knowing his friendship and close association with Vice President Humphrey would make it a difficult decision, but also knowing what O'Brien's endorsement would mean to the professional politicians who would dominate the Chicago Convention. He also discussed with Louis Martin, the most prominent Negro at the Democratic National Committee, the possibility of his joining the campaign staff.

Edward Kennedy was eating dinner in Indianapolis when he heard Johnson's announcement. He was incredulous. After checking with his brother, he, too, made calls to such figures as Senator Howard Cannon of Nevada, Governor William Guy of North Dakota, and Governor Warren Hearnes of Missouri. With President Johnson out, he said, prospects looked good for Robert Kennedy, and he would appreciate their support. He, too, found a reluctance to make commitments.

In the wake of the President's dramatic decision, the phone calls to political leaders were inappropriate, and probably some of those whom the senator tried to reach regarded the effort as rude and insensitive. Clearly it would have been better to measure the meaning of the withdrawal announcement, rather than seek its immediate personal advantages. The press conference the next morning was a mistake in the same sense. It had the uneasy aspect of a crown prince commenting on the personal implications of the king's death while the old monarch was still lying in state. But the press conference had been scheduled while Johnson was still a candidate, and no one had suggested canceling it.

Over the next few days, it became quite apparent that Johnson's decision was a mixed blessing to the Kennedy campaign. Undoubtedly, it opened up the nomination. No longer were the formidable powers of the presidency available for use by the incumbent in his own behalf. There was now a good chance that the nomination would go to the candidate who worked harder and won the primaries, a chance in Kennedy's favor.

But the immediate impact was to bring Kennedy's campaign to a standstill by removing the major issues. The new party leadership, for which he had entered the race, was now assured. The ultimate logic of his race, that only he could prevent the renomination of Lyndon Johnson, was prematurely valid. The new direction in Vietnam was evidently under way. The campaign tour that day of New Jersey and metropolitan Philadelphia found him groping unsuccessfully for new themes. Whatever Kennedy could say was out of keeping with what he had been saying. The crowds were large but much less responsive. He was operating in an atmosphere in which renewed hope had replaced the previous gloom about the prospects of peace, and the previous antagonism for Johnson had given way to strong sympathy for a man who had put his country above his ambitions. In December 1967, when Johnson had entered St. Patrick's Cathedral for the funeral of Cardinal Spellman, he had been received by the congregation with official respect and detached attention. Entering the same church for the investiture of Archbishop Cooke on April 4, he received a standing ovation, an unusual manifestation in an American Catholic cathedral and one last seen in St. Patrick's during the visit of Pope Paul VI.

Johnson's withdrawal compounded Kennedy's difficulties with McCarthy and the liberal wing of the party. Anti-Johnson coalition efforts quickly collapsed. With the immediate choice between Kennedy and McCarthy, many who were ready to support Kennedy as the only means of defeating Johnson drew back. Issues out of the way, the contest became one of personalities.

But the most significant thing, Kennedy found in checking around the country, was that most political leaders now expected that Hubert Humphrey would become a candidate, with the backing of the Administration. Although Humphrey delayed any declaration of intentions, Johnson made clear his own high regard for Humphrey by telling the Cabinet the day after he withdrew: "I am not going to endorse anybody. But I want to say that I was a B Vice President. Hubert Humphrey has been an A-plus Vice President." Backed by Johnson's remaining power, but bearing few of the antagonisms felt toward him, Humphrey could have considerable freedom of action. With his energy and his appealing over-all record, he would be a formidable candidate. Perhaps most important, he could not be defeated in the primaries, because almost all the filing dates had already passed.

On April 3, Kennedy met at Hickory Hill with top staff members of his campaign. It was the first and last review they were to have of where they stood and what had been done.

McCarthy had won the Wisconsin primary with 57 per cent of the vote the day before. Kennedy had just returned from the meeting he had requested with President Johnson. It had been surprisingly placid. Johnson had briefed him on the military situation in Vietnam and his plans for moving toward a peace conference. He assured Kennedy he would not get into the middle of the contest for the nomination. Kennedy asked him if this meant the top officials of the Administration would be free to participate. Johnson assured him every member of the Administration would be available to assist Kennedy with information on issues relating to their office, but he had asked them not to make their preference for the nomination public lest it look as if his Administration had fallen to fighting within itself over his successor.

Among those meeting at Hickory Hill, there was some feeling Humphrey might not run for the presidency. Dissatisfaction with the Administration, as expressed in the two primaries to date, might make him feel victory was not possible. It was agreed to send emissaries to the Humphrey camp, to see if the Vice President would be interested, instead of running himself, in taking an important position in the new Administration if Kennedy were elected. But these illusions were shattered later that afternoon, when AFL-CIO President George Meany informed Kennedy that there was no use in seeking his support because Humphrey was going to run and the presidents of all the International Unions in the AFL-CIO were going to endorse him within the next few days.

The discussion in the meeting turned to the main problems of the campaign. Kennedy reported he had called most of the party leaders but won no new commitments. Mayor Daley had said that he wanted to see how well Kennedy did in the primaries, and he would postpone making a commitment to anybody until June when the primaries were over. "And in June," Kennedy said, "he'll tell me he'll wait until August." The President's withdrawal had reversed the Convention strategy. Before March 31, the Kennedy organization was encouraging first ballot votes for McCarthy, to stop Johnson and throw the Convention open. Now Kennedy was the front runner, and the pressure was on him to win on the first ballot, to avoid the inevitable "stop-RFK" movement. Ironically, the big barrier to a first-ballot victory for Kennedy now appeared to be the seventy-two delegates of Massachusetts. As the only entry in the April 30 primary, McCarthy seemed assured of them. The meeting discussed the possibility of a write-in or sticker campaign[9] for Kennedy. Edward Kennedy supported the idea, but others pointed out it would mean a considerable expenditure of his time which was needed in other primary states. The suggestion was made that a change be proposed in the primary law to make it non-binding on the delegates elected. Edward Kennedy disagreed, saying any attempt to change the rules in the middle of the game would be resented by the public and vetoed by the governor. Final decisions were also made not to enter the primaries in New Jersey and Florida. O'Donnell felt confident that enough New Jersey party leaders were sympathetic to ensure the support of that delegation at the Convention. In Florida, where a McCarthy slate was running against a regular slate headed by Senator George Smathers, it was felt Kennedy had enough friends on both to insure the support he would need.

These matters out of the way, the main discussion turned to the primary states. The first was Indiana, and Kennedy was obsessed with it. He had decided to enter the primary after a poll showed him one point ahead of Governor Roger Branigin, who was running as a favorite-son stand-in for Johnson; McCarthy was far behind. Kennedy had never campaigned in Indiana before, and at this point had only the most rudimentary organization to support him. Kennedy felt that he could defeat Branigin, but that his real opponent would be McCarthy. "How am I different from McCarthy?" he asked several times, and in asking the question, he acknowledged the problem that had been made even more difficult by Johnson's withdrawal. "We have to be specific about this. I have to stress my experience and my capacity to deal with Vietnam, the race problem, our cities." He emphasized the student operation again. "It has to be decentralized. It can't look like we are moving in with an organization while the McCarthy kids are all volunteers. Just give the students my speeches and let them do whatever they want.

"I want new ideas in those speeches," he continued. "I want speeches—not lectures—speeches with lines that will get applause and that have news in them."

Then the manager left the room to become the candidate again.

9 The technique of getting votes for a candidate not on the ballot by passing out stickers bearing his name to place on the voting machines had been tried with some success in other Massachusetts elections.

One of the earliest critics of American involvement in Vietnam had been Reverend Martin Luther King, Jr. As early as the summer of 1965, he said publicly that the war must be stopped and a settlement negotiated, and wrote letters to this effect to both President Johnson and Ho Chi Minh. In doing so, he drew criticism from many who said that foreign policy was not a fitting subject for a civil rights leader, and that his strong position was undermining the effectiveness of his movement. For a time in 1966 and 1967, King was asked by the peace movement to run for President himself, with Dr. Spock as his running mate.

In November 1967, King privately told a Kennedy associate that the senator should challenge President Johnson. Although King's organization, the Southern Christian Leadership Conference, stayed out of partisan politics, King announced, early in March 1968, that the upcoming election was so important that he intended, for the first time in his life, to endorse a candidate in advance of the Conventions. The day before Kennedy announced, King told members of his family that Kennedy would be that candidate. By the first week in April, he was still clearing the endorsement with his associates in SCLC. On April 4, he was shot dead in Memphis.

Kennedy heard the news of Dr. King's assassination while en route to Indianapolis for a rally in the city's ghetto. He kept his schedule, and announced Dr. King's death to the crowd in a brief, intensely moving speech in which, for the first time, he referred publicly to his own brother's assassination.[10] He returned to his suite in the Sheraton-Lincoln Hotel, where he reached Mrs. King on the telephone. "I want to express my deep sympathy," he said. "I hope you understand that I know how you feel. Is there anything I can do to help

[10] "For those of you who are black and are tempted to be filled with hatred and distrust, at the injustice of such an act, against all white people, I can only say I feel in my heart the same kind of feeling. I had a member of my family killed, but he was killed by a white man. But we have to make an effort in the United States, we have to make an effort to understand, to go beyond these rather difficult times. My favorite poet was Aeschylus. He wrote: "Even in our sleep, pain which cannot forget falls drop by drop upon the heart until in our own despair against our will, comes wisdom through the awful grace of God.

"What we need in the United States is not division, what we need in the United States is not hatred, what we need in the United States is not violence or lawlessness, but love and wisdom and compassion toward one another, and a feeling of justice toward those who still suffer within our country, whether they be white or whether they be black."

you?" Mrs. King said she was trying to get an airplane to go to Memphis to bring her husband's body back to Atlanta. Kennedy told her he would make arrangements for this to be done. It was as simple as that. His critics tried to read all kinds of political calculations into Kennedy's providing a plane for the funeral flight of Dr. King's body. But his intervention came as a direct response to Mrs. King's request. Incredibly neither the White House nor anyone else had volunteered that kind of help.

The conversation over, he went into another room of the hotel suite where a group of fourteen black political activists had gathered, men his Indiana managers had wanted to meet him before beginning work in the campaign. They had been waiting for Kennedy for a long time. The news of King's death had made them restive, and they spoke disparagingly of all white leaders. They were in no mood for politics. "You're all the same," one of them said to Kennedy. "Our leader is dead tonight, and when we need you, we can't find you."

Kennedy responded harshly: "You think I like sitting here in this hotel? Wouldn't I rather be at home with my family? I happen to believe that I have something to offer to you and your people. Yes, you lost a friend. I lost a brother. I know how you feel . . . You talk about the establishment. I have to laugh. Big business is trying to defeat me because they think I am a friend of the Negro. You are down on me because you say I am part of the Establishment."

"How do we know we can rely on you?" they asked.

"I have only one thing to offer you—my word. I want and need your help. I wanted Martin Luther King's help and he gave me his help; not only to me but to other white people who were trying to help his people."

The visitors pledged their support.

The national reaction to King's death showed how fundamental was the gulf between the races. Black people had a deep sense of personal loss; some rioted in their fury. The despair of the more moderate blacks deepened, for if a moderate civil rights leader like Martin Luther King had been killed for his efforts, what hope could there be for improving the Negro condition?

Among the white population, the King assassination shocked and stirred sympathy and support for the Negro. But the subsequent riots created the opposite reaction—resentment and personal fear. The funeral and the riots, appearing together on split television screens, left a searing emotional ambiguity.

Kennedy was saddened by the riots, especially Washington's. But he had always believed each city contained riots "waiting to happen." Dr. King's murder crystallized them. He toured the Washington riot areas, talking to the residents. He was extremely concerned that in the aftermath of Dr. King's death, black leaders who advocated non-violence would be undermined, or become isolated, or worse yet, just give up. President Johnson had announced that he would speak to the Congress on April 8, the eve of the funeral, but the speech was canceled. There was little left for the President to say or offer. With the major Negro leaders assembling in Atlanta for the funeral, Kennedy offered to meet with them privately.

The senator met with three different groups beginning at 9 P.M. on April 8. For the most part, those present were already Kennedy's supporters, so the politics of the meetings were practically irrelevant. He began each session by saying he would be totally involved in the days ahead in primary campaigning and might not have another opportunity to see them soon. He wanted to know what they thought should be done, particularly to carry on the causes for which Dr. King had worked. The atmosphere was quite different from the angry meetings in New York in 1963. Many things had changed since that occasion, Kennedy, perhaps, most of all. No longer did he feel compelled to defend the white power structure. Five years had shown him ample justification for black bitterness.

A few suggestions were made—legislation for federal control of police weapons, which blacks thought were used against them; reform of the welfare program; changes in the highway program to prevent dislocation; more congressional representation for southern Negroes. But for the most part, the meeting served as an outlet for their frustrations. Most important was the clear determination that Dr. King's movement would go on. The fact that the meetings allowed Dr. King's shattered followers to turn their thoughts to future action was itself an accomplishment. It was past 3 A.M. when Ralph Abernathy, totally exhausted, weakened by a self-imposed hunger strike, and grief-stricken by the death of his close friend, stood up, embraced Kennedy and left to finish the funeral arrangements.

Kennedy returned to Hickory Hill from Atlanta tired and depressed.

He realized the riots had weakened his appeal to the white majority. But he continued to believe that in this, the most critical issue before the nation, he could make a contribution toward justice and reconciliation that no one else was attempting.

During the evening of April 6, Goodwin came to Hickory Hill to make his peace with Kennedy. It had been an incredible week. On Sunday, Johnson had withdrawn; on Tuesday, McCarthy had scored a decisive victory in Wisconsin; and on Thursday, Martin Luther King, Jr. had been assassinated, with riots and looting breaking out in Washington and a score of other cities. Washington was under siege. Smoke was still pouring from areas in the ghetto burned out by the rioters. An early curfew closed the city to traffic. Kennedy had to write out a special pass for Goodwin's passage over the bridge to McLean. As Goodwin commented, the scene was a backdrop to the drama that compelled Kennedy's candidacy. He alone among American political leaders could deal decisively with Vietnam, racial strife, and the urban rebellion. He outlined what he had learned from the "new politics" of New Hampshire and Wisconsin. He said he would join Kennedy, but not as a speechwriter. His work on McCarthy's television and radio advertising convinced him that area was far more important. He did not want to involve himself in jurisdictional conflicts with old associates who were already at work in the campaign organization. So for the rest of the campaign, Goodwin ran his own operation, producing television films for the campaign with John Frankenheimer, the gifted Hollywood director, disdaining any interference with his work, and insisting on dealing directly with the candidate.

The announcement of candidacy automatically placed Kennedy in the primaries of the three states, Nebraska, Oregon, and South Dakota, which require all active candidates to appear on the ballot. In addition, he entered the primaries in California and New York and chose to run in the District of Columbia, where he had many friends and the majority of the population was black. Several other non-binding primaries were available to him, but the only one he chose to enter was Indiana.

On March 16, the day he announced his candidacy, it was not his intention to enter the Indiana primary, but the continuing strength of McCarthy made him reconsider. If he skipped that state, he would have to wait to show his strength until the Nebraska primary, May 14, only three weeks before California. Nebraska was a small, atypical state, with only 300,000 registered Democrats. Indiana was the eleventh largest state, in many ways the heart of America, with a Democratic registration that included a broad spectrum of ethnic, religious, economic, and geographically widespread groups. Most important, Kennedy felt he had to do something to slow down McCarthy as soon as possible.

But were he to run in Indiana, he would be opposing not only McCarthy but also what was reputed to be the best Democratic state organization in the country. Branigin remained on the ballot after Johnson's withdrawal. He had 50,000 state jobholders beholden to him and had the endorsements of 91 of the 92 county chairmen. Kennedy had no known or trusted agents in Indiana. Equally important, the Indiana primary, a preference type, was binding on delegates for the first ballot only. The delegates themselves would be selected later by a state convention dominated by the governor's organization, and Kennedy's staff estimated that no matter who won the primary on the second ballot in Chicago, 55 of the state's 73 delegates would follow their governor to the candidate of the Johnson administration.

Kennedy's deliberations on whether to run in Indiana lasted through the last two weeks in March. The day after his brother announced, Edward Kennedy saw the state congressmen and senators. All of them advised him that Robert Kennedy should stay out. Even those who favored Kennedy for the nomination said they would be unable to endorse him, as they did not wish to forfeit organization support and funds in their own campaigns that year. He then sought advice from Gordon St. Angelo, the state chairman, who, professing warm friendship for the Kennedys, also advised him to stay out. Finally, he talked to Branigin himself, who combined political advice with a tirade against Robert Kennedy. There is still strong anti-Catholic sentiment in some parts of Indiana, Branigin noted, and most Hoosiers do not take to the Kennedy brand of liberalism; furthermore, he said, Kennedy's position on Vietnam was destroying the Democratic party. He ended by saying: "I don't care if I get beaten in this primary. It won't effect my position. But I don't think I will be."

Time was short, so even while opinions were being sought, Kennedy felt he should take the steps necessary to qualify for the ballot. Gerard Doherty, former Democratic State Chairman in Massachusetts, was given the task. Doherty, only thirty-seven, had graduated from Harvard and spoke Russian, but he belonged to the old school of Massachusetts politics. A skilled organizer, he knew how to count and vote a precinct. More than any other politician, he had been responsible for lining up the delegate majority by which Edward Kennedy defeated Edward J. McCormack, Jr. in the bitter Massachusetts Democratic Convention in 1962.

At 3 A.M. on Friday, March 22, in a blinding snowstorm, Doherty arrived at the Indianapolis airport. His main assignment was to obtain the 5500 signatures, 500 from each congressional district, each certified by the county clerk, which were required to put Kennedy's name on the ballot. He had a week in which to do it. St. Angelo had said it was impossible to get that many signatures, all over the state, in that time.

Doherty carried with him the names of the twelve people from Indiana who had written Kennedy volunteering their support after he announced. Doherty had never been in Indiana in his life and knew none of the twelve. He was met by Michael Riley, an Indianapolis attorney who was president of the Young Democrats, and two young workers. Together they began to arrange for signature petitions to be loaded on buses, destined for friends in outlying cities who would help circulate them. When petitions were intercepted and destroyed en route by the state organization, Doherty knew Indiana was going to be rough. He and Riley had them distributed by private automobile. Students for Kennedy organizations in Chicago and Ohio took them around their neighboring Indiana districts. In Fort Wayne, two seminarians from St. Francis College undertook the assignment, visiting services in Negro churches that Sunday so worshipers could sign up. By the end of the week, 12,000 Indiana voters had signed the petitions.

The certification requirements were a potential hazard. The Democratic county clerks were under the control of the state organization. Doherty told Edward Kennedy that St. Angelo, who was still posing as Kennedy's friend, was threatening to have the signatures declared invalid as fast as they were gathered. "Just tell him," Doherty advised, "that if he monkeys around with the signatures, you'll break him in two."

On Monday, March 25, with the petition campaign well under way, Sorensen, Smith, O'Donnell, and Edward Kennedy met in Washington to make a final decision on Indiana. All the points about the strength of the organization and the pro-war sentiment in the state were raised again; but Doherty insisted the voters were receptive. "It looks like we will have over 12,000 signatures. If we can do this, in one week, after meeting three guys in an airport in a snowstorm," he said, "it must be an O.K. state." His argument was reinforced by the results of a hastily ordered poll, showing Kennedy slightly ahead of Branigin and McCarthy well behind. Reaching Kennedy by telephone on the West Coast, the group recommended he enter the Indiana primary, and he agreed.

The organization of the Indiana campaign was Edward Kennedy's responsibility. He, in turn, relied primarily upon men who had worked with him and Doherty in Massachusetts. The tested devices of Kennedy campaigns reaching back to 1946 were recreated: outside coordinaters in each district, extensive radio and television, a tabloid newspaper on Kennedy's career and views, 2.5 million copies of which were prepared for distribution to every home in the state; saturation of the state with every available member of the Kennedy family, including Eunice Shriver, who was in the process of moving to Paris where her husband would be the new American ambassador. Jacqueline Kennedy's brother-in-law, Stanislas Radziwill, made his traditional tour of the Polish districts, this time in northern Indiana. Speaking at a rally in Gary, he was asked by one man, "Why does Robert Kennedy want to move a Negro family next to our homes?"

"Better a Negro than a Communist," Radziwill answered.

"That's right, Radziwill," shouted the crowd.

It was harder to program the students into this kind of campaign. Many refused to do something as menial as distributing tabloids. But most of the students willing to work for Kennedy were not trained for the "issue canvassing" that worked so well for McCarthy, and there was no time for them to be instructed. Large amounts of money were spent on the student effort, but the operation was only marginally effective.

On April 22, the political moratorium following Dr. King's assassination ended. Kennedy began two weeks of continuous campaigning in Indiana. He had still not found a theme, nor restored the urgency that had been deflated by Johnson's withdrawal, but he did have a specific strategy for that primary. Recognizing he was running as an Eastern outsider against a popular Governor, in a proud and somewhat insular state, he decided to identify himself as much as he comfortably could with Indiana history, landmarks and problems. Television commercials were filmed in Indiana settings, discussing problems of concern with Indiana housewives, students, and veterans. He began his tour by campaigning on the Lincoln Trail, the route Abraham Lincoln's family had traveled on its way to Illinois. He visited the home of Lincoln's mother, Nancy Hanks Lincoln, near Dale, Indiana, and the courthouse in Booneville where Lincoln had studied law. He ended that day with a rally in Evansville, where he drew his greatest applause with reference to the poor condition of the main highway leading north. A suggested tour of the pit stops on the Indianapolis 500 Speedway was ruled out, but a train trip on the route of the Wabash Cannonball through Central Indiana was scheduled, and proved the best stratagem of the campaign. It drew thousands of citizens to a relaxed, old-fashioned political ritual where crowd excitement was possible without mob frenzy."[11]

Kennedy also recognized that, in the aftermath of the riots following Dr. King's death, he was campaigning before a frightened electorate. As John Bartlow Martin called ahead to the areas Kennedy was to visit, no matter how small the community or how far removed from the disorders, he found that the overriding issue was "the backlash," white fear of black violence. Dutton, by this time Kennedy's most influential adviser and constant companion, also held this view out of his California experience in 1966, in which he attributed the defeat of Governor Brown exclusively to the backlash. At a dinner on April 21 at Hickory Hill, Kennedy outlined the theme he planned to use, emphasizing his concern with order as well as with justice. "We can't have violence. We can't have disorder. I was Attorney General of the United States. I know something about these problems."

11 The Wabash Cannonball, as well as later visits to the birthplace of Hoosier poet James Whitcomb Riley and a conservation tour of the Indiana Dunes, were originally suggested to Kennedy schedulers by P. J. Mode, a young Washington attorney and a native of Indiana, who worked in the research section of the campaign.

This theme was interpreted properly as a shift in his line. The pre-March 31 speeches had not dealt with the fear of violent division. Now it preoccupied the country. But Kennedy's was not a conservative shift, carefully measured to political necessity. As he saw it, blacks wanted a President who understood the injustice they suffered and would work to correct it; whites (as well as most blacks) wanted a President who would protect them. He offered to do both, but he made it clear in every speech that the price of domestic security to white America would be sacrifice—in terms of personal involvement in the community, taxes for social programs, and acceptance of a more integrated society. He believed that the causes of violence must be attacked if the violence itself was to diminish. The press emphasized the "law and order" part of his remarks, but these were prefatory in every appearance to his appeal to the white conscience.

It was "high risk" campaigning. A candidate could receive a tremendous emotional reaction talking about Vietnam, but for most Americans, "hawks" as well as "doves," the issue was still remote and impersonal. The black-white confrontation was a front-yard issue. It touched a voter's home, school, children, church, and conscience. Race tested the soul of the nation, bringing out fear and faith, hate and love, bigotry and brotherhood. It was not the kind of issue that professional politicians, or any of Kennedy's 1968 opponents, cared to talk about. Kennedy felt that he not only understood the issue but was the only candidate for President with real standing among both races, the only one who could bring them together toward understanding and action. This was the message and the promise he carried all over Indiana in the two weeks preceding the primary election.

Kennedy campaigning in Indiana was no different from the man who had traveled the country since 1966: he conveyed the same urgency, the same compassion. Television chose to highlight the frenzy, but there was another side to Kennedy as he campaigned. It was best described in an article by David Murray of the Chicago *Sun-Times:*

> At first, there was no joy at all on the faces of the dozen or so 5-year-olds in the tiny, dirty playground at the day nursery.
> They stared with wide, solemn eyes through the old cyclone fence topped with drooping barbed wire at Robert F. Kennedy, who had

walked a hundred feet down the street Tuesday to see them as they stood in their cage.

The place was the Day Nursery Association of Indianapolis, and it lies in a grubby section only a few steps away from James Whitcomb Riley's house. Kennedy had gone to the Riley house as part of his campaign for the Presidency.

Tentatively, they poked their fingers at him through the fence, and he pushed his fingers back at them and there was a smile or two, on both sides. But the children still didn't quite know what to make of this man who was surrounded by all the other people with the cameras and microphones and tape recorders and notebooks.

When he started talking to them, you could hardly hear what he said, it was so soft, and his eyes changed from those of a presidential candidate to something else. And he kept talking and stroking their fingers with his and then one little boy said: "Hey, you're on television, aren't you?" and Kennedy nodded and said yes, he was.

Kennedy walked in the bright sunlight to the day nursery and talked for a minute with the women who run it. They said it was mostly for children of broken homes and that the ones here were all 5-year-olds from different parts of the city.

So Kennedy stopped with the children for a minute, and they got to know him a bit better. The man who wants to be President pushed open a gate and went inside and hunkered down and talked to them some more.

Some of them continued to slide down the sliding board or climb on the jungle gym but the others clustered around Kennedy, not saying much, some of them, but just trying to hold onto him.

Two little girls came up and put their heads against his waist and he put his hands on their heads. And suddenly it was hard to watch, because he had become in that moment the father they did not know or the elder brother who couldn't talk to them, or more important, listen to them, because most elder brothers and most fathers don't know how to listen to 5-year-olds without thinking about other things.

He had gone to the Riley house because when you are fighting a campaign in Indiana, you have to pay homage to the Hoosier Keats. Before that, there had been a day of talking to union officials and a big walking tour, getting mobbed in this city's Monument Circle.

And after that there was going to be another visit to a factory and a reception and all the unusual paraphernalia of a big snazzy, first-class presidential primary campaign.

But this hiatus, in front of a gray, American Gothic house with the paint peeling off it, was something else. Gone, for just a moment, was the rhetoric and the playing with audiences and the motorcades and the adulation and the criticism.

The word that came on strongest, as he sat and listened to the children and made a quiet remark now and then, was the word "compassion."

This is because—and anyone who has ever dealt with 5-year-olds knows this—you can fool a lot of people in a campaign, and you can create phony issues if you want to, and you can build an image with a lot of sharpsters around you with their computers and their press releases.

But lonely little children don't come up and put their heads on your lap unless you mean it.

In the last ten days of the campaign, the diverse parts of the organization began to mesh. What began with Doherty and Riley a month before was now an organization of hundreds. The question-and-answer spots filled the television screen. There were Kennedys in every part of the state. The candidate himself kept up a brutal dawn-to-dark pace, urging his schedulers to "work me harder." In the final nine-hour motorcade across the northwest segment of the state, at least 100,000 hailed him in an emotional outpouring exceeding even the frantic first days in Kansas and California.

On election night, he was tense as he took the returns at the Holiday Inn Motel near the Indianapolis Airport. The first counts indicated his total might reach 50 per cent of the vote, the figure the press was generally predicting for him. But he was sure from the careful final polling supervised by Larry O'Brien that he would not achieve that figure. He was very upset when the first television network projections showed him under 40 per cent, with McCarthy close behind, despite the fact he was leading in all major cities but one, and was carrying all the major counties. This mis-estimate and the commentary that followed it would shape the impression formed by Democratic politicians around the country, diluting whatever impact his victory could have even before it was officially achieved. Nettled by the television editorializing that he knew was based on erroneous estimates, he went to the headquarters hotel in downtown Indianapolis to greet his precinct workers, telephoned key co-ordinators around the state, and re-established contact with the leaders of the Branigin organization. His resentment of the television coverage showed in a bitter interview with Roger Mudd of CBS, in which he turned a question about his campaign spending into an attack on the high rates networks charged for political commercials.

Kennedy won the primary with 320,485 votes (42 per cent) to McCarthy's 209,165 (27 per cent) and Branigin's 234,312 (30.7 per cent). It was a victory but not a triumph. His sister Eunice sent him a telegram: "Only one other person could have gotten over 42 per cent and she is on her way back to Paris." He and his associates realized that the major purpose of the primary—to slow down McCarthy—had not been accomplished. After the Wisconsin primary eight years before, one of John Kennedy's sisters had asked him what the results meant: "They mean we will have to go through the same thing all over again," he said. That was the story of Indiana.

An Indiana poll taken by Oliver Quayle for NBC news in the middle of April gave Kennedy 41 per cent and McCarthy only 19 per cent. If the poll was accurate, then in the last three weeks, despite a massive campaign, Kennedy had gained nothing, and almost all the undecided vote had swung to McCarthy. It may have been that this vote was a firm anti-Kennedy vote, just looking for the best alternative. Forty-nine per cent of the respondents to the Quayle poll had volunteered negative comments about Kennedy. In response to the suggestion that "Kennedy is too political," 55 per cent of the Democratic voters had agreed and only 36 per cent disagreed. The controversies of the last few years had taken their toll. His exhaustive campaign had brought the pro-Kennedy voters to the polls, but it had not broken down the broad opposition within his own party.

Most analyses of the Indiana primary stressed that at a time when racial feeling ran especially high, Kennedy had managed to forge an unlikely coalition of black and lower-middle-income white voters.[12]

[12] The source of this misconception was a column written by Rowland Evans and Robert Novak the day after the Indiana primary, entitled *Kennedy's Indiana Victory Proves His Appeal Defuses Backlash Voting*. The column stated that in Gary, "While Negro precincts were delivering around 90 per cent for Kennedy, he was running 2 to 1 ahead in some Polish precincts." This was picked up in most commentaries on the campaign, but in fact Kennedy only did that well in two precincts and lost 59 of the 70 white precincts in Gary. In *85 Days: The Last Campaign of Robert Kennedy*, Jules Witcover stated: ". . . Precinct breakdowns showed . . . [Kennedy received] more than the usual number of blue-collar whites for a Democrat in the backlash neighborhoods." In *The Unfinished Odyssey of Robert Kennedy*, David Halberstam stated: "The poles in Gary came through, 2 to 1 . . ." It should be added that the Kennedy campaign organization believed the misconception and encouraged it.

From this came the theory that many supporters of George Wallace, at least in the North, would have voted for Kennedy despite their racial views because he, like Wallace, was a strong figure running against the Establishment. A study of the actual voting shows a different picture. The area usually cited for this theory is Lake County, Indiana, the steel and heavy industry center next to Chicago, whose largest city, Gary, was sharply divided between blacks and lower-middle-income whites. Lake County had alarmed political observers in 1964 when it voted for Wallace in the Democratic primary. Kennedy carried Lake County by 15,500 votes over McCarthy. But the margin came entirely from Gary. Of the fifteen other Lake County cities and townships that Wallace had carried in 1964, thirteen were carried by McCarthy and only one by Kennedy. In Gary itself, 80 per cent of Kennedy's vote came from the black community. In the seventy precincts of Gary where all the white voters live, Kennedy received only 34 per cent of the vote. McCarthy received 49 per cent, Branigin 17 per cent.[13] The lesson of Lake County, then, was that the more personally involved the white voters were with the racial struggle, the more they identified Kennedy with the black side of it, and turned to his opponents as an outlet for their protest. His message of reconciliation had been powerfully articulated, but those whites who needed to hear it most desperately were not listening.

Kennedy's campaign for the Nebraska primary, May 14, was small compared to the scope of the Indiana effort, but it yielded a much more clear-cut victory. An effective grass-roots organization, a more conducive climate of opinion and a more homogeneous constituency allowed him to keep up his momentum of primary victories.

The Nebraska primary is a preference contest, not binding on the delegates. The delegates can run pledged to a candidate, but they do not have to vote for him if they are elected. Under Nebraska law, the secretary of the state is required to place all those he believes are candidates for President on the ballot. Kennedy's disavowal

[13] It is easy to isolate the white and black returns since the races live sharply apart, the blacks in 62 precincts in the center of the city, an area bounded by the railroad tracks and the Little Calumet River; The whites in seventy precincts both south and north of those demarcation lines. These seventy precincts gave Wallace 12,404 votes in 1964, 65 per cent of their total. In the bitter white-black mayoral contest in 1967, they gave the white candidate 36,166 of the 37,941 votes he received.

of candidacy on January 31 had persuaded the secretary of state to leave him off. He announced just in time to get back on before the ballots were printed.

There remained the question of whether he should campaign in the state. If he did not, a poor showing could be justified on the grounds that Kennedy had not sought votes because the primary had no binding effect. Furthermore, it could be argued that the delegate election presented a real dilemma because, by the time Kennedy announced, every major Democrat in the state had joined a slate pledged to Johnson and led by former Governor Frank Morrison. Only one candidate was running pledged to Kennedy, a coed from Creighton University in Omaha. This meant that those voters who favored Kennedy would have to be educated to vote, not for their accustomed party leaders, but for unfamiliar names who were running uncommitted. Moreover, they would have to find these names on a gigantic ballot that listed seventy contenders for the delegate-at-large positions alone.[14]

On the other hand, discontent with Johnson was widespread in the state. In January, when Kennedy was considering running, he had commissioned a poll in the urban areas of Omaha and Lincoln. Only 40 per cent of the Democrats expressed a preference for Johnson. Kennedy and McCarthy received far less support, but an unusually large number of voters said they were undecided. In addition to the usual issues, there was wide dissatisfaction in agricultural areas because grain and livestock prices had not kept up with the spiraling cost of farming.

The key to the organization for the Nebraska campaign were two sons of the late Charles Sorensen, former attorney general of the state. Besides Ted, there was Phil C. Sorensen, who had been lieutenant governor for two years and had run unsuccessfully for governor in 1966. What weighed most heavily in Kennedy's mind was the fact that the state-wide organization built by Phil Sorensen, which had won the 1966 gubernatorial primary, was intact and at his disposal. Kennedy decided to campaign. He made Nebraska the assignment of the Sorensen brothers, and they completed it handsomely.

[14] A few members of the Morrison-Johnson slate announced for Kennedy after the President withdrew, but the ballot, already printed, listed them as pledged to Johnson.

In March, Phil Sorensen, who had left the state to become a foundation executive in Indiana, returned to organize the campaign. He made minimum use of outsiders. Instead, in almost every community outside of Lincoln and Omaha, he sought out that person to whom local Democrats look for political guidance and asked him to become the district's co-ordinator. In the Third Congressional District, for example, a vast expanse of range land and the sugar beet country covering three quarters of the land area of the state, the co-ordinator was Donald McGinley, the only Democrat elected to Congress from that district in the last forty years.[15]

McCarthy paid one visit to Nebraska and decided essentially to abandon his campaign there. The labor unions were supposed to bring voters out for Johnson as a display of support for Humphrey. They did little. As a result, in most of the state's smaller communities, there was no activity for anyone but Kennedy. Co-ordinators reported that no one else was even being discussed.

Kennedy's own campaigning strengthened this impression. He covered the state extensively, creating greater political excitement than any presidential candidate since Nebraska's own William Jennings Bryan in 1896. The 14,000 people who heard him at the University of Nebraska Coliseum was the largest crowd in the state's political history. There were 5000 people at Hardington, a northeast Nebraska town of 1600; 6000 in Wayne, a town of 4200. He bore down hard on the causes of their discontent, urging de-escalation in Vietnam, offering a farm program which included firm price supports, more bargaining power for farmers in the market, and a redevelopment act for rural America. It was in Nebraska that he struck a major theme, decentralizing the federal bureaucracy, returning government to the people in their towns and neighborhoods. Again, he used a train, crossing the state on the main line of the Union Pacific Railroad, along which most of the larger towns had grown up. A rural populace, isolated and ignored in the middle of the nation, was thrilled by the excitement and pleased he cared enough about them to come.

Nebraska gave him 51 per cent of the vote to McCarthy's 31 per cent and a Johnson-Humphrey combined total of 14 per cent. On

[15] Others who worked with Sorensen in the campaign leadership were Eda Jo van Neste, James Green, and Helen Abdusch, a Nebraskan who had worked with Kennedy in the Justice Department.

May 14, primary night, for the first time he felt he could openly urge supporters of McCarthy to come over to him.

In Nebraska, the race problem was remote and the black vote in the primary was negligible. Nebraska was a triumph of sound tactics and good organization. Kennedy won because his liberal opponents were practically absent, the electorate' was small, and enough local citizens were willing to work for him, overcoming the handicap of his late entry.

As the primaries proceeded, the organization also tried to encourage support for Kennedy among the powerful interest groups whose support is always sought in national politics. Gathering business strength was not an immediate priority. The business community was not an important factor in the primaries he had to win, and few businessmen would be delegates to the Democratic Convention. It would be helpful, however, in creating a climate of popular support, and would be essential for the autumn in winning the election. A list was drawn up of leading businessmen whose endorsements would be solicited.

Antipathy to Kennedy in the business world ran very deep. His opposition to Johnson, in whose "consensus" business had occupied a prominent role, was not the dominant factor. Rather, as Goodwin had predicted over two years before, the cumulative effect of his views and the actions he had taken had resulted in the kind of publicity that led many businessmen to see Kennedy as someone who threatened their basic interests. The situation was summed up in an article in *Fortune* magazine of March 1968.

> During recent weeks, *Fortune* has surveyed the political views of business leaders in cities scattered across the nation. At each meeting with the businessmen, mention of the name Bobby Kennedy produced an almost unanimous chorus of condemnation . . . Although the traditional alignment of business with the Republicans has weakened, there is agreement that Kennedy is the one public figure who could produce an almost united front of business opposition . . . If Kennedy should become the Democratic candidate, this hostility would stuff the Republican coffers, and if he were elected it might seriously impair his ability to govern."[16]

[16] The article (written by a former staffer for Governor William Scranton of Pennsylvania) also contained an interview with Kennedy. If the interview had been filmed, an audience might have seen in his brief answers an attitude that

Thomas J. Watson, Jr., Chairman of IBM, was the most prominent business figure to support Kennedy's bid for the nomination. Watson never hesitated in committing his prestige and resources to his close friend, whose talents and integrity he admired so much. On April 2, Watson and Burke Marshall met with Kennedy at his apartment in New York to discuss the means of gaining support, or at least reducing the hostility. They agreed that priority should be given to presenting an objective version of some of the most "anti-business" Kennedy incidents, the most celebrated of which continued to be the early morning visits of FBI men to potential witnesses in their private homes, part of the government's fight to roll back the price of steel six years before. Business accepted this as evidence of Kennedy's ruthless use of power against its interests. It was decided to try to interest a major business publication like *Fortune* or the *Wall Street Journal* in conducting an independent investigation into the events of the 1962 steel crisis, in which the major participants, government and business, would be interviewed. Such an inquiry had to show it was the FBI, not Kennedy, which had ordered the agents to move in the early morning; and that it had been done without his knowledge, even though he had taken responsibility as the accountable cabinet official.

Watson and Marshall also advised Kennedy to make a major address before a business audience. Part of the speech would be reassurance, reiterating his commitment to the basic principles of free enterprise and the profit system, and to the accepted rule that the basic decisions of a company on products, investments, and operations should be made by its business managers and stockholders. He would also outline his proposals for the economy, knowing that much of his program would appeal to businessmen. A stronger effort to end the war would reduce the threat of both inflation and increased taxes. The ghetto development program showed his admiration for business managerial skills and offered attractive incentives to companies which involved themselves

---

was not altogether unhappy about the discomfiture he caused in the commercial world. An exchange like the following has to be read in that context:

FORTUNE: We have been talking to businessmen around the country about politics and government, and we find that in general businessmen have a bad reaction to you. Do you think that is a valid discovery?
KENNEDY: I am sure that some of it is, yes.
FORTUNE: Do you have any idea why they feel that way?
KENNEDY: I'm sure they could tell you.

in social problems. The address was tentatively scheduled for April 5, before the City Club of Cleveland, but the assassination of Dr. King on April 4 forced its postponement.

The effort to form a businessman's committee was a failure. Most businessmen, even those who were sympathetic, could not risk impairing their relations with the Administration by taking a public position. Many liberals in the commercial world, who agreed with Kennedy on Vietnam and the urban crisis, preferred to identify with Nelson Rockefeller's disjointed candidacy. Hubert Humphrey's assiduous cultivation of Wall Street brought a major dividend when a pro-Johnson group headed by Sidney Weinberg and John Loeb, probably the most powerful investment bankers in New York, agreed to raise his campaign funds. The national Citizens for Kennedy advertisement that appeared the end of May listed only two significant business names: Jerold Hoffberger, of the National Brewing Company, an old associate of Joseph P. Kennedy; and Harold Williams, President of Hunt Foods and Industries; and only one member of the New York Stock Exchange, Richard Weil.

A poor showing in the business community could be understood. It was predominantly Republican. Far more serious in terms of Kennedy's chances was the way the leaders of the large labor unions moved, almost in a body, to block his nomination. Ever since 1956, when President Eisenhower received over half the votes of union members, unions have no longer been able to deliver the votes of their members in presidential elections. But they have vast influence in Democratic Conventions. In the large industrial states east of the Mississippi, unions are the major source of funds for Democratic candidates. They are the political and financial base for many of the state and local officials, who are chosen to be delegates to the national conventions. Only approximately 300 delegates to the 1968 Convention were union members, but between 500 and 600 others were men whose votes could be influenced by the recommendations of the powerful unions in their area.

With the exception of the Teamsters Union, Kennedy's difficulties with labor leaders did not stem from the days of the Rackets Committee. An anti-labor climate had been created by those hearings, but memories had faded, and the only legislative product of the hearings, the Labor Management Reporting and Disclosure Act of 1959, had turned out to be a law labor could live with. In New York, moreover, Kennedy had established excellent relations with the leadership of all unions, including the Teamsters.

His difficulties derived instead from the politics of the labor movement itself. For several years, a bitter antagonism had been growing between AFL-CIO President George Meany, and UAW President Walter Reuther. It was both a personal and ideological rivalry, with the UAW fighting for more advanced social goals and more militant organizing among the poor. By the end of 1968, the break between AFL-CIO and its largest single union was complete.

Kennedy had always admired Reuther and his union. The UAW had an excellent record of honest and intelligent management for the benefit of its members; and it was a union that accepted blacks speedily and with a minimum of problems. In a 1964 speech in Detroit, Robert Kennedy had spoken of President Kennedy's great debt to Reuther for his help in 1960. Meany, who felt he had done much for John Kennedy and had developed an effective and warm relationship with him as President, was infuriated; from that day, Meany saw Robert Kennedy as an ally of his enemies. Opposition to Kennedy in the labor movement became a badge of loyalty to Meany over Reuther.

If this antagonism, along with labor's ties to Johnson, made things difficult, the entrance of Humphrey made them infinitely harder. Humphrey also had an impeccable pro-labor record, but unlike Kennedy, he enjoyed intimate personal associations with all important labor leaders. Even Walter Reuther, the friend for whom Kennedy had made the enemies, could not support Kennedy over Humphrey since he was indebted to both men. The other leaders of his union were evenly split. At the UAW Convention in Atlantic City on May 9, Kennedy received a warm demonstration, but Humphrey received a prolonged ovation. So dismal were the prospects that in the first week in April, O'Donnell, who was exercising general supervision over efforts among unions, advised against publicizing any labor leader endorsements of Kennedy, because they would look so insignificant compared to what Humphrey could produce.

Faced with almost solid opposition at the top, Kennedy's organizers sought support among the leaders of the local unions and the younger staff members in the offices of the large international unions. In the primary states, mailings were sent to every official of every local union. In Indiana and California, state UAW organizations as well as some steelworker locals helped; but in Nebraska and Oregon, union power and funds supported Humphrey, and in some instances Mc-Carthy.

Kennedy had less reason to hope for delegate support in the South than in any other part of the country. It never was considered part of the delegate coalition he would construct to win the nomination. Of the 510 votes from the eleven states of the Old Confederacy, including Texas, Kennedy strategists counted a maximum of five on the first ballot in Chicago, with perhaps another forty coming along later, most of them from an anticipated break in the Kentucky delegation after the state's county caucuses in late July.

On the surface, there should have been more support. Some of the South's most influential newspaper editors admired him greatly,[17] and in his southern trips over the past few years, he had received both objective coverage and friendly crowds. But the dynamics of social change had taken the South in a direction far different from the one he offered the nation.

For twenty years, the South had been changing from predominantly populist to a predominantly conservative area, a political transition fed both by the dominant issue of race and by the changes that came with the early stages of industrial expansion. In 1968, the first of these issues fueled the Wallace movement and the second the growth of the Republican Party. The moderate leaders of the Democratic Party had to contend with a shrinking white constituency. The black registration, spurred by new civil rights laws, was approaching three million, but it was not enough to offset these losses.

In addition to the attrition of the Democratic base, Kennedy had personal problems with the South. He was held responsible for the racial policies of President Kennedy's administration. His own positions on racial issues were considered far too radical. The South's military tradition and large number of military installations and defense industries made it more willing to go along with current policies in

[17] Eugene Patterson, former publisher of the Atlanta *Constitution*, the late Ralph McGill, the *Constitution*'s editor, the late Bill Baggs, editor of the Miami *Herald*, and John Siegenthaler, editor of the Nashville *Tennessean* were longtime friends and admirers.

Vietnam. Kennedy's role on tobacco advertising hurt him politically, especially in North Carolina and Kentucky. Perhaps most important, having been racked by social turmoil longer than the rest of the country, Southerners deeply desired a candidate who promised tranquillity.

Little of this seemed evident in the remarkable enthusiasm shown Kennedy on his trips in March to the universities in Nashville, Atlanta, and Tuscaloosa. Kennedy did not want to devote much of his overextended campaign resources to the South, but he did want to establish a political presence there. The only southern primary was to be in Florida, and his advisers argued back and forth about filing a slate in a place where the liberal vote was limited and a McCarthy slate was already entered. In the other ten states, it was largely a matter of flattering, cajoling, persuading, and courting the delegates or the leaders who controlled them. This kind of gentle exercise, typical of southern politics, was conducted on Kennedy's behalf by a small group of southerners close to him.[18] They broke bread with southern politicians to obtain what information they could about political lineups, and expressed their interest on Kennedy's behalf.

Only a handful of delegates were willing to commit themselves, none of whom had real political power, some of whom were considered chronic renegades. But Kennedy's spokesmen were encouraged by at least a willingness on the part of southern leaders to consider his candidacy. They hoped that local and personal loyalties or rivalries might persuade some elements to support Kennedy so they could advance their own power within the state if he were nominated. If things began to go Kennedy's way at the Convention, perhaps the southern delegates would come along.

Whatever small progress was made in the South disappeared after Humphrey entered the race. The repugnance and fear he had created in the South twenty years before had been largely dissolved. He drew none of the venom now directed at both Johnson and Kennedy. Most of the major political figures of the South happily lined up with him, either openly, in the case of former Governor Terry Sanford of

[18] The major figures working in the South were Siegenthaler, Troutman, James Wine of Kentucky (former ambassador to Luxembourg), Judge Edmund Reggie of Baton Rouge, Travis Glenn of South Carolina, Tom Johnston, and Ted McLaughlin.

North Carolina, or behind favorite-son candidacies, such as those of Governors Robert McNair of South Carolina and Buford Ellington of Tennessee, and Senator George Smathers of Florida.

By the end of May, Kennedy's estimates showed Humphrey with almost all of the southern delegates. The campaign's effort in the South turned to developing techniques for challenging the unit rule, or challenging the Mississippi and Alabama delegation on racial grounds, wooing alternate delegates, and currying strength for the second ballot. They were ingenious devices, but not what one tries when he has the votes.

Kennedy was also told that Jewish voters needed his special attention. Over 60 per cent of the Jews in the United States lived in New York and California, and the large majority of them were enrolled as Democrats. They had influence beyond their numbers, but in these critical primary states, their numbers alone were significant.

As soon as Kennedy's campaign began, his advisors sensed a recurrence of the same problems he had faced in 1964. Once again, Jewish voters had the luxury of a choice among attractive candidates. Hubert Humphrey had championed their causes for twenty years. He benefited from identification with the Administration's commitment to the security of Israel. To those who were attracted to sophisticated dissenters in politics, McCarthy was a powerful magnet.

Jewish leaders told Kennedy's campaign managers that one of his problems related to his stand on Israel. He could hardly believe it. If anything, as a senator, he had spoken more strongly than the White House on problems affecting Israel. On May 23, 1967, two weeks before the beginning of the Six Day War between Israel and the Arab states, he had electrified a B'nai B'rith audience by proposing a United Nations sea patrol to guarantee passage to vessels of all nations through the Gulf of Aqaba. He affirmed his own commitment to the pledge given by four Presidents of the United States to the "territorial integrity and political independence" of Israel, as of all nations in the Near East. He deplored the arms race that diverted the resources that could have given a better life to the Arab nations and economic stability to Israel; but in the aftermath of the War, with Russia re-equipping the Arab armies, he did not hesitate to urge American military assistance to Israel to maintain the balance of power. On January 9, 1968, he met privately with Premier Levi Eshkol in New York and repeated his public support of Israel's request for jet fighter planes. In light of all this, he could not understand how there could be any doubt about the firmness of his position, or why it was not well known to all who were concerned.

Kennedy's frustration erupted in an unpublicized meeting with Jewish leaders during his last visit to New York on May 8, the day after the Indiana primary. His New York managers were anxious he make a statement on Jewish affairs. He did not have time to make a speech, so an appointment was arranged in his apartment, early that afternoon, with a group of rabbis representing the spectrum of Judaism, who were in town for a meeting of the Synagogue Council of America.[19]

Kennedy was in a dark mood. Disappointed by the Indiana results, he had also been receiving reports of Jewish defections in California and New York and was most disheartened and sensitive whenever the subject was raised. Having been told to expect a friendly discussion about the Middle East and the current outbreak of anti-Semitism in Poland, the rabbis were surprised when Kennedy walked in and asked them, "Why do I have so much trouble with the Jews? I don't understand it," he continued. "Nobody has been more outspoken than I have. I have spoken out dozens of times. I spoke out before the war even began."

The rabbis were stunned as the accumulated frustrations surfaced under the tension of his campaign.

"Is it because of my father when he was in England? *That was thirty years ago.* What is it they have against me," he pleaded.

Rabbi Balfour Brickner of the Washington Hebrew Congregation and Rabbi Israel Klavan of the Rabbinical Council of America began patiently to explain that most Jews admired him very much. But the emotion of the Six-Day War had greatly heightened the nationalistic feeling of American Jews toward Israel. Admittedly, Kennedy's positions were beyond criticism, but with Israel's position so precarious, Brickner said American Jews needed continual reassurance that no

[19] The meeting was arranged by Rabbi Seymour Siegel of the Jewish Theological Seminary and attended by Henry N. Rapaport, President of the United Synagogue of America, Rabbi Israel Klavan, Executive Vice President of the Rabbinical Council of America, Rabbi Balfour Brickner of the Union of American Hebrew Congregations, Rabbi Irving Lehrman, and Rabbi Henry Siegman of the Synagogue Council of America.

matter who was President, the United States would not abandon its commitment. As to Kennedy, they needed to hear it from him in his new role as the possible next President. Jews were experienced enough to know that a senator's views sometimes changed when he assumed the responsibilities of the presidency. Perhaps Kennedy had given them these reassurances, perhaps very recently, but it had not reached them through the media, so as far as they were concerned he might as well have said nothing.

Brickner's explanation softened Kennedy. He dropped his defensive tone. He agreed to speak out again, and discussed when and how to give his views wider prominence in the Jewish press. In the middle of this discussion, he gave an eloquent exposition of why Americans should support the security of Israel:

"This is something I happen to feel very deeply about. I was in Israel during the War of Independence, and I have followed it very closely since that time. There are really three reasons:

"First is because of what happened in the 1930s and 1940s. A people were destroyed. It had never before happened in the history of mankind. The rest of the world failed in its moral responsibility to help save them, so the rest of the world has a deep moral responsibility to those who survived, to assure them a place of their own.

"Second, the United States had made a commitment to assure the security of Israel which it must honor. We made it in the Tripartite Declaration.

"Third, I believe in this because it is in the national interest of the United States. Israel is a democracy, with the same kind of tradition we have. If she is secure, she can help bring stability and progress in the Middle East—because she stands for what we stand for, and is doing the kinds of things we are doing."

The rabbis left, deeply impressed by a man who believed in Israel and whose beliefs, not formed by politics, would not be changed by political demands, and in fact resented those demands. It was precisely because Kennedy's views were so strong that he was so disappointed by those who doubted them.

But the political situation would force him to repeat his position time and again in weeks to come. At the Nevah Shalom synagogue in Portland, Oregon, at Temple Isiah in Beverly Hills, in the debate with Senator McCarthy on June 1, he spoke out to prove his credentials.

On the last page of his formal speech at Temple Isiah is this typed paragraph:

But no greater challenge waits this brave and determined people, than to struggle against two thousand years of hostility, and to begin to win the greatest victory of all: the victory over war in her homeland.

Added in Kennedy's hand at the bottom of the page are these words:

And in this we must work with Israel.

In this we in the United States have a responsibility to support Israel.

And we shall.

Soon, Humphrey's strength began to appear in all parts of the country. He had avoided the primary contests by postponing his entry until the last filing deadline had passed. His strategy was to get as many commitments in the non-primary states as he could, while his rivals were fighting each other in the primaries. He had the support of those party leaders and members of Congress still loyal to the Johnson administration, yet he seemed to inherit none of the personal antagonism that had been directed toward Johnson. With his credentials won through sixteen years as the liberal leader of the Senate, he was good enough to win support from the black mayor of Cleveland, Carl Stokes, and such independent liberals as Adlai Stevenson III.

But Humphrey's greatest strength was Kennedy's vulnerability. Robert Kennedy was a controversial candidate and a divisive force in 1968 politics. The leaders were impressed but not overwhelmed by his primary successes. He was more popular than any other Democrat, but there is an intensity of voter feeling which works its subtle influence on politicians by persuading them that one presidential candidate would lend the most strength to the ticket, or that his rejection by the convention would cause defections among the Democratic flock. The support for John Kennedy in 1960, especially among urban Catholics, was of this intensity. The support for Robert Kennedy was not. In the absence of pressure from the voters, and on their assumption that Nixon would be the opponent, the Democratic leaders felt Humphrey was a safer bet.

In April and May, several states which had supported John Kennedy in 1960—Maryland, New Jersey, Pennsylvania, Alaska—swung most of their delegates to Humphrey. The traditional Kennedy New England base also began to crack. In Connecticut, the first state to support John Kennedy in 1960, the leaders decided to remain uncommitted until the Convention. In Maine, the support of Governor Kenneth Curtis and Congressman William Hathaway could not offset the influence of Senator Edmund Muskie and active labor intervention, and the state convention chose a delegation favorable to Humphrey by a count of 20 to 7. Vermont gave a majority to Humphrey despite the pleas of Governor Philip Hoff, who supported Kennedy and campaigned for him.

Pennsylvania was the worst defeat. The two most powerful Democrats, Mayor Joseph Barr of Pittsburgh and Mayor James Tate of Philadelphia, were among those who urged Humphrey to run the second week in April. Barr was influenced by the United Steel Workers. Kennedy had wooed Tate strongly on his visit to Philadelphia on April 1, but Tate still remembered that when he asked Robert and Edward Kennedy to campaign for him the previous year, both had refused, while Humphrey had cheerfully toured Philadelphia with him.

Although the Pennsylvania delegation did not plan to meet until the Convention, Humphrey's managers, as part of their bandwagon strategy, arranged a special meeting in Harrisburg on May 25. The labor unions, main sources of campaign funds for the local office holders who were the delegates, applied intense pressure, and the Pennsylvania delegation cast a preponderance of its votes for Humphrey. It then voted to hold no more caucuses until the Convention. The Kennedy forces were successful only in preventing the adoption of a unit rule.

Kennedy had more success in a few states—without exception places where the party members had a greater voice in selecting the delegates. In Iowa, the delegate selection began at the precinct level caucuses, open to all registered Democrats. Kennedy supporters came out in force and held their strength up through the state convention. When the delegates were selected, they could count on 28 of the 45 votes. In Colorado, a Kennedy-McCarthy coalition succeeded in defeating such Humphrey stalwarts as Denver's Mayor Thomas Currigan in the congressional district caucuses, putting themselves in position to win a majority of the delegates at the convention to be held in July. Similar efforts were underway in Utah and Washington.

Just prior to the Oregon primary, *Newsweek* magazine could report that 1280 delegates were "committed or leaning" to Humphrey, with only 1312 needed to win. The same day, CBS claimed Humphrey already had 1483. Kennedy's own staff estimated Humphrey had approximately 1000 delegates. Thus, a month after his entry, without entering a primary, Humphrey had drawn to within striking distance of victory.

Two days before the Oregon primary, Edward Kennedy and Stephen Smith met in a restaurant in Portland to compare notes. It was the low point of the campaign. Edward Kennedy had just come from Pennsylvania, where the Humphrey forces had won a substantial victory. He had met the previous week with lieutenants in charge of the western states and received discouraging reports. The Oregon polls were very close; the momentum seemed to be with McCarthy. Now the Humphrey chieftains and the labor leaders were pushing for early caucuses in Illinois and Ohio. If those states went over, Humphrey would have a majority.

But this did not happen. Despite the Oregon results, Mayor Daley continued to wait, and the most influential leaders in Ohio, Morton Niepp and Burt Porter, refused to be pushed into a commitment. They had been impressed by Kennedy's reception in Cleveland in May and felt he might have the pulling power they needed. This gave the Kennedy forces a week's grace until the California primary. If California turned out well, and then New York, the pendulum would begin to swing back. It would be a contest once more.

In the midst of these difficulties came the results of the Oregon primary on May 28. Although only 300,00 votes were cast, one-tenth the expected turnout in California, and although a switch of fewer than 7000 votes would have changed the outcome, Oregon was considered a major defeat for Kennedy. His strategy had been to sweep the primaries and come to the convention as the choice of the people. Here was a state that had rejected him. Moreover, Oregon assured that the McCarthy candidacy, in some form, would survive to the Convention, continuing to split the liberal forces with the Democratic party.

What differentiated Oregon from the other primary states was its political traditions. Oregon was accustomed to a different brand of politics than Kennedy practiced. The state is one big neighborhood, where everyone seems to know everyone else. It is a state of political amateurs. Its last three governors have been a public relations man, a college professor, and a television news analyst; one does not come up through the ranks. Oregon politics are open, unsophisticated, and low-keyed, its people friendly and relaxed. Oregonians are proud of their state's beauty. Many of them are there because of it. Political workers think nothing of taking a three-day weekend in the middle of a campaign to go camping with their families.

Compared to most of the country, Oregon's politics are unstructured. State and county party organizations exist but are powerless. Voters disdain forceful organizations. Issues and personality considerations predominate. In recent years, the state's Democratic party had been torn by bitter factional strife in which the polarizing force was Senator Wayne Morse. A Republican originally, Morse had bolted to the Democratic Party in protest over the campaign of Dwight Eisenhower in 1956. It is typical of Oregon that he had been able to transfer to the Democratic Party and survive as an elected official with no difficulty.

Marked as a traditionally Republican state, Oregon emerged in the 1950s as a Democratic hope. The revival was sparked by the national candidacy of Adlai Stevenson, whose intellectual and independent manner was in the hero's mold of Oregonian democracy. The new faces included Senator Richard Neuberger and his wife, Maureen, former FPC Commissioner Howard Morgan, and Representatives Edith Green and Robert Duncan—and they all drew the wrath of Morse.

In 1960, Morse opposed John Kennedy's presidential bid, because of Kennedy's role in pressing for corrective labor legislation. When he entered the Oregon primary, Kennedy relied on Edith Green to organize his campaign. He beat Morse by a vote of better than three to two. By 1968, after twenty-three years in the U. S. Senate, Morse had accumulated enough enemies to put his political life in jeopardy. His primary opponent was former Congressman Robert Duncan, who had run for the Senate against Mark Hatfield in 1966 and lost, partly because Morse had endorsed Hatfield. The Morse-Duncan primary was to absorb much of the political energies of Oregon Democrats in May 1968.[20]

Robert Kennedy was a controversial figure to Oregonians even before he became Attorney General. In 1957, following up the investigations by two reporters of the Portland *Oregonian,* the Senate Rackets Committee held hearings on corruption among the Teamsters and other unions, after which a number of union leaders and public officials, including Portland's mayor, Terry Schrunk, were indicted and the city received a rash of unfavorable national publicity. Portlanders are extremely proud of their city, and they tended to blame Kennedy for their embarrassment. An incident involving Kennedy occurred in Portland in 1959 when he was subpoenaed as a witness in the trial of Mayor Schrunk (who was acquitted). As he finished his testimony, Kennedy went to the bench of the presiding judge and shook his hand. That breach of courtroom manners was recounted numberless times in Oregon in 1968, reflecting, if nothing else, the enduring quality of Oregonian memories and the state's special sensitivity to Robert Kennedy.

In 1968, Mayor Schrunk was still in office and the Teamsters was still the most powerful union in the state. But Kennedy had received enthusiastic receptions in Portland and elsewhere when he campaigned on behalf of Democrats in 1966, and he believed Oregon was a state where his stand on Vietnam and popularity among the general population could overcome the antipathy he knew existed among many of the leaders.

During the afternoon of March 16, Kennedy asked Mrs. Green to take charge of his campaign in Oregon. When she accepted, he was delighted. No other member of Congress offered assistance more quickly or with more personal commitment. She was tried and tested in her own state. In the midst of hectic preparations for primaries in other states, which had to be organized from scratch, the inclination

[20] Morse won the nomination by only 7000 votes. He was defeated by less than 3000 votes in the general election by an obscure Republican attorney, Robert Packwood. It was another example of the significance of a single vote. In August, 1969, Packwood's support of President Nixon gave the Administration its winning margin in its fight to deploy the antiballistic missile. If 1500 voters had chosen Morse instead of Packwood, the anti-ABM forces would have won the Senate struggle.

was to let Mrs. Green organize Oregon as she wished. Her judgment heavily influenced the issues, media techniques, and appearances chosen in Oregon. Her clearance was required for anyone from outside the state to work on the campaign.

Edith Green is probably the most powerful female politician in the United States. As chairman of the Education subcommittee in the House of Representatives, she has been a dominating influence on the unprecedented education and poverty legislation of the past decade. Her soft voice belies an eloquent speaker, and her popularity in the most populous part of her state gives her a commanding position in Oregon. In supporting Robert Kennedy, she had no illusions about how difficult a fight lay ahead. None of her advisers agreed with her decision. She knew that many of her oldest friends and associates were already committed to McCarthy or Johnson or Humphrey. There was little to gain and much to lose, but she admired Kennedy immensely, and on the issues that meant everything to her, he was the only candidate who could meet the tests of leadership.

By the standards required of a major presidential primary, Mrs. Green's personal organization in Multnomah County (Portland) was insufficient. In the rest of the state, where 65 per cent of the vote was to be cast, no organization existed. Experienced help was virtually unavailable. Most of the liberal activists had already joined the McCarthy effort. The local managers of the McCarthy campaign, Mr. and Mrs. Roger Bachman, had preferred Kennedy but enlisted for McCarthy the previous December when they concluded Kennedy would not run. The same was true of the students. The political apparatus of labor was even cooler to Kennedy in Oregon than elsewhere because of what had happened ten years before. When his campaign committee sent 800 letters to local union officials asking for individual endorsements, fewer than 10 responded.

Kennedy's organization was aware of all this. As early as mid-April, Steve Smith had visited Oregon and was disturbed by the slow progress he saw. But his real professionals were already thinly spread, and the call had gone out for almost everyone in the campaign to drop what they were doing to go to Indiana. By the time Indiana reached the point where people could be spared, distress signals started coming out of California, necessitating the emergency dispatch of personnel to shore up a crumbling organization there. Oregon seemed to be the one state where effort could be spared. It was assigned a low priority and a low budget.

By the time John Kennedy had reached the Oregon primary in 1960, the issue had already been decided in West Virginia. Now there was a lingering hope, fed by the desperate shortage of experienced professionals available to the campaign, that 1960 would be repeated, and by May 28 the McCarthy candidacy would have disappeared in the wake of the Indiana and Nebraska results. In any event, everyone's attention was concentrated on "tomorrow"—and Oregon was weeks away.

On April 28, 1968, the Kennedy headquarters in Oregon consisted of two desks and three people. A telephone company strike added to the difficulties of installing campaign communications equipment. The McCarthy campaign, in contrast, had begun in December, and hundreds of volunteers were organized in a statewide effort. The McCarthy strategists mobilized for an all-out effort in Oregon, correctly understanding the possibilities of victory that awaited them. In many ways, Oregon was the perfect state for the McCarthy candidacy. With his low-key, modest, reassuring manner, he had a special appeal to an electorate that resented pressure. He was a maverick in a state fond of mavericks, a Midwesterner in a state resentful of Easterners, a college professor in a state where education was the major industry, an independent politician in a state resentful of professional organization, a literate man in a state whose citizens have the second highest level of educational attainment in the country, and a teacher in a state with a tradition of electing academics to public office. Finally, Oregon had led the nation in its early opposition to the Vietnam war, and New Hampshire had made McCarthy the most dramatic symbol of that issue.

There was another factor that was crucial in Oregon. Lyndon Johnson's name was on the ballot. His withdrawal as a candidate for renomination came too late to affect this. In the polls before Johnson's withdrawal statement, the President ran ahead of Kennedy with McCarthy far behind. After March 31, the erosion in Johnson's poll strength was largely in McCarthy's favor. By the end of April, the polls showed: Kennedy, 29.0 per cent, McCarthy, 28.5 per cent; Johnson, 27 per cent. It was clear to those who studied these polls that McCarthy was really much stronger in Oregon than he had been in any other primary state at a comparable date, and that both a major effort and a lot of luck would be necessary to pull it out for Kennedy. Moreover, the same polls indicated that while McCarthy was a generally acceptable figure, Kennedy's negative impressions were more pronounced in Oregon than elsewhere. Large numbers of voters considered him impulsive, power-hungry, and immature. Highly publicized campaign activities, such as his impulsive plunge into the cold Pacific surf, reinforced those impressions.

Another element that deserves mention was the strategy of the Humphrey forces. There was an abortive attempt in April to make the Johnson name on the ballot the magnet for Humphrey votes, but the Vice President's tacticians soon learned that such an effort would take considerable resources and would probably be unsuccessful. They understood that the best result in Oregon for Humphrey would be a Kennedy defeat. Since McCarthy was never considered by the White House-Humphrey forces to be a serious challenger, they could help him beat Kennedy—and Hubert Humphrey would be the real winner.

The standard explanation for Kennedy's defeat is that Oregon was too white, too Protestant, "one vast suburb" unaffected by the social forces sweeping the nation. This theory does not account for the liberal and sensitive nature of the Democratic electorate in Oregon; it also assumes the candidate of "reconciliation" needed votes from the poor and black to cancel out opposition from the middle class. Had Kennedy been able to concentrate on his political problems in Oregon, had he more time to get a sense of the style required and reshape his style (not his policies) to Oregon's expectations, he might have won. But he was too busy elsewhere. The frenetic aura which marked his personal campaigning since 1964, and which was continued successfully in Indiana, carried over to Oregon and proved to be disastrous. What happened in Oregon was exactly what he had predicted would happen had he entered New Hampshire: the noise, the glamour, the excitement which accompanied his presence alienated the voters. In addition, the crowds delayed his schedule, causing resentment in a state with a passion for punctuality. The widespread appearance of his family, which Mrs. Green had urged him to restrict, contrasted unfavorably with McCarthy's image as the "lonely man." But he had a campaign formula which had worked in three states, and it was natural to stick to it. Moreover, his campaigning in Oregon was being televised on daily news shows in Southern California, where voters were also making up their minds. He could not be a different candidate in different states at the same time.

Two incidents occurred during the critical last week of the campaign which contributed to his defeat. The Friday before the election, Portland's *Oregon-Journal* devoted banner headlines to a column by Drew Pearson charging that Kennedy, as Attorney General, had placed a wiretap on Martin Luther King. The same charge had been made by Pearson two years before, and had aroused little interest. Now, in the aftermath of Dr. King's death, it was powerful political ammunition. Civil liberties issues had a special appeal for Oregon Democrats. The Pearson column served to revive the image of a man who had worked for Joe McCarthy, hounded Hoffa, and compromised the reputation of the city of Portland. As usual, Kennedy's explanation and rejection of Pearson's charge were lost in the weekend coverage of more important events.

The second incident was related to McCarthy's challenge to a debate. McCarthy held the underdog's initiative on the issue. He purchased television time for debate, drawing an effective contrast between Kennedy's tumultuous campaigning and his refusal to debate the issues. For the last ten days of the campaign, political advertisements on radio and television repeated: "He wouldn't stand up to Johnson in New Hampshire. Now he won't stand up to McCarthy in Oregon." Kennedy reacted to the challenge with the front runner's standard disinterest. By this point, he felt the trend in Oregon had set in for him. The CBS poll taken five days before the election gave him a 2 per cent lead, 34 per cent to McCarthy's 32 per cent; but the large undecided vote loomed ominously at this late stage of the campaign. He accepted the argument that any major confrontation could only jeopardize what looked like a narrow victory.

Most of his campaign associates urged him to change his mind. Kennedy's decision was supported by Mrs. Green and by Dutton, who was keenly conscious of the fact that almost six weeks of non-stop campaigning had left the candidate groggy with fatigue. Dutton felt Kennedy should not appear in a debate until he had had a chance to refresh himself, physically and mentally, and prepare himself for the questions, an impossible assignment in the last frantic days before the election. Nevertheless, on May 23 Dutton gave instructions to the research staff in Los Angeles to prepare debate material, saying "it seems more and more likely McCarthy is going to confront Kennedy on some occasion . . . he must have the material to handle such a situation quickly and decisively." On Saturday, May 25, Kennedy finally rejected the possibility of a debate in Oregon. McCarthy appeared alone for the half hour of television time that he had purchased and spoke informally and extemporaneously about the issues as he saw them. Given the Kennedy image of candor and competition, the whole scene was wrong, and before the weekend was over, it would be worse.

The next day, Sunday, two days before the election, Kennedy campaigned among the crowds at the Portland Zoo. Learning of Kennedy's schedule, the McCarthy forces sent their candidate to the same campaign ground to force a face-to-face meeting. Kennedy was about 300 feet from his car, preparing to leave for the next scheduled stop, when McCarthy and his advance men spotted him and started to run toward him. Kennedy jogged to his car and drove off with insults and taunts of "coward" echoing behind from McCarthy supporters. Meanwhile, McCarthy boarded the Kennedy press bus to make the most of Kennedy's exit. The television news reports that evening covered the occasion thoroughly.

On May 28, primary day in Oregon, Kennedy campaigned in California. He left Los Angeles for Portland at 7 P.M., two hours late, and as he boarded the aircraft, he was handed the television network reports which projected his defeat. He had two hours of flight to consider this news. When he arrived in Portland, it was confirmed. For the first time in his career as a manager and a candidate, he had lost an election.

In the beginning of the 1964 campaign Jack Rosenthal, who had worked for Kennedy in the Department of Justice and knew him as a ferocious competitor, said he hoped Kennedy would never fall behind because "if he ever thought he was going to lose, he would be absolutely terrifying." Now that the moment had come, he was amazingly mild, calm, and generous. In a conference in the bedroom of his hotel suite, he was the manager again, deciding what statement he should release to the press, how he should change his strategy, deciding to accept a debate in California, but otherwise changing nothing. In his statement in the hotel ballroom, he had nothing but praise for

Oregon's people and generous comments for McCarthy. But he was terribly tired and occasionally he uttered an expression of despair. He was cheered by a call from Charles Evers: "Hey, man, it's the best thing that ever happened to you. It shows you're mortal." He comforted Mrs. Green and the other Oregonians who, having worked for him so hard, blamed themselves. The next day he said simply: "I lost because I didn't do well enough. The only fault is me."

It was a strangely relaxed candidate who flew back to Los Angeles to begin the final days of the campaign in California. He could see the end of the primary road ahead. Beyond it stretched three months until the Convention, a time of reduced tensions in which he would make what he could of his primary victories in the final competition for delegates.

Kennedy had always considered California the ultimate test. To the winner would go 174 pledged delegates, more than in all the previous contested primaries combined. Victory here, in the largest, most urban of the states, would be an enormous lift. By anchoring California to the bulk of the delegates from New York, he would form his base for the Convention.

Kennedy assumed he could win the California primary; had he believed otherwise, he would not have run. Indeed, the poll Jesse Unruh brought him early in March, showing he could easily defeat both McCarthy and a favorite son pledged to Johnson, had touched off the final sequence of decisions that led to the announcement of his candidacy.

Kennedy always had a special appeal to the California electorate. They liked his style. They were accustomed to mass-appeal politics, liberal Democratic programs, and glamorous candidates with celebrities in their retinues. Expensive campaigns were taken for granted. Voters in smaller states may be put off by these qualitites, but Californians welcome them.

In January the leading Democrats of the state, after delicate negotiations, had joined together to form a slate pledged to State Attorney General Thomas Lynch as a stand-in for Johnson. Only one major Democrat had stayed off the slate: Assembly Speaker Unruh. Through the month of February, his aloofness was the only hard political fact pointing to the possibility Kennedy might run. Kennedy's triumphant tour in March had installed him as the clear favorite to win the primary. Several leading political figures deserted the Lynch slate for the Kennedy slate hastily formed by Unruh. Other Lynch delegates indicated their preference by putting their wives on the Kennedy slate.

At first it was hoped that Kennedy's California supporters could mount their own campaign, raising their own money. Unruh was given a free hand. He was the most astute political manager in the state's Democratic party, and the one man who knew how to produce the vote in Los Angeles County, which cast 38 per cent of the ballots. But for all his experience, Unruh did not do enough to broaden the organization beyond his own followers. Volunteers from party factions hostile to Unruh in the past, and others from college campuses, complained they were being excluded from the campaign.[21] It looked as though Unruh was using the primary for his own purposes in the state's politics. Through many stormy years, Unruh had acquired a reputation as a tough, no-nonsense "boss." As Californians began to view the campaign as Unruh's exclusive property, Kennedy's earlier appeal dimmed.

The crisis came when Kennedy visited California the third week in April to find that his lead over McCarthy had dropped drastically, and that insufficient funds had been raised for the final weeks. At that point Kennedy decided Steve Smith must spend full time in Los Angeles. Frank Mankiewicz was shifted from his duties as traveling press secretary to help stimulate activity among southern California's influential Jewish voters, with whom McCarthy was well entrenched. John Siegenthaler was dispatched to northern California with full authority to manage the campaign there.

On May 11, Kennedy settled down for intensive campaigning in California, broken only by eight days in Oregon. Dutton, who came from California and had managed two state-wide campaigns for Governor Brown, molded a schedule that took Kennedy to both parts of the State each day with the purpose of reaching the television audience in each area.

---

[21] The man Unruh assigned to manage the campaign in Northern California, Congressman Phillip Burton of San Francisco, followed a similar policy of exclusion. His office manager kept campaign buttons, posters, and materials under lock and refused to give them to anyone for distribution without Burton's written authorization.

Once again, those closest to the issues reported that race was predominant. California's migrants had come from small towns in the Midwest or Southwest, bringing their racial fears with them. In 1966, California had repealed, by public referendum, its law forbidding discrimination in the sale of housing. So it was not surprising that Kennedy's identification with Negroes hurt him in California. When pollsters asked respondents to react to the statement that "Robert Kennedy is the man who can bring peace to the cities," 71 per cent disagreed. To the statement "Robert Kennedy spends most of his time courting minority groups," 61 per cent agreed. Ed Guthman, who had spent the last three years in California as national news editor of the Los Angeles *Times,* recommended that Kennedy should de-emphasize outdoor rallies and instead meet with small groups of whites in the suburbs, exposing them to his remarkable gifts of reason and per-suasiveness on race relations. These meetings, heavily televised, could give white voters a better understanding of the problem, as well as great confidence in Kennedy.

But there was only a week to go. It was too late to change. Perhaps the techniques which had hurt him in Oregon would work to his ad-vantage in California. He concentrated on rallies and motorcades in the low-income districts, choosing to get out the vote in his areas of strength instead of seeking converts in his areas of weakness. The campaign in California was ending, as it had begun, in an outpouring of frenzied adulation.

On Thursday, May 30, Kennedy campaigned through the Central Valley by train and, late at night, attended an unannounced meeting in the ghetto of East Oakland. Assemblyman Willie Brown of San Francisco had called together a loose association of black leaders, named the "Bay Area Black Caucus." It included many black mili-tants (Oakland is the home of Eldridge Cleaver and the Black Panthers) whose goals of separatism and contempt for white people were the ultimate results of discrimination; and whose symbols—the beard, the dark glasses, the gun—had become the primary symbols of fear among white Americans.

Kennedy had learned a great deal since the meeting with James Baldwin's group in 1963. He had watched black militancy develop and learned to discriminate between the handful of blacks dedicated to violence, and the militant organizations like the Muslims and the Panthers, which often enforced restraint and group discipline in the ghetto. When he campaigned in Watts, for example, members of the Sons of Watts guarded him. These organizations offered an institution bigger than self, to which blacks could attach themselves.

On the way to the meeting, Kennedy said to John Glenn, who was accompanying him: "I don't know whether you have been to any of these, but they can get pretty mean. These people have a lot of pent-up hostility. I suspect they will take some of it out on me."

After Brown had opened the meeting, Kennedy spoke briefly about ghetto problems and what was going on in Bedford-Stuyvesant. He was interrupted almost at once by a man in a red sweater who shouted: "Talk, talk, talk; go ahead, baby—talk, talk, talk, talk." The man launched into a long attack on Kennedy and his family, who represented, he said, the worst things about white people. "If you like the black man as much as you say you do," he demanded, "why don't you give us some of that money your family has?"

When Kennedy finished and asked for questions, one man after another rose to attack him, as a symbol of the white society they despised. At one point Rafer Johnson, watching from the back, said he "had enough" and moved toward the front where Kennedy was sitting. Kennedy restrained him. "I've come here to listen," he said softly.

The meeting lasted until early morning. On the way across the Bay Bridge to San Francisco, Kennedy turned again to Glenn. "What did you think, John?" he asked.

Glenn could only shake his head slowly. Kennedy smiled and said: "That's the kind of situation I really enjoy."

He turned to Rafer Johnson and Fred Dutton, "Are you glad I went?" he asked. They said they were not. He had had an unpleasant time, and he hadn't won any votes.

"Well, I am," he said. "They need to know someone will listen to them. I'd feel better about it if I knew Gene McCarthy and Hubert Humphrey were having these sessions. But whether they are or not, I feel better because I went, and heard what they said, and they know that while no one is going to solve their problems overnight, I at least will listen to them and I won't make any false promises, and I'll work to try to help them."

In fact, his appearance had won converts. The next day, a man who styled himself "the Black Jesus," and who had attacked him the night before, could be seen clearing the way for him at a rally in the Oakland ghetto, saying "I'm Senator Kennedy's personal representative."

The day after the Oregon primary, Kennedy had accepted the challenge to debate McCarthy, and an arrangement was hastily agreed on for the candidates to appear on a special program of ABC's "Issues and Answers." An enormous amount of work had gone into preparation for the debate. The remaining members of the research staff in Washington, working under William Smith, former assistant to Senator Joseph S. Clark, had prepared extensive briefing papers, including a detailed analysis of McCarthy's stands, where they differed from Kennedy's, and how they could be criticized. Several others contributed ideas and proposals. In all, the material weighed about two pounds. One memo said:

> McCarthy will come on as a mild, kindly fellow presenting rather radical views in a way that sounds thoughtful and credible. He will be witty. His disadvantage is that he gives no feeling of being able to lead anyone or produce any results; he projects no sense of commitment and has command of few facts to back up his philosophy.
> In general your strategy should be:
> 1. To show a greater command of the facts.
> 2. Not to attack him. We are being told by reporters that he is saying he hopes you will go after him hard.
> 3. To nevertheless draw the differences in policy between yourselves sharply. The audience is hoping for a real contest with differences.
> 4. Make the point, without laboring it, that you have had experience in fields that he has only talked about.

The policy differences between the men were few, and the briefing papers spelled them out: McCarthy opposed any tax increase. Kennedy felt, in the currently "overheated" state of the economy, a surtax was needed to help stave off inflation. McCarthy wanted Dean Rusk and J. Edgar Hoover dismissed. Kennedy did not feel cabinet members should be held responsible for decisions made by a President. McCarthy had asked sweeping reductions in America's commitments abroad. Kennedy believed many were essential (in the debate, he was to point to the security of Latin America and Israel as examples of pledges the United States should uphold. McCarthy was to agree as to Israel.) The chief difference on Vietnam was whether a coalition government was essential to the initial peace moves. McCarthy believed that an agreement for a coalition government was a necessary condition for successful negotiations. Kennedy believed that the U.S. had to guarantee NLF participation in the procedure in which a new government was selected, but this gave more options than just insistence on a coalition government.

On racial issues, McCarthy felt only integration could offer meaningful opportunity to blacks. He criticized Kennedy's stress on improving the ghetto as dodging the more critical issue of residential integration in middle-income neighborhoods and in suburbs. He called Kennedy's program "ghetto colonialism." Kennedy felt McCarthy's program was unrealistic, not because whites might resist it, but because conditions were not yet appropriate. There were no jobs available in the suburbs, and the older generation of black Americans was simply unprepared to cope with life outside the ghetto.

On Saturday, June 1, the day of the debate, Kennedy cleared his schedule. It was a perfect spring day in San Francisco and the clear air gave a special brilliance to the sunlight. From Kennedy's suite on the top floor of the Fairmont Hotel on Nob Hill spread the greatest urban view in the world: San Francisco Bay, with the Golden Gate to the West, the Coast Range to the North and Sausalito nestled in the golden brown hills of Marin County. Kennedy, dressed in a silk kimono, sat curled up at the end of a couch, absorbed in the scene.

Nine advisers[22] were there to try to anticipate the questions that might be asked and offer suggestions on Kennedy's answers. An atmosphere of gloom pervaded the room. Most of the participants had not recovered from the Oregon primary, and were unsettled by the progress of the campaign so far. They were apprehensive that McCarthy, who had proven so unpredictably strong so often, might also carry the debate.

Kennedy had rested well the night before, and would nap again that day. He would be alert for the debate itself, but he was not in a

[22] Burke Marshall, Sorensen, Edelman, Goodwin, Mankiewicz, Schlesinger, Unruh, Dutton, and Gwirtzman.

mood to stuff his mind with materials, and the two pounds of preparation was scarcely read. He did listen carefully to the strategy recommended by the advisers: use the debate to remind the audience that, in the chief areas of national concern, he was more knowledgeable and far more experienced than McCarthy.

"Are you comfortable talking about yourself?" Sorensen asked. "Yes," Kennedy said. "I will be today." His deep reluctance to be self-serving would yield to the demands of this occasion.

When the issue of integration as opposed to ghetto development was raised, Unruh observed that in Los Angeles, the McCarthy "ghetto dispersal" program would have to be implemented by moving Negroes en masse into Orange County, the Los Angeles suburb. He suggested Kennedy could point up his position for the California audience by asking whether Negroes would really gain by such a move.

Kennedy allowed less than a day to prepare for the debate. At noon on Saturday he broke away for two hours of campaigning at Fisherman's Wharf, partly to taste the beauty of the day, which was distracting him. An hour before air time, he huddled privately with Sorensen while dressing, receiving last-minute briefing and advice, including the professional's reminder to shake hands at the end.

The debate itself went as expected. They disagreed about installing a coalition government in South Vietnam prior to elections (Kennedy opposed imposing one on the current government; McCarthy urged the Administration "to state now that it would accept" such a government). Kennedy forced McCarthy to admit that the advertisement appearing in California under his campaign committee's sponsorship which said Kennedy was "part of the decision" to invade the Dominican Republic, was unfair; but McCarthy counterattacked by assailing wiretapping, tying Kennedy to the embarrassment about Dr. King.[23]

Kennedy emphasized his experience:

[23] Kennedy approved an FBI request for a tap on King on October 10, 1963. The FBI had been requesting the tap the preceding two years, on the grounds that King was influenced by associates who were Communists. The authorization was made to verify or disprove the FBI allegations. Kennedy's successors, former Attorneys General Nicholas Katzenbach and Ramsay Clark, have since put Kennedy's role in a much different light than did the Pearson article. ". . . To say or imply that this tap was the original conception of Robert Kennedy . . . is false," Katzenbach said in a statement in June 1969.

"When I was Attorney General of the United States we had a riot at the University of Mississippi and yet no one fired a gun—the marshals and the troops. We kept a mob under control at the University of Alabama. I have had some experience in dealing with these problems."

Kennedy had not been told there would be concluding statements.[24] After the last question, the timekeeper had signaled his time was up, so he had to improvise when asked to talk briefly on "why you should be President." It was the kind of self-serving question he answered least well. He offered his credentials in 250 words. McCarthy took 440 words, also gave his credentials, but went on to make a brilliant statement about what his candidacy had meant to the country.

"I think I sensed what the country needed in 1968 . . . I sensed what the young people needed . . . the campaign has brought a genuine reconciliation of old and young, and because of it there is a new confidence in the future of America."

The debate showed up how much the two agreed, and the press considered it tame. President Johnson, viewing the debate at his ranch with Henry Ford, Gregory Peck, and their wives, felt Kennedy had won. At a steak dinner in his suite afterward, Kennedy's friends told him he had scored points and had discharged his obligation to debate. Kennedy felt the debate had come too late and been too even to change many votes.

On Monday the contact with the people began again. A San Francisco motorcade, and then to Long Beach, through Watts and the Mexican section of San Diego. KE-NE-DEE, KE-NE-DEE. The cry he had heard in Poland and Japan, Chile and Brazil—the cry of excitement and belief. The faces of the poor he liked so much, anxious and flushed in their desire to see, to get closer, to touch. North to San Francisco, then Sacramento and south to San Diego in a final circuit of the state. In his final appearance of the day, he collapsed from fatigue.

Election day he rested beside a pool at Malibu, trying to shake the exhaustion from his eyes as Goodwin talked of a plan to bring

[24] The printed ground rules said: "There will be no formal opening or closing statements, but a general first question and a wrap-up question."

McCarthy's supporters to his side. That night, in his suite in the Ambassador Hotel, the returns looked good, and the atmosphere was hope and expectation. It seemed as though he would win a clear majority of the vote. His mind anticipated the next moves. From his bedroom, calls were going out—to Lowenstein about McCarthy, to O'Donnell about Daley and the city leaders. The room was crowded with the friends of many years. In the midst of the noise and excitement, he reviewed the latest estimate of delegate strength his staff had prepared in Washington. It purported to show how Kennedy could end up with 1432 votes and the nomination.[25] He did not believe it, but tomorrow he would listen to the reports on which it was based.

Just before midnight, he decided to go down to the ballroom to make his statement. Stepping into the hallway, clogged with people waiting to go downstairs with him, he saw his daughter Courtney walking down the stairs with his secretary, Swani von Heinegg. He asked where she was going. "To help with the speeches," she said. He asked whether she had had a good time that day, and what she had done, and how she liked Los Angeles. For ten minutes, while a country waited to see him after his most important victory, there was no one else in that hall, no crowd in the ballroom below, no campaign. There was only a father and his daughter absorbed with one another, sharing the unlimited adventure of a child's day.

The final totals were Kennedy 1,472,166; McCarthy 1,322,608; Lynch 380,286. Kennedy's performance in the debate did not stop another fast-closing finish by McCarthy. The results showed that while Kennedy had maintained the 46 per cent he held in the Unruh poll in March, McCarthy had picked up almost all the votes which had abandoned the Lynch slate. The California primary supported the claim Kennedy would be the strongest nominee because he could bring out the low-income voters. It also supported McCarthy's claim that he could best cut into the independent and Republican vote.[26]

[25] The chart Kennedy saw appears as Appendix.
[26] An analysis of the California returns showed Kennedy's victory margin had been fashioned in Los Angeles, among the Negroes and Mexican-Americans who turned out in very high numbers for a primary. (In some Mexican-American precincts he received 100 per cent of the ballots.) McCarthy carried the suburban areas around Los Angeles and San Francisco and those metropolitan areas, like San Diego, which tend to be more conservative and have specially high proportion of white voters who moved to California from the South or

The day after the California primary, a meeting was to be held at Steve Smith's bungalow at the Beverly Hills Hotel to plan the strategy of the rest of the campaign. For the first time since early April, Kennedy would be able to devote full attention to the total picture. The Washington staff, under Sorensen, had been planning the agenda for weeks. David Hackett would begin by explaining the delegate count, state by state.[27] Next on the agenda were such items as "Relations with Senator McCarthy," followed by "National Public Opinion Polls"—how to use them, now that the primaries were over, to show Kennedy was the first choice of Democrats, the candidate of the people against the bosses, and the man most likely to be elected. The future travel schedule would have been discussed, and the position to be taken on issues like the Vietnam peace talks. There would have been discussions of national television appearances, arrangements for the Convention, and a reorganization of the campaign staff to make it more efficient.

Another issue might have come up, an unwelcome visitor on the agenda. After the Oregon primary and the defeats in the Michigan and Pennsylvania caucuses, some of Kennedy's advisers felt that unless he received over 50 per cent of the vote in the California primary, it made no sense for him to continue. Humphrey would be nominated. Continued resistance after an issue has been settled was not a posture Kennedy tolerated for himself.

Most probably, the possibility of abandoning the campaign would not have been raised. It would have been discussed privately, earlier, with his brother, Steve Smith and a couple of others, and forgotten. If it had come up, Kennedy would have rejected the suggestion. He had come too far to drop out now. The prospects of winning the nomination were not bright, but they were visible. He would go on

---

Southwest. In the counties of the Central Valley, the Mexican-American vote stimulated by Chavez had given Kennedy majorities, but in all the other ranching, agricultural and sparcely-settled areas of the state he did poorly. Intensive organizational efforts in the final weeks allowed Kennedy to draw even with McCarthy among the state's Jewish voters. Kennedy ran better among the older Jewish voters (in, for example, Los Angeles' Fairfax area) than he did among the young, better-educated—repeating his familiar pattern among Jews, a pattern which almost certainly would have held in the New York primary.

[27] Hackett would give no estimate that was not backed up by two independent sources outside his staff.

until the realistic possibilities had been exhausted. The meeting would have turned to the future.

As soon as the primaries were over, Kennedy would make some national television appearances—relaxed, reflective "fireside chats" where he would not be buffeted by screaming crowds and could discuss the issues as he really saw them. Later in the summer, his book on the Cuban missile crisis would be published, reminding the public of his experience in presidential decision-making and his coolness under pressure. If it could be arranged, he wished to make a trip to Moscow at the end of July, speaking to the Russian people on television, perhaps being received with the same dramatic jubilation the Poles had given him years before. He would come back by way of Prague, Berlin, Western Europe, and the Middle East. The trip would dominate the headlines for two weeks. Just before the convention, he would hold receptions at Hyannis Port for delegates and their wives from the northeastern states, and perhaps from the South.

He would go to the Convention as the candidate of the people—not the front runner, as he had thought in early April, but the dramatic underdog and challenger. He would challenge any Humphrey delegation that had excluded black Democrats. He would challenge the unit rule. Somewhere along the way would come one key test on a preliminary issue, perhaps involving Charles Evers' Mississippi Democrats. The issue of principle would be clear enough so that the big northern delegations would have to support him. If so, he could break Humphrey's grip on the Convention. The psychology of conventions being what it is, it might well turn toward him.

By the morning after Robert Kennedy's greatest primary triumph, the plans for the summer and the hopes and dreams of future years were all dissolved. One young man, a refugee from history, decided to take history into his own hands; and by one insane act, struck down the most dramatic public figure of the time.

16

A SUMMING UP

The question of whether Robert Kennedy could have been elected President, had he lived, is too bound up in both speculation and grief to consider at length. Kennedy's hopes depended on McCarthy stepping aside in his favor. No one but McCarthy can say when, or if, this would have happened. McCarthy has said that the Kennedy supporters and his own "would have dominated the Convention on the issues," had Kennedy lived, but he does not know what this would have meant in terms of the candidate. Nothing McCarthy had done up to June 4 indicated he would step aside. His respectable showing in California, and the 25 to 35 delegates he would have won in New York would have given him sufficient justification to continue if that had been his wish.

Humphrey's campaign sagged badly in the summer weeks before the Convention. This would have helped Kennedy's chances, but Humphrey's decline was traceable to the lack of competition and the malaise that affected the party after Kennedy's death. Some of Humphrey's sag may have been the rub-off of the Johnson policies, but Humphrey was not bound to them forever, as he showed in his campaign. A real challenge in the summer of 1968 might have forced his independence from the Johnson policies earlier than it came. The Kennedy and McCarthy forces might have been able to write the Democratic platform, but Humphrey could still have run on it.

Thus, Kennedy's chance of winning the nomination must be assessed as remote. His chance of being elected President if he had been nominated, however, was excellent. With Kennedy the nominee, the apocalypse of the Chicago riots would not have happened. Most of the participants would not have felt excluded from the convention proceedings. With Daley supporting Kennedy, the mayor would have had to handle the fringe demonstrators who remained differently than he did. In fact, at the first reports of trouble, Kennedy would have offered Daley the help of the men who had negotiated similar incidents in the South and in the 1963 March on Washington, to help move the demonstrations into peaceful channels.

So Kennedy could have pursued Nixon from the outset, instead of having to repair a party divided by the riots, which was Humphrey's lot, free from the burden of Johnson's failures. Facing another Kennedy, Nixon would have lost command of the political situation. Johnson would have been an ignored figure, his polices and chosen successor repudiated by his own party. He might not have tried to help Kennedy, as he did Humphrey, by announcing a bombing halt a few days before the election. But whatever votes Humphrey gained by this move, Kennedy would have already had. On election day, Kennedy would have cut deeply into Nixon's share of the massive protest vote of 1968. The millions of urban dwellers who sat out the election would have had a man to vote for, and would have helped give him a healthy plurality over Nixon.

The theory has been advanced that Kennedy could easily have been nominated had he rejected the "voices of the old politics" and followed his instinct when it said to enter the race—either in November, before McCarthy did, or at the end of January. This theory belittles Kennedy, implying as it does that in his most difficult decision, he subordinated his own judgment to those of his advisers. Anyone who sat with him in these difficulties knows this is not the way he worked. At each stage he, as Lincoln, "listened to everyone and then did what he thought best."

Kennedy himself rejected this theory. Even after the defeat in Oregon, when the full impact of the consequences of his delay was felt, he told his brother Edward that he could not have made the decision to run any earlier than he did.

There is no point at which an earlier announcement would have helped him. The first week in March? It would have been charged that he was doing it because he felt McCarthy was going to do well in New Hampshire; after New Hampshire, those who made McCarthy their champion would have done so anyway. In December or January? He would have had to run in the primaries in New Hampshire and Wisconsin, splitting the anti-Administration vote with McCarthy. That vote included many conservative, hawk Democrats, not friendly to Kennedy. McCarthy's share might have been larger than expected.

The fall of 1967, so McCarthy would not have had to run? If Kennedy had been his first opponent, Johnson would not have retired. He would have used the power of his office to keep the large-state delegations in line and alleviate the conditions of discontent which might have placed him behind Kennedy in the opinion polls. Pleading the pressure of his duties, he could have by-passed the primaries. Uncontested primary victories would have given Kennedy 350 votes on the first ballot, but no significant push toward the nomination. (The late Estes Kefauver won twelve primaries in 1952 and went nowhere.) By striking his "bargain" with the North Vietnamese sooner, Johnson could have run a stronger race than Humphrey. This would have been sufficient to keep him in the White House for four more years. Kennedy would have supported Humphrey, if he had not been nominated himself. His support in a close election would have made Humphrey President. Kennedy's death demoralized the McCarthy campaign, and did much to create the despair and riots that ruined Humphrey's chances and elected Richard Nixon.

But none of his hopes were fated to be. And so Robert Kennedy can only be measured by what he did, and what he inspired the nation to do. Like many great and complex leaders, he meant different things to different people. The radicals will claim him as their own, but so will nuns and hospital attendants and workers. His name will be applauded at political county dinners in New York as well as rallies of the poor. And each will have something important to show his identification with them. He was a radical and a revolutionary, but he will be remembered as a practical idealist. He sensed his country was living through revolutionary times. Because he was free of the fears of older men, the fears of Munich and depression, he could see the way to new directions of domestic justice and international restraint.

Robert Kennedy's politics turned out to be prophecy. A year after his voice was silenced, the bombing of North Vietnam had stopped, the President of the United States had offered the Vietcong a chance to participate in elections, the plight of the grape pickers was on the cover of *Time* magazine, and an Indian had been chosen to head the Bureau of Indian Affairs. The broadcast networks, which had opposed so fiercely his suggestion to limit the hours of cigarette commercials, decided to phase them out completely. The minimum income tax, which he recommended in his campaign, had been proposed to Congress by a Republican administration, along with the principle of national minimum standards for welfare. Southern senators could be seen traveling through their own states in search of hunger, on a trail he had blazed years before. The Administration could be seen recommending a $1 billion program to fight hunger and appointing as its administrator the Harvard University nutritionist who had been Robert Kennedy's chief adviser on the problem. This is not to say the new Administration, or the American people, had become converted to Kennedy's views. Neither was ready to make the commitment to the poor, or to the peace, that he represented.

In Berlin in 1964, during the first grief-filled months after President Kennedy's death, Robert Kennedy said:

"There were many who felt that a light had been snuffed out, that the torchbearer for a whole generation was gone . . . But I have come to understand that the hope President Kennedy kindled is not dead, but alive . . . The torch still burns, and because it does, there remains for all of us the chance to light up the tomorrows and to brighten the future. For me, that is the challenge that makes life worthwhile . . ."

In his four years on his own, he had kept these hopes alive and gave them meaning in areas beyond John Kennedy's vision. He was less successful in changing feelings toward himself; not until the last months of his life, when millions finally saw the personal dimensions of his passionate commitment to the weak and underprivileged, did the image of ruthlessness begin to fade.

He kept the image of America alive in other lands. His words carried great weight abroad because of who he was. His trips and speeches reminded other peoples what was good and generous about America, at a time when American policies were showing other traits.

When he joined the opposition to the war policies in Vietnam, beginning in February 1966, dissent received legitimacy. From then on, there would be a serious and powerful alternative to the policies of escalation. His views were rejected in the White House, but they had their effect. If American policy did pursue a course between

all-out war and withdrawal, as its architects will contend, it was because men of the weight of Kennedy were on the side of moderation.

At home, he broke new ground in the problems of modern civilization. In his projects for the ghettos, as in the way he drew people
to him campaigning, he tried to show that in a huge and mecha-
nized society, the individual could participate in the processes of
government, and that people could come together, not alone for
personal achievement, but for the benefit of the community.

These years of Robert Kennedy will be remembered not for achievement in the Senate, nor for any legislation that bears his name, but
for a new consciousness that embodies his spirit. At a time when a nation desperately needed to hear a voice of compassion and concern
toward those who were hurt by society, he provided it.

Robert Kennedy believed his greatest achievements in government
had been his role in the Cuban missile crisis and his management
of the 1960 election. But his unique contribution to American politics
was his dramatization of the plight of the poor. In placing his power
behind their aspirations, especially those of the blacks, he alienated a
large segment of the comfortable middle class. If blacks and Mexican-
Americans were his margin of victory in California, the voters he
frightened were his margin of defeat in Oregon and his source of
weakness throughout the country; and he knew this better than anyone.
But he believed the quality of a nation's government should be
judged by what it did for those who were the most powerless to help
themselves.

In an interview just before the Oregon primary, he was asked how
he would want to be remembered. "I hope it will be because I made
some contribution . . . to those who are less well off." he said. He
quoted Camus: "Perhaps we cannot prevent this world from being a
world in which children are tortured. But we can reduce the number
of tortured children. And if you don't help us, who else in the
world can help us do this?

"I would like to feel," he said, "that I did something to lessen their
suffering."

To all, he will be remembered as a generous, wise and passionate
man. At a time of life when most accede to the pressure of convention,
he used his last years to change himself and all who knew him, and
show his country what it could and ought to be.

EPILOGUE

A long, low, red brick school building stands in the fold of a gentle hill in McLean, Virginia. It is like thousands of schools newly built in the same functional style, except for a plain cross rising above the entrance, and the words "St. Luke's School" in aluminum letters on the wall below.

One half of the auditorium of the school is used as a gymnasium. Basketball backboards are on the wall. The other half is used as a sanctuary, and it was here that Robert and Ethel Kennedy used to come on Sunday evenings for folk mass. Sitting on a bench of West Virginia pine, they enjoyed the simple service, especially the joy of faith that the guitars and singers expressed so well. The folk mass had a special spirit and spirituality for them. After the liturgical change authorized by Vatican II, the church has sponsored the mass as a way of reaching out to young people. The rector told Kennedy he might not like the untraditional form, but he had, and from then on the folk mass was the only one he attended.

To this church, on a raw and wintry day in January 1969, Ethel Kennedy brought her newborn daughter, Rory Kathleen Elizabeth, to be baptized. It was a Kennedy occasion, attended by family and close friends who together made the mosaic of the eventful years that each of them now recalled. The children of President John F. Kennedy kneeled in prayer with their mother. Mrs. Robert Kennedy entered, accompanied by Senator Edward Kennedy of Massachusetts. The young, pure voices of the singers sang out:

> "Enter, rejoice and come in.
> Lift up your hearts to the Lord.
> Today will be a joyful day.
> Enter, rejoice and come in.

This is the day of new birth.
This is the day of new life.

Today will be a joyful day.
Enter, rejoice and come in."

The newest prince of the Roman Catholic heirarchy, Terence Cooke, Archbishop of New York, began: "Who gives this child to be baptized?"

Mary Kerry Kennedy, age nine, held her new ward with eyes wide with wonder. The godfather, Michael Kennedy, age ten, stood by her side protectively.

The Archbishop performed the rite of baptism, placing the salt in the baby's mouth and oil on her hand to purify her, pouring holy water to wash away original sin.

After the sacraments, the Reverend Carey Landry sang:

"See this child before you, Lord;
You who gave her life
Keep her in your sight, O Lord;
Now and all her days
Child of pain, child of love,
Child of sorrow and joy
Child of two who lived as one
Born again today."

The child of sorrow and joy cried softly, then quieted and gradually closed her eyes in sleep.

At the end his friends left as they had come, speaking quietly, in the gathering darkness, of the pain and love of a man whose life had meant so much to them; and of this child, who was now his extension to eternity.

And life goes on, generation after generation, passed like a spark of flame through the void of infinity. Who is to live and who to die is in the wisdom of the Lord. But do not grieve, for life on earth is but a prelude to life everlasting. He who gives life and hope to others will be the most blessed of all.

<u>Fifth</u>:   Support for all
efforts toward joint Arab-Israeli
cooperation in promoting economic
development. ///

Perhaps the day of peace is
still years away. ///

Perhaps the shadow of war will
still darken the promise of Israel.///

But no greater challenge awaits
the brave and determined people,/ than
to struggle against 2000 years of
hostility,/ and to begin to win the
greatest victory of all:/ the victory
over war in her homeland. ///

And in this we must work with Israel.

In this we in the United States have a responsibility to support Israel. And we shall

Last page of the reading text of a speech delivered by Robert Kennedy at Temple Isiah in Beverly Hills, California on June 1, 1968, four days before his assassination. The conclusion, written in Kennedy's hand at the bottom of the page reads:

"And in this we must work with Israel.
"In this we in the United States have a responsibility to support Israel.
"And we shall."

Reproduced by permission of the Reverend Carey Landry.

APPENDIX

CHART OF STATUS OF DELEGATES
TO DEMOCRATIC CONVENTION
COMPILED BY KENNEDY ORGANIZATION,
SHOWN TO ROBERT KENNEDY
ON EVENING OF JUNE 4, 1968

State	Number of Votes	Preference now				Objectives	
		RFK	HHH	EMc	UnD	RFK	HHH
ALABAMA	32	5	27			7	25
ALASKA	22	3	7	1	11	12	10
ARIZONA	19	5	10	1	3	7	12
ARKANSAS	33		33				33
CALIFORNIA	174	174				174	
COLORADO	35	3	5	3	24	20	15
CONNECTICUT	44				44	38	6
DELAWARE	22	6	16			10	12
FLORIDA	63		59	4		4	59
GEORGIA	43		43				43
HAWAII	26	4	22			5	21
IDAHO	25				25	8	17
ILLINOIS	118				118	108	10
INDIANA	63	57			6	63	
IOWA	46	26½	11½	5	3	40	6
KANSAS	38	17	13		8	28	10
KENTUCKY	46				46	34	12
LOUISIANA	36		36				36
MAINE	27	(8)	(18)	(1)			
MARYLAND	49		49			49	
MASSACHUSETTS	72			72		66	6

The figures in parentheses represent the "educated estimates" of relative strength as analyzed by the Kennedy organization.

APPENDIX

State	Number of Votes	Preference now				Objectives	
		RFK	HHH	EMc	UnD	RFK	HHH
MICHIGAN	96	40	47	2	7	50	46
MINNESOTA	52		37½	14½		13½	28½
MISSISSIPPI	24				24		24
MISSOURI	60	12	30	3	15	35	25
MONTANA	26				26	13	13
NEBRASKA	30	24	3	3		26	4
NEVADA	22	3	11	1	7	5	17
NEW HAMPSHIRE	26		6	20		15	11
NEW JERSEY	82	(25)	(25)	(32)		75	7
NEW MEXICO	26	1	3		22	14	12
NEW YORK	190	(132)	(47)	(11)		174	16
NORTH CAROLINA	59		59				59
NORTH DAKOTA	25	(10)	(12)	(3)		16	9
OHIO	115	13	25	4	73	77	38
OKLAHOMA	41		41				41
OREGON	35			35		35	
PENNSYLVANIA	130	27	71	17	15	59	71
RHODE ISLAND	27	22	5			22	5
SOUTH CAROLINA	28		28				28
SOUTH DAKOTA	26	26				26	
TENNESSEE	51		51				51
TEXAS	104		104				104
UTAH	26	2	3		21	13	13
VERMONT	22	7	10	5		15	7
VIRGINIA	54		54				54
WASHINGTON	47	(9)	(25)	(13)	47	26	21
WEST VIRGINIA	38	11	16		11	21	17
WISCONSIN	59			49	10	39	20
WYOMING	22	3	19			8	14
DIST. OF COL.	23	23				23	
GUAM	5	1			4	2	3
VIRGIN ISLANDS	5	5				5	
PUERTO RICO	8	3	3		2	5	3
CANAL ZONE	5	1	1		3	5	
Total	2,622						
Needed to win	1,312						

The figures in parentheses represent the "educated estimates" of relative strength as analyzed by the Kennedy organization.

Regions	Number of votes	Preferences now				Objectives	
		RFK	HHH	EMc	UnD	RFK	HHH
NEW ENGLAND	218	29	27	97	44	156	35
MID-ATLANTIC	132	40	81		11	54	78
MID-WESTERN	339	150½	65	71½	52	251½	87½
ROCKY MT.	201	17	51	5	128	88	113
PACIFIC	130	7	64	1	58	78	52
SOUTH-S.W.	614	5	535	4	70	45	569
LARGE STATES	965	266	173	26	500	743	213
TERRITORIES	23	10	4		9	17	6
Total		524½	994	204	872	1432½	1153½

PHOTO CREDITS

L8